W9-BMB-135

The Complete
Home
Decorating
Book

The Complete
Home
Decorating
Book

NICHOLAS BARNARD

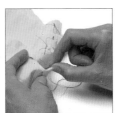
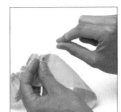

DORLING KINDERSLEY
LONDON • NEW YORK • STUTTGART

A DORLING KINDERSLEY BOOK

Project Editor Lee Stacy
Art Editor Gurinder Purewall
Managing Editor Krystyna Mayer
Managing Art Editor Derek Coombes
DTP Designer Cressida Joyce
Production Controller Rosalind Priestley
U.S. Editor Ray Rogers

Photography by Tim Ridley
Soft furnishings demonstrations by Alison Kingsbury

First American Edition, 1994
2 4 6 8 10 9 7 5 3

Published in the United States
by Dorling Kindersley Publishing, Inc., 95 Madison Avenue,
New York, New York 10016

Copyright © 1994
Dorling Kindersley Limited, London
Text copyright © 1994 Nicholas Barnard

All rights reserved under International and Pan-American
Copyright Conventions. No part of this publication may be
reproduced, stored in a retrieval system, or transmitted in any
form or by any means, electronic, mechanical, photocopying,
recording, or otherwise, without the prior written permission
of the copyright owner. Published in Great Britain by
Dorling Kindersley Limited.
Distributed by Houghton Mifflin Company, Boston.

Library of Congress Cataloging-in-Publication Data

Barnard, Nicholas.
The complete home decorating book / by Nicholas Barnard.
--1st American ed.
p. cm.
Includes index.
ISBN 1-56458-667-7
1. House furnishing. 2. Textile fabrics in interior decoration.
3. Machine sewing. 4. House painting. 5. Paperhanging. I. Title.
TT387.B37 1994
747--dc20
94-639
CIP

Color reproduced by J. Film Process Pte. Ltd., Singapore
Printed and bound in Germany by Mohndruck GmbH, Gütersloh

CONVERSIONS

Throughout the book, measurements are
given in metric and imperial equivalents,
either of which can be used. Within a
technique, do not mix the two systems.

CONTENTS

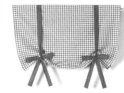

DECORATING

PAINTING

WALLPAPERING

TILING

HARD FLOORS

CARPETS AND RUGS

SHELVING

LIGHTING

HOUSEPLANTS

INTRODUCTION

DUE TO THE AVAILABILITY of an enormous diversity of decorating materials, tools, and equipment, it is possible to give every room in your home precisely the look that you desire. The style of decoration is very much a matter of individual taste. However, whether you wish to convey a traditional atmosphere or to strike a modern note in your home, you will be able to achieve the most satisfying results only if you have a thorough understanding of the fundamental principles and techniques of home decorating. As this book demonstrates, a professional finish is easily within your grasp, provided you execute each technique correctly and use the appropriate equipment for each task.

PERFECT RESULTS

The guiding principle behind all home decorating projects should be to create high-quality, enduring results. This is all-important because decorating is not about making a temporary veneer that you have to put up with for a short time. Good-quality decorating can transform your home, improving its visual quality and comfort and increasing its value. This book explains how to achieve high-quality results from the outset. It describes exactly which tools and equipment you will need for each task and recommends the most appropriate materials. Each technique is clearly demonstrated with step-by-step photographs and instructions, giving you the confidence and skills to undertake all manner of decorating jobs and to create the look you desire. Also included are ideas on how to create particular looks around the home by combining colors, styles, and many of the techniques demonstrated in this book in a variety of ways.

SOFT FURNISHINGS

There is an enormous range of furnishing fabrics available today, so that making your own soft furnishings is more rewarding than ever before. For those who need guidance in the fundamental techniques of sewing and in the methods involved in joining fabrics, this section begins with a detailed, clear explanation of these techniques. Well-made curtains and shades can make a dramatic difference to your existing decor. Two chapters show how to make and mount in position a selection of curtains and shades in different styles, suitable for dressing every type of window. The bedroom is a special place that benefits from a very decorative but practical treatment. The chapter on bed furnishings shows you how to make sheets, pillowcases, and comforter covers that are both functional and decorative. Cushions are invaluable accessories, bringing comfort and color to the home. The chapter on cushions demonstrates how to make cushion

covers in various shapes, fabrics, sizes, and styles and with different edgings. Making a cover for an armchair or sofa can improve its look immeasurably. In addition, a loose cover is easy to remove and clean, and you can make several covers to use on the same piece of furniture at different times. The chapter on simple upholstery includes detailed instructions for making both a fitted cover and a slipcover. Making tablecloths and napkins is also demonstrated in this section, as are the techniques for constructing paper and fabric lampshades.

DECORATING

A room will stay looking good for a long time if you decorate it correctly and take the time to prepare the surfaces carefully and properly. This section of the book uses clear, step-by-step techniques, combined with useful tips and charts, to show you how to complete every decorating project successfully. The painting chapter stresses the importance of thorough surface preparation and gives instructions for achieving perfect paintwork. Both elementary and more specialized techniques, such as dragging, stenciling, stippling, and rag-rolling, are covered. As demonstrated in the chapter on wallpapering, this can be surprisingly simple, once you have mastered the techniques of measuring, cutting, pasting, and hanging wallpaper. Tiling helps protect walls in moist environments, such as kitchens and bathrooms. The chapter on tiling explains how to achieve a long-lasting and professional finish using wall tiles. When you refer to the chapters on flooring, you will find invaluable information that enables you to choose the most appropriate types of floor tile, wooden flooring, or carpets and rugs for every kind of floor surface in your home. Also included are detailed instructions for putting up shelving soundly and for incorporating the most effective type of lighting into your decorative scheme. This section concludes by recommending how to choose and site foliage, flowering, and scented houseplants around the home for a variety of complementary effects. Finally, you will find a handy reference section that covers the care and maintenance of fabrics and surfaces, as well as a glossary of terms and techniques.

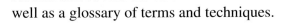

SOFT FURNISHINGS

Basic Sewing Techniques
Curtains
Shades
Bed Furnishings
Cushions
Simple Upholstery
Table Linen
Lampshades

TYPES OF FABRIC

ϒOUR CHOICE OF A FABRIC DEPENDS BOTH ON its use and on how it will affect a room's character. Although the range of natural fibers for textiles is essentially limited to wool, silk, linen, and cotton, fabrics are available in more textures, colors, and patterns than ever before. This is because manufacturers are able to blend fibers together, and with synthetic materials, to make fabrics that are easier to care for, stronger, and more shrink resistant than fabrics made from only one type of natural fiber. When choosing fabrics, bear in mind that texture and the way a fabric drapes are as important as color and pattern.

LINING FABRICS
When you make a window dressing, you may wish to use lining fabric to protect the main fabric from harsh sunlight, add insulation, or provide a neat finish to the draping. Cotton sateen is suitable for lining. Blackout lining will shut out all light. Muslin is a coarse cotton used for inner covers.

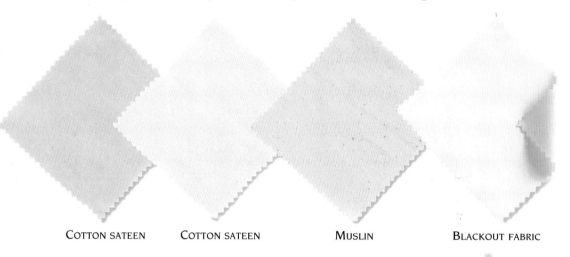

COTTON SATEEN   COTTON SATEEN   MUSLIN   BLACKOUT FABRIC

SHEER FABRICS
These thin and lightweight fabrics are often used as translucent window dressings or decorative edgings. They include nets, lace, batiste, voile, and English embroidery. They gather much easier than thicker materials of a heavier weight, and many are inexpensive. Sheer fabrics are available in a wide range of plain colors, printed patterns, and mixed weaves, and can be difficult to work with.

WHITE BATISTE PRINT   NATURAL BATISTE PRINT   NATURAL COTTON MIXED WEAVE

LIGHTWEIGHT FABRICS
Lightweight fabrics are made from cotton, silk, and synthetic fibers. Like sheers, they are often translucent and can usually be gathered in quantity. If you use silk for a curtain or shade, consider lining it – silk can be damaged if exposed to sunlight for a prolonged period.

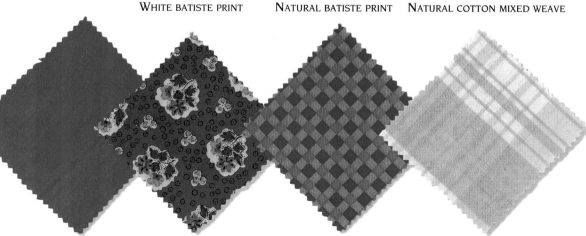

SILK   COTTON FLORAL PRINT   COTTON CHECK PRINT   WOVEN COTTON CHECK

LIGHT TO MEDIUM FABRICS
Possessing a finely woven surface texture, which is an ideal medium for printing detailed patterns, these fabrics are known for their decorative appearance and practical qualities. You can use them for a wide variety of projects, including window dressings, bed furnishings, tablecloths and napkins, and cushion covers. Many of the fabrics in this category handle well and are easy to clean.

WOVEN COTTON CHECK   COTTON FLORAL PRINT   PLAIN COTTON   FLORAL CHINTZ

PLAIN COTTON   COTTON BROCADE   BROCADED TWILL   PRINTED COTTON

MEDIUM-WEIGHT FABRICS
The majority of general-purpose furnishing fabrics are produced in a medium weight. Easy to work with, these fabrics are adaptable and useful throughout the home. Popular fibers include cotton, linen, and mixtures of synthetic and natural fibers that contain wool and silk. Many medium-weight fabrics are suitable for simple upholstery.

LINEN UNION PRINT   PATTERNED WEAVE WITH PRINT   WOOL-AND-COTTON WOVEN PAISLEY

HEAVYWEIGHT FABRICS
Heavyweight fabrics are bulky and present a warm and comfortable appearance to all manner of soft furnishings. Because they are generally very durable, they are often used for upholstery. Many of these fabrics can be very difficult to work with and shape, particularly when making large curtains or loose covers.

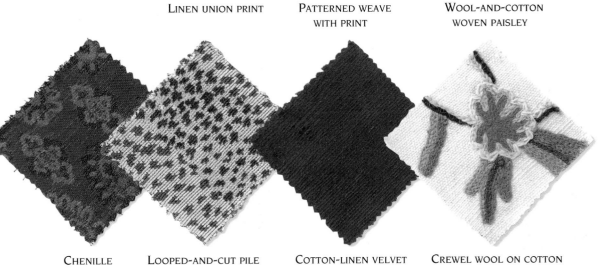

CHENILLE   LOOPED-AND-CUT PILE   COTTON-LINEN VELVET   CREWEL WOOL ON COTTON

BASIC SEWING KIT

To ACHIEVE A PROFESSIONAL FINISH for your soft furnishings, proper equipment and a clean, well-ordered work surface are essential. Keep your sewing equipment separate from your other household tools, and use it only for sewing tasks. Having a work surface large enough for the task is vital – when making extremely long curtains, the floor may be the only suitable surface on which to work. Bear in mind comfort when establishing a work area. Sit on a chair with firm support, and position the table high enough to avoid backache. Work in a well-lit room, particularly when there is limited daylight available.

CUTTING TOOLS

Fabric must always be cut accurately to ensure perfect hanging and fitting. Select scissors that are sharp, durable, and comfortable to use. Avoid using fabric scissors for household chores, since they will quickly become blunted. Use dressmaker's scissors for cutting out patterns and fabric, embroidery scissors for cutting detailed work, and pinking shears for neatening raw edges.

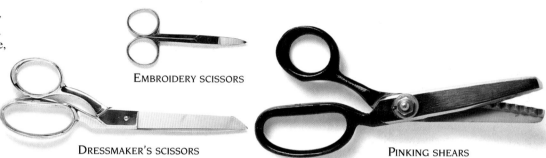

EMBROIDERY SCISSORS

DRESSMAKER'S SCISSORS

PINKING SHEARS

IRON AND IRONING BOARD

An iron should be used not only at the finish but throughout the process, for tasks such as flattening seams, hems, and turnings. Select an iron with a steam feature, if possible: it is not the weight of the iron but the moisture and heat that flattens the fabric. An ironing board should be height adjustable and possess a padded cover that is easy to keep clean.

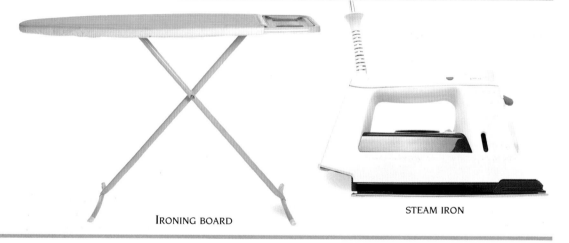

IRONING BOARD

STEAM IRON

SEWING MACHINE

In most cases, a sewing machine is faster and easier than sewing by hand. Modern sewing machines are simple to operate and provide an extensive range of useful options, including straight stitch, zigzag stitch, and reverse settings. Most machines are available with sewing attachments like a zipper foot, which is used for such tasks as securing a zipper to a seam. Keep spare bobbins nearby, and wind the thread on before you begin to work.

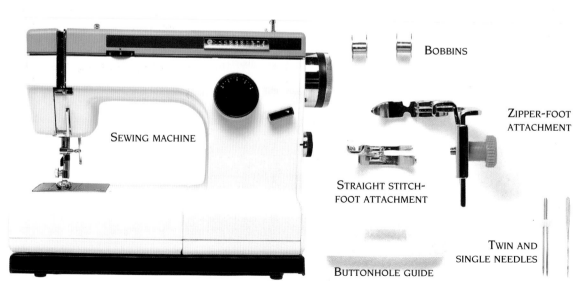

SEWING MACHINE

BOBBINS

ZIPPER-FOOT ATTACHMENT

STRAIGHT STITCH-FOOT ATTACHMENT

BUTTONHOLE GUIDE

TWIN AND SINGLE NEEDLES

SEWING EQUIPMENT

Use plain, stainless steel pins or, for greater visibility on the fabric, pins with colored glass heads. For safety and easy access, keep pins in a box or in a pincushion. A wide range of sewing needles is available for fabrics of different thicknesses. A threader facilitates threading a needle. Select thread according to the project, and to the color, type, and weight of the fabric. Tacking thread is available in a range of colors and is easier to break than other threads.

PINCUSHION

HAND-SEWING
NEEDLES

STRAIGHT
PINS

SEWING THREADS

TACKING THREAD

THREADER

MEASURING AND MARKING EQUIPMENT

Accurate measuring and marking are essential for sewing. A stretch-resistant cloth tape measure enables you to work easily around curves and corners. Mark fabric with a clearly visible color that is easy to remove – use tailor's chalk or a vanishing-ink pen for this purpose. Do not press fabric before vanishing ink has disappeared completely. Many soft furnishings require the fabric to be cut at perfect right angles; a large, transparent try square is ideal for helping you to mark right angles accurately.

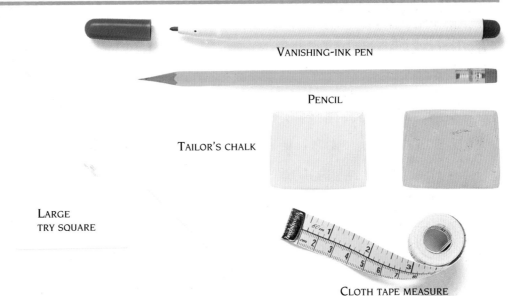

VANISHING-INK PEN

PENCIL

TAILOR'S CHALK

LARGE
TRY SQUARE

CLOTH TAPE MEASURE

MISCELLANEOUS

A bodkin is a blunt, thick needle with a long eye, used for threading cord, ribbon, or elastic through heavy fabric or casings. Unpick seams quickly and easily using a seam ripper. Clothespins are helpful when you need to temporarily secure fabric to stiff objects such as buckram or a lampshade frame. You can use brown paper, tracing paper, or graph paper for making a pattern or template.

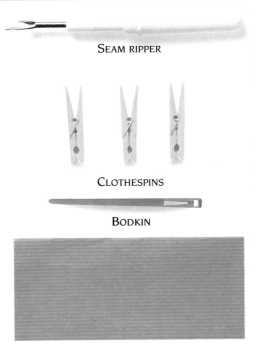

SEAM RIPPER

CLOTHESPINS

BODKIN

PAPER FOR PATTERN MAKING

UPHOLSTERY TOOLS

Few special tools are required when making most cushion covers or simple upholstery. For attaching buttons or tufts to a cushion cover, you will need a long upholstery needle – these are available in a range of sizes. To fit a fabric cover to a simply shaped piece of furniture such as a footstool, use upholstery skewers to stretch and hold the material firmly in place before securing. These upholstery tools should be used only on thick fabric – do not use skewers or upholstery needles on sheer fabric, because they will tear the material.

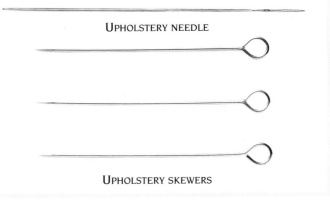

UPHOLSTERY NEEDLE

UPHOLSTERY SKEWERS

HAND SEWING

*A*LTHOUGH SEWING MACHINES can produce almost every variety of stitch, there are always times when you need to sew by hand. Sometimes a hand-sewn effect is desired, and hand sewing can also complement machine sewing – tacking, for instance, is the best way of aligning and holding together layers of fabric for machine stitching. Needle marks and stitches can be hidden by careful preparation: before undertaking any hand sewing, select the finest needles possible and a thread of suitable color and weight. Right-handed people should work from right to left, left-handed people from left to right.

PINNING AND TACKING

Pinning and tacking is used to hold fabric pieces together before sewing. Pin perpendicular to stitching. Use tacking thread in contrasting color. Remove tacking after sewing.

JOINING FABRICS
Pin the fabric pieces together. Secure the end of the thread either by stitching over it or by tying a knot in it. Make all the tacking stitches about ⅜ in (1 cm) long, or alternate stitches ⅝ in (1.5 cm) long at the front with stitches ³⁄₁₆ in (5 mm) long at the back.

SLIPSTITCHING

The slipstitch is used for hems or where a seam must be sewn from the right side of the fabric: for example, to close the opening through which something was turned right side out.

CLOSING A GAP
Secure the thread and take the needle across the opening. Make a stitch ¹⁄₁₆ in (2 mm) long in the seam-line fold. Bring the thread back across the opening and make a similar stitch in the first side. Continue this process to the end, and fasten off in the seam.

TAILOR'S TACKS

Tailor's tacks are used to mark fabrics that need to be joined accurately, or to transfer a pattern mark to one layer of fabric or two identical pieces. Make tailor's tacks with doubled thread in a contrasting color to the fabric. When a number of different marks are needed on one section of fabric, use a different color for each to help you to distinguish them.

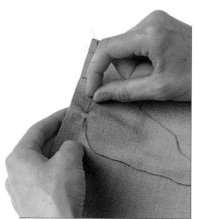

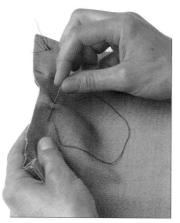

When finishing, cut excess thread to ⅝ in (1.5 cm) to match length of start of tack

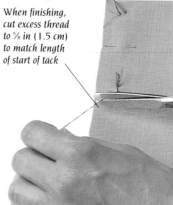

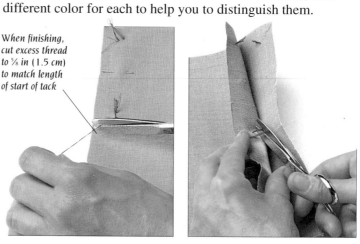

1 STARTING OFF Make a stitch about ⅜ in (1 cm) long through the fabric. Pull the thread through, leaving a ⅝ in (1.5 cm) length of thread on the surface. Insert the needle into the first hole of the stitch again.

2 FORMING A LOOP Make a second stitch through the same holes. Pull the thread through, but leave a loop of tacking thread large enough to fit around your index finger standing out from the fabric.

3 FINISHING OFF A few stitches make a loop of many threads on the fabric. Finish the tack with the needle at the front of the fabric, and cut the thread to leave an end of ⅝ in (1.5 cm), matching the start of the tack.

4 SNIPPING THE THREADS If the tacks are marking two layers of fabric, ease the layers apart and snip the threads as above. If they are made through a pattern lying on the fabric, cut the loop to remove the pattern.

LADDER STITCH

The ladder stitch is ideal for joining two pieces of patterned fabric, ensuring that the pattern matches exactly across the seam prior to a more permanent sewing. Essentially, it is tacking the fabric sections together from the right, or patterned, side. Although the ladder stitch may result in a certain waste of fabric, it is an essential technique for achieving a neat and professional finish when joining pieces of patterned fabric. You will need an iron for this task.

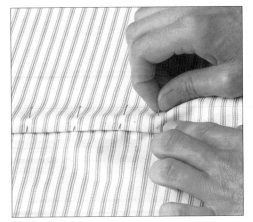

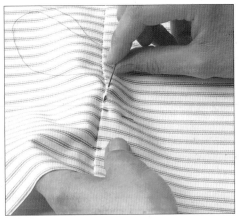

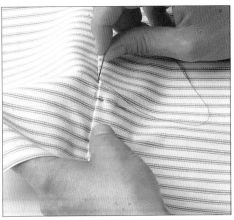

1 ALIGNING PIECES Lay the fabric right side up, overlapping the edges. Fold the edge of the top piece under by ¾ in (2 cm), or more for a heavy fabric. Press the fold, align the pattern, and pin the pieces.

2 STARTING SEAM Thread a needle with tacking thread, and secure the end of the thread on the seam line. Make a stitch ⅜ in (1 cm) long inside the seam-line fold in the top piece of fabric.

3 FORMING LADDER Make a stitch ⅜ in (1 cm) long in the bottom piece of fabric. Make ladderlike stitches to the seam end and fasten off. Fold the fabrics right sides together, sew, and remove ladder stitches.

BLANKET STITCH

The blanket stitch is used mainly for neatening raw edges of fabric, but it can also be used decoratively. Use a thick thread for decorative blanket stitch, especially if the thread is the same color as the cloth, so that the texture of the edging is clearly evident. Closely worked blanket stitch is used to secure the edges of buttonholes: proper buttonhole thread, which is fine but very strong, should be used for this.

BACKSTITCH

This stitch is used for strong, permanent seams, particularly in awkward places such as tight corners, where a machine is difficult to use. It can also be used to sew in zippers, if a machine cannot be used. A backstitch every so often in a hem ensures that even if the hem catches and rips, only a short length will come undone and need resewing.

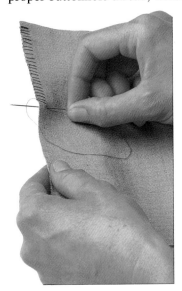

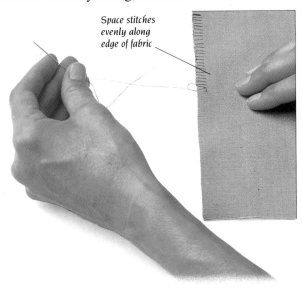

Space stitches evenly along edge of fabric

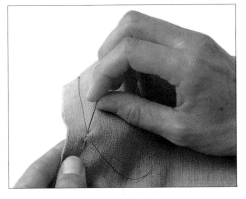

1 MAKING STITCH Make the blanket stitches about ⅜ in (1 cm) in from the raw edge for heavy fabrics, ³⁄₁₆ in (5 mm) for light fabrics, and ⅛ in (3 mm) for buttonholes. Catch the thread behind the needle.

2 TIGHTENING STITCH Pull the needle through. The caught loop of thread runs along the edge of the fabric before turning into the stitch away from the edge. Tighten gently to avoid puckering the edge of the fabric, and repeat the stitch all along the edge. Space the stitches widely on heavy fabrics, closer on light fabrics, and right next to each other for buttonholes.

THE STITCH
From the front, make a stitch ⅜ in (1 cm) long. Push the needle to the back of the fabric ³⁄₁₆ in (5 mm) back along this stitch, and bring it to the front ³⁄₁₆ in (5 mm) beyond the stitch. Repeat sewing each stitch into the end of the previous one. At the front, the stitches should be ³⁄₁₆ in (5 mm) long; at the back, they should be ⅜ in (1 cm) long and overlap.

SEAMS

*W*HEN MAKING ANY SOFT FURNISHING, it is necessary to use a number of specific hand- and machine-sewing techniques to create a durable and neatly finished article. The choice of a suitable seam for joining the pieces of fabric, from a variety that includes French, overlocked, plain, and flat fell seams, is most important. Consider the task ahead before selecting the most suitable method for the purpose and appearance of the seam.

BASIC SEAMING

The plain seam is the most simple and versatile means of joining together two lengths of fabric. Always pin and tack the lengths of fabric together along the seam line before sewing. Neat corners and curves are achieved by cutting and clipping: at a corner, cut away a triangle of fabric; along a curve, cut a serrated edge or snip into the seam allowance.

PLAIN FLAT SEAM

Pin and tack, then position the fabric under the machine needle and clamp it in place with the presser foot. Secure the thread in the seam by sewing forward and backward along the seam line for ⅜ in (1 cm) several times. Sew along the seam as required, and finish by stitching back and forth on the seam line again. Remove the tacking stitches and press the seam open. When using a new stitch or type of fabric, sew a short length of test seam on a scrap first, to check that the machine settings are correct.

CLIPPING CORNERS

At corners, cut across the seam allowance after sewing the seam. Leave about ¼ in (6 mm) between the seam and the cut edge of the fabric, or the seam allowance may fray away when the piece is turned right-side out.

CLIPPING CURVES

Clip a convex seam into a serrated edge, as above, to reduce its bulk and prevent distortion. Snip into the seam allowance of a concave seam to ease the fabric and prevent pulling. Be careful not to cut too close to the seam.

NEATENING RAW EDGES

The raw edges of pieces of fabric should be finished to prevent them from fraying – this is called neatening. It is particularly important on furnishings that will have to endure hard wear. You can neaten a raw edge in one of several ways – by oversewing or overlocking it, by sewing a zigzag stitch along it, by applying bias binding to it, or simply by serrating it with pinking shears.

Probably the easiest and the most commonly used neatening technique is zigzag sewing with a machine. Bias binding ensures that no raw edges are visible. Overlocking also hides raw edges, but you must allow extra fabric for this. When the reverse of a fabric and, therefore, any seams will be visible, it may be worth using a self-neatening seam *(see opposite)*.

MACHINE ZIGZAG

Set the machine to the zigzag stitch and clamp the raw edge under the needle. Secure the thread, stitch along the fabric as close to the edge as possible, and fasten off.

OVERSEWING BY HAND

Make evenly spaced stitches from the back to the front of the fabric, bringing the thread over the raw edge. Do not pull the stitches too tight, or the fabric will pucker.

BIAS BINDING

Unfold one edge of the binding and align it with the raw edge. Pin, tack, and sew on the binding fold. Fold the binding over the edge, and sew through all the layers.

OVERLOCKING

Make seam allowances 1–1¼ in (2.5–3 cm) deep. Trim one to ³⁄₁₆ in (5 mm) after sewing, and fold the wide edge over it, tucking the raw edge under. Pin, then stitch along the fold.

PINKING

Pinking shears cut a serrated edge. Pinking is a quick and easy way to neaten a raw edge, but it is not hard wearing and is therefore best used only on internal seams.

FRENCH SEAM

This is a strong, self-neatening seam that does not show any additional stitching line from the right side of the fabric. It can, however, be used only on straight edges, and you must allow ⅝ in (1.5 cm) for the seam allowances. A French seam is ideal to use if both sides of the fabric will be visible, as is the case when sewing with sheer fabric.

1 FIRST SEAM Pin and tack the pieces of fabric wrong sides together. Machine sew a plain seam (*see opposite*) ³⁄₁₆ in (5 mm) from the edge. Take the fabric from the machine and remove the tacking stitches.

2 TRIMMING SEAMS Carefully trim both of the seam allowances to ⅛ in (3 mm) with a pair of sharp scissors. Turn the pieces of fabric right sides together, fold along the seam line, and press.

3 SECOND SEAM Tack the layers of fabric right sides together close to the folded edge. Sew a second seam ⅜ in (1 cm) from the first (which is now the folded edge), enclosing the raw edges.

4 FINISHED SEAM Remove the tacking stitches and unfold the fabric right side up. The neat seam will be visible, with no stitching evident. Press the seam allowance flat to one side of the seam.

FLAT FELL SEAM

The flat fell seam is extremely useful where both strength and a flat finish are required, which is often the case with upholstery. The stitching will, however, be visible on the right side of the fabric with this seam.

1 SEWING SEAM Sew the pieces of fabric right sides together, ⅝ in (1.5 cm) from the aligned edges. Trim one allowance to ³⁄₁₆ in (5 mm).

2 FOLDING SEAM Fold the wide allowance over the narrow one. Lay both to one side, the raw edge underneath, and tack.

3 SECOND SEAM Sew along the tacking from the right side and press the seam flat. One row of stitches will show.

TOPSTITCHING

This is a simple technique that can be used to emphasize a line such as a seam. A thick, contrasting thread or a long stitch can be used to give more emphasis. Pin, tack, and sew a plain seam, remove the tacking stitches, and press the seam open. Run a line of stitching along either side of the seam from the right side.

QUILTING

Quilting not only provides an extra thickness of insulation, it also gives a decorative finish. Wadding can simply be stitched between the layers of fabric, as here, and the edges bound.

Alternatively, you can tack the wadding to the wrong side of one piece and put the pieces right sides together. Seam on three sides, turn right sides out, and slipstitch (*see page 14*) the fourth edge.

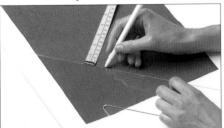  

1 MARKING PATTERN Decide on the pattern. Diagonals are simple and prominent, but you might quilt around designs on a fabric. Mark the quilting lines on the fabric with a suitable marker.

2 ASSEMBLING LAYERS Cut the wadding, the backing fabric, and the main fabric to the same size, and sandwich the wadding between the layers of fabric. Pin and tack the layers together.

3 SEWING QUILTING Run lines of tacking across the fabric to hold the wadding firmly in place. Sew along the quilting lines. Remove the tacking and trim wadding out of the seam allowances. Bind the edges.

USING FABRIC

*B*EFORE YOU BEGIN A SOFT FURNISHING TECHNIQUE, there are a few basic rules that you need to bear in mind about handling and estimating amounts of fabric. Cutting out fabric and joining panels are skills that are essential for almost every sewing project. When using patterned fabric, you must match the design motifs between joins in panels, and between pieces of fabric that will be positioned side by side, as in the case of curtains. Before you cut out the fabric, assess the final appearance of the pattern by placing it against the object that it will cover and adjusting it until the design motif is positioned to your satisfaction.

PLACING THE PATTERN

When you intend to make a soft furnishing using a patterned fabric, first consider the placement of the pattern in relation to the item you are decorating, such as a window or piece of furniture. You should match the pattern across any seams in the fabric, as well as over panels of fabric. Use a tape measure to determine the size of the pattern repeat on a fabric. It is important to bear in mind the size of the pattern repeat when calculating the amount of fabric required.

MEASURING PATTERN REPEAT

Manufacturers indicate the size of the pattern repeat on the selvage, or on a ticket attached to the bolt. To establish the dimension of the pattern yourself, measure the distance between identical motifs.

MATCHING ACROSS PANELS

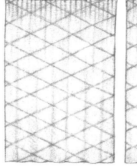

When making a pair of furnishings to hang side by side, such as curtains, consider how the pattern matches across the drops. Make sure the pattern will match edge to edge when the curtains are closed. Cut out one curtain, then match the second to the first *(see page 41)*.

PARTIAL REPEATS

When dressing a window with a curtain or shade, it may be impossible to avoid having a partial pattern repeat at the top or bottom. For a short curtain *(left)*, place the partial pattern above the heading and the full pattern at the bottom hem. A full-length curtain should have a full pattern at the heading *(right)* and a partial pattern along the bottom hem.

CUTTING OUT FABRIC

Cutting out fabric is not difficult as long as you are careful and use a sharp pair of scissors. The most effective and comfortable method of cutting out fabric is to lay it out on a smooth, flat surface. You may need to use a clean floor as a work surface when cutting out a large piece of fabric. To cut out fabric accurately, you will need the basic sewing kit.

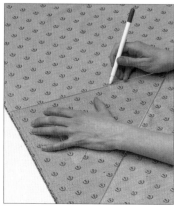

1 MARKING FABRIC Fabric should be cut on the grain – along the weft threads and across the warp threads. Lay a try square at right angles to the selvage, and mark the cutting line using a vanishing-ink pen.

2 CUTTING FABRIC Using a pair of dressmaker's scissors, cut steadily along the marked line. Some loosely woven fabrics can be cut following the gap made by pulling out a single thread *(see page 41)*.

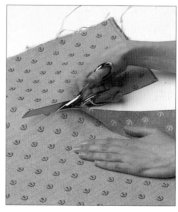

NOTCHING FABRIC

You may need to join lengths of fabric from the bottom edge to the top edge. To identify the direction of the lengths, and to continue any pile or shading from length to length, cut notches at the top edges.

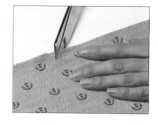

JOINING PLAIN FABRICS

For most soft furnishing techniques, you will need to join panels of fabric to form a single large piece. Most techniques require joins to be made with plain flat seams *(see page 16)*.

When greater strength or flatness is desired, however, use flat fell seams or French seams *(see page 17)*. To join panels, you will need matching thread and the basic sewing kit.

1 TACKING PANELS After the fabric has been cut to size, lay out the panels right sides together, and match their raw edges. Pin and tack the panels together, making a seam ⅝ in (1.5 cm) from the edges.

2 SEWING SEAM Remove the pins before machine sewing along the tacked line. Remove the tacking stitches after you have finished sewing.

3 FLATTENING SEAM Press the seam allowance flat to smooth the finished join.

JOINING PATTERNED FABRICS

When you are using patterned fabric, you will need to match the pattern repeat across seams. Before cutting out the fabric, decide where you want the pattern to lie when the soft furnishing is complete. Cut out the first piece, then cut the second piece by matching the pattern with reference to the first. Join panels after all of the required pieces of fabric have been cut out. To align the pattern repeat when joining fabric, you will need matching thread and the basic sewing kit.

1 MATCHING PATTERN Along the edge of one panel, press a ⅝ in (1.5 cm) seam allowance to the wrong side. Turn the panel over and place the pressed edge on top of the raw edge of the other panel, right sides up. Match the pattern over the panels. Keeping the edges together, fold the pressed panel onto the other panel, right sides facing. Pin the panels together along the fold line.

2 STITCHING PANELS Open out the panels, and make sure the pattern remains aligned. Ladder stitch *(see page 15)* along the fold line to temporarily secure the panels together. Fold the panels right sides together again, and sew a plain flat seam *(see page 16)* along the fold line. Remove the ladder stitches.

PLACING JOINS

The placement of joined panels of fabric on or across large pieces of furniture or windows is as important as the positioning of pattern repeats. Place the fabric against the furniture or window, and decide what looks most appropriate for each type of furnishing and fabric. Across a window, place the fabric joins to the sides. For bed and table furnishings, center a complete fabric panel down the middle of the length of the furniture.

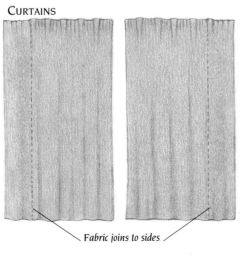

CURTAINS

Fabric joins to sides

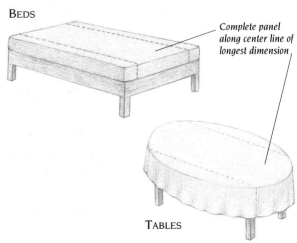

BEDS

Complete panel along center line of longest dimension

TABLES

HEMS AND MITERING

*F*INISHING A HOMEMADE FURNISHING with suitable hems and correct mitering is an important part of achieving a neat and professional look. The careful preparation and execution of hems is as vital as choosing the right fabric or the best type of seam to use. When deciding on a hem, it is important to select the appropriate depth for the fabric and the scale of the furnishing: deep for large items and heavy fabrics, shallower for lighter fabrics and smaller pieces. Mitering is a vital skill to master, because it is the only effective way of achieving a neat corner on deep hems.

HEMS

Hems can vary from ³⁄₁₆ in (5 mm) to 6 in (15 cm) in depth. If it is not important to hide the sewing, you can sew the hem by machine. Use a straight or zigzag stitch, or (if the machine has the option) a blind hem stitch. For inconspicuous stitching, it is best to hem by hand. Use a thread slightly darker than the fabric: hemming stitches catch the light more than the fabric.

HERRINGBONE STITCH, SINGLE HEM

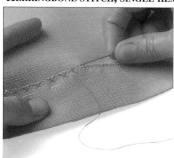

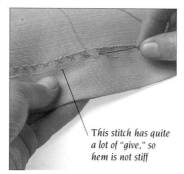

This stitch has quite a lot of "give," so hem is not stiff

1 **STITCHING FABRIC** This method is used for heavy fabrics and on lined curtains. Neaten the edge by oversewing or with a zigzag stitch. Turn the hem up to the required depth, pin, and tack. Secure the thread, and catch up a few threads of the main fabric against the direction in which you will sew.

2 **STITCHING HEM** Pull the needle through. Crossing the thread over the first stitch, push it into the hem farther along. Make a stitch through the hem turning – again, working in the opposite direction to the seam. Repeat this procedure along the hem, with each stitch crossing over the last.

DOUBLE HEM WITH CONCEALED STITCHING

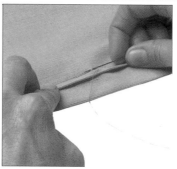

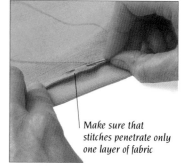

Make sure that stitches penetrate only one layer of fabric

1 **STITCHING FABRIC** This method is suitable for finer fabrics. Turn up the hem to the required depth, press, and turn up by same amount again. Pin and tack a little way from the top. Fold back the top of the hem by ³⁄₁₆ in (5 mm). Secure the thread, and catch up one or two threads from the main fabric.

2 **STITCHING HEM** Sew a small stitch through one layer only of the folded back top of the hem. Continue this way, stitching alternately through the hem and the main fabric. When the hem is finished, fold the top part of the hem flat and press it: the stitching will be concealed within the hem.

TWICE-TURNED AND SLIPSTITCHED HEM

This hem uses less fabric than a double hem

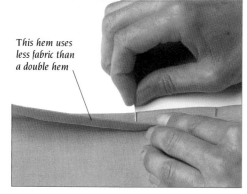

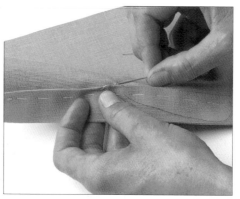

1 **PINNING HEM** Use this method for hiding raw edges on medium-weight and lightweight fabrics. Turn the raw edge up by ³⁄₈–³⁄₄ in (1–2 cm) and press. Turn the edge up again to the required depth, pin, and tack.

2 **STITCHING HEM** Slipstitch the hem by alternately catching up a few threads from the main body of the fabric and making a stitch of ³⁄₈ in (1 cm) in the hem fold. Continue along the length of the hem.

MACHINE-STITCHED HEM

This is a quick way to hem if the stitching need not be hidden – for example, on curtain linings. Turn the hem up to the required depth, as for a double or twice-turned hem, pin, and tack. Machine sew close to the top of the hem.

MITERING CORNERS

Mitering hem turnings at corners ensures a neat and tidy finish, no matter how bulky the fabric. It must be done before the rest of the hems are sewn. Mitering is an important technique and is particularly useful when making curtains. It is not difficult, but the method does vary according to both the type of hem used and the depth of the turnings. Folding the corners to make a miter can be an awkward task with some particularly thick and difficult-to-handle fabrics. Cutting excess fabric out of the corner miters will reduce the quantity of layered fabric and help to make a neater finish.

SINGLE HEM MITER

1 MARKING CORNER Neaten the raw edges. Fold the hems to the required depth, one over the other, and press. Mark the points where they cross with a pin in each turning.

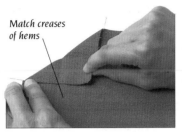

Match creases of hems

2 FOLDING CORNER Unfold the hem turnings. Make a fold across the corner from one pin to the other – the creases from the hem turnings should align. Press the fold.

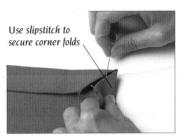

Use slipstitch to secure corner folds

3 STITCHING MITER Refold both of the hems over the diagonally folded corner to give a neat miter. Slipstitch the corner folds together, and sew the hems as required.

DOUBLE HEM MITER

Fold hems twice. Mark where the one on top falls on the other with a pin. Repeat with the other hem on top. Unfold the second hem folds, fold from pin to pin, press, refold hems, and slipstitch miter.

TWICE-TURNED MITER

1 FOLDING EDGES Lay the fabric wrong side up. Fold the edges to be hemmed to the wrong side by ⅜ in (1 cm) and press the turnings. Fold them up to their required finished depths and press again.

2 FOLDING CORNER Unfold the second turnings and fold across the corner diagonally. Align the second turning creases on the folded corner with the same creases running along the edges. Press flat.

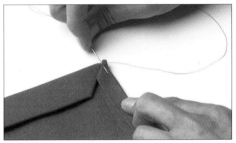

3 COMPLETING MITER Refold the hems along the fold lines of the second turning, with the corner folded inside the hems. Slipstitch the mitered corner and sew the rest of the hems.

CUTTING A SINGLE-HEM MITER

1 FOLDING CORNERS Follow steps 1and 2 for the single-hem miter. Unfold the fold across the corner, and refold the whole piece of fabric on a diagonal into the corner, with the right sides together and the adjacent sides aligning.

2 CUTTING ACROSS The crease left by the fold across the corner is now folded double on itself. Sew along it, and trim away the excess corner fabric beyond the seam, leaving a seam allowance of ¼ in (6 mm). Press the seam open.

3 TURNING OUT Unfold the fabric and turn the mitered corner right side out. Carefully push out the corner with the end of a pair of scissors: use scissors with rounded, not sharp, tips. Sew the rest of the hems as required.

CUTTING AN UNEVEN MITER

1 FOLDING IN Follow steps 1 and 2 for the twice-turned miter. Open the corner. Fold the piece on a diagonal, right sides together. The fold runs through the point where the creases of the second turnings cross, not into the corner.

2 COMPLETING CORNER Sew along the crease across the corner, and cut away the excess fabric. Press the seam open, turn the corner right side out, and refold the hems. Push out the corner with the end of a pair of scissors.

TRIMMINGS

A VARIETY OF EASY-TO-APPLY EDGINGS can be used for decoration. Trimmings are not structurally important, but when used with imagination, binding, piping, or a frilled or pleated edging can add a smart and individual finish to curtains, cushions, bed linen, or blinds. In addition to these hand-finished edgings, there is also a host of ready-made trimmings available, such as braids, fringes, lace, ribbons, and cords, that can be stitched onto or into a seam or hem to provide extra color and texture.

BINDING AND PIPING

These edgings add both decoration and strength to soft furnishings. Binding is made from strips of fabric that are cut on the bias – a line diagonal to the grain, or weave – and will not pucker on curves. Ready-cut bias binding can be bought in a variety of weights and colors, but it is easy to cut strips from most kinds of fabric. Piped edging is made by covering a length of piping cord with strips of bias binding. Piping cord is sold in a range of diameters, suitable for different furnishings and weights of fabric. Always preshrink piping cord and bias strip by washing them.

BIAS STRIPS

Snip off corners of pressed seam to reduce bulk

1 FINDING THE BIAS Check that the edges of the fabric are cut along the grain. Fold the fabric diagonally, so that one straight raw edge lies parallel to the adjacent edge. This fold is the bias line. Press in place.

2 MARKING STRIPS Calculate the length and the width of binding needed – allow extra for joins. Rule measured lines parallel to the bias crease, marking with vanishing ink or tailor's chalk, and cut the strips.

3 JOINING STRIPS Join strips by placing them right sides together at right angles to each other. The raw edges and the straight grains should align. Pin, tack if necessary, and sew ³⁄₁₆ in (5 mm) from the raw edges.

4 TRIMMING JOINS Open the seam and press it flat. You now have a bias strip with two corners sticking out at the seam. Snip off these corners. Join pieces as necessary to make up the required length of strip.

CONTINUOUS BIAS STRIP

1 FINDING THE BIAS This is a useful way of making a long length of bias binding. Take a rectangle of fabric with straight edges, and fold one short side down diagonally to meet the adjacent edge. Press in place and cut along the bias-line crease.

2 SEWING PIECES Lay the triangle on the other piece, right sides together and short straight edges aligned, so that when sewn they will form a diamond. Sew the pieces together, using a plain seam with a ¼ in (6 mm) allowance, and press the seam open.

3 MARKING STRIPS Lay the fabric right side up. Mark lines parallel to the bias across the whole of the fabric, spaced to the desired width for the finished strip. Use a straight edge and either vanishing ink or tailor's chalk to mark the lines on the fabric.

4 FORMING A TUBE Fold the fabric right sides together, aligning the marked edges. Align the ends of the marked lines, offsetting them by one: they will form a spiral. Pin along these edges to form a tube: the seam will spiral. Turn the tube right side out.

5 CUTTING A STRIP Check that the bias lines on the pinned edges meet. Turn the tube inside out again, tack, and sew a plain flat seam ¼ in (6 mm) from the edge. Press the seam flat. Starting at one end, cut along the marked line in a continuous spiral.

COVERING PIPING CORD

1 MEASURING CORD Choose a cord and wash to preshrink. Measure around it and add 1¼ in (3 cm) for seam allowances: this is the width of bias strip that is required. Cut a strip to this width and the required length.

2 COVERING CORD Lay the cord along the center of the wrong side of the bias strip. Fold the strip over the cord, and pin and tack. Sew close to the cord, using a zipper attachment if you use a machine.

APPLYING PIPING

1 PINNING PIPING Cut and cover the required length of piping cord, adding 4 in (10 cm) for joining lengths if necessary. Lay the piping on the right side of one piece of fabric, with the raw edges aligning. Pin in place, snipping the seam allowance at corners, and tack.

2 SEWING IN Lay the second piece of fabric on top of the piece with the piping attached, right sides together and raw edges aligning. The piping will be sandwiched between them. Tack and sew through all the layers close to the cord, using the zipper attachment.

JOINING PIPING STRAIGHT ACROSS

1 THINNING CORD Sew the piping to the right side of one piece of fabric. Allow a 1 in (2.5 cm) overlap, and leave 2 in (5 cm) of each end free. Open a few stitches on each end to reveal the cord. Unravel the ends, and cut half the strands from each.

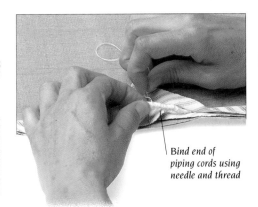

Bind end of piping cords using needle and thread

2 BINDING CORD Twist the ends of the cord together and bind with thread. With the piping ends flat and wrong side up, fold one end to the wrong side by ¼ in (6 mm). Lay the other end of the binding on top of it and trim the overlap to ⅝ in (1.5 cm).

3 SEWING JOIN Fold the overlapping ends of the binding around the cord. Sew along the seam line, over the join, securing the piping to the fabric. Slipstitch the join in the binding. To disguise a join, make it at a seam or in a central position on a panel.

JOINING PIPING DIAGONALLY

1 MATCHING UP This is the neatest way to join piping. Sew piping to the right side of one fabric piece, with a 4 in (10 cm) overlap free and with seam unpicked. Fold back the corner plus ¼ in (6 mm) of one end of the bias strip diagonally, on its straight grain, and press.

2 PINNING BIAS STRIP Lay the other end of the bias strip on top of the folded end. Make sure that the straight grain of the two ends matches, and that both ends lie flat. Carefully pin the two pieces of bias strip together along the fold in the bottom end.

3 JOINING ENDS Tack and sew along the pinned fold line, and trim off the excess fabric from the ends of the bias strips. Press the finished seam flat. Unravel the ends of the piping cord, cut strands away from each to thin them, and twist them together.

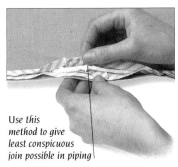

Use this method to give least conspicuous join possible in piping

4 FINISHING JOIN Stitch and bind the two ends of the piping cord together securely with a needle and thread. Fold the diagonally stitched bias strip over the bound piping cord ends. Tack the joined piping to the main fabric, using a zipper attachment if machine sewing.

FRILLS AND PLEATS

Frills are most often used on bed linen and scatter cushions. Use single frills for a delicate effect, double frills for a robust finish or for furnishings with different fabrics on each side. Frills need from one and a half to three times their finished length in fabric: gather heavy fabrics gently, light ones more tightly. Pleats, which need two and a half to three times their finished length in fabric, give a formal look. Use tailor's tacks *(see page 14)* to align pieces, and allow extra fabric at corners.

SINGLE FRILL

Cut a strip of fabric to the width and length required, allowing extra fabric for the seam you choose for joins. Hem the bottom edge by hand or machine, as shown here. Neaten the top edge of the fabric and gather it using one of the methods shown here.

DOUBLE FRILL

Double thickness of fabric gives this frill body

Cut a strip of fabric to the length required and to double the finished depth plus 1¼ in (3 cm). Join lengths as necessary and press the seams flat. Fold the strip in half lengthwise, wrong sides together, and press. Gather the fabric through both edges.

HAND GATHERING

Use small stitches for fine or close gathering

1 **GATHERING STITCH** Use this method for medium- to heavyweight fabrics and double frills. Using a strong thread, tie a knot in the end that will not pull through the fabric. On the seam line, make stitches as if tacking, adjusting the length to suit.

2 **GATHERING FABRIC** When you reach the end, hold the free end of the thread firmly. Ease the fabric toward the knotted end to the correct length and fullness, and knot the free end. Even the gathers out and pin and tack in place.

MACHINE GATHERING FOR LIGHTWEIGHT FABRICS

1 **LONG STITCHING** Set the machine to the longest stitch. Slightly increase the top tension to make the gathers easy to pull up. Sew ⅜–⅝ in (1–1.5 cm) from the edge, leaving the end free.

2 **GATHERING FABRIC** Run a second row of stitches close to the first. Pull up the free ends of the threads, making sure that the secured ends stay in place. Knot the gathering threads.

MACHINE ZIGZAG FOR HEAVYWEIGHT FABRICS

1 **SECURING THREAD** Cut a piece of strong thread or fine twine to the length of the fabric band, and lay it on the band about ⅝ in (1.5 cm) from the raw edge. Carefully zigzag over it.

2 **MAKING GATHERS** Stitch over one end of the strong thread several times, and gather the fabric by holding the free end and easing the fabric along toward the secured end.

SINGLE- OR DOUBLE-LAYERED KNIFE PLEATS

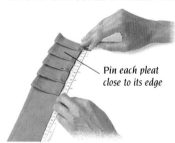

Pin each pleat close to its edge

1 **MAKING A SAMPLE** Decide on the size of pleat, make a strip of four or five pleats, and pin and press it. Make the pleats deep enough to give a firm edge, but do not overlap them, except at corners. Measure the length of the sample section.

2 **CALCULATING LENGTHS** Unpin and measure the strip. Divide the length of edging you need by the length of the pleated strip. Multiply this by the length of the sample piece when unpleated. The result is the length of fabric needed.

3 **MARKING PLEATS** Make up the edging, joining with plain or flat fell seams as required. Mark up the wrong side with lines for folding as you join the lengths, ensuring that joins will be hidden in the folded back section of a pleat.

4 **STITCHING PLEATS** Fold the pleats on the lines and pin them. When all the pleats are pinned, tack along the seam line about ⅝ in (1.5 cm) from the top edge. Press the strip. Sew along the seam line and remove the tacking stitches.

BOX PLEATS

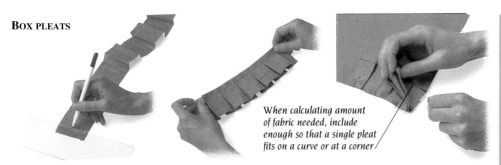

1 MARKING UP Box pleats take three times the final length in fabric, so multiply the length to be edged by three for the fabric needed. Mark lines for pleating on the wrong side of the strip.

2 MAKING UP Fold and pin the fabric on the marked lines to form the box pleats. To secure the pleats, tack along the seam line, and press and sew the pleated strip.

When calculating amount of fabric needed, include enough so that a single pleat fits on a curve or at a corner

3 TURNING CORNERS At a corner, fold the pleated strip, and attach as necessary. The corner fold should run down the middle of a pleat. Finished box pleats make a very formal decoration.

BOWS

A bow can either be used as a simple trimming or act as a fastener. Cut a strip of fabric to the length and double the finished width required, adding ¾ in (2 cm) each way for seam allowances. Fold the strip in half lengthwise. Pin, tack, and sew ⅜ in (1 cm) from the raw edge. Leave a gap in the center of the seam on the long edge to allow for turning right side out, and sew across the ends diagonally. Snip the seam allowances at the corners, turn right side out, and press. Slipstitch the opening closed and tie in a bow.

READY-MADE TRIMMINGS

Fringes, colorful ribbons and cords, and delicate lace can be found in department and sewing stores. Allow for seams, corners, and neatening, and check that trimmings are preshrunk and colorfast if they will be washed. If a trimming needs two rows of machine sewing, sew the same way both times, to prevent puckering.

FRINGING IN A SEAM

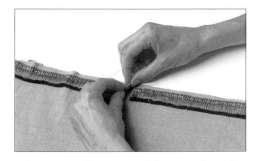

1 APPLYING FRINGE If there is a line of "stay" stitches on the fringe edge, leave them in. Lay the fringe face down on the right side of the fabric, with the part you will sew through on the seam line. Pin and tack in place, butting the ends at any joins.

2 STITCHING IN Lay the second panel of fabric right side down on top of the first piece and the fringe, aligning the edges. Pin and tack through all three layers along the seam line. Sew along the tacking line and remove the tacking. Turn right side out.

3 FINISHING SEAM If necessary, remove the manufacturer's stay stitches from the fringe by unfastening them at one end and gently pulling them out. Fringes can also be sewn on the edge of a fabric, or over the stitches of a hem, on the right side.

LACE

1 FOLDING CORNERS If lace is sewn into or onto an edge, it must be mitered at corners. Fold it back on itself, right sides together, and press. Fold one end back diagonally, and press.

2 SEWING ACROSS Fold the top end flat on the other again. Pin, tack, and sew along the diagonal fold. Remove the tacks and trim the excess lace. Press, and neaten the edges.

RIBBON

1 TACKING Always mark the position and tack ribbon first. Needles mark some satin ribbon, so tack this at the edges. At corners, fold narrow ribbon, and miter bulky ribbon as for lace.

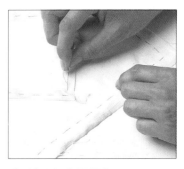

2 JOINING ENDS At corners, diagonally fold one end under and sew it on top of the other. On a straight length, fold one end under by ⅜ in (1 cm), lay it over the other, and slipstitch.

FASTENINGS

A COVER THAT HAS TO BE REMOVED from time to time for cleaning needs a suitable fastening. Fabrics for removable covers range from sturdy materials suitable for a sofa to fine cottons and delicate textiles used for bed linen and cushions, so take care to match the fastening to the type of soft furnishing. For a heavy-duty closure, use a zipper or sturdy hooks and eyes. More lightweight, decorative fasteners include fabric ties and buttons. Hide snaps and Velcro tabs or strips within a seam. When a cover needs only infrequent cleaning, consider slipstitching one seam, opening it when necessary.

VELCRO

Velcro is also known as "touch-and-close" fastening. Two strips of material, one covered with tiny hooks, the other with small loops, adhere to each other when brought together.

Although easy to apply and use, it is too stiff for light- or medium-weight materials. Continuous lengths of several widths and colors and tabs of various sizes are available.

VELCRO SPOTS

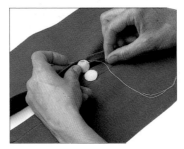

VELCRO TAPE

1 FIRST SIDE The seam allowance must be wider than the tab. Mark sites for the tabs and pin half a tab to one allowance. Hand sew in place.

2 SECOND SIDE On the opposite allowance, align the second half of the tab with the first. Pin and sew in place. Space tabs 2–4 in (5–10 cm) apart.

1 FIRST STRIP Use a tape slightly narrower than the seam allowance. Place one half on the allowance and pin, tack, and sew it in place.

2 SECOND STRIP Pin the other half of the tape on the opposite allowance. Check the alignment and adjust if necessary. Tack and sew in place.

SNAPS

Snaps are available in both metal and plastic, and in a limited variety of colors and sizes. They are sold either loose, to be stitched on individually, or mounted to a tape, which is more convenient for long openings. Although they are a simple

means of fastening two edges together, snaps are not very sturdy and will pop open under any moderate strain. They are suitable for bed linen and scatter cushions, where they can be unobtrusively mounted for a neat finish.

SEW-ON SNAPS

SNAP STRIP

1 THE SOCKET Mark positions ¼ in (6 mm) from the edge with pins every 2–4 in (5–10 cm). Place the socket of a snap on the seam underlap, and work a few stitches through each hole.

2 ALIGNING HALVES Place the ball half of the snap on the overlapping fabric in the position marked by the pin. Check its alignment with the socket half, and sew in position.

1 FIRST STRIP The seam allowance must be wider than the strip. Turn under the raw edges on the ends of the strip, position it on the seam allowance, and pin in place.

2 ALIGNING STRIPS To align the two strips accurately, lay the second one on the first and close the snaps. Pin the second strip in place, working from the back, and turn under the raw ends.

3 SEWING ON STRIPS Open the snaps and tack and sew both edges of the strips. Work in the same direction each time to prevent puckering, and use the zipper attachment on a sewing machine.

HOOKS AND EYES

Hand-sewn metal hooks and eyes are a simple fastening for edge-to-edge or overlapping fabric pieces. These easy-to-hide fasteners are available in a number of different sizes, and are sold either loose or mounted on a plastic strip. They are strong enough to take quite considerable strain, making them particularly suitable for furniture covers.

INDIVIDUAL HOOKS AND EYES

1 THE EYES Mark positions for the fasteners with pins every 2–4 in (5–10 cm). Hold the eye in place, and sew five or six times through each metal loop.

2 THE HOOKS Check the hooks' alignment. Stitch over the hook neck and through the loops. If the seam allowances gape, slipstitch the edges.

HOOK-AND-EYE STRIP

1 FIRST SIDE The seam allowance must be wider than the strip. Neaten the raw edges of the strips. Place the eye strip on the allowance and pin, tack, and sew in place. Use a zipper attachment if necessary.

2 SECOND STRIP Fasten the hooks and eyes to align the strips. Pin the hooked strip from the back, undo the hooks, and tack. Sewing through both layers of fabric will leave visible stitching. If sewing through one layer only, slipstitch the seam allowance to prevent gaping.

TIES

Fabric ties make an unusual change from ready-made fasteners. Flat fabric ties are easily made up and attached and make a decorative fastener for lightweight furnishings such as bed linen and scatter cushions. Rouleau strips are narrow tubes made up from bias strips, which can be tied or mounted as loops along an opening as an alternative to buttonholes.

FLAT TIES

Cut across inner corners diagonally to reduce fabric bulk

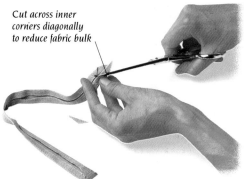

1 CUTTING ENDS Cut the length and twice the width of the tie, plus ⅜ in (1 cm) all around. Fold the edges of the long sides to the wrong side by ⅜ in (1 cm) and press. Cut across the corners diagonally and fold the ends down to wrong side. Press.

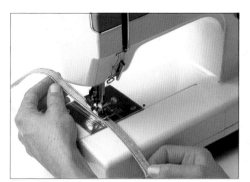

2 SEWING Fold fabric in half lengthwise, wrong sides together. Pin, tack, and sew all sides, about ¹⁄₁₆ in (2 mm) from edge. Make up the other tie. Pin one end of each tie to each side of the opening, sew in place, and tie into a bow or knot.

ROULEAU STRIPS

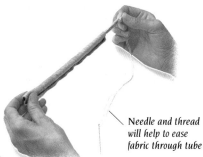

Needle and thread will help to ease fabric through tube

1 SEWING A TUBE Fold the required length of bias strip, using a strip 1–1¼ in (2.5–3 cm) wide, in half lengthwise, right sides together; press and sew ¼ in (6 mm) from the edge.

2 ATTACHING THREAD Thread a large, blunt needle with strong thread or fine twine. Secure the thread to one end of the rouleau and push the needle into the opening of the tube.

3 TURNING TUBE Work the needle and thread along the tube and out at the other end. The end of the rouleau will follow: take hold of it and pull the tube right side out.

4 FINISHING STRIP Snip the thread from the tube, and tuck the raw edges of the rouleau back to the inside. Oversew the ends neatly with small stitches to finish off.

BUTTONS

Although they are associated with clothing, many buttons are eminently suitable for soft furnishings. They are made from plastic, wood, leather, and shell, or may be fabric-covered.

Buttons can be both functional and decorative. They are not very strong, so use them where they will not receive a great deal of strain: bed linen and scatter cushions are ideal.

BUTTONS WITH SHANKS

1 MARKING UP Mark up for buttons and buttonholes, and make holes. Check the button position through the hole, and secure a thread.

2 STITCHING ON Sew on the button, making stitches through the hole in the shank. Make 12 to 14 such stitches before fastening off.

BUTTONS WITH HOLES

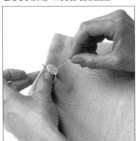

Sew parallel stitches over a pin under the button. Take out the pin. Wind the thread around the slack to form a shank. Fasten off on wrong side.

COVERING BUTTONS

1 FITTING FABRIC Cut fabric to cover the button and overlap. Lay button face down on the wrong side, and fold the fabric over the teeth.

2 SECURING Snap the back of the button into place. These buttons are sold in a variety of types and sizes. Read the instructions; they vary.

BUTTONHOLES

Position buttonholes and buttons very carefully to prevent openings from gaping. To give a buttonhole strength, make the fastening edge from a double thickness of material and

use the buttonhole stitch. Many sewing machines have a special attachment for sewing buttonholes. For an unusual finish, you can use rouleau loops instead of buttonholes.

MACHINE-SEWN BUTTONHOLES

1 MARKING UP Mark the center of the buttonhole and align the button with the mark. Mark the width plus the thickness of the button, plus a little for oversewing the ends of the hole.

Seam rippers are useful tools for helping you start to open up buttonholes

2 CUTTING OUT Sew a buttonhole stitch along either side of the mark and across the ends. Cut a hole at the end of the mark with a seam ripper or small, sharp scissors. Cut open the hole.

HAND-SEWN BUTTONHOLES

1 CUTTING HOLE Mark the position and length of the buttonhole as required with tailor's chalk or vanishing ink. Use a seam ripper or small, sharp pair of scissors to cut open the length of the buttonhole.

2 STARTING EDGE Thread a needle with buttonhole thread. Secure it at one end of the slit; if the hole is at a right angle to the edge, start at the end that will take the strain. Oversew across this end.

3 STITCHING EDGES Working in the buttonhole stitch (see *blanket stitch, page 15*), sew closely along one side of buttonhole. At the far end, oversew again. Work along second side and fasten off.

BUTTON LOOPS

First, sew the buttons in place on one edge of the opening. Pin the rouleau strip *(see page 27)* in place along the other edge of the opening, folding it to form loops. Adjust the loops to fit the buttons' size and spacing. Tack and oversew the rouleau in place.

ZIPPERS

Ideal for strength and invisibility, metal and plastic zippers are available in a wide variety of weights, lengths, and colors. They are suitable for all but the most lightweight furnishings.

Metal zippers are strongest, but plastic zippers are available in a wider color range and are more flexible, although you must take care not to damage them when ironing.

CENTERED ZIPPER

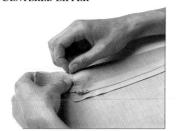

1 **POSITIONING** Select a zipper for the fabric, taking wear and tear into consideration. Make sure that the zipper is long enough for the task. Lay zipper on the seam line on the wrong side of the fabric, and mark the point where each end lies.

2 **SEWING IN** Pin, tack, and sew the fabric pieces at both ends of the zipper, starting at fabric edges and stopping at pin markers. Tack the opening for the zipper between the pins closed along the seam line, and press the seam allowances open.

3 **PINNING ZIPPER** Lay the fabric right side down with seam pressed open. Place the zipper right side down on the tacked part of the seam. Make sure that it is placed centrally, with the teeth lying on the join. Pin and tack the zipper in place.

4 **SEWING ON ZIPPER** Turn fabric right-side up. Using the zipper attachment on a sewing machine, sew through all layers of fabric around the zipper. Keep the stitching about 5/16 in (8 mm) from the zipper teeth. Remove the tacking stitches.

OFFSET ZIPPER

1 **TACKING IN PLACE** Follow steps 1 and 2 for centered zipper. Place zipper on the tacked section and set to one side so that teeth are on one seam allowance. Pin and tack in place.

2 **SEWING ON ZIPPER** Turn fabric right side up. Using the zipper attachment on a sewing machine, stitch through all layers of fabric around the zipper. Follow the tacking stitches closely.

3 **FINISHED ZIPPER** Take out the tacking stitches. An offset zipper is less visible than a centered one, so this is a particularly useful way of hiding a zipper that does not match the fabric.

ZIPPER IN A PIPED SEAM

1 **PIPED SIDE** Lay one edge of the open zipper right side down on the inside of the allowance of the piped edge. Pin, tack, and sew 1/8 in (3 mm) from the zipper teeth, using the zip attachment on a sewing machine.

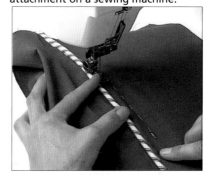

2 **PLAIN SIDE** Close the zipper. Turn back the seam allowances of both edges. Lay the unpiped edge on the zipper to meet the piping. Pin, tack, and sew the zipper in place.

LAPPED ZIPPER AT THE END OF A SEAM

1 **PLACING** Sew allowances wider than the zipper. Leave opening for zipper at seam end. Fold both allowances to one side. Lay fabric right side up, and fold back top piece. Pin, tack, and sew one side of zipper right side up on bottom allowance.

Fold back allowance with zipper attached

2 **SECOND SIDE** Lay the top fabric piece over the zipper, and line up the seam allowances. Turn the fabric pieces over. Pin and tack free edge of zipper to free seam allowance. Turn right side up again, open zipper, and sew along tacked edge of zipper.

3 **FINISHED ZIPPER** Seam allowances both lie to one side of seam, with the zipper between them, concealed beneath the top seam allowance. This method is generally used for loose covers on chairs and sofas.

CURTAINS

BECAUSE A WINDOW IS one of the focal points of a room, it should be dressed with great care and attention. Curtains have long been accepted as one of the most appropriate means of providing this dressing. As a decorative and functional window dressing, curtains create privacy, conserve heat, and reduce external noise. Nowadays, dressing a window involves establishing decorative schemes with fabrics and taking advantage of the visual potential of curtain accessories such as edgings, tiebacks, cornices, and valances. There is an enormous range of curtain styles and fabrics to choose from, and modern developments in heading tapes and hanging systems – rods, poles, and tracks – have made the process of making curtains easier than ever before. Whether you wish to make sophisticated lined drapes or a simple sheer or net curtain, a professional finish is not difficult to achieve.

CHOOSING A STYLE

*T*HERE ARE VARIOUS FACTORS TO CONSIDER before making a curtain. There is an extensive range of fabrics to choose from, as well as the style of hanging system and a suitable type of heading tape. Begin by examining your practical requirements. Take into account the shape and size of your windows, the need for privacy, and the overall decorative style and color scheme of the room. If you are at the point of decorating the room, you may wish to base the decoration on the curtain fabric. Bear in mind that curtains can set the style and mood of a room and create the illusion of more, or less, space.

PLAIN AND SIMPLE
When you wish to dress a window with a curtain that is not only practical but also elegant, choose a simple heading and a plain fabric with a lining, and hang the curtain from rings on a pole.

Pole or track with generous overhang on each side permits curtains to be drawn well back from window

ELEGANT AND OPULENT
The lavish dressing of windows reached a climax in the 19th century, when different accessories such as tiebacks, tassels, and trimmings were introduced. In a home of that period, high windows are perfectly suited to elaborate curtains with swags and cascades.

Multiple folds of fabric are emphasized when curtains are held back by tiebacks

DECORATIVE AND PRACTICAL
If your window is not exposed to view and you do not require the insulating and lightproof properties of lined curtains, consider furnishing a window with a purely decorative dressing. You can combine a drape with a plain shade that rolls out of sight when it is not in use. The shade provides a practical solution to a predominantly decorative window dressing.

Shape of window is outlined and softened by draping curtain pole with swags of sheer fabric that cascade to each side

Shade screens off damaging effects of sun's rays on furniture

EFFICIENT SCREENS
Curtains do not need to be restricted to windows. They can be used to conceal openings such as a cupboard front or an alcove. Easy to draw aside for access and ideal as a dust barrier, a screening curtain also adds texture and color to a room.

Curtains conceal cupboards and provide attractive decorative element to room

SMALL-SPACE DIVIDERS
Suspended from separate poles, these curtains divide the bathing and sleeping areas within a bedroom. This concept has many applications, particularly in a studio apartment, where one room has to accommodate various activities.

Curtains are tied back when they are not in use

MULTIPLE-WINDOW TREATMENTS
When making up curtains for multiple windows – either a straight row of single windows or a large bay window – you will not only need a large quantity of fabric but must also consider how best to arrange the curtains so that they can be drawn away from the windows. The most effective solution is to hang a number of individual curtains, so that when they are drawn open they rest to the side or in between the windows. This way, when drawn closed, the curtains form one continuous spread of fabric over the window area.

Valance conceals lengths of curtain track – contrasting binding fabric at edge of valance emphasizes its shape

Curtains are hung singly from a continuous length of track

Bunching curtain on floor helps to accentuate curtain's fullness, as well as increasing level of insulation

CHOOSING A HANGING SYSTEM

BEFORE YOU BEGIN TO MAKE YOUR CURTAINS, you must decide on the type of hanging system you intend to use. It is important to make this decision first, because the hanging system and heading tape that you choose, along with the size of the opening to be covered, determine the measurements of the curtains. For a visible hanging system, choose a rod or pole made of wood or metal. Track systems, by contrast, are usually plastic and designed to be concealed by the curtain heading, a valance, or a cornice.

RODS AND POLES

Rods or poles with matching rings and finials are available in a wide range of woods – painted or natural – and brass and iron, and provide a decorative way to hang curtains. They can only be used to span straight openings. Choose an appropriate thickness of rod or pole to support the weight of fabric. Rods and poles are usually attached to the wall with two supporting side brackets, but when hanging heavy or wide curtains, you should consider attaching an additional central bracket.

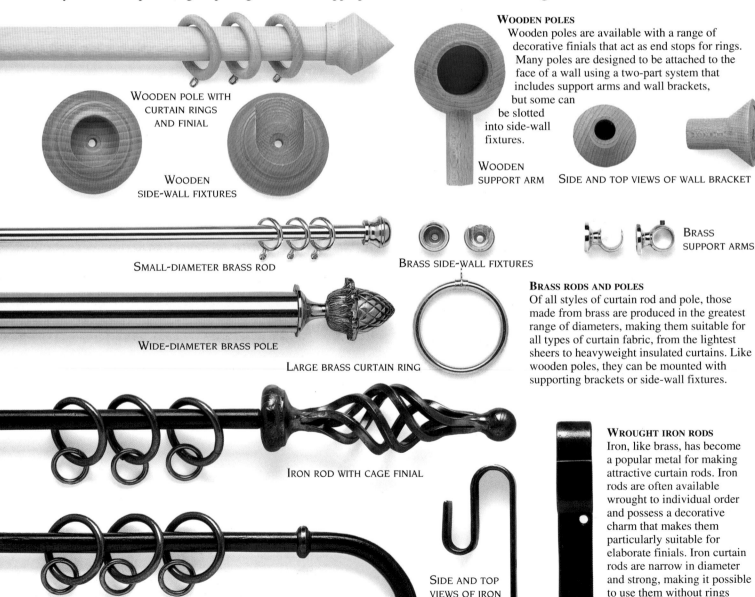

WOODEN POLE WITH CURTAIN RINGS AND FINIAL

WOODEN SIDE-WALL FIXTURES

WOODEN POLES
Wooden poles are available with a range of decorative finials that act as end stops for rings. Many poles are designed to be attached to the face of a wall using a two-part system that includes support arms and wall brackets, but some can be slotted into side-wall fixtures.

WOODEN SUPPORT ARM

SIDE AND TOP VIEWS OF WALL BRACKET

SMALL-DIAMETER BRASS ROD

BRASS SIDE-WALL FIXTURES

BRASS SUPPORT ARMS

WIDE-DIAMETER BRASS POLE

LARGE BRASS CURTAIN RING

BRASS RODS AND POLES
Of all styles of curtain rod and pole, those made from brass are produced in the greatest range of diameters, making them suitable for all types of curtain fabric, from the lightest sheers to heavyweight insulated curtains. Like wooden poles, they can be mounted with supporting brackets or side-wall fixtures.

IRON ROD WITH CAGE FINIAL

WROUGHT IRON RODS
Iron, like brass, has become a popular metal for making attractive curtain rods. Iron rods are often available wrought to individual order and possess a decorative charm that makes them particularly suitable for elaborate finials. Iron curtain rods are narrow in diameter and strong, making it possible to use them without rings for curtains made with a simple slot heading.

IRON ROD WITH CURVED FINIAL

SIDE AND TOP VIEWS OF IRON MOUNTING BRACKET

SIMPLE HANGING SYSTEMS AND TRACKS

When hanging lightweight, stationary curtains, choose a simple support such as a narrow-diameter rod. For other types of curtain and weights of fabric, several systems are available. Tracks can be mounted on a wall or ceiling using multipurpose brackets. Curtains hang from a track on slides with hooks, or combined slides and hooks.

SIMPLE HANGING SYSTEMS
For net and sheer curtains that remain in a fixed position, use a custom-made spring wire or sash rod. Both can be attached to the face of a wall or to a side wall using screw eyes or brackets. Spring-tension rods can be extended to fit a variety of openings.

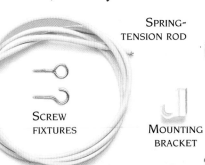

SCREW FIXTURES

SPRING-TENSION ROD

MOUNTING BRACKET

PLASTIC-COATED SPRING WIRE

SASH ROD

PULL-ROD AND CLIP

TRACK WITH CONCEALED SLIDES
This track conceals slides behind a flat fascia. Curtain hooks are inserted into the heading tape and hooked onto the slides. The end stop secures the last curtain hook.

WALL OR CEILING BRACKET

END STOP

TRACK AND SLIDES

TRACK WITH COMBINED SLIDES AND HOOKS
In this system, slides move along the track face and support separate hooks inserted into the tape, or they can be inserted directly into the tape.

END STOP AND WALL BRACKET

COMBINED HOOKS AND SLIDES

TRACK WITH COMBINED HOOKS AND SLIDES

VALANCE ROD
The simplest rod for supporting a valance in front of a curtain heading, with clip-on brackets and linking bars. This is adaptable for any length and shape of window.

COMBINED VALANCE HOOK AND SLIDE

METAL LINKING BAR

VALANCE ROD WITH COMBINED HOOKS AND SLIDES

TRACK FIXTURES

Optional fixtures enable hanging systems to fit all openings. Extension brackets can be used to mount a track away from a wall or to support a second track or a valance rod.

FIXED-LENGTH EXTENSION BRACKET

MULTIPURPOSE BRACKET

VALANCE ROD BRACKET

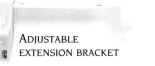

ADJUSTABLE EXTENSION BRACKET

BUILT-IN VALANCE ROD
When making up a matching curtain and valance, it is possible to use a curtain track supplied with a built-in valance rod. This system is easy to assemble and can be mounted either on the wall or the ceiling.

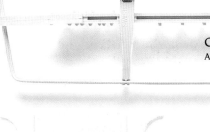

CONVENTIONAL TRAVERSE AND VALANCE ROD

CORD TIEBACK

TRACK WITH BUILT-IN PULL-CORD

PULL-CORDS AND PULL-RODS
Track systems are available with pull-cords to ease the opening and closing of curtains, and a cord weight prevents pull-cords from entangling. A master slide with an overlap arm ensures that curtains overlap slightly in the center. Alternatively, pull-rods can be clipped to the master slide at the central edge of each curtain.

HANGING-SYSTEM ACCESSORIES

You may wish to add accessories and fixtures to your curtain hanging system that allow you to completely personalize your curtains. A variety of finials and support brackets is available for use with poles or rods. Similarly, there are several tieback accessories, which can be used for drawing curtains away from windows and securing them to walls.

FITTINGS FOR POLES

Choose from a range of decorative finials and support brackets to use in conjunction with your curtain pole or rod. Brass – or brass-effect – poles in particular can be purchased as lengths of tube, which you can accessorize with fixtures to complement your hanging system.

ACORN-SHAPED BRASS FINIAL

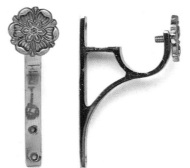

DECORATIVE BRASS END-SUPPORT BRACKET

SPHERICAL BRASS FINIAL

DISK-SHAPED BRASS FINIAL

MATCHING BRASS CENTRAL-SUPPORT BRACKET

TIEBACK HOOKS AND CLASPS

If you wish to use tiebacks that are fitted with rings, you will need a pair of wall hooks to secure the tiebacks to the wall. These curtain accessories are available in both simple and elaborate designs. Alternatively, you can secure a curtain to a wall by means of various styles of metal clasp, or you can hold a curtain away from a window or other opening by draping it over a tieback arm and knob.

SIMPLE TIEBACK HOOK

FLEUR-DE-LIS TIEBACK HOOKS

TIEBACK ARM AND KNOB

DECORATIVE BRASS CLASPS

CURTAIN HOOKS

Curtain hooks are manufactured according to their function. Choose hooks best suited to your heading tape. Most ready-made tapes can be hung from standard plastic hooks. Elaborate pleats, however, require split hooks, while handmade headings need pin-on or sew-on hooks.

STANDARD PLASTIC HOOKS

BRASS SEW-ON HOOK

PIN-ON HOOKS

SPLIT HOOK

MOUNTING HANGING SYSTEMS

*W*HEN SECURING A HANGING SYSTEM TO A WALL, you should allow enough space for the apparatus to overhang on each side of the opening, so that the curtains can be drawn away from the window. The hanging system should be attached either to the wall or to the window frame. Rods and poles are meant to be seen; tracks are designed to be hidden by the curtain. Always be sure to align the pole, rod, or curtain track so that it is parallel to the top of the opening, or to the ceiling. Use a carpenter's level if your walls and windows are perfectly squared; if they are not, align the hanging system to the opening by eye.

MOUNTING RODS OR POLES

Metal or wooden rods and poles, complete with supports, are manufactured in a range of standard lengths and can be cut to size. First measure the width of the opening and frame, and add enough for the curtains to overhang on each side. Select a pole or rod at least as long as this measurement, and calculate the number of rings needed. Make a series of marks at least 2 in (5 cm) above the opening, and join these with a guideline the same length as the width of the opening, plus the overhang. Mount supports to the wall using a drill with a masonry bit, screw anchors and screws, and a screwdriver.

1 MARKING POSITION Mark the position for the wall bracket on the guideline, allowing for curtain overhang. You will also need to consider a further 2–4 in (5–10 cm) at each end of the pole for the finial, which extends beyond the wall bracket. Drill a hole in the mark and mount an anchor in it.

2 POSITIONING BRACKET Align the bracket with the anchor. Screw the wall bracket in place. Mount a wall bracket on the other side of the window. When hanging a long pole, prevent it from sagging under the weight of the curtains by attaching a central-support bracket above the window.

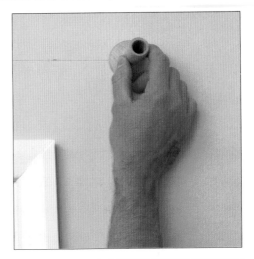

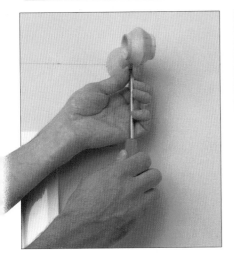

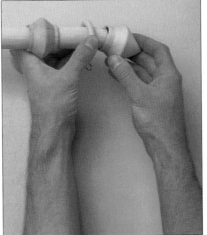

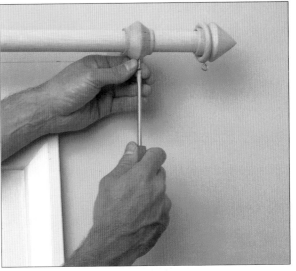

3 SECURING BRACKETS Slide the support brackets into the wall brackets. Secure with the small screws provided. Slide the pole through a support bracket. Place all but two rings on the pole. Push it into position through the second support bracket.

4 ADDING FINIALS Slide one of the remaining curtain rings over the end of the pole and push the finial into place on the end of the pole. Add the last curtain ring and the finial to the other end of the pole. Centralize the pole within the brackets.

5 SECURING POLE Finally, you should drive home the small screw provided by the manufacturer into the hole on the underside of each ring support bracket. Once the small screws have bitten into the wood, the pole will be held securely in position.

MOUNTING A TRACK TO A WALL

Choose the track most appropriate for the heading tape or handmade heading of the curtain *(see page 35)*. Measure the width of the window and add enough for an overhang on each side. If necessary, cut the track to the exact size. Tracks are

held in place by small brackets. Use a tape measure, pencil, and straightedge to mark the positions of the brackets on the wall. Mount the brackets in place, using a power drill with a masonry bit, suitable anchors, screws, and a screwdriver.

1 MARKING TRACK POSITION Make a series of pencil marks along the top edge of the window, of equal distance from the ceiling. If mounting the track very close to the ceiling, you must ensure that there is sufficient room remaining for attaching and securing the track.

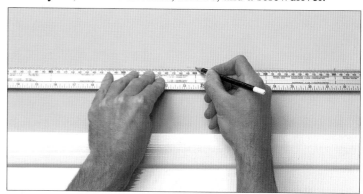

2 MARKING GUIDELINE Using a straightedge as a guide, join the measured marks with a pencil line directly on the wall. Refer to the track manufacturer's instructions to establish the minimum recommended distance between the mounting points for the brackets that will hold the track in place, and mark these on the wall.

3 POSITIONING ANCHORS Beginning at the side of the window, and allowing for the overhang, mark the drilling positions for the anchors with a pencil. Here, the overhang is 4 in (10 cm). The first point for a bracket should be 2 in (5 cm) in from the end of the track. Drill first position mark and push in an anchor.

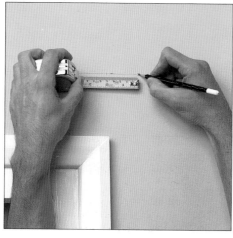

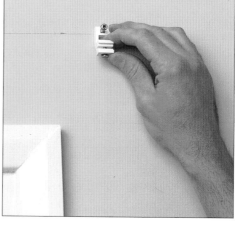

4 SECURING BRACKETS Place the track bracket and a suitable screw on the first fixing point. Lightly push the tip of the screw into the anchor, then drive it home with a screwdriver. Work along the mounting points, drilling, plugging, and screwing the brackets in place.

5 POSITIONING TRACK Make sure that each of the brackets is correctly aligned, then clip or slot the track into place. If the track is not centered above the window opening, remove the track and reposition it onto the brackets.

6 SECURING TRACK Once you have put the curtain track in the correct place, secure it to the wall fixtures by tightening the screws on each bracket.

FRAME-MOUNTED TRACK

As an alternative to fixing tracks to a wall, brackets can be mounted onto a wooden window frame, although the width of frame may make it difficult to draw curtains back fully. Mark bracket positions, make pilot holes, and screw brackets in place.

MOUNTING ON THE FRAME

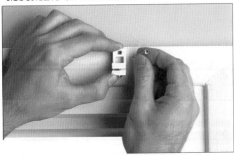

Consult the manufacturer's instructions for positioning the brackets. Mark the position of each bracket. Make a pilot hole in each mark with an awl or, for longer screws, an electric drill and wood drill bit. Push each screw into the bracket and screw it into place.

FRAME EXTENSIONS

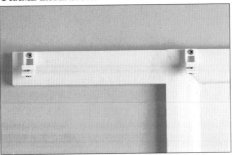

If you wish to draw the curtains away from the window to allow the maximum amount of daylight into the room, you can extend the width of the window frame by mounting a pair of short wooden battens onto the wall. Mount the brackets onto the extensions as before.

SLIDES AND END STOPS

Once the track has been correctly positioned and attached to the brackets, calculate how many slides you will need. You can then slide these onto the track. Fit the end stops or finials. When hanging the curtain, it is a simple task to remove an end stop and add or remove extra slides.

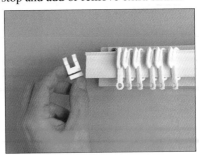

ATTACHING A WIRE TO A FRAME

Sheer and net curtains can be hung across a window or door opening with a lightweight hanging system, such as plastic-coated spring wire. This can be attached by a hook and eye at each end to the side or face of the frame. If you wish to use this system, first mark the positions for the eyes, then use an awl to make pilot holes for the fixtures. Cut the wire to the correct length with a pair of pliers.

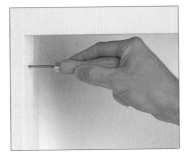

1 MAKING PILOT HOLES Push and twist the awl into the pencil marks on both sides of the window frame to make two small pilot holes to guide the threaded metal eyes.

2 SETTING SCREW EYES Screw eyes into the wood by hand, so that they lie flush with the frame. Measure the distance between the eyes and cut wire to this length, minus the hooks.

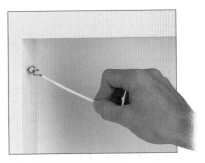

3 HOOKING WIRE Screw the hooks onto each end of the wire. Attach one hook to one of the eyes on the frame. Stretch the wire across the window and join the other hook and eye.

PUTTING UP A CORNICE BOARD

First determine the location for a cornice board by aligning it with the window or the ceiling. If the ceiling and window are not parallel, use a level as a guide. Drill into the wall with an electric drill and masonry drill bit. Attach the board to the wall above the window with brackets that are secured by screws and anchors.

1 MARKING DRILL HOLES Center the cornice board over the opening and, using a level as a guide for correct alignment, mark the drilling points through the bracket holes with a pencil. Remove the cornice, drill the holes, and push anchors into them.

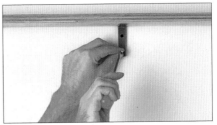

2 ATTACHING BRACKETS Place the cornice board on the wall, align the brackets with the correct anchors, and screw them in place. You may need an assistant for a large cornice board.

PLANNING AND PREPARATION

*H*ANGING FABRIC OVER A WINDOW or door creates a strong visual focus in any room. For the most part, the effect of a curtain will determine the character of a room. It is therefore well worth taking plenty of time to plan and prepare the look of a curtain in relation to its window or door opening, and to the whole of the room, before you begin working. The decorative appearance of a curtain is subject to a number of factors other than just the type of fabric that you choose, including the style of the curtain heading tape, the dimensions of the window or door opening, and the width and length of the curtains.

CHOOSING A HEADING TAPE

The type of heading tape determines the curtain's character by governing the way the fabric hangs in folds. Ready-made heading tapes are available in many gathered or pleated styles. They are easily applied to the fabric, and the pleats or gathers are made by drawing up sets of cords within the tape. These folds can be released to allow the curtains to be washed or dry-cleaned flat. Some tapes are constructed with rows of pockets into which the curtain hooks can be inserted.

SHEER AND NET TAPE

This tape forms thin pencil pleats on sheer or net fabrics. It is approximately 2½ in (6 cm) wide. Use standard curtain hooks, or slide a curtain rod through loops in the tape. For measuring, allow twice the track length.

SIMPLE GATHERED HEADING

Often used for small-scale curtains, this narrow tape – approximately 1 in (2.5 cm) wide – forms gathers. When using a track, position the tape to hide the fixture. Allow one and a half to two times the track length.

BOX PLEATING

Use this tape for fixed-position curtains and valances. It is 3 in (7.5 cm) wide, which enables you to hide the track. This tape has two rows of hook pockets, to be used with split hooks. Allow for three times track length.

GOBLET PLEATING

An extra-wide heading tape that forms deep, goblet-shaped pleats, this is ideally suited to full, floor-length curtains. You should use metal split hooks with this heading tape. Allow two times the track length when measuring.

CARTRIDGE PLEATING

Designed to produce rows of cylindrical pleats, cartridge tape, which is 3½ in (9 cm) wide, is most suitable for curtains that have a long drop. Use split hooks to hang this tape. Allow two times the track length when measuring.

PENCIL PLEATING

The most popular heading tape, pencil pleating is 3 in (7.5 cm) wide and produces multiple folds in the curtain fabric. Standard hooks can be placed in one of three rows of pockets. Allow two and a half times the track length.

SMOCKED PLEATING

A heading tape 3 in (7.5 cm) wide, designed to produce a "smocked" effect, this is made for valances and curtains. Standard hooks can be placed into one of two rows of hook pockets. Allow two and a half times the track length.

TRIPLE PINCH PLEATING

This tape is 3¼ in (8.5 cm) wide and creates groups of triple pleats. Suitable for curtains with a long drop, it can be used with any fabric. Fit split hooks into either of the two rows of pockets. Allow twice the track length.

MEASURING

The amount of fabric needed is affected by the width of the opening, type of hanging system *(see pages 34–36)*, style of heading tape, length of the finished curtains, and size of any pattern repeats on the material. For floor-length curtains to clear the floor, deduct ½ in (12 mm) from the track-to-floor measurement (B). To bunch curtains on the floor, add 2–8 in (5–20 cm) to measurement B. For a window sill, hang the curtains either ½ in (12 mm) above the sill (C), or to an apron length of 2–4 in (5–10 cm) below.

The curtain heading should obscure, or stand slightly above, a track. If you are using a pole, curtains should hang just below it. From the curtain top or the hanging system, measure to the bottom edge of the required curtain drop. Add to this 3 in (7.5 cm) for top turnings and 6 in (15 cm) for the lower hem.

To find the fabric width, measure the span of the hanging system (A). If the curtains are to overlap, add the extra necessary. Multiply this by the fullness of the heading tape. Add 12 in (30 cm) for side turnings. Divide this by the fabric width to find the number of fabric panels needed for the curtain width. Round up to the next whole number. For the total amount of fabric required, multiply the number of panels needed by the length calculated above.

SILL-LENGTH CURTAINS

APRON-LENGTH CURTAINS

Floor-length curtains are very good insulators, but should not be hung too close to an electric heater

FLOOR-LENGTH CURTAINS

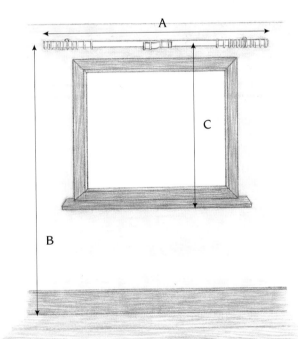

MEASURING REQUIREMENTS
The length of the hanging system and curtain are the bases for calculating the amount of curtain fabric needed. Use a wooden ruler or steel tape measure for accuracy. To calculate the width of fabric, measure the span of the hanging system between the end stops (A). To find the track-to-floor measurement (B), or the track-to-sill length (C), measure carefully, starting from the pole or track. You will need to add or deduct from B or C, depending on the required length of the curtains.

A HANGING SYSTEM LENGTH

B TRACK-TO-FLOOR MEASUREMENT

C TRACK-TO-SILL MEASUREMENT

MATCHING PATTERNS

When calculating the widths for a patterned material, allow for the pattern repeat so that you can accurately match the pattern across the curtain. You should always try to centralize the pattern on each curtain.

MEASURING PATTERN REPEAT

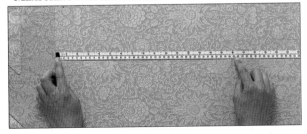

You will need to spread out the fabric onto a smooth, flat work surface and carefully measure the whole of one pattern repeat on the material. You can allow for the matching of the pattern across the seams and from one curtain to another by simply adding a single pattern repeat for each drop of curtain.

CUTTING OUT

Cutting out with accuracy is as important as taking careful measurements. Lay the fabric on a flat surface. Cut square and straight to the grain or, if necessary, the pattern. For cutting out fabric, you will need the basic sewing kit. When cutting loosely woven fabric, cut along a pulled thread.

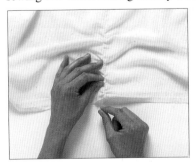

1 PULLING THREAD Make a small cut through the selvage. Pull out a single thread at this point and smooth the fabric.

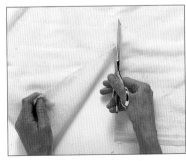

2 CUTTING FABRIC Using the channel left by the pulled thread as a guideline, cut across the fabric with a pair of dressmaker's scissors.

SHEER AND NET CURTAINS

*T*RANSLUCENT FABRICS MAKE IDEAL CURTAIN material when daytime privacy is desired. When drawn, sheer or net fabrics will obscure a window, but at the same time allow daylight to illuminate the room. Available in various weights and colors, sheers and nets can be made up as the only curtains in a window or as secondary daylight drapes accompanying a set of curtains in a lightproof fabric. Make a handmade heading *(see page 49)* or use a ready-made heading tape. Hang the curtains from a lightweight pole, sash rod, or plastic-coated spring wire, attached by hooks to eyes screwed into the frame *(see page 39)*.

MAKING THE CURTAIN

Choose a sheer or net heading tape, and calculate the quantity of fabric required *(see page 41)*. For translucent curtains, try to find a wide fabric needing few joins. Cut the fabric straight, using the pulled-thread method. Using a new, fine sewing needle, make joins with French seams. You will also need appropriate hooks and the basic sewing kit.

1 HEMMING EDGES Lay the fabric on a large, smooth, flat surface. To neaten the edges of the fabric, pin a ⅜ in (1 cm) double hem at each side edge. Tack, sew, and press the hems.

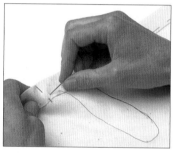

2 HEMMING BOTTOM EDGE Turn over and pin a ¾ in (2 cm) double hem at the bottom edge. Tack, sew, and press the hem. At the top, or heading, edge of the curtain, turn over the fabric the same width as the tape and pin the tape in position.

3 ATTACHING TAPE Turn under the raw ends of the heading tape by ¾ in (2 cm), and sew it to the wrong side of the curtain. Sew across the ends of the threads at the leading edge. Pull up loose gathers. Arrange fabric evenly across the curtain *(see page 48)*. Secure free ends of cords using a cord tieback.

THE FINISHED CURTAIN

OTHER OPTIONS

The easy-to-work and lightweight nature of translucent fabrics allows for a wide range of curtain styles to be quickly made up and hung over a window or doorway. A simple effect can be quickly achieved with a narrow heading tape or sleeve. Sophisticated ideas include draping the curtain pole and cutting the drops too long so that the fabric cascades onto the floor.

CROSSOVER SHEER

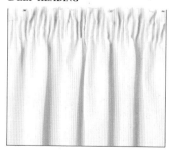

Sew two curtains to one piece of heading tape. The leading edge of each should be the length of the diagonal of the window. The sides should be the sill length.

DEEP HEADING

This is a formal style using wide heading tape on a sheer fabric. A deep frill such as this looks very effective and elegant on curtains with a long drop.

DRAPED HEADING

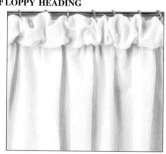

Drape a pole or rod above an opening with sheer fabric. The effect is purely decorative and is ideal for windows where privacy is not very important.

FLOPPY HEADING

When using a wooden or metal pole or rod, attach heading tape below the top edge of the fabric so that the frill flops forward, revealing the hanging system.

UNLINED CURTAINS

*W*HEN MADE OF AN OPAQUE FABRIC, unlined curtains are the simplest and least expensive lightproof drapes for a window or other opening. Unlined fabric may be well suited to frequent washing, so curtains made from this material are particularly appropriate for the most extensively used rooms of a home, such as the kitchen and bathroom. An unlined curtain is also quick and easy to make, and it provides an ideal way to practice fundamental curtain-making techniques before attempting the demanding lined varieties. To enable these curtains to hang properly, you may have to add weights in the hems or miters.

MAKING THE CURTAIN

Decide on the type of hanging system and curtain heading *(see page 40)* and the fabric fullness. Measure the window and calculate your fabric requirements *(see page 41)*. Clear a flat surface to work on and have ready the heading tape, matching hooks, and the basic sewing kit. Cut the fabric to size, allowing extra for joining panels. Remove the selvages.

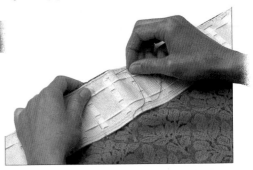

1 JOINING PANELS Sew together panels of fabric, aligning any pattern *(see page 41)*. Fold the hem and sides of the fabric by ⅝ in (1.5 cm) to the wrong side and press in place. Fold the sides over again by 1 in (2.5 cm) and press. Fold up the hem by 3 in (7.5 cm) and miter the corners *(see page 21)*. Then slipstitch the side turnings.

2 TURNING TOP EDGE Along the top edge of the curtain, fold over, pin, and press a strip of fabric 1½ in (4 cm) wide to the wrong side. Cut the heading tape to the same width as the finished curtain, allowing ¾ in (2 cm) at each end for turning under.

3 ATTACHING TAPE Pin and tack heading tape in position, just below top fold of the curtain. Sew along both sides of the tape in same direction, and across leading edge to secure the drawstrings. Knot individual drawstrings to prevent them from being pulled through when you draw up gathers *(see page 48)*. Cut a length of medium-density chain weights to the curtain width.

4 SECURING WEIGHTS Unfold the hem so that the topmost fold is exposed. Lay the length of chain weights along the crease in the fabric. Then sew the weights in place at regular intervals.

5 FINISHING OFF To finish off the curtain, refold the hem and pin it in place. Then slipstitch along the hem to secure it. Fit the curtain hooks to the tape, and hang the curtain on the track, rod, or pole. Dress the finished curtain.

THE FINISHED CURTAIN

WEIGHTS

The draping quality of lightweight or opaque curtains will be improved by securing weights within the hem. Weights are available either as chains to lay along a hem or as button-shaped disks to secure in the miters.

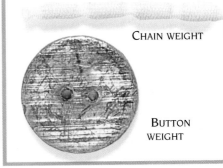

CHAIN WEIGHT

BUTTON WEIGHT

LINED CURTAINS

*T*HERE ARE MANY ADVANTAGES to lining a curtain. First, the lining will give body to the main fabric so that the curtain hangs with pleasing fullness. Second, a curtain composed of layers will be much more lightproof than an unlined curtain. Last, if the appropriate interlining material is inserted between the two fabrics, the curtain will possess excellent insulating properties. You can line a curtain using the simple tube method *(see opposite)*, which is best for small, light curtains, or by hand sewing the lining to the main fabric – a technique known as locked-in lining. This technique is best suited to wide, deep curtains.

LOCKED-IN LINING

You should use the locked-in lining technique to achieve the most professional finish, particularly when making wide and deep curtains from widths of fabric that need to be joined together. Lock the lining in place with rows of lockstitches *(see below)* running at regular intervals down the length of the back of the main fabric. You will need curtain and lining fabrics, heading tape, hooks, and the basic sewing kit. First cut out the panels for the curtain, making joins with plain flat seams if necessary *(see page 16)*. Next, cut out the panels for the lining 5 in (13 cm) shorter than the length of the curtain fabric. Allow 3½ in (9 cm) at the hem edge and 1½ in (4 cm) at the heading edge. Join the panels of lining fabric with plain flat seams, and trim 1½ in (4 cm) from each side edge of the completed lining sections.

1 HEMMING FABRIC Turn fabric sides under by 1½ in (4 cm). Turn a 2 in (5 cm) hem along bottom edge and miter corners. Press hem and add weights. Herringbone stitch hem *(see page 20)*. Turn sides and hem of lining under by ⅝ in (1.5 cm) and press.

2 MARKING GUIDELINES Using a triangle or straightedge as a guide, along with a vanishing-ink pen or tailor's chalk, draw full-length, vertical lines on the wrong side of the curtain fabric at intervals of about 12–20 in (30–50 cm).

3 PINNING LINING Pin the lining material to the curtain fabric, wrong sides together, along each of the marked lines. Beginning 6 in (15 cm) from the top of the curtain fabric, tack the lining in position along the first of the vertical lines.

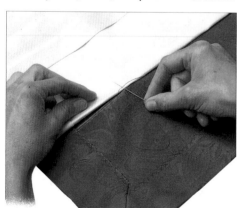

4 LOCKSTITCHING LINING Fold back the lining and lockstitch along the first line of tacking, beginning 6 in (15 cm) from the top. To lockstitch, sew loose stitches wide apart to avoid puckering. Stitch the lining in place down the lines. Remove the tacking stitches.

5 FINISHING OFF Pin, tack, and slipstitch the lining fabric to the curtain at the sides and hem. Remove the tacking stitches. Finish off by applying the chosen heading tape *(see page 48)*. Attach the appropriate hooks, then hang and dress the curtain.

THE FINISHED CURTAIN

TUBE LINING

This is a quick and simple means of lining a curtain, in which lining is attached to the main fabric, only by its side seams, to form a tube. Tube lining is best suited for small curtains and light fabrics. You will need curtain and lining fabrics, heading tape complete with hooks, and the basic sewing kit. Cut out the curtain and lining as described opposite.

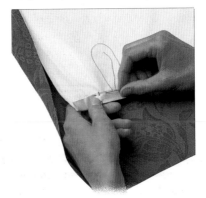

1 ATTACHING LINING Place the lining on top of the curtain, right sides together. The top edge of the lining should lie 1½ in (4 cm) from the top of the curtain. Pin, tack, and sew down one side with a plain flat seam, ⅝ in (1.5 cm) from the edge. Leave 6 in (15 cm) of the bottom of the lining unsewn to allow for turning up hems. Align the other side edge of the lining with the unsewn curtain edge. Pin, tack, and sew lining to curtain as before. Press both seams open.

2 HEMMING LINING Continue to work with the curtain laid wrong side out. Fold a double hem ⅝ in (1.5 cm) deep along the bottom edge of the lining. Pin, tack, and sew the hem in place.

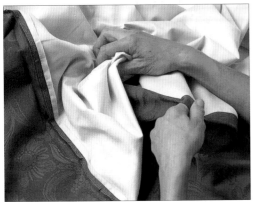

3 TURNING OUT Turn the curtain and lining right side out. Lay the tube flat, lining side up, and adjust it so that the side seams lie on the reverse of the curtain and the lining is centered. An equal amount of curtain fabric – about 1½ in (4 cm) – should be visible at each edge. Pin to hold in place if necessary and press. Turn up the curtain hem by ⅝ in (1.5 cm), and then by 3 in (7.5 cm), and press.

4 MITERING CORNERS Miter the hem corners *(see page 21)*, adding curtain weights if required *(see page 43)*. Then pin and tack the miters in position. Next, pin and tack the hem in place. Attach the heading tape *(see page 48)* and hang the curtain. Check the length of the lining and the curtain fabric and adjust if necessary.

OTHER LINING OPTIONS

SELF-LINED

Rather than using white or cream lining fabric, consider self-lining the curtain with the same material as the front. Here, for instance, the reverse of a brocaded fabric makes an ideal lining.

CONTRASTING PATTERN

Fabrics with a pattern containing a range of colors harmonious with the curtain fabric or similar to it make an interesting lining. Suitably colored stripes and checks are possibilities.

5 FINISHING OFF Once the two fabrics have been correctly aligned, you can finish off the curtain by slipstitching the hem, the mitered corners, and the remainder of the lining in place. Remove any tacking stitches. Then press the curtain on both sides and rehang it.

THE FINISHED CURTAIN

INTERLINED CURTAIN

An interlining between a curtain fabric and lining provides efficient insulation and gives bulk and durability to a curtain. For an interlined curtain, you will need curtain and lining fabrics *(see page 10)*, interlining, heading tape with hooks, and the basic sewing kit. Measure and cut out the curtain, if necessary joining panels of fabric with plain flat seams.

1 CUTTING OUT Fold up the fabric hem by ⅝ in (1.5 cm), then by 3 in (7.5 cm) to the wrong side, and press. Fold in the other edges by 1½ in (4 cm) and press. Open out the turnings. Lay the interlining on the fabric and trim it to fit within hem folds. Cut lining to the same size as the interlining.

2 ATTACHING INTERLINING To join sections of interlining, simply overlap the edges of the pieces, and pin, tack, and sew through both. Attach the interlining to the curtain fabric with parallel vertical rows of lockstitching, as for locked-in linings *(see page 44)*.

3 SEWING HEMS Fold hems over interlining and miter the corners. Use a herringbone stitch *(see page 20)* to hem the sides, and slipstitch the bottom hem to the interlining *(see page 14)*. Stop short of the corners if you are using curtain weights.

4 ADDING WEIGHTS Sew curtain weights onto the inside of the corners of the bottom hem allowance, and finish slipstitching the hem. Hem the bottom of lining fabric by turning it up twice by ⅝ in (1.5 cm) and machine stitching it.

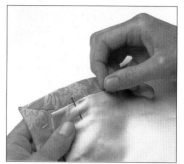

5 ATTACHING LINING Fold under the side edges of the lining by ⅝ in (1.5 cm) and press. Slipstitch the folded side edges to the curtain *(see page 44)*. Fold the fabric over the lining at the top edge and attach the heading tape *(see page 48)*.

THE FINISHED CURTAIN

LOOSE-LINED CURTAIN

Loose-lining is an easy way of adding a detachable layer to a curtain. To make up this curtain, you will need fabric and heading tape, lining fabric and lining heading tape, hooks for both tapes, and the basic sewing kit. Make up the curtain and cut lining to the size of the finished, ungathered curtain. Turn under the sides by ⅝ in (1.5 cm) twice and machine sew them.

1 POSITIONING TAPE Lining heading tape is folded double lengthwise. Slip the raw top edge of the lining into the fold in the heading tape. Check that the tape is the right way around, and that the raw edge is against the inside of the fold in the tape. Pin it in position.

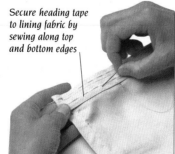

Secure heading tape to lining fabric by sewing along top and bottom edges

2 ATTACHING TAPE When the lining is enclosed within the tape, tack along the top and bottom edges. Sew along the tacking lines, working in the same direction each time to prevent puckering. Remove the tacking stitches and gather the lining *(see page 48)*.

3 HEMMING LINING Hook the lining to the curtain tape. Lay both layers flat, and trim the lining length so that a double hem of ⅝ in (1.5 cm) will make it 1¼–1½ in (3–4 cm) shorter than the curtain. Hem and attach the lining, and hang and dress the curtain *(see page 51)*.

THE FINISHED CURTAIN

ADAPTABLE CURTAIN

Versatile curtains, ideal for seasonal use, can be made by layering fabrics. You will need curtain and sheer fabrics, fabric for binding edges and for ties, heading tapes, and the basic sewing kit. Measure for the curtains, and cut out fabric one and a half times the width of the finished curtain by the full length, plus 1¼ in (3 cm) for the heading. Allowances are not necessary for other edges, because they will be bound *(see page 53)*. Make joins with French seams *(see page 17)*. Cut out the sheer fabric to same fullness, adding 2½ in (6 cm) to the width and 5⅛ in (13 cm) to the length for turnings.

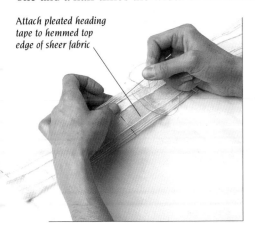

Attach pleated heading tape to hemmed top edge of sheer fabric

1 SEWING TAPE Fold, tack, and sew ⅝ in (1.5 cm) double hems on the sides and bottom of the sheer fabric. Fold a double hem 2 in (5 cm) deep at the heading edge, and press. Pin, tack, and sew a pleated sheer heading tape just below the top fold, and gather up the sheer curtain *(see page 48)*.

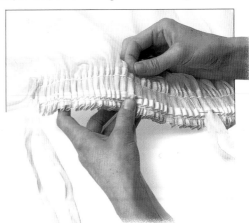

2 SEWING TIES Count how many ties you need, spacing them about 4 in (10 cm) apart with one at the very edge of each end. Mark the positions. Make ties *(see page 27)* long enough to hold the curtain at the right height when folded in half. Fold each tie double and slipstitch the fold to the tape.

3 SEWING BINDING Make a bias strip 1½–2½ in (4–6 cm) wide to go all around the heavier fabric, adding 4 in (10 cm) for joining ends. Fold ⅜ in (1 cm) of each long edge of the binding to the wrong side, and press. Bind the edges of the fabric *(see page 16)*. Join the ends of the binding on the bottom edge, where they will be least visible.

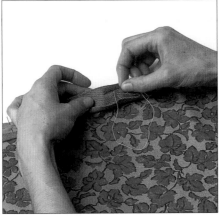

4 ATTACHING TAPE Measure and mark a line 1¼ in (3 cm) from the top of the main curtain fabric. Pin, tack, and sew a simple heading tape along this line, and gather it up. Estimate the positions for the ties, as for the sheer curtain, ensuring that they will alternate with the sheer ties. Fold the ties in half and slipstitch them to the tape's top edge.

5 HANGING CURTAIN Attach the ties of the sheer curtain and the main curtain to alternate curtain rings. Remove the main fabric and the rings to which it is tied during the summer months, when an insulating layer is not required. This leaves the sheer curtain in place to ensure privacy.

THE SHEER CURTAIN

THE TOP CURTAIN WITH SHEER LINING

HEADING TAPES

*T*HE FINAL TASK, ONCE YOU HAVE assembled your curtains, is to attach the heading tape that you chose when deciding on the style of the curtains *(see page 40)*. Every type of ready-made heading tape, from the simplest pencil pleat to the most sophisticated triple pleat, is made of a strip of strong, stiff fabric. Ready-made heading tape has one or more rows of pockets, through which the curtain hooks are threaded, and two or more drawstrings that run along the length of the heading tape and are designed for gathering up the curtain fabric to the desired fullness.

APPLYING HEADING TAPE

You will need the curtain, the heading tape and hooks, and the basic sewing kit. Measuring from the bottom edge up, mark the desired length on the fabric at the top of the curtain. Turn the fabric down at the mark, and press. If necessary, trim the folded part to the depth recommended for the tape. Cut the heading tape to the width of the curtain, plus 1½ in (4 cm).

UNLINED CURTAIN

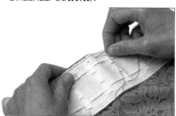

1 PLACING TAPE Lay the tape with its top edge just below the top fold. At the leading edge, knot the drawstring ends.

2 TACKING TAPE Turn under the fixed end of the tape by ¾ in (2 cm) and align the fold with the curtain edge. Tack the tape in place. At the side edge, turn the other end of the tape under by ¾ in (2 cm), leaving the drawstring ends free.

3 SEWING TAPE Machine sew along the top and bottom edges of the tape to secure it to the curtain. Sew in the same direction both times, to prevent the fabric from puckering. Sew across the ends of the tape, securing the knotted ends of the drawstrings at the leading edge and leaving them free at the side edge. Remove the tacking stitches.

LINED CURTAIN

1 FOLDING FABRIC Trim the lining fabric at the top, so that its edge aligns with the mark that indicates the top of the curtain drop. Fold the top of the curtain fabric over at the mark, covering the raw edge of the lining fabric. Pin the folded fabric in place over the lining, and press. Remove the pins.

2 SEWING TAPE Lay the heading tape along the top of the curtain, just below the top fold. Knot the drawstring ends at the leading edge, turn under the end of the tape by ¾ in (2 cm), and align the fold with the curtain edge. Pin and tack the tape. At the side edge, turn the end of the tape under but leave the drawstrings free. Sew the tape in place as for an unlined curtain.

GATHERING UP THE TAPE

1 PULLING STRINGS Grasp the free ends of the drawstrings at the side of the curtain. Hold the tape and curtain steady with your other hand, and pull the strings to one side. As you pull out the drawstrings, the tape will gather and form pleats. As you pull, ease the pleats along the whole length of the tape, until the curtain heading is gathered to the required width.

Use a ready-made cord tieback or a piece of cardboard

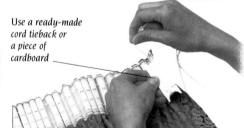

2 TYING OFF Tie the ends of the drawstrings in a slipknot to hold them. Wind the free lengths of drawstring around a cord tieback so that they will lie neatly out of sight. Do not cut off the drawstring ends: when the curtains are taken down to be cleaned, the drawstrings must be released and the heading tapes pulled out again so that the curtains will lie flat.

Use recommended hooks

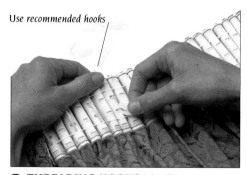

3 THREADING HOOKS Distribute the curtain's fullness evenly along the width of the curtain by adjusting the pleats. Decide on the position and spacing of the hooks, and insert them into one of the rows of woven pockets in the tape.

HANDMADE HEADINGS

*U*NTIL RELATIVELY RECENTLY, the majority of headings were handmade, forming
an integral component of a curtain. Nowadays, most types of pleated headings can be
purchased as commercial heading tapes. There remain, however, a range of curtain
headings that either can or must be made by hand. In some cases, for example the looped
and scalloped treatments, this is because they are very specialized. In other cases, such as
cased headings, it is because they are simple. Assembling your own handmade heading also
allows you to customize curtains and maintain greater control over the look of your room.

CASED HEADING

A cased or slot heading provides the simplest method of hanging a curtain. It is suitable for treatments where the curtains will be held open with tiebacks, while the heading remains closed. You will need one and a half to two and a half times the width of the finished curtain (if necessary, join widths with French seams), the curtain rod or wire that you intend to use, and the basic sewing kit. Hem the bottom and side edges of the curtain first *(see page 42)*.

(see page 42)

1 TURNING TOP Fold a double hem deep enough for the slot and the desired frill. Mark a seam line to the depth for the slot, which should fit the rod loosely, and tack along it.

2 TACKING HEADING Tack close to the bottom of the turning. This will now form the case, or slot, for the rod. Before sewing, check the fit of the casing, and adjust if necessary.

3 SEWING SLOT Machine sew along the tacked lines. Work in the same direction each time to prevent puckering. Remove the tacking stitches and press. Insert the rod, gather the curtain, and hang in place. A heading with a frill will hang better on a rod than on a wire.

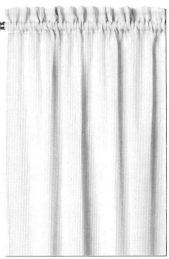

THE FINISHED CURTAIN

OTHER CASED HEADINGS

Making a turning in the top edge of a curtain fabric to form a slot for a rod or wire is a simple and versatile heading technique. It can easily be adapted to make a variety of heading treatments, both plain and decorative. All of these headings are ideally suited for hanging sheer, net, or lightweight fabrics that are not intended to be drawn: cased headings do not draw very easily.

UNGATHERED CURTAIN

Some curtains, such as pictorial lace panels, look best if they are made up without any gathers at the heading. Cut the fabric slightly narrower than the width of the rod or wire to prevent wrinkles. Turn a double hem to fit the pole or wire, and stitch along its edge.

GATHERED CURTAIN

A simple casing will hang better on a wire than one with a frill. Cut the fabric to the fullness desired. Make a double turning for the slot, deep enough to fit loosely over the eyes at the ends of the wire. Tack and sew along the lower edge.

GATHERED DOUBLE FRILL

Press a turning in the top edge to wrong side for the slot. Fold two pleats wrong sides together for each frill. Align the inner fold of pleats with the raw edge of the slot. Sew two seams for the casing: bottom one through the slot fold; top one through raw edge and pleats.

SCALLOPED HEADING

A fabric heading cut into a scalloped pattern is popular for ungathered café curtains covering the lower half of a window. Be sure to cut the fabric straight, particularly when using a striped pattern. Estimate the width desired for the scallops and the strips between them. The strips should be no less than 2 in (5 cm) wide, and the scallops about 4¾ in (12 cm) wide.

Divide the finished curtain width by combined measurement of scallop and strip, remembering to make one more strip than scallops to provide a strip at each end. You will need curtain and lining fabrics to the width of the window and depth desired plus allowances for hems, cardboard for the template, café curtain rings, and the basic sewing kit.

1 MAKING TEMPLATE Use a compass to draw a circle to the width of the scallop on a piece of cardboard. Draw a pencil line across the cardboard at the required depth, and cut out the template.

2 MARKING UP Pin curtain and lining right sides together. Lay fabrics with lining facing up. Mark seam line ⅝ in (1.5 cm) from raw heading edge. Mark width of one strip in from side of curtain. Place template against the mark, straight edge against heading seam line, and draw around it. Work along curtain top, spacing scallops one strip-width apart. Pin and tack along scalloped line.

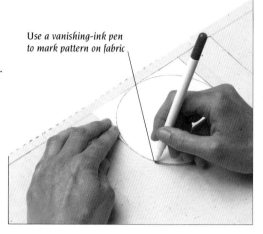

Use a vanishing-ink pen to mark pattern on fabric

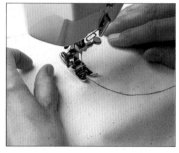

3 SEWING SCALLOPS Sew along the pinned and tacked line of scallops and continue around the other sides of the curtain. Leave a gap in one of the seams, large enough for the whole curtain to be turned right side out through it.

4 CUTTING OUT Use a pair of sharp dressmaker's scissors to cut away the fabric inside the scallops, leaving a ⅝ in (1.5 cm) seam allowance. Snip into the allowance on all curves, and clip the fabric at the corners.

Carefully cut fabric ⅝ in (1.5 cm) inside tacking line of scallops

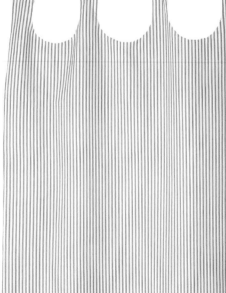

5 TURNING OUT Turn the whole curtain right side out through the opening left in one of the seams. Gently push out all the corners to a neat point – a blunt knitting needle is ideal for this task. Slipstitch the opening closed and press the curtain.

6 SEWING RINGS Sew café curtain rings in place at the center of each of the strip between the scallops. If you are using café clips, follow the manufacturer's instructions. Slide the pole or rod through the rings, mount the end stops, and hang the curtain.

THE FINISHED CURTAIN

LOOPED HEADING

Flat or gathered curtains can be given a heading of simple fabric loops. Cut the curtain fabric to the size required, joining pieces with flat fell seams *(see page 17)*, if necessary. Hem the sides and bottom *(see page 20)*. The loops should be stitched to the wrong side of the top of the curtain, and the ends covered with a facing strip. Decide on the number and

size of loops required. Cut each fabric strip for the loops to double the distance from the top of the curtain and pole and double the width required, plus ⅝ in (1.5 cm) all around for seam allowances. Allow enough fabric for a facing strip 2½ in (6 cm) wide, and as long as the curtain width, plus 1¼ in (3 cm) for turnings. You will also need the basic sewing kit.

1 SEWING LOOPS Fold each strip in half lengthwise, right sides together. Pin, tack, and sew each strip ⅝ in (1.5 cm) from the edge to form a tube. Press the seam open.

2 TURNING OUT Turn each strip right side out. For narrow strips, stitch a piece of thread to one end, pass it through the tube, and pull. Press flat, with the seam in the middle of one side.

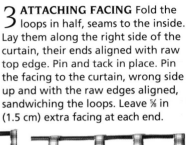

3 ATTACHING FACING Fold the loops in half, seams to the inside. Lay them along the right side of the curtain, their ends aligned with raw top edge. Pin and tack in place. Pin the facing to the curtain, wrong side up and with the raw edges aligned, sandwiching the loops. Leave ⅝ in (1.5 cm) extra facing at each end.

4 SEWING Tack and sew a seam ⅝ in (1.5 cm) from the top, securing the fabric, the loops, and the facing. Fold under ⅝ in (1.5 cm) on the other edges of the facing strip. Press and tack.

5 FINISHING FACING Press the facing strip and curtain wrong sides together, with the loop end hidden. Slipstitch the folded edges of the facing to the curtain. Press the curtain.

THE FINISHED CURTAIN

ADDING BOWS
To decorate the loops with fabric bows, make up rouleau strips *(see page 27)* to the required length, and tie them around the base of each loop to form bows. Alternatively, you could use ribbon or cord.

HANGING AND DRESSING CURTAINS

To achieve the best results, finished curtains must be hung correctly, and then dressed. Hang heavy curtains for at least 24 hours before hemming to allow the fabric to stretch fully.

Dressing curtains involves tying the folds in place: bind the folds securely, but not so tightly that the fabric will crease. After the ties have been removed, the curtains will hang in neat folds.

INTEGRAL CURTAIN HOOKS

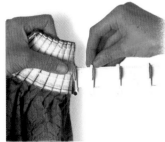

To ensure that the hooks will be evenly spaced, count the pockets to be hooked and mark them before hanging the curtain.

HOOKS AND EYELET RUNNERS

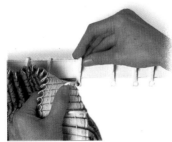

Curtain hooks are threaded through pockets in the header tape and hooked through eyelets in the bottom of each runner.

DRESSING CURTAINS

1 ARRANGING FOLDS Fold curtain into an accordion. Grasp each fold at heading. Pull down in one smooth motion.

2 BINDING Bind folds with fabric strips tied at the top, center, and bottom. Leave for 48 hours, then remove ties.

TRIMMINGS

*A*DDING TRIMMINGS IS A QUICK, easy, and effective way of decorating window dressings. An extraordinary variety of trimmings, such as fringing, tassels, cord, and binding, is available ready-made; alternatively, you can make your own curtain trimmings. Finding a trimming of a certain weight, size, pattern, and color to suit your particular curtain fabric should not be difficult because of the wide range of trimmings that exists. The same trimmings can be applied not only to curtains but also to the furnishings that accompany them, such as tiebacks, cornices, and valances.

PICOT EDGING ON A SHEER CURTAIN

Because sheer curtains are usually used to give privacy or to obscure an unattractive view, they are often kept drawn across the window permanently. It is therefore worth using a decorative style of hanging or a simple trimming to make them more attractive. A crossover hanging *(see page 42)* is one way of making sheer curtains more interesting, and its look can be strengthened by emphasizing the diagonal lines

with a trimming. For these crossover sheer curtains with a simple edging trim, you will need the made-up curtains, your chosen trimming (picot edging is used here), and the basic sewing kit. Measure the lengths of the edges of the curtains that will drape diagonally across the window, and cut two pieces of the trimming to these measurements, allowing an extra 1¼ in (3 cm) on each length for turnings.

1 POSITIONING TRIMMING
Neaten the trimming by turning under and sewing ⅝ in (1.5 cm) of each of the raw ends. Lay the curtain fabric wrong side up on a large, smooth surface and carefully pin and tack the trimming in position along the leading edge. Repeat for the other curtain.

2 ATTACHING TRIMMING
Machine sew or slipstitch the trimming along each edge. Remove the tacking stitches and press. Hang the curtains and draw back each panel. To add further interest to a sheer curtain, use an unusual tieback.

Ready-made edging such as picot adds subtle elegance to cross-over curtains

THE FINISHED CURTAIN

CORDED EDGING

This type of trimming is applied to a finished curtain, so it can be used to give a new look to existing curtains. You will need cord and the basic sewing kit. Mark a line for the cord

on the curtain fabric ⅜ in (1 cm) from the leading and hemmed edges. Measure along the marked line and cut the cord to this length, adding 1¼ in (3 cm) for turnings.

1 PREPARING CORD Take the measured length of cord and secure one of the ends. To do this, wrap strong matching thread around the frayed end of the cord to bind it.

2 SECURING END Fold the end of the cord under itself to hide the binding. Lay the cord on the line, folded end against one edge of the curtain, and oversew it in place by hand.

3 SEWING ON Slipstitch the cord along the marked line. Keep the cord and the fabric flat to avoid puckering when hung. When you reach the end, turn the cord under and oversew.

THE FINISHED CURTAIN

FRINGED EDGING

You will need fabric and lining as for a lined curtain, fringing, and the basic sewing kit. Cut the curtain fabric and lining fabric as for a lined curtain *(see page 44)*. Lay the curtain fabric right side up on a large, flat surface. Sew the lining to the fabric along the unfringed side, its top 1½ in (4 cm) from the top of the fabric. Fold the opposite edge of the lining to the wrong side by ⅜ in (1 cm), and press. Measure the leading edge of the curtain, starting 1½ in (4 cm) from the top edge and ending 3½ in (9 cm) from the bottom. Cut the fringe to this size.

1 ATTACHING FRINGE Sew fringe to right side of the curtain's leading edge with its sewing line aligned with the seam line. Press seam allowance to the wrong side so that the fringe sticks out. Fold the bottom edge of the curtain by ⅝ in (1.5 cm) and by 3 in (7.5 cm) to enclose the fringe seam, and press. Miter the corner of the fold and slipstitch the hem.

2 SECURING LINING Lay the curtain wrong side up and bring the free edge of lining to fringed edge. Align with fringe stitching line. Slipstitch to secure.

3 ATTACHING TAPE Fold and slipstitch lining along the bottom edge. Trim and fold the lining and fabric at the top. Attach the heading tape *(see page 48)*.

THE FINISHED CURTAIN

BIAS BINDING

This edging stiffens and strengthens the edges of an unlined or loose-lined curtain, giving a smart finish. It is not suitable for lined curtains. To make up a curtain with bound edges, you will need curtain fabric, binding, heading tape, fabric for a loose lining if required, and the basic sewing kit. Cut out the curtain fabric as for an unlined curtain *(see page 43)*, but do not add seam allowances on edges that will be bound (here, all the edges are bound). Measure around the edges to be bound and buy or make a bias strip *(see page 22)* to this length, adding 1¼ in (3 cm) for turning under raw ends.

1 FOLDING BIAS STRIP Fold both edges of the bias strip to the center of the wrong side and press flat. Bias binding can also be bought ready-folded.

Choose binding fabric that complements curtain fabric

2 POSITIONING BIAS STRIP Lay the bias strip and the curtain fabric right sides together, edges aligned, and pin the bias strip to the curtain edges. Tack and sew along the fold line in the strip nearest to the raw edges. Remove the tacking stitches.

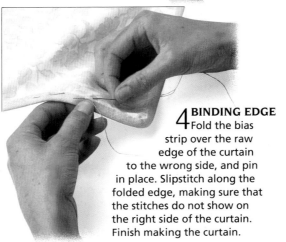

3 TRIMMING ALLOWANCES When all of the bias strip has been sewn in position, trim the edge of the curtain fabric and the strip to ¼ in (6 mm) from the seam to reduce the bulk of the edge.

4 BINDING EDGE Fold the bias strip over the raw edge of the curtain to the wrong side, and pin in place. Slipstitch along the folded edge, making sure that the stitches do not show on the right side of the curtain. Finish making the curtain.

THE FINISHED CURTAIN

TIEBACKS

*T*IEBACKS ARE USEFUL AND DECORATIVE curtain accessories. A tieback holds a
curtain away from a window, allowing as much daylight as possible to enter a room
during the day, and it also breaks up the straight vertical line of a curtain. Hooks or cleats
are fixed to the wall to anchor the tieback, and should be positioned far enough out from
the window to pull the curtain clear, and high enough to allow a generous sweep of fabric
to hang below them. Ready-made tiebacks of cord and rope, complete with tassels, can
be bought, or you can make your own out of fabric in a variety of shapes.

MEASURING

Hang and dress the curtain, then draw
it to one side. Hold a tape measure
around the curtain at the chosen level
for the tieback. Hold the ends of the
tape against the wall where you want
the hook. Decide on the size and
position for the tieback. Note the
measurement around the curtain, and
mark the hook position on the wall.

SIMPLE V-SHAPED TIEBACK

To make the V-shaped tieback, you will need the fabric for the tieback, and
lining if desired, interfacing, suitable rings and hooks for fixing the tieback
round the curtain and to the wall, as well as the basic sewing kit.

1 **MAKING PATTERN** Measure for the tieback and
mark a rectangle on the paper that measures half
the required length by 11 in (28 cm) wide. Mark a point
5½ in (14 cm) up from the bottom left-hand corner of
this rectangle, and mark a straight line from this point
to the top right-hand corner. Measure 2 in (5 cm) down
from the top right-hand corner, and mark a straight
line from this point to the bottom left-hand corner.
Cut out the wedge shape for the paper pattern.

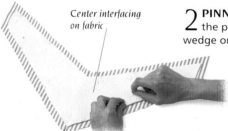

*Center interfacing
on fabric*

2 **PINNING PIECES** Fold the fabric double, and lay
the paper pattern on it with the wider end of the
wedge on the fold. Cut out the fabric, adding ⅝ in
(1.5 cm) all around for seam allowances.
Cut out a piece of lining fabric in the same
way. Cut a piece of interfacing to the exact
size of the paper pattern. Unfold the fabric
piece and lay it right side down on a flat
surface. Unfold and place the interfacing
on the fabric, and pin and tack in place.

3 **SEWING FABRIC** Place
the tieback fabric and the
lining right sides together. Pin,
tack, and sew them together,
keeping close to the edge of
the interfacing. Leave a gap
in the seam large enough to
turn the tieback right side out.

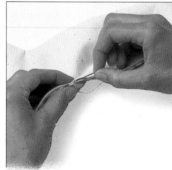

4 **FINISHING** Trim corner
seam allowances to reduce
bulk. Pull the tieback right side
out and press it. Turn in the raw
edges of the gap and slipstitch
the edges together. Topstitch
¼ in (6 mm) in from around the
edge to hold interfacing in place.

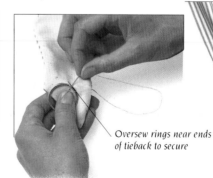

*Oversew rings near ends
of tieback to secure*

5 **FIXING RINGS** Attach rings
at either end of the tieback,
oversewing to secure. The rings
can be positioned far enough in
so that they are almost hidden,
or at the ends to make them
visible. Fix the hook to the wall,
and hang the tieback in place.

THE FINISHED TIEBACK

PADDED TIEBACK

The padded tieback, a simple tube with filling, can add a three-dimensional feel to your finished curtain. Determine the length of the tieback required, as described opposite, and decide on the width of the tieback. Cut out the fabric to the length of the tieback and double the width, adding ⅝ in (1.5 cm) all around for seam allowances. To make this tieback, you will need fabric for the tieback, padding, rings and retaining hooks, and the basic sewing kit.

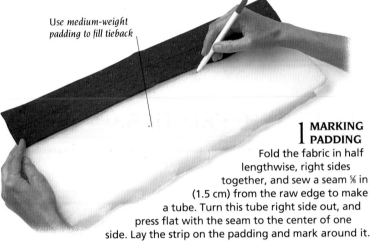

Use medium-weight padding to fill tieback

Tie a thread to one end of padding to help pull it through fabric tube

1 MARKING PADDING
Fold the fabric in half lengthwise, right sides together, and sew a seam ⅝ in (1.5 cm) from the raw edge to make a tube. Turn this tube right side out, and press flat with the seam to the center of one side. Lay the strip on the padding and mark around it.

2 FILLING TUBE Cut out the padding to the same size as the strip. Tie a strong thread around one end of the padding and pass the thread through the tube. Carefully pull on the thread to ease the padding into the tube.

Rings are attached to ends of tieback

3 SECURING ENDS When the padding is in position and well into the tube, remove the thread from it. Turn the two raw ends of the tieback fabric to the inside, and then slipstitch their folded edges together.

4 FIXING RINGS Place the securing rings at each end of the tieback and mark their positions according to whether you want them to be visible or not. Oversew them securely in place. Fix the hook to the wall and hang the tieback in place.

THE FINISHED TIEBACK

ROPES, TASSELS, AND CLASPS

Ready-made ropes and cords with tassels are available in a wide variety of thicknesses, colors, textures, and sizes to match or attractively contrast with every type of curtain fabric. Often, these rope tiebacks incorporate one or more elaborate tassels. Fixed hooks and holdbacks can be found in a range of finishes and styles, and they can provide another decorative means for holding a curtain open.

HOLDBACKS
Hooks and knobs are available in both wood and metal, often made to match decorative curtain poles. These fixtures are usually sold with screws and anchors for mounting them to a wall. Hook the curtain fabric behind the holdback and move it up and down the wall to determine the best position.

ROPES AND TASSELS
These elegant tiebacks can be bought ready-made in standard lengths, but you could buy tassels separately and combine colored cords to make a tieback to match your curtains. Attach the hook to the wall and loop the rope around the curtain, leaving the tassel to hang down against folds.

CRESCENT TIEBACK WITH CORDED EDGE

The edge of a tieback can be decorated with a range of trimmings to highlight its shape. To make this tieback, you will need fabric, decorative cord, iron-on interfacing, lining if required, rings, hooks, and the basic sewing kit. Measure for the tieback. On a piece of pattern paper, mark a strip 4¼ in (11 cm) wide by half the length required.

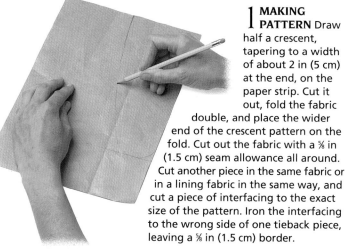

1 MAKING PATTERN Draw half a crescent, tapering to a width of about 2 in (5 cm) at the end, on the paper strip. Cut it out, fold the fabric double, and place the wider end of the crescent pattern on the fold. Cut out the fabric with a ⅝ in (1.5 cm) seam allowance all around. Cut another piece in the same fabric or in a lining fabric in the same way, and cut a piece of interfacing to the exact size of the pattern. Iron the interfacing to the wrong side of one tieback piece, leaving a ⅝ in (1.5 cm) border.

Attach edging just inside seam line

2 TACKING EDGING Unfold the fabric and measure around the seam line to find the length of cord required. Cut the cord to this length, adding 1 in (2.5 cm) extra for overlapping the ends. Pin and tack the cord just inside the seam line on the right side of the piece of fabric that will be the outside of the tieback.

Pin and tack pieces together along seam line

3 ALIGNING PIECES Lay the back piece of fabric on top of the front piece, right sides facing, and align the edges. Pin and tack the fabric pieces together along the seam line, sandwiching the corded edging between them.

4 SEWING PIECES Machine sew along the tacking line on the tieback, stitching through the corded edging to secure the pieces together. Remember to leave a gap large enough to allow the tieback to be turned right side out through it.

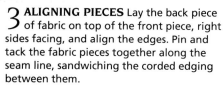

5 CLIPPING ALLOWANCES Using a pair of sharp dressmaker's scissors, make snips into the seam allowance around the tieback to ease the fabric and reduce bulk *(see page 16)*. Turn the tie-back right side out through the opening and press flat.

6 FINISHING OFF Fold in the raw edges of the opening and slipstitch it closed. Sew the curtain rings securely in their required positions at the ends of the tieback, then mount the hook to the wall and wrap the tieback around the finished curtain. Adjust and dress the curtain as necessary.

Make sure slipstitching is on inside when hanging tieback

THE FINISHED TIEBACK

BOW-TRIMMED TIEBACK

To add a bow to a tieback, you will need fabric for both, iron-on interfacing, rings, hooks, and the basic sewing kit. Cut two strips the length of the tieback by 3⅛ in (8 cm) wide, plus ⅝ in (1.5 cm) for allowances. Cut out interfacing to the same size minus the seam allowance. Iron it to the wrong side of one of the fabric strips, leaving a ⅝ in (1.5 cm) border.

1 SEWING TIEBACK Lay the tieback strips right sides together and pin, tack, and sew together ⅝ in (1.5 cm) from the cut edge, close to the edge of the interfacing. Leave an opening in one side for turning the band right side out. Trim the seam allowances to ¼ in (6 mm) and clip them at the corners.

Stitch close to, but not through, interfacing

Pull tieback band right sides out through opening in seam

2 FINISHING TIEBACK Turn the tieback band right side out through the opening in the seam, and press flat. Finish making the tieback by neatly slipstitching closed the opening in the seam.

3 MAKING BOW BAND Lay two cut strips of fabric – 1 yd x 4¼ in (93 x 11 cm) – right sides together. Pin, tack, and sew ⅝ in (1.5 cm) from edges. Leave a gap. Trim seams to ¼ in (6 mm), and clip corners. Turn right sides out and press. Slipstitch the opening closed.

4 CROSSING ENDS Fold the strip in half, bringing the ends together, and mark the center of it with a pin. Fold the ends of the strip over each other across the center mark, to form a bow shape. Adjust the placing to change the size of the loops and tails.

5 STITCHING BOW When the bow is the shape desired and the loops and tails are even, pin layers in place at the center. For a bigger bow, just use larger pieces of fabric. Try out your bow with inexpensive material before cutting it out in the fabric.

6 SEWING CENTER STRIP Cut out a 4¼ in (11 cm) square of fabric. Fold it in half, right sides together. Pin, tack, and sew ⅝ in (1.5 cm) from the long edge of the rectangle to make a tube. Turn right side out, and press flat with the seam in the center of one side.

7 SECURING BOW Wrap strip around center of folded band, with seamed side inside. Overlap and fold under ends at back. Bring together folded ends to grip center of bow. Slipstitch ends together.

8 ATTACHING BOW Lay the completed tieback band face up on a flat surface and mark the center. Sew the bow in place at the mark, making sure that it lies straight on the tieback. Sew the rings in place at the ends of the tieback and wrap it around the finished curtain. Hook the tieback to the wall and adjust or dress the curtain as necessary.

THE FINISHED TIEBACK

CORNICES AND VALANCES

A CORNICE OR A VALANCE provides an additional decorative finish to the heading of a curtain and also helps to prevent drafts from coming through a window. A cornice is made of rigid or semi-rigid panels covered with fabric, which usually matches the curtain fabric. It is hung or tacked over the window on a board that is held on right-angled brackets, with side pieces attached under the board at each end. The cornice board does not need to be very strong, because it carries little weight. A valance is a deep frill of fabric that either hangs over the curtain heading on a rod or is attached to the curtain fabric itself.

SIMPLE CORNICE

The cornice should be slightly wider than the curtains, so that they do not look cramped by it, and its front should be far enough away to ensure that the curtains do not drag against it when they are opened or closed. The depth of the cornice will depend on the length and style of the curtain: a good rule is to make the cornice one-eighth of the depth of the finished curtain. To make up this cornice, you will need the curtain and lining fabric, medium-weight interlining, buckram, Velcro, a permanent marker pen, a decorator's brush, heavy-duty shears, staple gun, and the basic sewing kit.

1 CUTTING BUCKRAM Measure and cut the buckram to the length (including the sides, or returns, of the cornice) and depth required. Use heavy-duty shears – buckram is very tough and will blunt good dressmaker's scissors.

2 SCORING SIDES Mark lines on the buckram at the point where the sides meet the front corners of the cornice. Score along these two lines with the back of a scissor blade. Cut out the interlining and the lining ⅝ in (1.5 cm) larger than the buckram panel all around. Assess the placement of any design motifs and pattern repeats on the cornice's covering fabric, and ensure that the straight grain will run straight on the finished cornice. Cut out the curtain fabric 1¼ in (3 cm) larger than the buckram panel all around.

3 DAMPENING EDGES Lay the buckram centrally onto the interlining, and lightly dampen its edges with water: a small decorator's paintbrush is ideal for this purpose. The dampened buckram will be lightly adhesive.

4 CLAMPING INTERLINING Fold the edges of the interlining over and then onto the dampened edge of the buckram panel. Press the interlining edges down firmly with your fingertips, and fix it in place with clothespins.

5 TRIMMING INTERLINING Press the edges with an iron over a damp cloth, removing the pins as you work around the buckram panel. The heat from the iron will cause the interlining to adhere to the buckram. Trim off the excess interlining at the corners so that the cornice's covering fabric will fit easily and smoothly over the interlining.

6 ATTACHING FABRIC Lay the panel centrally on the wrong side of the fabric. Dampen the edges of the buckram to the inside of the interlined edge. Fold the fabric over the panel, overlapping the interlining. Miter it at the corners. Smooth fabric taut and pin in place. Iron the edges over a damp cloth.

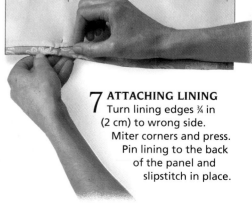

7 ATTACHING LINING Turn lining edges ¾ in (2 cm) to wrong side. Miter corners and press. Pin lining to the back of the panel and slipstitch in place.

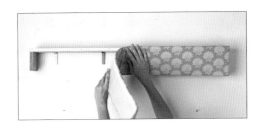

9 ATTACHING CORNICE
Fold along the scored lines marking where the cornice sides meet the front. Attach the fabric-covered panel to the cornice board by aligning the two Velcro strips and then pressing them together firmly.

8 MOUNTING VELCRO
Attach the frame over the window *(see page 39)*, ensuring that the cornice will cover the curtain heading. Cut Velcro to the length of the frame. Staple the hooked strip along the frame. Slipstitch the fuzzy strip to the top edge of the back of the cornice.

THE FINISHED CORNICE

CASTELLATED CORNICE

Cut buckram to the size of the panel, including sides. Make a pattern to the size of the front of the cornice. Fold in half and mark the center, then fold into quarters or eighths. You will need curtain and lining fabric, medium-weight interlining, buckram, Velcro, a marker pen, tape, decorator's brush, heavy-duty shears, and the basic sewing kit.

1 DRAWING PATTERN
Draw a right-angled shape from the side to the bottom edge of the paper pattern. If you draw the shape from the side that has the marked central fold, there will be an indentation at the center of the panel; if, however, you draw from the other side of the paper pattern, there will be a castellation at the center, as below.

2 CUTTING PAPER
Cut out the pattern and open up the paper. If the pattern shape was half the width of the folded paper, the castellations and indentations will be of equal size.

3 TRACING PATTERN
Secure the pattern on the buckram with tape. Draw around the pattern with a marker pen. At each end of the pattern, mark on the buckram where the sides of the cornice meet the front.

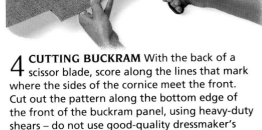

4 CUTTING BUCKRAM
With the back of a scissor blade, score along the lines that mark where the sides of the cornice meet the front. Cut out the pattern along the bottom edge of the front of the buckram panel, using heavy-duty shears – do not use good-quality dressmaker's scissors on buckram.

5 CUTTING INTERLINING
Cut the interlining, lining, and fabric ⅝ in (1.5 cm) larger than the buckram all around, carefully assessing the placement of pattern repeats and the alignment of the straight grain on the cornice fabric before cutting. Lay the buckram centrally on the interlining, and snip the internal corners.

6 TRIMMING EXCESS
Dampen the buckram edges with a brush, and clothespin the interlining in place. Press the interlining over a damp cloth. Trim the excess at the corners. Lay the panel centrally on the wrong side of the covering fabric and carefully snip the internal corners.

7 ATTACHING FABRIC
Fold the fabric over the cornice edge and pin it to the interlining. Smooth the fabric taut and sew it to the interlining with small tacking stitches. Trim excess fabric at corners. Hang the cornice as for a simple cornice.

THE FINISHED CORNICE

SHAPED WOODEN CORNICE

Decide on the size of the cornice *(see page 58)*, then cut panels of board to shape for the front and sides. Cut out lining and interlining to the same shape, but ⅝ in (1.5 cm) larger all around than the panels. To make a shaped cornice, you will need thin board, curtain and lining fabrics, interlining, curtain rings, cord, fabric glue, tape, and the basic sewing kit.

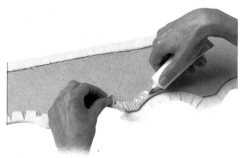

1 ATTACHING INTERLINING Lay the front board panel centrally on the interlining, and clip the edges of the interlining all around the curves and corners. Spread fabric glue along the edge of the board, and fold the edges of the fabric onto the glue, pressing down firmly with your fingertips. Attach the interlining to the two side panels in the same way.

2 CUTTING FABRIC Taking into account the alignment of any patterns and the straight grain of the fabric, lay the panel in position, interlined side face down, on wrong side of the fabric. Cut out the fabric 1¼ in (3 cm) larger than the panel all around. Repeat this procedure for the side pieces.

3 ATTACHING FABRIC Clip fabric edges at the curves and fold them over the interlined edges. Pin in place, stretching the fabric taut and laying it square on the panel. Secure fabric edges to the panel with glue, and press. Cover side pieces in the same way.

4 PREPARING LINING Lay out the lining fabric for the front and the side panels. Clip the edges around the curves and fold all edges under to the wrong side by ¾ in (2 cm). Miter the corners, and press.

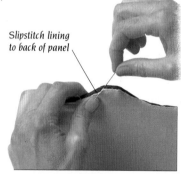

Slipstitch lining to back of panel

5 ATTACHING LINING Lay the lining fabric right side up on the back of the prepared front panel. Slipstitch it in place along the edge, leaving a section at one end unstitched. Repeat for the two sides, leaving the front edges open.

6 EDGING FRONT PANEL Measure around the edge of the front panel and cut the cord to this length. Starting at the opening in the lining seam, tuck the ends under the lining. Slipstitch the cord to the edges of the front panel, stitching through the open section to close it as you attach the cord.

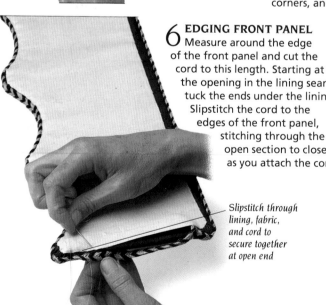

Slipstitch through lining, fabric, and cord to secure together at open end

7 EDGING SIDES Measure around the top, back, and bottom edges of each side piece, and cut cord to size. Slipstitch the cord to the three edges of the sides, tucking in the ends and closing the opening as for the front panel. Slipstitch the lining to the fabric along the front edges.

8 MOUNTING RINGS Mount screws into the top of the cornice board. Sew curtain rings in place on the back of the front and side panels, below the cord, to align with these fixtures. Hang the panels on the board by the rings.

THE FINISHED CORNICE

SIMPLE VALANCE WITH BOUND EDGE

For this technique, you will need fabric, lining fabric, bias strip, heading tape, curtain rod, hooks, and the basic sewing kit. Decide on the heading tape and estimate the fabric width (the valance should have more fullness than the curtain). For joins, center the largest panel of fabric, joining panels with plain flat seams. Decide on the valance length and cut out the valance fabric, allowing 1 in (2.5 cm) for side turnings and

1½ in (4 cm) for the heading turning. Cut out the lining fabric ¾ in (2 cm) smaller all around than the fabric. Place the fabric and lining right sides together, aligning bottom edges. Pin, tack, and sew both side seams. Press seams open and turn right side out. Press flat, centering the lining so that the seams lie on the lined side, ¾ in (2 cm) in from the folded edges. Fold the top 1½ in (4 cm) of fabric down over the lining, and press.

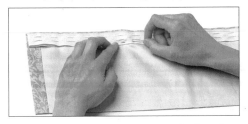

1 ATTACHING HEADING Lay the heading tape on the valance to align it with the top edge. Pin, tack, and sew the tape in place as for a curtain heading (see page 48).

2 BINDING EDGE Make up bias strip to the length of the bottom edge of the valance. Attach the bias strip (see page 16). Gather and secure the heading tape, attach the hooks, and hang the finished valance on the separate curtain rod.

THE FINISHED VALANCE

INTEGRAL VALANCE

You will need a tube-lined curtain without heading tape, fabric, fringe, binding, heading tape, and the basic sewing kit. Cut the fabric to the curtain width, plus 4¼ in (11 cm) for turnings and joins. For the length, allow one-sixth to one-fifth of the curtain drop, adding ⅝ in (1.5 cm) for turnings: cut lining 3⅛ in (8 cm) less in width and to the same depth. Cut a

fringe strip to 2¼ in (5.5 cm) less than length of the valance hem edge. Attach fringe to right side of fabric, ⅝ in (1.5 cm) from hem edge, facing away from the edge. Lay lining and fabric right sides together, aligning top edges, and sew a 1.5 cm (⅝ in) seam at the sides. Press seams open and turn right sides out. Fold fringed edge allowance to wrong side and press.

1 ATTACHING LINING Turn the bottom edge of the lining under by ⅝ in (1.5 cm). Press the turning and slipstitch it in place along the back of the fringed edge.

Slipstitch bias strip to lined side of curtain

2 ATTACHING VALANCE Lay the curtain right side up on top of a large, flat surface. Lay the valance right side up on it. Align the top edges, and pin and tack the valance to the curtain along the heading edge.

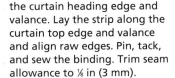

3 FIXING BINDING Cut bias strip to the length of the curtain heading edge and valance. Lay the strip along the curtain top edge and valance and align raw edges. Pin, tack, and sew the binding. Trim seam allowance to ⅛ in (3 mm).

4 STITCHING BINDING Fold the bias strip over the raw edges of the valance and curtain, and pin. Slipstitch in place along the seam line on the lined side of the curtain.

5 ATTACHING TAPE Pin, tack, and sew the heading tape to the curtain just below the bound edge, sewing through all the layers of fabric. Gather the heading tape, fit the hooks, and hang and dress the finished curtain (see page 51).

THE FINISHED VALANCE

SWAGS AND CASCADES

*A*MONG THE MOST SOPHISTICATED and luxurious window dressings, swags and cascades (also called tails or jabots) complement and enhance functional curtains. To benefit from their full decorative effect, swags and cascades should preferably be hung over a long window in a room that has a high ceiling. Swags and cascades are constructed individually and then attached to the cornice board above a window to form an independent curtain furnishing. It is appropriate to make them in the same fabric as the curtain – the edges of the cascades can be highlighted with a frill, contrasting piping, or ribbon.

MAKING UP A SWAG

For the swag and binding, you will need the same fabric as used for the curtain, lining fabric, masking tape, a cornice board with sides in position *(see page 39)*, and the basic sewing kit. Measure the front panel of the cornice: this will be the width of the finished swag. To calculate the drop, measure the height of the window. The drop at the deepest point of the finished swag should be between one sixth and one eighth of this measurement.

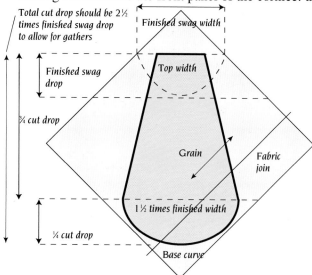

Total cut drop should be 2½ times finished swag drop to allow for gathers

Finished swag width

Finished swag drop

Top width

¾ cut drop

Grain

Fabric join

1½ times finished width

¼ cut drop

Base curve

1 DRAWING PATTERN
Using the diagram as a guide, draw a pattern on paper to the proportions shown for use as a template, adding ⅝ in (1.5 cm) for seams. You will need to cut out the pattern and pin it in place on the bias of the lining fabric.

2 CUTTING FABRIC Cut out the lining fabric around the pattern. Remove the pattern. Pin the lining fabric to the main fabric, again on the bias. Cut out main fabric, making joins, if necessary, on the straight grain with plain flat seams *(see page 16)*.

3 TURNING HEM Remove pins. Turn ⅝ in (1.5 cm) hem to wrong side along all edges of main fabric. Tack and sew, using herringbone stitch *(see page 20)*. Clip the seam allowance along the base curve to reduce its bulk *(see page 16)*. Turn a ⅝ in (1.5 cm) hem to the wrong side along lining fabric edges, and press.

4 TACKING FABRICS With the wrong sides together, tack the lining fabric to the main fabric along the three straight edges.

5 STITCHING BASE CURVE On the finished swag, the base curve will be visible. Make sure lining does not show on the right side of the swag by slipstitching panels together along base curve.

6 HANGING FABRIC Using masking tape, attach a strip of spare fabric longer than the ultimate width of the swag to the edge of a table. Mark the center and the ultimate width of the finished swag on the fabric strip as a guide. Pin the central point of the top edge of the swag to the marked center of the fabric strip. Pin the outer edges of the swag to marked width points on the fabric strip.

7 FOLDING FABRIC Working toward the center, make even folds up one long side of the fabric, allowing the fold nearest to the center to lie over the top edge of the center swag. Repeat on the other long side, mirroring the fold at the center to create a symmetrical swag. Pin all the folds securely in place. It may also be helpful to mark the fold edges at the top with a vanishing-ink pen. Remove the pins securing the swag to the tabletop fabric.

8 SEWING FOLDS Tack and sew along the tops of the folds to hold them firmly in place. To bind the top edge of the swag, cut a strip of the main fabric 2 in (5 cm) wide, and to the same length as the cornice, plus 1¼ in (3 cm). Lay one edge of binding *(see page 16)* against top edge of the swag, right sides together. Sew the binding ⅝ in (1.5 cm) from the edge.

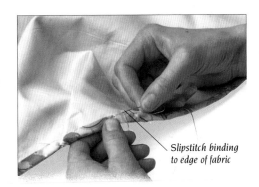

Slipstitch binding to edge of fabric

9 STITCHING BINDING
To complete the swag, fold the binding over the edge of the main fabric. Tuck in the raw edges of the binding, and slipstitch along the edge to secure.

MAKING UP CASCADES

Cascades are fitted to the cornice board and fall at each side of the swag. They can be self-lined or lined with contrasting fabric. As well as cascade and binding fabrics, you will need to use a staple gun and the basic sewing kit. Make cascades in mirroring pairs. Decide on finished length of cascades (A).

The length of the shorter edge (B) should be about 6 in (15 cm). Estimate width of top edge (C), allowing for the sides of the cornice to be covered. Select the number of pleats and their width. Double the number of pleats, and multiply this by the pleat width to give finished width of the top edge.

1 MAKING PATTERN Draw and cut out a full-size paper pattern to the required dimensions for a cascade, adding ⅝ in (1.5 cm) all around for seam allowance. Use a try square to draw the corners.

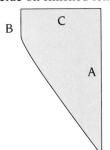

2 CUTTING OUT FABRIC Pin the pattern to the straight grain of the lining fabric. Cut out the fabric. Remove the pattern from the lining fabric, and pin it in place on the straight grain of the main fabric, aligning designs, if necessary. Cut out the fabric. Make the piping *(see page 22)* to the length of the leading edge.

3 TRIMMING PIPING Pin and tack piping to right side of main fabric, then trim ends. Lay right sides of main and lining fabrics together. Pin, tack, and sew along three edges. Leave top open for turning out. Use zipper foot to sew along piped edge. Turn right side out, and press. Tack top edge.

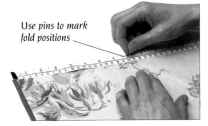

Use pins to mark fold positions

4 MARKING FOLDS Lay the fabric on a flat surface, with the right side facing up. Starting from the short edge, measure and then mark the positions for the folds with pins along the top edge.

Use staple gun to secure swag and cascades to cornice board

5 PINNING FOLDS Pin the folds in place, leaving the last fold open in order to position it around the side of the cornice board. Tack and sew along the top edge to secure the folds. Cut out a strip of the same fabric 2 in (5 cm) wide by the width of the top edge for the binding. Attach the binding as in steps 8 and 9, above.

6 FITTING SWAG AND CASCADES Secure the swag and cascades to the cornice with staples or tacks. Make sure that the swag is correctly centered, and staple or tack it in position along the top edge of the cornice front. Attach the cascades to the top edge of the sides and front of the cornice.

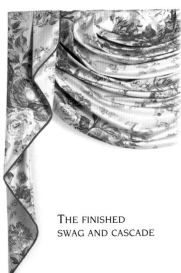

THE FINISHED SWAG AND CASCADE

SHADES

CONCEIVED OVER FOUR CENTURIES AGO, the first shades were little more than pieces of fabric draped over windows, designed to protect furnishings from the destructive effect of sunlight. Today, by contrast, shades are firmly established in their own right as a means of decorating windows. As well as being inherently practical, shades are easy to make in a variety of styles, sizes, and materials, ranging from the simplicity of a plain roller shade to the period character of elegant gathered Austrian or balloon shades. A shade can be used either on its own or as a useful supplement to a curtain. When combined with a set of purely decorative curtains, a simple shade helps keep out the light and reduces noise and drafts, offering an ideal, utilitarian solution to covering a window. In this chapter, you will find all the information you need to make and fit roller, Roman, and gathered shades.

CHOOSING A STYLE

WINDOW SHADES CAN BE CATEGORIZED into two basic groups: plain and gathered.
The first category consists of roller, simple tied, hooked, and Roman shades, all of which
give a flat surface when lowered. Plain shades have a tailored appearance, and draw up
to allow the maximum amount of daylight to enter a room. Gathered shades include
Austrian and balloon shades, and provide fuller and more opulent window dressings
than plain shades. When choosing a style, bear in mind that, even when fully
raised, a gathered shade will always obscure a section of the window.

PERMANENT FIXTURES

If you have a window that is exposed to view or has a poor view, consider hanging a shade that will remain permanently drawn. This simple shade, made from a shawl stretched flat, has been secured to the frame of a recessed window on a pair of battens.

PRACTICAL AND POPULAR

Ideal for recessed windows that need to be screened but not insulated, roller shades are a popular choice for the most frequently used rooms, such as kitchens and bathrooms. A roller shade hangs most effectively if it is constructed from specially made shade fabric, or a fabric made semi-rigid with commercial stiffening fluid, which gives the material a durable surface that is easy to wipe clean.

SCREENS FOR PRIVACY

Roller shades are among the most versatile shades. Because they self-wind onto unobtrusive poles, roller shades are ideal for use in bathrooms, where privacy is essential. If you need a lightproof roller shade for privacy, use specially made blackout fabric.

Flat surface of shade is best suited to material with simple, small pattern, or to plain fabric

Shape of roller shade is enhanced by decorative base below batten

SECONDARY SHADES
When you wish to preserve your furnishings, upholstery, and other light-sensitive objects from the damaging effect of sunlight, combine flat shades, such as these Roman shades, with curtains, to provide secondary daytime cover.

MULTIPLE SHADES
For aesthetic purposes, a shade should be longer than it is wide, otherwise it would appear stunted and distorted. When dressing a wide window or a series of windows, you can divide a large shade into a series of swags, or hang several shades in a row.

LUXURIOUS GATHERED EFFECTS
The most sophisticated shades are undoubtedly of the gathered variety. Unlike a balloon shade, which is lightly gathered from top to bottom, an Austrian shade is gathered and heavily swagged along the bottom edge only, making it most appropriate for a tall window. If fitted above the window, as here, the shade will allow more daylight into the room than if it is fixed within the window recess. Lightweight fabrics, such as net, lace, cotton, and silk, are most effective for these shades.

HIDDEN HEADINGS
Roller shades wrap around a pole suspended between a pair of small metal brackets that are attached over a window. Although this assembly is relatively unobtrusive, it can be hidden behind a simple cornice. Made of wood and fastened to a wall, ceiling, or window frame by metal brackets, cornices can either be decorated with fabric that matches the shade, or painted.

Shade made from furnishing fabric matches style of room

Simple heading has been used to gather fabric of the shade

Shade is attractively illuminated from behind by sunlight

Frills at bottom edge of shade help to emphasize swags

MAKING SHADES

ONE OF THE FIRST CRITERIA FOR deciding on which style of shade to choose is the effect it will have when lowered and raised. When lowered, roller, Roman, tie-up, and hooked shades present flat surfaces of fabric. They also expose a greater window area when raised than gathered shades. Balloon and Austrian shades, on the other hand, are more shapely and pronounced at full length, dominating the window and its surrounding area. When raised, they remain gathered and highly decorative. Regardless of which shade you are making, it is important to take accurate, relevant measurements of the window area before starting.

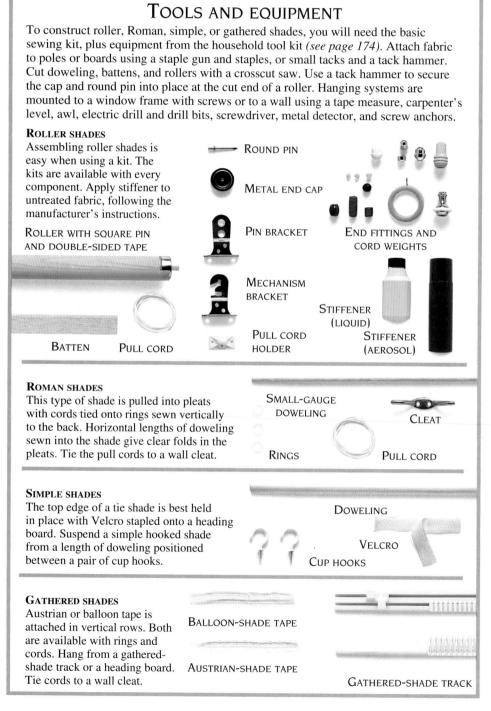

TOOLS AND EQUIPMENT

To construct roller, Roman, simple, or gathered shades, you will need the basic sewing kit, plus equipment from the household tool kit (*see page 174*). Attach fabric to poles or boards using a staple gun and staples, or small tacks and a tack hammer. Cut doweling, battens, and rollers with a crosscut saw. Use a tack hammer to secure the cap and round pin into place at the cut end of a roller. Hanging systems are mounted to a window frame with screws or to a wall using a tape measure, carpenter's level, awl, electric drill and drill bits, screwdriver, metal detector, and screw anchors.

ROLLER SHADES
Assembling roller shades is easy when using a kit. The kits are available with every component. Apply stiffener to untreated fabric, following the manufacturer's instructions.

ROLLER WITH SQUARE PIN AND DOUBLE-SIDED TAPE

ROUND PIN

METAL END CAP

PIN BRACKET

END FITTINGS AND CORD WEIGHTS

MECHANISM BRACKET

STIFFENER (LIQUID)

STIFFENER (AEROSOL)

PULL CORD HOLDER

BATTEN   PULL CORD

ROMAN SHADES
This type of shade is pulled into pleats with cords tied onto rings sewn vertically to the back. Horizontal lengths of doweling sewn into the shade give clear folds in the pleats. Tie the pull cords to a wall cleat.

SMALL-GAUGE DOWELING

CLEAT

RINGS

PULL CORD

SIMPLE SHADES
The top edge of a tie shade is best held in place with Velcro stapled onto a heading board. Suspend a simple hooked shade from a length of doweling positioned between a pair of cup hooks.

DOWELING

VELCRO

CUP HOOKS

GATHERED SHADES
Austrian or balloon tape is attached in vertical rows. Both are available with rings and cords. Hang from a gathered-shade track or a heading board. Tie cords to a wall cleat.

BALLOON-SHADE TAPE

AUSTRIAN-SHADE TAPE

GATHERED-SHADE TRACK

MEASURING WINDOW AREA

If the shade is to fit inside the recess, measure from the mounting position to the windowsill for the drop required. The finished width should be 1¼ in (3 cm) less than the width of the recess. For a shade hanging outside the recess, measure from the top of the hanging system to 2 in (5 cm) below the windowsill for the drop. The finished width should be 2 in (5 cm) wider than the window at the sides to keep light from spilling in around the shade.

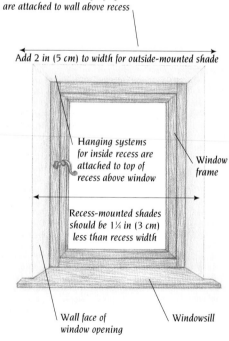

Outside-mounted hanging systems are attached to wall above recess

Add 2 in (5 cm) to width for outside-mounted shade

Hanging systems for inside recess are attached to top of recess above window

Window frame

Recess-mounted shades should be 1¼ in (3 cm) less than recess width

Wall face of window opening

Windowsill

ROLLER SHADES

THE SPRING MECHANISM THAT CAUSES a roller to raise and lower the fabric is what distinguishes this type of shade from others. At its full length, the shade should cover the window while allowing some daylight into the room – providing the fabric is not too thick. When the roller is attached above the window and the shade is rolled up, the entire window will be on view. You can embellish a roller shade with a decorative edging along the bottom.

SIMPLE ROLLER SHADE

Choose from a range of roller-shade fabrics, or apply stiffener to thin fabric. Brackets can be mounted to a window frame or to a wall. Purchase a roller that is too long – you can cut it down to size. When mounting the brackets, align them horizontally with the window. Cut the roller to the distance between the mounted brackets, less ⅛ in (3 mm), to allow for

the end cap. Fit the end cap and hammer the pin home, following the manufacturer's instructions. Measure for the shade (see opposite), checking that the roller hangs correctly in the brackets. Add 12 in (30 cm) to the length to allow for the roller to be covered with fabric when the shade is down, and for the hemmed channel for the batten at the lower edge.

3 SEWING CHANNEL Zigzag stitch the lower edge (see page 16). Place batten on wrong side of fabric. Fold lower edge over it. Mark the turning. Remove the batten. Press, tack, and sew near the stitching to form a channel. Leave sides open.

1 ATTACHING BRACKET If mounting the hanging system within a window recess, allow a space of ¾ in (2 cm) from the brackets to the top of the recess. Mount the bracket for the square pin to the left of the window, and the bracket for the round pin to the right. In a wooden frame, mark the positions for the screws, then awl the holes before driving home the screws. On a wall, use a metal detector to confirm that there are no electrical wires. Mark, awl, drill holes, and insert an anchor into each hole.

2 MARKING FABRIC Measure the shade and mark the dimensions (see opposite). Cut out the fabric, making sure that the corners are at perfect right angles so that the shade will hang and roll correctly. Join widths by overlapping edges by ⅜ in (1 cm) and sewing close to the raw edges (take such measurements into account when calculating the fabric).

4 TAPING ROLLER Lay the fabric flat, right side up. Mark the place for the roller. Center it along the top edge of the fabric. Align the roller with the mark. Tape the top of the fabric along its length, or attach using double-sided tape, if supplied.

5 ATTACHING FABRIC Work a half-roll of fabric onto the roller, ensuring that the fabric is aligned. Using small upholstery tacks or staples, attach it to the roller, following the manufacturer's instructions.

6 ATTACHING CORD Cut batten ¼ in (6 mm) shorter than shade width. Center it in the channel. Secure cord in cord holder, and attach this to center of batten on wrong side of the fabric.

7 ATTACHING WEIGHT Thread the cord weight and end fitting onto the cord, and knot to secure. Wind the fabric onto the roller. Fit the roller into the brackets. Test the operation of the shade, altering the amount wound around the roller in order to obtain a perfect drop; if necessary, adjust the tension, following the manufacturer's instructions.

THE FINISHED SHADE

FRINGE-EDGED ROLLER SHADE

To give a roller shade a decorative lower edge, you will need the edging and the basic sewing kit. Measure for and make a roller shade *(see page 69)*. Consider the edging size in relation to the window, allowing for the edging to drop below the sill if the roller is to be mounted onto the molding or wall, or to the sill if it is to be recess-mounted.

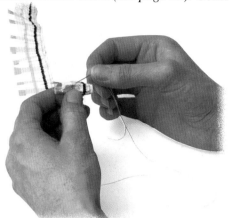

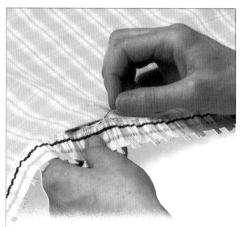

1 NEATENING FRINGE Cut out the fringe to the same width as the shade, adding 2 in (5 cm) for turnings. Trim the raw edges at each end, turn them to the wrong side, and oversew to secure.

2 ATTACHING FRINGE Remove the batten and lay the lower edge of the shade on a flat surface. Using matching thread, slipstitch the fringe to the lower edge of the batten channel, with the wrong side facing the right side of the shade. Finish the shade by following steps 4–7 on page 69.

THE FINISHED SHADE

SCALLOP-EDGED ROLLER SHADE

There are several shapes, such as scallops, that can be used to decorate the lower edge of a roller shade. For this technique, you will need fabric for the shade and the facing strip, iron-on interlining to give body to the lower edge, a saucer for use as a template, and the basic sewing kit. Measure for the shade *(see page 68)*. Add the desired depth of the scallops to the dimension for the shade drop. The scallop depth here is 1¼ in (3 cm). Cut out and stiffen the shade fabric *(see page 69)*.

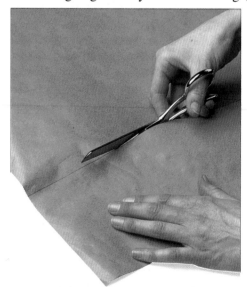

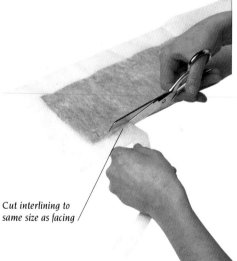

Cut interlining to same size as facing

1 CUTTING PATTERN Cut out a strip of pattern paper to the width of the shade by the depth of the batten plus 3 in (7.5 cm), adding 1¼ in (3 cm) for the depth of the scallops.

2 TRIMMING INTERLINING Cut out a strip of fabric for the facing to the same size as the paper pattern. Cut a strip of interlining to match the facing. Press the interlining to the wrong side of the facing.

3 MARKING BATTEN LINE Machine sew a row of zigzag stitches *(see page 16)* along the top edge of the facing. Mark lines on both sides of the facing ⅜ in (1 cm) from the top edge. Mark a second line away from each marked line equal to the batten width. The batten used here is 1¼ in (3 cm) wide.

4 DRAWING CURVE

Fold the paper pattern into equal lengths. Place the saucer on the folded pattern and draw a smooth curve for the scallop outline.

5 CUTTING PATTERN

Hold the folded pattern firmly in one hand and cut out the scallops, carefully following the marked line.

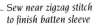

Cut out scallops in pattern by following marked lines

6 PINNING PATTERN

Pin the facing and shade fabric right sides together, aligning the raw edges. Unfold the paper pattern and pin it to the facing, aligning the straight edge of the pattern with the neatened edge of the facing.

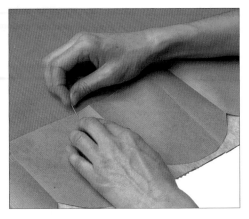

7 MARKING FACING

Use a vanishing-ink pen to trace the outline of the scallops onto the facing. Remove the pattern. Sew a row of tacking stitches ¼ in (6 mm) inside the scallop line.

8 SEWING FABRIC

Machine sew along the tacked line. Cut out the scallops, following the marked line. Notch the curved seam allowances *(see page 16)*. Turn the shade fabric and the facing right sides out, and press.

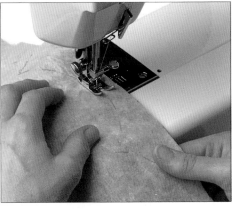

9 STITCHING BATTEN LINE

Sew facing and shade fabric together along the lower batten line *(see step 3)*. Lay out the shade and place the batten between the fabric pieces and against the stitched line. Fold the facing over the batten to check that there is space left for the batten.

10 FINISHING CHANNEL

Remove the batten. Complete the batten channel by machine sewing the fabric close to the zigzag stitching. Finish the roller shade by following steps 4–7 on page 69.

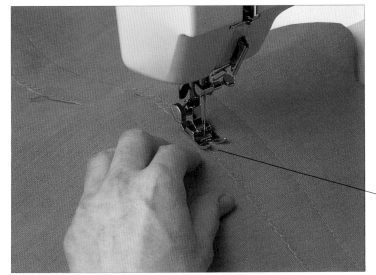

Sew near zigzag stitch to finish batten sleeve

THE FINISHED SHADE

SIMPLE SHADES

SIMPLE SHADES ARE WELL SUITED FOR covering windows in rooms where privacy is needed, such as bathrooms. These basic shades are easy to assemble, and they lend themselves to various decorative style options. The tie shades consists of unlined fabric held up by strips of fabric or ribbon, and is attached to a heading board with Velcro. The double-sided, hooked shade is more versatile than the tie shade. It is suspended from a piece of doweling supported between hooks attached above the window frame, and can be lowered, drawn halfway, reversed, and removed easily from the window.

TIE SHADE

To make this simple shade, you will need fabric for the shade, ribbon, Velcro strips, and the basic sewing kit. Alternatively, you can make ties from the fabric scraps. Measure the width and drop required, allowing for a 2 in (5 cm) overlap at all edges if the shade is to hang outside the recess. Add 2½ in (6 cm) to the width and drop measurements for turnings. Mount the heading board in position.

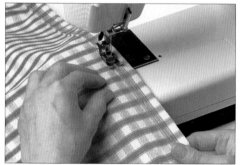

1 SEWING HEM
Cut out the fabric. Sew a double ⅝ in (1.5 cm) hem to the wrong side on the sides and lower edge. Make four fabric ties to the width required, 2 in (5 cm) longer than the shade (see page 27).

2 MARKING FABRIC
Lay out the fabric on a flat surface. Measure and mark a quarter of the shade width from both corners on the top edge.

4 ATTACHING VELCRO
Cut the Velcro strip that has the tiny, smooth loops to the width of the shade. Turn 1¼ in (3 cm) of the shade fabric to the wrong side along the top edge and press. Pin, tack, and sew the Velcro strip to this turned edge of the fabric.

5 STAPLING VELCRO STRIP Staple the other Velcro strip to the heading board. Hold the shade up to the board, align the Velcro strips, and push the shade into place. To tie up the shade, gather the fabric loosely and knot the ties at the required height.

ATTACHING A HEADING BOARD

Upon deciding the position for the shade, look at the window setting and choose where to mount the heading board. If the shade is to be fitted inside the recess, mount the board to the top face of the recess with screws, as shown here. If the shade is to be fitted to the outside of a window, mount a board using angle brackets, as for the curtain cornice (see page 39). The heading board shown here is also used for hanging Roman or gathered shades – the shade cords are threaded through the eyes screwed into the underside of the board.

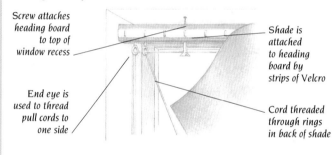

Screw attaches heading board to top of window recess

End eye is used to thread pull cords to one side

Shade is attached to heading board by strips of Velcro

Cord threaded through rings in back of shade

3 POSITIONING TIES Pin, tack, and sew the four ties to the top edge of the fabric on both sides, aligning them with the quarter marks.

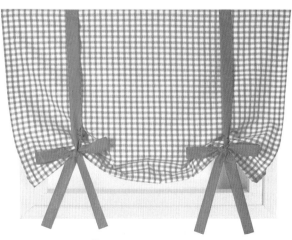

THE FINISHED SHADE

REVERSIBLE SHADE

This shade works well when lined with a complementary fabric, since the back of the shade is visible when the shade is folded up. Here, the back of the shade is bordered with the main fabric. To make this shade, you will need the main fabric, lining fabric, braid edging, and the basic sewing kit. For securing the hanging system to the window frame, use two lengths of ½ in (12 mm) doweling for the top and bottom edges of the shade, a crosscut saw, two cup hooks, and an awl. For securing the hanging system to the wall, use a drill, drill bits, and screw anchors. Measure as for the Roman shade (see page 74), allowing space within a recess for the doweling to protrude ¾ in (2 cm) at each end of the shade width, top and bottom. If hanging the shade outside the recess, allow a 2 in (5 cm) overlap at each side to exclude the light.

1 CUTTING OUT FABRIC Cut out the main fabric to the required measurements, adding a border allowance, here 3 in (7.5 cm) all around. Cut out the lining fabric to the exact size of the finished shade.

Turn each edge ⅝ in (1.5 cm) to wrong side

2 TURNING EDGES Lay out the main fabric wrong side up. Fold a ⅝ in (1.5 cm) hem to the wrong side on all edges, and press.

3 FOLDING AGAIN Turn the folded edges of the fabric by 2 in (5 cm) to the wrong side. Fold and press a miter in each corner (see page 21).

4 MITERING CORNER Unfold the 2 in (5 cm) hems. Lay the lining fabric and main fabric wrong sides together. Align the raw edges of the lining within the creases of the hems of the main fabric. Refold the 2 in (5 cm) hems and the mitered corners, and pin in place.

Refold edges and corners once lining has been positioned

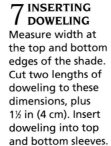

Stitch folded edge to lining to form border

5 STITCHING EDGES Tack and slipstitch close to the inner folded edge to form the border. Leave the inside edges of the mitered corners at the top and bottom unsewn to form a sleeve for inserting the pieces of doweling.

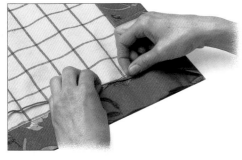

6 ATTACHING BRAID For the braid edging, measure and cut a length of braid to the same length as the inner edge of the border. Slipstitch the braid in place along this edge.

7 INSERTING DOWELING Measure width at the top and bottom edges of the shade. Cut two lengths of doweling to these dimensions, plus 1½ in (4 cm). Insert doweling into top and bottom sleeves.

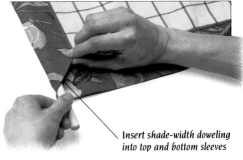

Insert shade-width doweling into top and bottom sleeves

8 MOUNTING CUP HOOK Add ⅜ in (1 cm) to the shade width dimension, and mark this on the wall or window frame for the hook positions. With an awl, make pilot holes in a wooden frame, then screw the cup hooks into position. On a wall, mark, awl, drill, and use screw anchors to secure the hooks. Hang the doweling between the hooks.

THE FINISHED SHADE AT FULL LENGTH

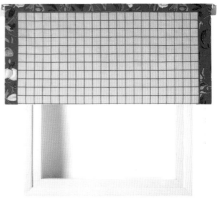

THE FINISHED SHADE WHEN FOLDED UP

ROMAN SHADES

ROMAN SHADES ARE THE MOST ELEGANT of the flat-faced shades and complement almost any decorative scheme. When raised, Roman shades gather into folds of deep horizontal pleats; these are formed by pieces of doweling that are sewn into sleeves in the lining fabric. Because the doweling gives firmness to this type of shade, there is no need to treat the fabric with stiffener. The hanging system for a Roman shade includes pull cords that run vertically up the back of the fabric and are threaded through a series of metal eyes screwed into a heading board. The same hanging system can also be used for gathered shades.

MAKING A ROMAN SHADE

Decide on the shade position and measure the window width. If the shade is to hang outside the recess, add an extra 2 in (5 cm) for a light-excluding overlap. Mount the heading board *(see page 72)*. Measure the drop from the heading board to the windowsill, or 2 in (5 cm) below if the shade is to hang outside the recess. To make this shade, you will need shade fabric, lining fabric, pull cords, crosscut saw, doweling, screw eyes, rings, Velcro strips, cleat, and the basic sewing kit.

CONSTRUCTION OF THE SHADE
The pull-up system applies to Austrian, balloon, and Roman shades. Cords are attached near the lower edge and threaded up through rings sewn to sleeves containing pieces of doweling. At the top, the cords are worked through eyes screwed into the underside of the heading board. These eyes are aligned with the vertical rows of rings at the back. An extra eye is screwed to the side on which the cords will hang. The distance between the topmost piece of doweling and the top of the shade should be greater than the distances between the other pieces of doweling. This part is made larger so that the rest of the shade will pull up neatly behind it.

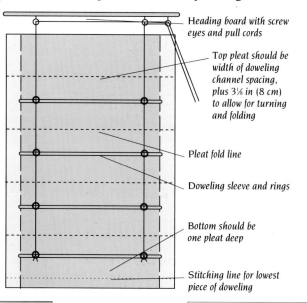

Heading board with screw eyes and pull cords

Top pleat should be width of doweling channel spacing, plus 3⅛ in (8 cm) to allow for turning and folding

Pleat fold line

Doweling sleeve and rings

Bottom should be one pleat deep

Stitching line for lowest piece of doweling

1 CUTTING FABRIC Cut out the fabric on the straight grain to the required size, adding 2½ in (6 cm) to the length and width. Cut the lining to the same size as the main fabric, less 3⅛ in (8 cm) widthwise, and add the sleeve widths – the circumference of each piece of doweling, plus ¼ in (6 mm) – to the length. You will need a piece of doweling for the bottom of the shade and for each sleeve. The top of the shade does not require a piece of doweling.

2 STITCHING SIDE HEM Lay out the lining fabric and turn the side edges by ⅝ in (1.5 cm) to the wrong side. Press, pin, tack, and sew both of the side hems.

3 MARKING SLEEVE POSITIONS On the right side of the lining, mark a line 1¼ in (3 cm) from the bottom. From there, measure and mark the sleeve positions. The distance between the pieces of doweling will be twice the pleat depth.

4 FOLDING SLEEVE Following the sleeve marks, pinch the sleeves together, wrong sides facing. Pin, tack, and sew along these marks. Turn and press the sides and bottom edge of the main fabric 1¼ in (3 cm) to the wrong side.

5 MARKING SLEEVE Fold the bottom corners of main fabric into miters *(see page 21)*. From the lower folded edge, make a mark for each sleeve position. At lower edges of the fabrics, mark the midpoints.

6 **PINNING FABRICS** Lay the fabrics right sides together, aligning the midpoints. Sew a plain flat seam 1¼ in (3 cm) from lower edge. Trim seams to ⅝ in (1.5 cm). Fold lining and main fabric wrong sides together. Press along lower edge of seam line.

7 **ALIGNING SLEEVE MARKS** Align the sleeve seam line on the lining with the sleeve marks on the main fabric. Pin the lining to the main fabric along the edges.

8 **ATTACHING LINING** Tack together the lining and main fabric, just above or below each sleeve line and close to stitching. For the bottom doweling, tack a line ¹⁄₁₆ in (2 mm) plus the diameter of the doweling from the lower edge of the shade.

9 **SEWING LINING** Sew the lining and the main fabric together along the tacked lines. Cut doweling pieces, except the bottom one, ⅜ in (1 cm) shorter than the sleeve length. Cut the bottom doweling to the width of the shade, less ¼ in (6 mm).

10 **STITCHING SIDES** Insert each piece of doweling into a sleeve, including the longer piece at the bottom. Slipstitch the ends closed. Slipstitch the sides of the lining to the sides of the main fabric.

11 **ATTACHING RINGS** Sew the rings to the doweling sleeves, 4 in (10 cm) from the edges and 12–16 in (30–40 cm) apart. Make sure that they are aligned vertically. At the top edge of the shade, turn the fabric 1¼ in (3 cm) to the wrong side, press, and tack. Cut strips of Velcro to the same width as the shade.

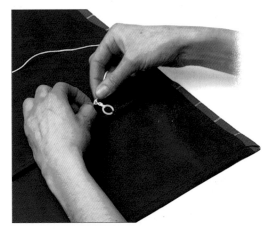

12 **STITCHING VELCRO** Sew the loop strip of Velcro to the top hem. Cut each cord length to twice the blind length plus the necessary amount for the cord to run along the top of the blind to the pull-up side.

13 **SECURING CORD** Tie one end of a cord to the lowest ring. Thread the cord up through the vertical line of rings to the top of the shade. Tie and thread the remaining cords in place across the shade. Staple the hook strip of Velcro to the heading board.

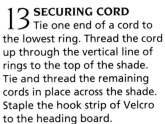

14 **SECURING EYES** Mark on the heading board the placement for the screw eyes. All of the eyes, except one, should line up with the rows of rings. Screw the eyes to the underside of the board corresponding with these dimensions. Fit one eye at the edge of the board on the side you wish the cords to hang. Attach the shade to the board.

15 **MOUNTING SHADE** Thread the cords through the eyes on the heading board, working toward the side where the cords will hang. Let the shade hang down and tie the cords together at the top, 1 in (2.5 cm) from the last eye. Trim the cords at the bottom and knot together again to neaten. Draw the shade, and mark and attach the cleat to the wall or window frame.

THE FINISHED SHADE WHEN DRAWN

GATHERED SHADES

THERE ARE TWO TYPES OF GATHERED SHADES, the Austrian and the balloon, and the headings of both are gathered in the same way as a curtain heading. Although the shades are similar in appearance, a balloon shade is gathered only at its lower edge, while an Austrian shade is gathered along its entire length. Gathered shades are drawn up by a system of parallel rows of cords threaded through rings or loops that are attached to the back of the shade, in the same way as a Roman shade *(see page 74)*. You can make gathered shades with or without a lining. Of the two shades, the balloon type is more suitable for heavy fabrics. To enhance the ruffled effect of the shade, add a frill or fringe at the lower edge and sides.

BALLOON SHADE

Measure the window and estimate the size of the finished shade *(see page 68)*. Decide on the shade fullness, and the width and number of finished swags – lightweight fabric provides the fullest swags. You will need shade fabric, lining fabric, heading tape *(see page 40)*, fringe, shade tape strips with loops or rings, pull cords, a cleat, a hanging system, heading board, and the basic sewing kit. Cut the main fabric to the required drop, adding 1½ in (4 cm) to the length for turnings and 6–24 in (15–60 cm) for gathering at the bottom edge. For the width, cut fabric to one to two and a half times desired width, depending on the fabric used and on the heading, plus 1¼ in (3 cm) for side turnings. If it is necessary to make joins to the fabric, allow 1¼ in (3 cm) for French seams *(see page 17)*. Join panels by making seams along the vertical lines where the edges of the swags will fall, and place half widths at the sides. Cut the lining to the same size as the main fabric, and stagger joins in the lining and main fabric to ease the gathering of the shade.

1 ATTACHING LINING Place the lining fabric and the main fabric right sides together. Pin, tack, and sew a seam ⅝ in (1.5 cm) from the side and lower edges of the material. Clip the corners *(see page 16)*. Turn the fabrics right side out and press.

2 ATTACHING HEADING Lay the shade out on a flat surface, with the lining side up. Turn the heading edge allowance by 1½ in (4 cm) to the wrong side, then press. Pin, tack, and sew the heading tape in place *(see page 48)*.

3 POSITIONING TAPE Mark the positions for the tape strips on the lining, beginning 1¼ in (3 cm) in from the sides. Decide on the spacing for the strips. If the fabric is one and a half times the finished shade width, the strips should be positioned apart one and a half times the finished swag width. Cut the strips to the length of the shade less the heading, allowing ⅝ in (1.5 cm) at ends for turning.

4 POSITIONING LOOPS Pin and tack the first tape strip in position with a line of stitching down each side. Turn under raw ends. Attach the remaining tape strips, making sure that the loops align horizontally. Measure from the lower edge of the shade and mark the loop positions.

5 ATTACHING TAPE Sew each of the tape strips in position, again making sure that the loops align across the shade.

6 FITTING EDGING For the fringe edging, measure the width of the shade, adding 1¼ in (3 cm) at each end for turnings. Cut the fringe to this length.

7 SECURING ENDS Turn each end of the fringe ⅝ in (1.5 cm) twice to the wrong side. Slipstitch the ends to secure them in place, taking care since the fringing can unravel easily. Slipstitch the length of fringe along the bottom edge of the front of the shade.

Slipstitch turned ends of fringe to secure in place

8 ATTACHING CORD Cut a length of cord for each tape strip to twice the finished shade length, plus the necessary amount for the cord to run along the top of the shade to the pull side. The cords are used to pull up and gather the shade.

9 THREADING LOOPS For each strip, tie one end of the cord to the loop nearest to the base of the shade. Leave a long end free when tying off – this loose end will be secured to a loop two or three loops from the bottom to make the bottom swag. Thread the cord up to the heading edge through the loops in the tape strip.

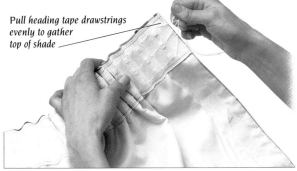

Pull heading tape drawstrings evenly to gather top of shade

10 GATHERING HEADING Pull up the heading tape and wind the drawstrings around a cord tieback *(see page 48).* Insert the curtain hooks and hang the shade on a track, or attach it to a heading board as for Roman shades *(see page 75).*

11 THREADING TRACK Decide which side of the shade the pull cord is to hang. Thread the cords through slots on the track corresponding to the top of the line of each tape. Feed the cords through the slots to the side edge where the pull cord will hang. Attach the track to its brackets on the wall *(see page 38),* and mount the cleat in position *(see page 75).* Hang the shade in position. To form the swag, tie the loose end of the cord to the bottom two or three loops of the tape strip – depending on the depth of gathering required.

Thread pull cords through corresponding track slots, and feed cords to side where they will hang

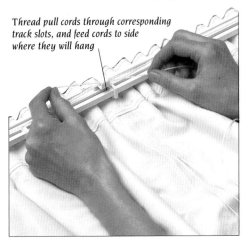

THE FINISHED SHADE

PIPED AND FRILLED AUSTRIAN SHADE

You will need fabric for the shade, frill, and piping, lining fabric, piping cord, shade tape, pull cords, cleat, and the basic sewing kit. Mount a hanging system *(see page 38)*, and measure as for a balloon shade *(see page 76)*. For the gathers, multiply the finished length by up to three for sheer and fine fabrics or one and a half for heavier materials. Add 1½ in (4 cm) for the heading tape. Cut the lining to the same size as the shade fabric. For the piping, measure the length of the shade fabric, multiply by two, and add the width. Cut a bias strip and make the piping *(see page 22)*. Multiply the piping length by two to give the frill length. Cut fabric for the frill to this length by twice the width of frill required, plus 1¼ in (3 cm). Join fabric with plain flat seams *(see page 16)*. Press the seams open. Turn each end of the frill ⅝ in (1.5 cm) to the wrong side. Press, then fold in half lengthwise. Sew across each end ¹⁄₁₆ in (2 mm) from the edges.

1 ATTACHING PIPING Lay the shade fabric right side up on a flat surface. Pin and tack the piping to the shade fabric along the two side edges and the lower edge.

2 TACKING FRILL Gather the frill at the raw edges *(see page 24)*. Pin and tack the frill to the shade right sides together along the piping seam line. Start and finish the frill 1½ in (4 cm) from the top edge of the shade.

Attach gathered frill to piping seam line

3 PINNING LINING Lay the lining and shade fabrics right sides together. Pin, tack, and machine sew them together along the piping and frill seam, using a zipper foot. Leave heading end open. Turn right side out and press.

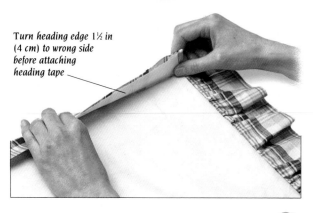

Turn heading edge 1½ in (4 cm) to wrong side before attaching heading tape

4 TURNING HEADING EDGE Turn the allowance at the heading edge 1½ in (4 cm) to the wrong side, and press.

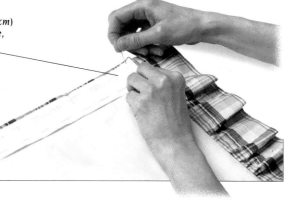

Turn under end of tape ¾ in (2 cm) and align fold with edge of shade, but leave drawstrings free

5 ATTACHING HEADING TAPE Apply the chosen heading tape to the wrong side of the top edge of the shade *(see page 48)*.

6 POSITIONING TAPE Lay the shade out flat with the lining side up. Mark positions for the tape strips, starting 1¼ in (3 cm) from the side edges. When the shade has been made to two and a half times the width of the window, the tape strips will need to be positioned two and a half times the required finished scallop-width apart from each other. Cut the number of tape strips required to the length of the shade, less the heading, allowing ⅝ in (1.5 cm) at each end for turning under raw edges.

7 PINNING TAPE
Pin, tack, and sew tape strips in position with a line of stitching down each side, turning under raw edges. Make sure that the loops (or rings) are aligned horizontally by measuring and marking loop positions from the shade's lower edge.

8 SECURING TAPE ENDS
Sew across the bottom edge of each tape strip to secure the ends of the gathering cords. When all the tape strips have been sewn in place, draw the gathering cords until the shade measures the required length.

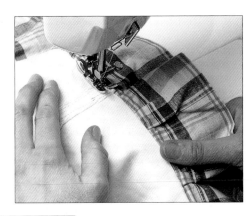

9 SECURING CORDS
Tie ends of gathering cords to themselves and roll spare cord neatly. (Do not cut the ends, since it will be necessary to ease out the gathers for cleaning.) Cut a length of pull cord for each tape strip to twice the finished shade length, plus the necessary shade width.

10 ATTACHING CORDS
Tie the end of each pull cord securely to each bottom loop of the tape strips. Thread each of the pull cords vertically through each row of loops.

Thread pull cord through tape strip and secure at bottom loop

11 TYING DRAWSTRINGS
Gather the heading tape. Do not cut the drawstrings – you can neaten them by winding them onto a cord tieback. Insert the curtain hooks and hang the shade on the track.

Thread pull cords through corresponding track slots

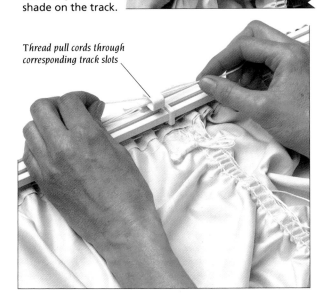

12 ATTACHING TRACK
Decide on which side of the track the pull cords will hang. Following the manufacturer's instructions, position slots on the track to align with the top of each tape strip. Thread the cords through the slots, then to the sides toward the edge where the cords will be. Attach the track to its brackets (see page 39). Mount the cord cleat (see page 75).

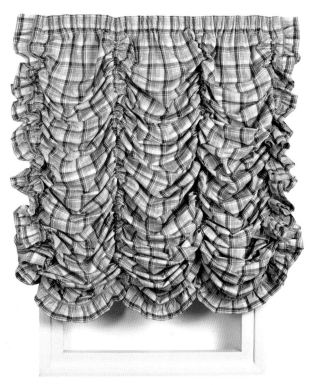

THE FINISHED SHADE

BED FURNISHINGS

THE CENTERPIECE OF THE MOST personal room in the home, a bed and its furnishings should be chosen with an attention to detail that reflects the preferences of its owner. Once a prestigious item, constructed from wood and ornately crafted, the bed has now assumed a more utilitarian role. This evolution has been matched by changes in the way that beds are furnished. Four centuries ago, beds were draped with draftproof curtains. These practical considerations gave way to fanciful styles of bedding, more concerned with decoration than insulation. Today, bedding can be produced in a wide-ranging choice of styles, due to the enormous selection of fabrics available. Whether you wish to furnish a simple divan or an ornate four-poster, there are many plain or patterned fabrics to choose from. This chapter describes how to make pillowcases, comforter covers, sheets, valances, and bedspreads that are both highly practical and attractive.

CHOOSING A STYLE

*B*ECAUSE A BED FORMS THE FOCAL POINT IN A BEDROOM, bed furnishings should fulfill two functions: they should make a bed comfortable and warm to sleep in, as well as complementing its size and the overall decorative scheme of the room. You can use plain or discreetly patterned fabrics to create a crisp, tailored look. To achieve a more sumptuous effect, use ornately patterned fabrics with contrasting piping, edgings, or frills. Coordinating valances will add decorative touches while concealing unsightly bases. To create a unified look, always make sure that the bed linen complements the style of the coverings.

LAYERED EFFECTS
With their narrow, rectangular shapes, single beds lend themselves well to a variety of decorative furnishings, either fitted or loosely laid over the mattress. Here, the loose gathers of a simply patterned valance, tailored to fit the perimeter of the bed, are complemented by the straight edges of a simple throw bedspread.

Randomly patterned patchwork cover and cushion provide an informal accent

OLD-STYLE FORMALITY
Most appropriate in a period home with high-ceilinged bedrooms, a four-poster bed forms an imposing centerpiece. Once dressed with patterned fabric drapes, frilled valances, and gathered backdrops, the period-style sumptuousness becomes even more marked. A white throw bedspread can provide a contrast to the heavy fabrics and lighten the look of the room.

TIMELESS ELEGANCE
There is nothing quite like the pleasurable feel and simple elegance of layers of crisp white cotton or linen sheets and bedspreads. Fine white linen and a variety of plain and patterned white cottons are well suited for sheets, since these fabrics are available extra-wide. Decoratively edged pillowcases can be used to add softness to an otherwise rather stark effect.

Antique lace forms decorative edging to plain pillowcase

Loose spread is folded back into pleats, allowing patterned cotton sheet to be visible underneath

CRISP AND TAILORED
Traditionally associated with elaborate bed furnishings and sumptuous fabrics, some contemporary four-poster beds can appear striking if left undraped and starkly dressed. Here, the simple architectural style of the four-poster is emphasized by the neat tailoring of the corner-pleated valance.

Fabric with clearly defined, generous check compounds geometrical structure of bed

Valance is fitted to hang as flat face of fabric, creating a smooth skirt at the bed base

MODERN COMFORTS
Highly practical and cozy, comforters are designed to make life simple, since they obviate the need for tedious bedmaking. Whether plain or patterned, comforter covers have a decorative appeal that is well suited to modern bedrooms.

OPULENT FABRICS
One way of creating a grand centerpiece of a bed is to make a throw bedspread and a padded headboard in a fabric that complements the curtain material. A curtain hanging on the wall behind will serve to enhance the proportions of the bed.

ANTIQUE STYLE
For antique cast-iron bedsteads, the most appropriate bed furnishings are those that highlight the sturdy yet elegant shape of the bed. For a period emphasis, combine a traditional quilt with generously cut white cotton or linen sheets, matching pillowcases, and a layer of blankets for insulation.

Decorative patchwork quilt, thrown over made-up bed, complements style of iron bedstead

Bed has been made up to reveal as much of ornamental cast-iron framework as possible

PILLOWCASES

MAKING YOUR OWN COLORFUL PILLOWCASE is a simple and inexpensive method of decorating a bed. Only a small amount of fabric is needed for assembling a pillowcase, and you can choose the fabric from a great variety of durable and easy-to-wash sources, ranging from elegant linens to printed dress materials. A pillowcase can be fastened with a concealed inner fold of fabric or by means of simple or fanciful buttons or ties. In addition to decorative fastenings, you can give a pillowcase a personal touch by adding an edging, such as a flange or a frill, to complement your bed furnishings.

PLAIN PILLOWCASE

This simple pillowcase is made from a continuous length of fabric and is therefore quick and easy to make up. One end of the fabric is folded over to the inside, forming a hidden flap that holds the pillow in position. To make this pillowcase, you will need suitable fabric that is more than twice the length of the pillow itself, plus the basic sewing kit.

1 **MEASURING** Measure the pillow length and width. Cut out fabric to twice the length, adding 9½ in (24 cm) for turnings and the fold-over flap. Add 1¼ in (3 cm) to the pillow width for seam allowances. Turn, pin, and tack a ⅝ in (1.5 cm) double hem along the width at one end of the fabric, and press.

2 **MAKING HEM** Turn the fabric around so that you are working at the opposite end, then fold over a hem to the wrong side by ⅜ in (1 cm), followed by a 2 in (5 cm) turning, to form a wide-hemmed edge. Pin, tack, and sew.

Pillowcase fabric should be durable and easy to care for

3 **MAKING POCKET** Turn the fabric around again so that you are working at the ⅝ in (1.5 cm) double hem. Make the internal pocket that will hold the pillow by folding over a 6 in (15 cm) flap of fabric to the inside. Pin and press. Fold the fabric in half along the width, so that the wrong sides are together.

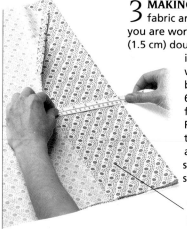

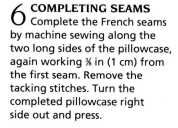

Wide internal pocket of fabric will act as fastening

4 **SEWING SEAMS** Align the sides then the wide-hemmed edge with the edge of the flap. Pin, tack, and sew a ¼ in (6 mm) seam on each long side of fabric – this is the first stage of a French seam (*see page 17*). Trim the seams and remove all of the tacking stitches.

5 **ENCLOSING EDGES** Turn the pillowcase wrong side out, and press before pinning and tacking the long sides of the fabric together, ⅜ in (1 cm) from the first seam. This second seam will enclose the raw edges.

6 **COMPLETING SEAMS** Complete the French seams by machine sewing along the two long sides of the pillowcase, again working ⅜ in (1 cm) from the first seam. Remove the tacking stitches. Turn the completed pillowcase right side out and press.

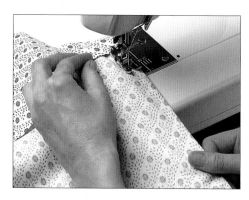

THE FINISHED PILLOWCASE

PILLOWCASE WITH FLANGE EDGING

Unlike the plain pillowcase opposite, this is constructed from separate sections of fabric and incorporates a fastening consisting of buttons and a strip of looped rouleau. Select the fabric for the pillowcase, and have ready the basic sewing kit.

Measure the pillow, then cut out one piece of fabric to the same size, plus ⅝ in (1.5 cm) all around. For the facing strip, which conceals the pillow, cut a length of fabric to the same width as the pillow, plus ⅝ in (1.5 cm), by 2½ in (6 cm) wide.

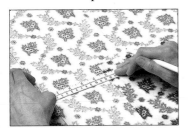

1 MEASURING FABRIC Mark and cut out the fabric for flanged-edge panel to the same size as pillow, plus 5 in (12.5 cm) all around. Make a rouleau strip 2 ft (60 cm) long *(see page 27)*.

2 HEMMING STRIP Turn, press, and pin a ⅜ in (1 cm) double hem on a long edge of facing strip. Take smaller panel and mark ¾ in (2 cm) intervals along right side of a short edge.

3 POSITIONING ROULEAU Pin and tack rouleau strip to this edge, making loops between marks. Lay facing strip over rouleau, with right sides together. Match the raw edges.

4 PINNING FACING STRIP Secure the facing strip in place over the rouleau strip by pinning, tacking, and sewing it ⅝ in (1.5 cm) from the edge of the panel of fabric.

5 FOLDING FACING STRIP Fold the facing strip over the edge of the pillowcase panel, so that the facing and the fabric panel now lie wrong sides together. Carefully press the rouleau edge flat.

6 FOLDING EDGES Take the larger of the two panels, fold over the edges by ⅝ in (1.5 cm) to the wrong side, and press flat. Fold the edges over again to the wrong side by 2 in (5 cm) and press.

Tuck straight edge of back casing under flange fold

7 MITERING CORNERS Neaten the folds of the fabric at the corners by machine mitering *(see page 21)*.

8 TRIMMING CORNERS Trim the excess fabric at the mitered corners *(see page 21)*. Press the seams open. Turn the corners right side out, and press.

9 JOINING SECTIONS Lay the pillowcase back with the rouleau onto the mitered pillowcase front, wrong sides together. Line up the rouleau edge with the inside edge of the flange on one of the short sides. Tuck the other three edges of the back under the fold of the flange. Pin in place and tack.

10 STITCHING EDGES On three sides, topstitch around the edges close to the turning edge of flange. Do not sew over the rouleau edge. After the first row, topstitch a second row ¼ in (6 mm) in from the first.

BUTTON AND
ROULEAU FASTENING

11 ATTACHING BUTTONS Sew the buttons to the flange edge, corresponding to the rouleau. Make sure the buttons are aligned with the loops. Press the finished pillowcase.

THE FINISHED
PILLOWCASE

FRILLED PILLOWCASE WITH TIE FASTENINGS

To make this pillowcase, you will need suitable fabric and the basic sewing kit. First, cut out two panels to the same size as the pillow, plus ⅝ in (1.5 cm) all around. Cut out a strip of fabric for the internal flap; the length should measure the same as the pillow's width, plus ⅝ in (1.5 cm), by 6 in (15 cm) wide. Cut out a piece of fabric for the frill to twice the entire perimeter of the pillow. The width of the frill fabric should be twice the width of the finished frill, plus 1¼ in (3 cm) for seam allowances. Make the frill as a continuous strip *(see page 24)*. Mark divisions at the frill seam-line with tailor's tacks in order to align the frill with diagonally opposite corners; this will ensure an even distribution of gathers.

1 MEASURING TIES Cut out ties from the pillowcase fabric. The number required depends on the size of the pillowcase. Here, there are three pairs of ties, made from six fabric pieces, each 2 x 10 in (5 x 25 cm). Make ties to the size required *(see page 27)*.

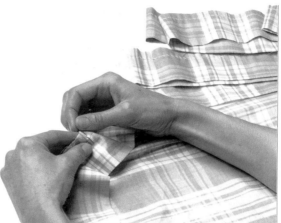

2 ALIGNING FRILL Take one of the panels and, on the right side, align the tailor's tacks made on the frill to one corner of the panel, and pin the frill to the panel at this point. Align the tailor's tacks to the corner diagonally opposite, and pin.

3 GATHERING FRILL Pull on gathering stitches from pinned corner so that one long and one short side of frill is same length as corresponding sides of panel. Arrange gathers so they are evenly distributed *(see page 24)*. Pin and tack. Align, pin at corners, gather, and secure other half of frill to remaining two sides.

4 TURNING HEM On the back panel of the pillowcase, turn under and pin a double hem of ³⁄₁₆ in (5 mm), followed by ⅜ in (1 cm), to the wrong side of one short edge. Press, tack, and sew along this hemmed edge – this will be the open edge. Remove tacking stitches.

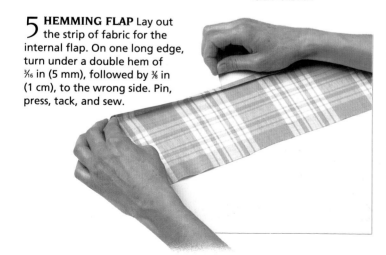

5 HEMMING FLAP Lay out the strip of fabric for the internal flap. On one long edge, turn under a double hem of ³⁄₁₆ in (5 mm), followed by ⅜ in (1 cm), to the wrong side. Pin, press, tack, and sew.

6 ATTACHING TIES Pin and tack three of the fabric ties to the frilled edge of the pillowcase opening. Position one of the ties centrally, and the other two ties equidistantly to either side.

7 JOINING PANELS Lay the pillowcase back panel over the front panel on top of the frill, right sides together, matching the hemmed edge to the seam line of the frill. Pin and tack along the three unhemmed sides.

Match seam lines on three sides of pillowcase

8 ATTACHING FLAP Place the flap fabric, right side down, at the open end of the pillowcase, on top of the frill, ties, and hemmed edge of the back panel. Pin and tack in place, taking care not to sew through the hemmed edge of the opening. Machine sew all around the pillowcase, ⅝ in (1.5 cm) from the edges. Remove the tacking stitches, and turn the pillowcase right side out.

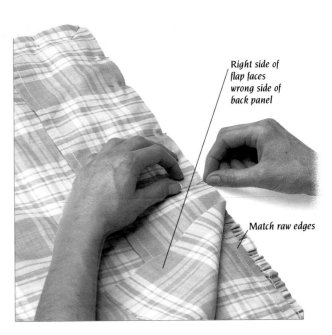

Right side of flap faces wrong side of back panel

Match raw edges

9 COMPLETING TIES Complete the fastenings by pinning, tacking, and sewing the other three ties to the open edge of the pillowcase, adjacent to the ties secured within the frill. Press the finished pillowcase.

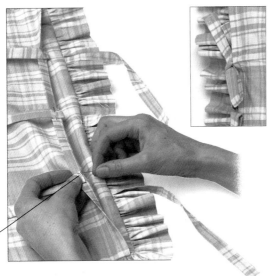

Pin ties to underside of open edge

THE FINISHED PILLOWCASE

ENGLISH EMBROIDERY

As an alternative to making a frill, you can use a piece of ready-made edging, such as English embroidery, for this type of pillowcase. English embroidery does not need to be gathered as much as a frill; use a strip one and a half times the length of the pillow's circumference. To make this pillowcase, you will need fabric, English embroidery, and the basic sewing kit.

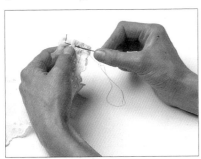

1 JOINING ENGLISH EMBROIDERY Tack the strips of English embroidery together, right sides facing.

2 SEWING FRENCH SEAMS Sew a French seam ³⁄₁₆ in (5 mm) from the edge. Remove the tacking stitches, trim the seams, and press.

THE FINISHED PILLOWCASE

PILLOWCASE WITH MATCHING BORDER

For this pillowcase, you will need fabric – including a matching border – and the basic sewing kit. Cut out one piece of fabric for the front to the same dimensions as the pillow, plus ⅝ in (1.5 cm) all around for seam allowances. Cut out another piece for the back to the same dimensions as the pillow, plus ⅝ in (1.5 cm) for seam allowances on the two long sides and one of the short sides. For the opening edge, allow an extra 2½ in (6 cm) for the hem. Cut out a piece for the hidden flap to the same length as the pillowcase panel width, by 6 in (15 cm) wide. For the border, cut out two strips of fabric to the same length as the front panel, and two to the same width, plus 1¼ in (3 cm). The width of the four border strips should be the same as the finished width of the border – this depends on the chosen border fabric – plus 1¼ in (3 cm).

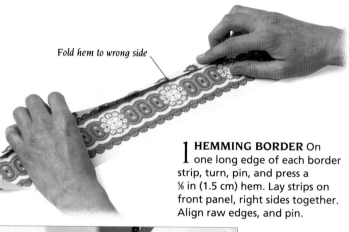

Fold hem to wrong side

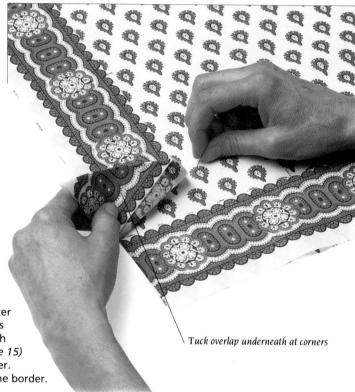

Tuck overlap underneath at corners

1 HEMMING BORDER On one long edge of each border strip, turn, pin, and press a ⅝ in (1.5 cm) hem. Lay strips on front panel, right sides together. Align raw edges, and pin.

2 MITERING CORNERS Fold the corners of the overlapping border underneath at 45 degrees, to miter them. Pin the corners in place. Ladder stitch the corners *(see page 15)* to tack them together. Unpin and remove the border.

3 SEWING CORNERS Fold the border strips right sides together, and machine sew the tacked diagonal corner seams close to the tacking lines. Trim the excess fabric at the mitered corners of the border, and press the seams open.

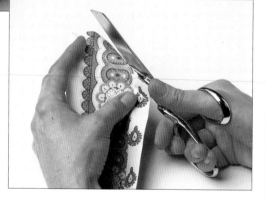

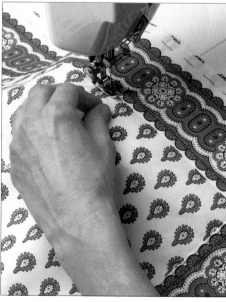

4 REPOSITIOING BORDER Reposition the border frame on the right side of the pillowcase front panel. Pin and tack the border along the four inner edges.

Pin and tack along four inner edges of border

5 ATTACHING BORDER Secure the border to the pillowcase front panel by machine topstitching along the four inside tacked edges. Remove all tacking stitches.

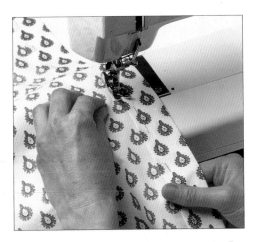

6 HEMMING BACK PANEL On one short edge of the pillowcase back panel, turn under, pin, tack, and sew a ⅜ in (1 cm) double hem, followed by 2 in (5 cm), to wrong side.

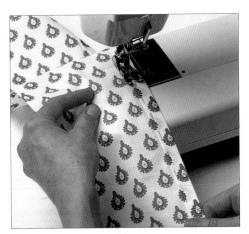

7 HEMMING FLAP On one long edge of the flap panel, turn under, pin, tack, and sew a ⅝ in (1.5 cm) double hem to the wrong side.

8 JOINING PANELS Place the front and back panels right sides together, aligning the raw edges on three sides of the panels. Pin and tack the pillowcase front panel to the back on three sides, leaving the hemmed edge open.

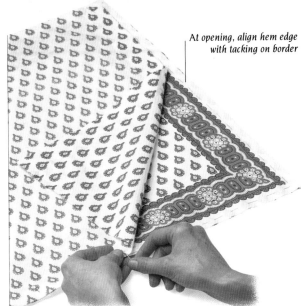

At opening, align hem edge with tacking on border

9 ATTACHING FLAP Lay the flap on the pillowcase back so that the right side of the flap is facing the wrong side of the back panel. Match the raw edges of the flap and the front panel along the opening side, then pin and tack along them and through the flap and front and back panels along the sides. Take care not to sew through the flap at the open end.

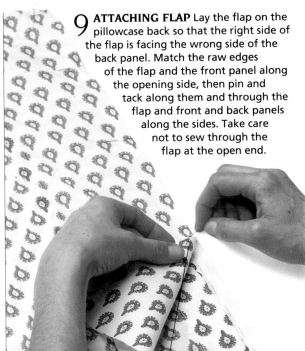

Lay right side of flap facing wrong side of back panel, aligning raw edges of front panel and flap

10 MACHINING EDGES Machine sew around all four sides, taking care not to sew through the hemmed opening edge. Remove the tacking stitches and trim the four corners to reduce the fabric bulk.

11 PUSHING OUT CORNERS Turn the pillowcase right side out and tuck in the flap. Using your finger, push the corners out.

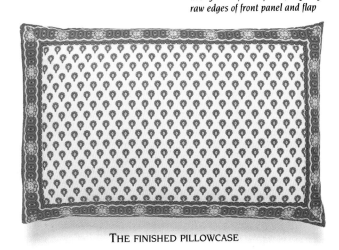

THE FINISHED PILLOWCASE

COMFORTER COVERS

COMFORTERS ARE WARM IN THE WINTER and lightweight in the summer, and in many households a comforter has taken the place of blankets and a top sheet as a comfortable and decorative bed covering. When combined with a fitted bottom sheet, a covered comforter allows for easy and quick bedmaking, needing only to be lightly shaken or turned over each morning. To cover a comforter, you can use either an extra-wide sheeting fabric or other easy-care material. It is well worth bearing in mind that many fabrics will have to be seamed to make up the required width.

BUTTONED COMFORTER COVER

Made from one length of fabric, this simple comforter cover is suitable for all types of comforter. Measure length and width of your comforter, which should overlap the bed by about 10 in (25 cm). Cut out a piece of fabric to twice the comforter length, adding 6 in (15 cm), by the width of the comforter, adding 4 in (10 cm). These allowances are for seams and fastenings, and provide space for the comforter, which is important if it is filled with feathers and down. In addition to the cover fabric, you will need buttons and the basic sewing kit.

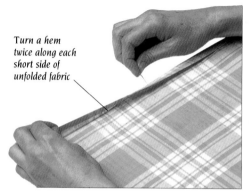

Turn a hem twice along each short side of unfolded fabric

1 PINNING HEM Lay the covering fabric right side down on a flat surface and turn under the two short sides of the fabric by ⅜ in (1 cm) and then ⅝ in (1.5 cm) to the wrong side. Press, pin, tack, and sew these hems. Remove the tacking stitches.

2 SEWING SEAMS Fold fabric in half along width, wrong sides together. Align hemmed edges. Pin, tack, and sew first part of French seam *(see page 17)* down each side 3/16 in (5 mm) from edges. Trim allowances to ⅛ in (3 mm) along sides. Turn wrong side out and press seams. Finish French seam at each side, ⅜ in (1 cm) from the folded edge.

3 MARKING OPENING Using a tape measure, triangle, and vanishing-ink pen, measure and draw a line on the wrong side of the fabric along both sides of the cover 2 in (5 cm) from, and parallel to, the folded edge of the hemmed opening.

4 SEWING OPENING From each edge of the cover, pin, tack, and sew 8 in (20 cm) along the marked guideline. This will leave an opening in the cover large enough to insert the comforter. Remove the tacking stitches.

5 FOLDING OPENING Fold both unsewn edges of the comforter cover at the opening end to the wrong side along the marked guidelines. Press the folded edges. Turn the comforter cover right side out and press again. Mark the positions for the buttonholes along one edge of the folded opening. Make the buttonholes to the appropriate size *(see page 28)*.

6 ATTACHING BUTTONS Use the buttonholes as a guide to mark the button positions on the opposite edge, then sew the buttons in place. Fill the cover with the comforter, shake it into place, and fasten the buttons.

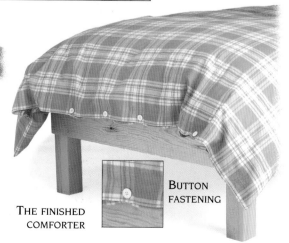

THE FINISHED COMFORTER

BUTTON FASTENING

PIPED COMFORTER COVER WITH TIE FASTENINGS

This comforter cover with piping is made up of two panels of material, with a side opening secured by matching fabric ties. Begin by cutting out two pieces of fabric to the dimensions of your comforter, adding 4 in (10 cm) all around for seam allowance. Make piped edging to the circumference of the cover at seam line, adding 4 in (10 cm) for joining *(see page 22)*. To make the comforter cover, you will need fabric for the cover, facing, ties, and piping, and the basic sewing kit.

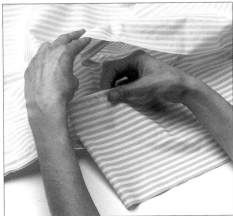

1 **ATTACHING PIPING** Pin and tack the piping to the right side of the front cover panel along the seam line. Clip the corners of the piping and join the ends *(see page 23)*.

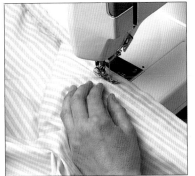

2 **SEWING PANELS** Place the fabric panels right sides together. Pin, tack, and sew them together along the seam line, leaving an opening of approximately 1 yd (1 m) in the center of one side seam. Clip the excess fabric at the corners *(see page 16)*.

3 **MAKING FACING** Cut out a strip twice the length of the opening, adding 1¼ in (3 cm) to the length for allowances, and 7½ in (19 cm) to the width. Sew a ⅝ in (1.5 cm) double hem to the wrong side along a long edge of the strip. Join the fabric length with a seam ⅝ in (1.5 cm) from short edges. Make ties from eight strips *(see page 27)*, each measuring 2 x 14 in (5 x 36 cm).

4 **ATTACHING TIES** Mark four equidistant points on each side of the opening to show the positions for the ties. Pin and tack the ties in place, making sure that they are aligned in pairs.

Ties should be aligned in pairs before sewing in place

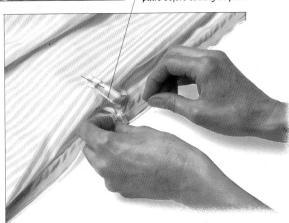

5 **POSITIONING FACING** Turn the facing strip right side out and tuck it into the cover opening. Pin and tack the facing strip to the inside of the cover opening along one side. Make sure you have aligned the raw edges of the facing with the raw edges of the opening.

6 **SECURING FACING** Machine or hand sew the facing strip in place, ensuring that the raw edges are aligned. When you have finished sewing, remove the tacking stitches. Turn the comforter cover right side out.

7 **TUCKING IN FACING** Tuck the facing strip inside the cover opening. Press the finished comforter cover and fill it with the comforter. The corners of the cover should be well filled with the comforter. Tie the fabric ties neatly into secure but decorative bows.

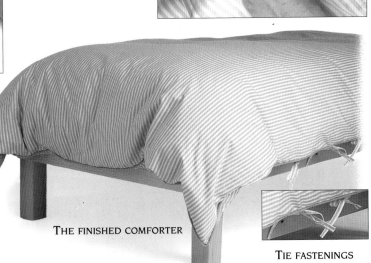

THE FINISHED COMFORTER

TIE FASTENINGS

SHEETS

*M*AKING YOUR OWN SHEETS is an economical and satisfying project. You can use any fabrics that are light, durable, and easy to care for. Fabrics that are too narrow for your mattress can be joined lengthwise. Reduce the impact of the seams by making up a central full-width panel seamed with cut-down side panels. Extra-wide fabric for sheeting is also available in a range of widths, such as 7½ or 9 ft (228 or 274 cm). Traditional flat sheets are the most versatile type of sheet because they can be used as either top or bottom sheets. Fitted sheets are, however, much easier to handle when making a bed.

FLAT SHEET WITH DECORATIVE STITCHING

If you are going to use a flat sheet as a top sheet, consider decorating the top seam line of the fabric with a satin stitch sewn in a matching or contrasting colored thread. Choose fabric from a range of suitable cottons, linen, or poly-cottons, and calculate the amount of fabric needed. To make this sheet, you will need fabric for the sheet and the basic sewing kit.

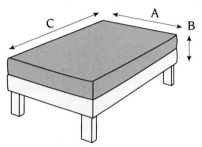

1 CALCULATING FABRIC Measure the length and width of the mattress. Add 16 in (40 cm) to the width (A), plus twice the mattress depth (B), and 20 in (50 cm) to the length (C), plus twice the mattress depth (B). Add a ¾ in (2 cm) allowance for side hems, if these are required.

Wide hem will make an attractive band at top edge of sheet

3 FOLDING TOP HEM Make a wide hem at the top edge of the sheet by turning a 2 in (5 cm) double hem to the wrong side. Press, pin, and tack the hem.

4 STITCHING TOP HEM Machine stitch the wide hem edge, using satin stitch, which is a close, tight zigzag *(see page 16)*. Remove the tacking stitches and press the finished sheet.

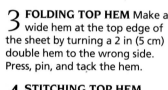

2 SEWING HEMS Turn and press ⅜ in (1 cm) double hems to the wrong side along each long edge. Pin, tack, and sew. Turn the fabric around and fold a ⅝ in (1.5 cm) double hem to the wrong side along the bottom edge. Press, pin, tack, and sew.

THE FINISHED SHEET

FLAT SHEET WITH PIPED TOP SEAM LINE

To make this sheet, you will need sheet fabric, piping cord, a bodkin, and the basic sewing kit. Select piping cord to the width of the fabric, plus 2 in (5 cm). Make a flat sheet *(see above)*.

Topstitch along, and ⅜ in (1 cm) in from, the edge of the wide hem at the top edge of the sheet. Topstitch again, ½ in (12 mm) from the first row of stitches, to form a narrow channel.

1 THREADING CORD Thread the piping cord onto a bodkin, then ease the cord through the channel in the top seam line.

2 TRIMMING CORD Once the piping cord is positioned along the length of the channel, cut off the excess cord close to the edge of the sheet.

3 SECURING ENDS Secure the ends of the cord by oversewing either by hand or with a sewing machine. Press the finished sheet.

THE FINISHED SHEET

FITTED BOTTOM SHEET

A fitted bottom sheet requires slightly less material overall than a flat sheet, because the elasticized corners keep the sheet firmly in place. Fitted sheets also greatly facilitate the task of making up a bed. To make this type of sheet, you will need fabric for the sheet, 1 yd (1 m) of elastic that is ¼ in (6 mm) wide, as well as the basic sewing kit.

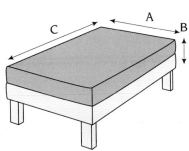

1 CALCULATING FABRIC

Measure the length and width of the mattress. Add 8 in (20 cm) to the width (A), plus twice mattress depth (B), and 8 in (20 cm) to the length (C), plus twice the mattress depth (B). Cut out the sheeting fabric to these dimensions.

2 REMOVING CORNERS Lay

fabric wrong side up. From corner along each edge, mark mattress depth plus 4 in (10 cm). Form a square at the corner by drawing lines from each marked edge. Draw lines ⅝ in (1.5 cm) to inside of first lines. Cut along the second set of lines. Repeat on remaining three corners.

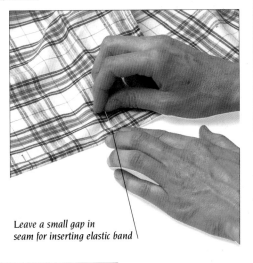

3 SEWING CORNERS Position wrong

sides of cut edges of corner together, and pin, tack, and sew a seam ³⁄₁₆ in (5 mm) from edge, as first part of a French seam (see page 17). Trim allowance to ⅛ in (3 mm). Turn right sides together, press, and finish French seam. Repeat on three remaining corners.

Leave a small gap in seam for inserting elastic band

4 PINNING HEM Turn a

³⁄₁₆ in (5 mm) and then a ⅜ in (1 cm) hem to the wrong side along all edges of the sheet. Pin, tack, and sew the hem. Along each edge, leave a ⅜ in (1 cm) gap in the seam, 6 in (15 cm) from all four corners. You will insert the elastic band through these gaps to form the fitted corners. Remove the tacking stitches.

5 INSERTING ELASTIC Cut

four 10 in (25 cm) lengths of elastic and thread each through corner hems from gap to gap. To do this, pin one end and pull the other end to gather corners. Oversew to secure elastic at openings. Sew up openings. Repeat at other corners. Press finished sheet.

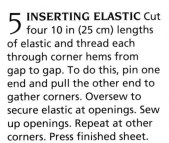

FITTED TOP SHEET

Cut fabric to mattress width, adding twice mattress depth plus 16 in (40 cm), and to length of mattress, adding mattress depth plus 8 in (20 cm). Cut out and sew two corners at the foot end as above. Sew a ⅜ in (1 cm) double hem along the long edges and one short end of the sheet, leaving gaps for elastic at two corners as described above. Insert and secure the elastic.

HEMMING TOP EDGE

Next, turn the fabric to work at the raw edge. Neaten this edge by turning a 2 in (5 cm) double hem to the wrong side. Finish the top sheet by pinning, tacking, pressing, and sewing the hem in place.

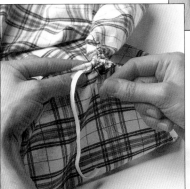

THE FINISHED SHEET

VALANCES

$\mathscr{A}$ VALANCE IS A BED FURNISHING accessory that provides a decorative cover for the sides and foot of a bed, particularly those with a solid base. You can choose to make a valance with either an informal-looking gathered skirt or a plain-sided panel, complete with corner pleats. The style that you opt for will depend on the character of your bedroom. For both types of valance, the technique involves sewing a three-sided skirt onto a piped top panel that fits over the bed base and under the mattress.

GATHERED VALANCE

Choose a decorative fabric for the gathered skirt; for economy, use a plain material for the top panel, which will be hidden from view, and edge it with a border of the same fabric as the skirt. You will also need prewashed piping cord, piping fabric, and the basic sewing kit. Prevent uneven shrinkage by prewashing both the skirt and the panel fabrics. Measure the length and width of the bed, and cut out a piece of plain fabric for the top panel to this size, less 8 in (20 cm) all around. To choose the length of the skirt drop, measure from the bed base down to where you want the skirt to finish.

B — Facing over end of bed-head
Bed base
C
Piping
A
Top panel with border strips
Gathered skirt

1 MEASURING Cut out a length of fabric for the skirt to three times length of top panel (A), plus one and a half times its width (B), by the skirt drop (C). If necessary, join fabric using French seams *(see page 17)*. Cut out five strips of fabric, all 5 in (12.5 cm) wide: two to length of A, plus 1¼ in (3 cm); two to length of B, minus 9¼ in (23 cm); and one to length of B, plus 1¼ in (3 cm), for facing.

2 SEWING ENDS Pin, tack, and sew a short border strip to each end of the top panel, right sides together, ⅝ in (1.5 cm) from edges. Press seams open.

3 ATTACHING SIDE STRIPS In the same way, attach a long border strip to each side of the top panel to form an edging. Press the seams open.

4 MARKING CORNERS Use a saucer or a glass to draw a curve at each corner. Cut along the curves. Make up piping *(see page 22)* to twice the length of A, plus B, adding 9½ in (24 cm) for the two corners at the bed-head end. Cut the piping cord ¾ in (2 cm) short of the bias strip at each end. Turn ¾ in (2 cm) at the ends to the wrong side.

5 STITCHING PIPING Fold the bias strip over the piping cord at each end, and slipstitch the edges together so that the ends of the cord are enclosed.

6 ATTACHING PIPING Pin and tack piping to the right side of the top panel. Turn the extra around the head-end corners. Turn ⅝ in (1.5 cm) double hems at the ends and bottom edge of the skirt. Press, pin, tack, and sew hems.

7 SECTIONING SKIRT On the top edge of the skirt fabric, measuring from one hemmed end, mark a point at one and a half times the length of A, plus 7 in (18 cm). This section will fit one side of the top panel. From this point, measure one and a half times the length of B and mark, to correspond with the opposite corner. The remaining length of fabric fits the other long side of the panel.

8 SEWING GATHERING STITCHES Sew gathering stitches between the marks along the top of the skirt fabric, ⅝ in (1.5 cm) from the edge *(see page 24)*. Overlap the stitches at the corners to make it easier to pull up the gathers.

9 PINNING SKIRT Align one end of the skirt with one end of the piping on the top panel, with the right sides of the fabric together. Pin ⅝ in (1.5 cm) from the edge.

10 ALIGNING MARKS Match the first mark to the first corner, and pin at this point. Pull up the gathers. Distribute evenly along the fabric. Repeat along the remaining sections of the skirt, finishing at the other end of the piping. Tack and sew the skirt in place, using the zipper attachment on the machine.

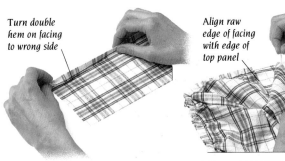

11 HEMMING FACING
On one long edge of the strip of fabric for the facing, turn, pin, tack, and sew a double hem of 3/16 in (5 mm), followed by 3/8 in (1 cm).

12 ATTACHING FACING
Pin, tack, and sew, right sides together, the raw edge of the facing to the head end of the top panel, over the border strip and along the skirt seams.

13 FITTING VALANCE Turn right side out. The facing strip lies over the head end of the top panel and neatens the valance's appearance. Press the valance, and fit it in place.

THE FINISHED VALANCE

CORNER-PLEATED VALANCE

This plain-sided bed valance is constructed with corner inserts that together form box pleats. Make up the top panel by following the directions to the end of step 6, opposite, but do not cut out the fabric for the skirt. For this valance, you will need three separate pieces of fabric for the skirt. Two pieces should measure the length of the bed, plus 8 in (20 cm); the length of the third piece should be equal to B (see diagram opposite), plus 8 in (20 cm). Measure the length required for the skirt drop (C), and add 1¾ in (4.5 cm). This measurement is the width of the three skirt panels.

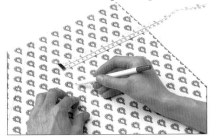

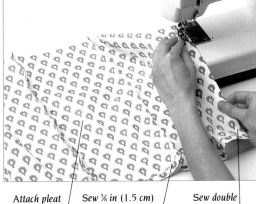

1 MEASURING Cut out four panels for the pleat inserts to the same width as the skirt fabric, by 8 in (20 cm). For the corner panels at the bed-head end, cut two panels to the same width as the skirt, by 10½ in (26.5 cm) wide.

Attach pleat inserts to skirt panels

Sew ⅝ in (1.5 cm) double hems on lower edges of all skirt panels

Sew double hems to wrong sides on edges of corner panels

2 ATTACHING INSERTS Starting at the bed-head end, pin, tack, and sew a top corner panel to a pleat insert, ⅝ in (1.5 cm) from the edge, right sides together. Join this insert to one of the side skirt panels in the same way. At the foot corner, join this side skirt panel to another pleat insert. In this way, continue around the valance, finishing with the other bed-head corner panel. Trim all seam allowances.

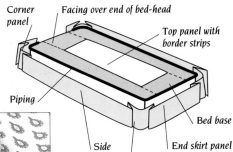

Corner panel
Facing over end of bed-head
Top panel with border strips
Piping
Side skirt panel
Pleat insert
End skirt panel
Bed base

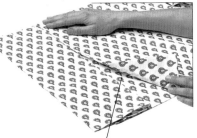

Fold ends of side panels to center of inserts to form box pleats, and press, pin, and tack ⅝ in (1.5 cm) from top edge to secure pleats while attaching them to top panel

3 FOLDING PLEATS
At each corner, fold side panels to centre of insert to form a box pleat. Press, pin, and tack 1.5 cm (⅝ in) from top edge to secure them in place while attaching to top panel.

4 ATTACHING SKIRT Pin, tack, and sew the skirt with pleated corners, right sides together, to piped edge of the top panel. Turn a double hem of 3/16 in (5 mm), followed by 3/8 in (1 cm), on one long edge of the facing panel. Pin, tack, and sew the facing panel to the head end of the top panel, right sides together, along top edge and skirt seams. Turn right side out and press. Trim all seams before fitting valance in place.

Align pleats with corners of piped panel

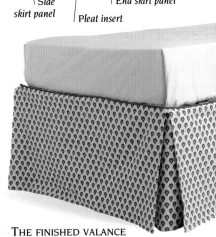

THE FINISHED VALANCE

BEDSPREADS

*T*HE PURPOSE OF A BEDSPREAD IS PRIMARILY to decorate a bed when it is not in use. A throw cover is easy to prepare and presents a casual, comfortable dressing. This style of cover can be made in a heavyweight fabric, so that it can double as an extra blanket. Alternatively, fitted covers, which are made to fit the shape of a mattress exactly, neaten the appearance of a bed, allowing you the option of using it as a seat. For a tailored finish, you can make a cover with a straight skirt and box-pleated corners. Choose a cover with a gathered skirt and contrasting piping for a more relaxed effect.

REVERSIBLE THROW COVER

To make a reversible cover, use matching or contrasting fabrics for the top and lining panels. If you wish the bedspread to have insulating properties, either quilt material *(see page 17)* or select a medium- to heavyweight fabric. Allow the fabric to drape to the length you wish. Select a fabric for the binding, and have the basic sewing kit ready.

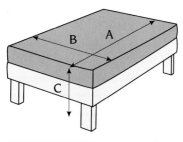

1 MEASURING With the bed linen in place, measure the length of the bed (A) and the width (B). Decide on the length of drop you require (C). Add to A the measurement of C; if you wish the cover to extend over a pillow, add a further 6 in (15 cm) to A. Add to B twice the length of C. Cut the top and lining panels to these dimensions, if necessary allowing for joins *(see page 19)* and pattern matching.

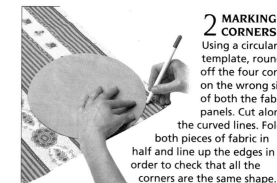

2 MARKING CORNERS Using a circular template, round off the four corners on the wrong side of both the fabric panels. Cut along the curved lines. Fold both pieces of fabric in half and line up the edges in order to check that all the corners are the same shape.

3 JOINING PANELS Lay the wrong sides of the top and lining fabrics together. Pin and tack the two fabrics to each other all around, ⅜ in (1 cm) from the edges.

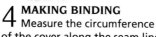

Fold ⅜ in (1 cm) to wrong side on both edges, and press flat

4 MAKING BINDING Measure the circumference of the cover along the seam line, and make a strip of binding to this length *(see page 22)*, adding 4 in (10 cm) for joins. Decide on the width of the binding, and add ¾ in (2 cm) for turnings.

5 ATTACHING BINDING With the right sides together, pin, tack, and sew one edge of the binding to the top panel of fabric, ⅝ in (1.5 cm) from the edge, along the fold line of the binding. Trim the seam allowance to ⅜ in (1 cm), or just under half the finished width.

6 COMPLETING BINDING Turn the cover over. Fold the binding over the edge. Pin, tack, and slipstitch the folded edge of the binding to the lining ⅝ in (1.5 cm) from the edge.

7 TOPSTITCHING BINDING You may prefer to finish the binding by machine topstitching. These stitches will, however, be more visible. Press the finished cover and place it over the bed.

THE FINISHED BEDSPREAD

FITTED BEDSPREAD WITH GATHERED SKIRT

When choosing fabric for a fitted cover for a daybed, choose a durable material that will withstand wear and tear. You will also need prewashed piping cord, fabric for the piping – the one shown here is in a complementary color to the main fabric – and the basic sewing kit. Measure the dimensions of the bed with the bed linen in place to make sure that the finished cover fits neatly. To find the dimensions of the top panel of fabric, measure the length (A) and width (B) of the bed, and then add 1¾ in (4.5 cm) to the length for seams and hem, and 1¼ in (3 cm) to the width for seams.

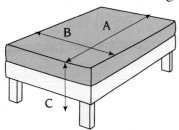

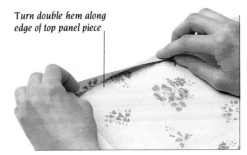

1 MEASURING SKIRT For the width of the skirt fabric, measure the skirt drop (C), and add 1¾ in (4.5 cm) for seams and hem. The length should be three times the length of the bed (A), plus one and a half times the width (B), plus 2½ in (6 cm) for hems. If you need to join fabric, add ⅝ in (1.5 cm) for seams.

Turn double hem along edge of top panel piece

2 HEMMING PANEL Lay the top panel right side down on a flat surface, and turn and press a ⅝ in (1.5 cm) double hem along its top edge.

Turn ¾ in (2 cm) to wrong side at end, and slipstitch folded edges

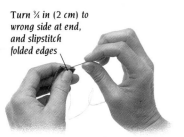

3 SEWING PIPING Cut a bias strip to twice A, plus B. Add 1½ in (4 cm) for turnings. Make up piping *(see page 22)*, leaving 1½ in (4 cm) unsewn at each end.

4 ATTACHING PIPING Pin and tack the piping to the right side of the top panel, along one short and two long edges, matching raw edges of fabric.

5 HEMMING SKIRT EDGE Join skirt fabric using French seams *(see page 17)*. Turn, pin, tack, and sew a ⅝ in (1.5 cm) double hem to the wrong side.

6 HEMMING SKIRT ENDS At both ends of the skirt, turn ⅝ in (1.5 cm) double hems to the wrong side. Pin, tack, and sew the hems.

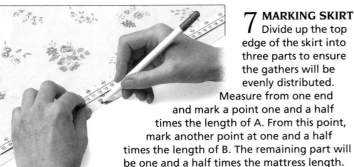

7 MARKING SKIRT Divide up the top edge of the skirt into three parts to ensure the gathers will be evenly distributed. Measure from one end and mark a point one and a half times the length of A. From this point, mark another point at one and a half times the length of B. The remaining part will be one and a half times the mattress length.

8 SEWING GATHERING STITCHES Sew a line of gathering stitches *(see page 24)* ⅝ in (1.5 cm) from the top of the unhemmed edge of the skirt. Sew separate lines of stitching along each of the three marked lengths. Overlap the lines of gathering stitches at the corner marks, so that the fullness will not be lost when gathering up.

9 GATHERING SKIRT Align the ends of the skirt with the ends of the piped top panel, and pin in place at these points. Align the corner marks on the skirt with the corners of the panel, and pin in place at these points. Starting at one of the long edges, pull up the gathers, distribute evenly, and pin and tack the skirt in place along the piped edge. Repeat this procedure on the remaining two sides.

10 ATTACHING SKIRT Machine sew the skirt to the piped panel along the tacking using the zipper foot. Trim the seam allowances. Press the cover, and fit it to the bed.

THE FINISHED BEDSPREAD

FITTED BEDSPREAD WITH BOX PLEATS

To make this bedspread, you will need fabric for the spread and piping, piping cord, and the basic sewing kit. Cut out the fabric for the top panel to the width (A) and length (B) of the mattress, adding 1¼ in (3 cm) to the width for seams and 1¾ in (4.5 cm) to the length for seams and hems. At the foot end of the top panel, use a vanishing-ink pen to round off corners (see page 94). For the sides, cut out three strips of fabric to the mattress depth (C). Add 1¼ in (3 cm) to the width for seams. Cut two strips to B, adding 1¾ in (4.5 cm) for hems and seams, and one strip to A, adding 1¼ in (3 cm) for seams.

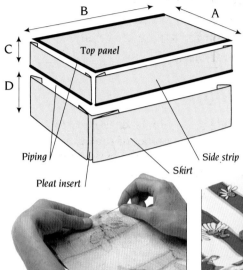

Top panel

C

D

Piping

Pleat insert

Side strip

Skirt

1 CUTTING OUT SKIRT Measure drop (D) from lower edge of mattress to floor, adding 1¾ in (4.5 cm) for hems and seams. This is the required width of skirt pieces. Cut out two pieces to this width by same length as B plus 1¼ in (3 cm) for top edge hem, adding 4 in (10 cm) to each for pleats. Cut one piece of fabric to D by same length as A, adding 8 in (20 cm). For corner pleat inserts, cut two pieces to D by 8 in (20 cm). Cut out two bias strips for piping to twice B plus A, adding 1¾ in (4.5 cm) for turnings. Make two strips of piping (see page 22).

2 ATTACHING PIPING Pin and tack one length of piping to the right side of the top panel, matching the edges of the piping allowance and the top panel. Clip the piping seam allowance at the corners (see page 16).

3 SEWING STRIPS Sew a long side strip to a short side strip along their widths, right sides together. Leave a ⅝ in (1.5 cm) seam. Similarly, attach other long strip to other side of short strip.

4 PINNING SECOND PIPING Pin and tack the second length of piping to the edges of the mattress side strips. In step 9 below, the skirt piece will be attached to these edges.

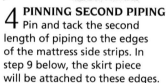

5 ATTACHING PANEL Place unpiped edges of side strips and piped edges of top panel right sides together. Pin, tack, and sew them to each other, leaving a ⅝ in (1.5 cm) allowance.

6 TURNING HEM Turn a ⅝ in (1.5 cm) double hem to the wrong side of the bottom edges of the three skirt pieces, and the insert pieces.

7 SEWING INSERTS Sew insert pieces to ends of short skirt piece, leaving a ⅝ in (1.5 cm) seam. Attach each long skirt piece to insert pieces on either side of short skirt piece, leaving a ⅝ in (1.5 cm) seam. Trim seams.

8 FOLDING PLEATS At each corner, fold side panel to center of insert to form a box pleat. Press, pin, and tack ⅝ in (1.5 cm) from top edge to secure the pleats in place while attaching the skirt.

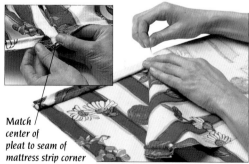

Match center of pleat to seam of mattress strip corner

9 ATTACHING SKIRT Pin, tack, and sew the top edge of the skirt to the piped edge of the mattress side strip, right sides together. Match the centers of the pleats to the seams of the mattress strip corners. Press all seams and hems and, where necessary, trim seams.

10 SLIPSTITCHING END At the bed-head end of the cover, trim away any excess fabric to form a straight line along the edge. Turn a ⅝ in (1.5 cm) double hem to the wrong side of the bed-head end, and pin, tack, and slipstitch it in place. Press the cover and fit it to the mattress and bed.

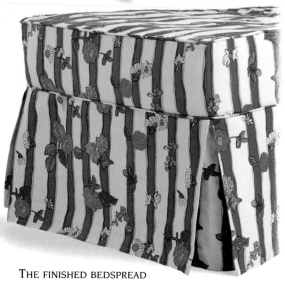

THE FINISHED BEDSPREAD

PATCHWORK AND QUILTING

PATCHWORK COVERS ENABLE YOU to combine patterns, colors, and shapes to create your own personalized furnishing. When you are contemplating the design for your patchwork, let your imagination take over, and do not be afraid to use the shapes and colors that inspire you. Bear in mind that a patchwork cover made up of simple shapes such as squares can be machine stitched, but that more complex patchworks have to be sewn together by hand. Quilting the fabric provides effective insulation for the cover. This is a simple technique that involves layering wadding between two fabrics (*see page 17*).

SQUARE PATCHWORK SPREAD

This bedspread is easy to make up by machine but, as with all patchwork, needs careful preparation. Accuracy in measuring and cutting out is essential. To make this spread, you will need fabric for the patches, lining fabric, and the basic sewing kit. Decide on the sizes of the bedspread and the patchwork squares. Consider the scale of the squares in relation to the size of the bed. Calculate the number of squares needed to fill the cover area, adjusting the quantity to the nearest square. After you have cut out the squares, lay them on a flat surface and work out the placement of the squares.

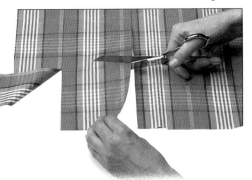

1 CUTTING OUT SQUARES Add ⅝ in (1.5 cm) all around to the required finished size of each square. On the fabric, carefully measure and draw out the number of squares required for the patchwork. Cut out the squares.

2 JOINING SQUARES Assemble the patchwork by working across the width of the cover, one row at a time. Pin, tack, and sew the squares right sides together, and 1.5 cm (⅝ in) from their edges. To prevent seams from pulling apart, secure the stitching by reversing the sewing at start and end of seams. Press open seams.

Sew rows of patchwork together ⅝ in (1.5 cm) from edges

3 SEWING ROWS Once the rows are completed, pin, tack, and sew them right sides together, ⅝ in (1.5 cm) from the edges. Press the seams open. Measure the finished spread and cut a panel of fabric for the lining to the same dimension.

4 ATTACHING LINING Lay the lining and cover right sides together. Pin and tack ⅝ in (1.5 cm) from edges. Leave a 20 in (50 cm) gap in a seam for turning the spread right side out.

5 TURNING OUT Turn the spread right side out and press it. Fold the edges of the opening by ⅝ in (1.5 cm) to the inside, then pin and slipstitch the edges together.

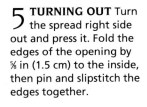
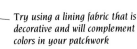

Try using a lining fabric that is decorative and will complement colors in your patchwork

THE FINISHED BEDSPREAD

HEXAGONAL PATCHWORK BEDSPREAD

Decide on the finished design. The patches can be sewn together randomly, arranged in patterns of color, or carefully placed to form configurations. Measure the size of the finished bedspread, and choose the appropriate size of the patchwork pieces. Estimate the number required to fill the area of the spread. Because the patchwork will not form a straight edge around the cover, make a straight line by cutting out partial hexagons, or choose a backing fabric for the border. As well as the fabrics and the basic sewing kit, you will need a piece of stiff cardboard, and a standard compass.

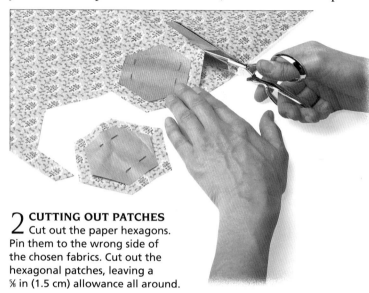

1 DRAWING PATTERN
Make a pattern to the size required. Draw a circle on the cardboard. Mark the circumference with six equally spaced points. Join the points with straight lines to form a hexagon. Cut out pattern. Use it to draw the number of hexagons required on paper.

Draw circle on cardboard with compass

Mark six equidistant points, and draw straight lines between them

2 CUTTING OUT PATCHES
Cut out the paper hexagons. Pin them to the wrong side of the chosen fabrics. Cut out the hexagonal patches, leaving a ⅝ in (1.5 cm) allowance all around.

3 SEWING SEAMS
Leaving the paper in position, fold the seam allowances over the edges of the paper, and tack and press. Make sure that the hexagons are identical in size and shape.

4 STITCHING PATCHES
Lay out the patches in the pattern you have chosen. Working on the wrong side, slipstitch the edges together. It is worth taking the time to do this very carefully.

5 REMOVING PAPER
After patches have been stitched together, press and remove tacks and paper pieces. Measure length and width at widest points of panel. Cut out lining to these dimensions, plus diameter of one hexagon, plus 1¼ in (3 cm) all around.

6 MARKING LINING
Lay patchwork and lining wrong sides together. Mark outermost edges of patches on the lining. Fold lining to wrong side under the patchwork along the marked points. Fold the corners into miters (see page 21), and press.

7 STITCHING LINING
Keeping the lining and patchwork wrong sides together, pin, tack, and slipstitch the lining and the patchwork together along all the edges.

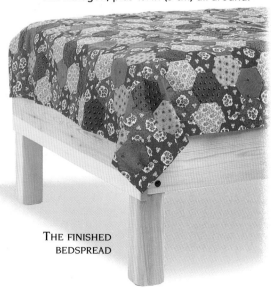

THE FINISHED BEDSPREAD

REVERSIBLE QUILTED BEDSPREAD

The size of this spread depends on the bed dimensions and on whether or not the spread reaches to the floor. To calculate the fabric dimensions, measure the length and width of the bed with the bedclothes in place. Add the required amount for the drop to the length measurement, and twice this amount to the width. Add 2 in (5 cm) to the length and width to allow for the fabric that gets taken up in quilting. Cut the top and lining panels to this size. Make any joins in the fabric with plain flat seams *(see page 16)*. You will also need fabric for the binding, wadding, a quilting pencil, and the basic sewing kit.

1 CUTTING WADDING Cut out a section of wadding to the same size as the fabric panels. When it is necessary to join pieces of wadding, use large herringbone stitches *(see page 20)*.

Make small overlap on wadding and secure widths with large herringbone stitches

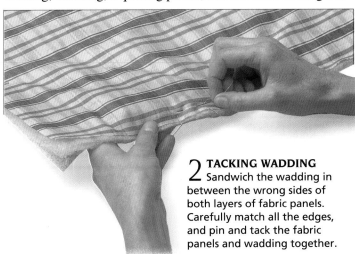

2 TACKING WADDING Sandwich the wadding in between the wrong sides of both layers of fabric panels. Carefully match all the edges, and pin and tack the fabric panels and wadding together.

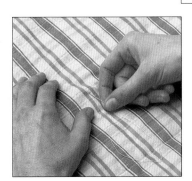

3 MAKING SECURING TACKS Lay the quilt flat. Using long tacking stitches, tack along the center from the top to bottom, and across the width, from the center of one side to the other. Use tacking thread of the same color as the sewing thread that you intend to use. Repeat the process, this time tacking halfway between the previous tacking lines and the edges of the quilt. These tacks will prevent the fabrics and wadding from slipping while you make the quilting tacks.

4 TACKING QUILTING LINES Decide on the style and size of the quilting pattern. Measure and mark lines for the quilting on the top panel of the fabric, using a quilting pencil. Tack along these marked lines through all the layers.

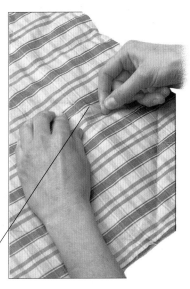

Tack along quilting lines through all layers of fabric and wadding

5 SEWING QUILT Sew along the tacking lines. Remove the tacking. Measure the perimeter of the quilt. Cut bias fabric for the binding to this length, adding 4 in (10 cm) for the join. The width of the binding fabric should be the ultimate binding width, plus 1¼ in (3 cm).

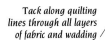

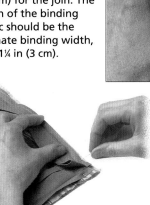

6 TACKING BINDING Fold the long edges of the binding by ⅝ in (1.5 cm) to the wrong side, and press. With the right sides together, pin and tack the edge of the binding to the edge of the top side of the quilt. At corners, snip the binding to fit. Miter, and join the ends of the binding *(see page 21)*. Trim the seam edges to ⅜ in (1 cm). Fold the binding over the edge of the cover. Pin and slipstitch the folded edge.

THE FINISHED BEDSPREAD

CUSHIONS

$\mathcal{B}$ECAUSE OF THEIR INHERENT MOBILITY and versatility, cushions are among the most useful of soft furnishings, bringing comfort to seating areas such as sofas, chairs, and floors and providing decorative focal points of color, texture, and pattern to a room. There are two basic types of cushion. Tailor-made types, such as box seat cushions, are used where a fitted shape is required – for example, on a wicker chair. Scatter cushions, on the other hand, are not made to fit and can be moved around. Of the two categories, scatter cushions are the more adaptable and popular and are commonly used on beds, chairs, and sofas. This chapter shows how to make up a variety of scatter cushions, bolsters, and fitted seat cushions; describes how to make inner pads, decorative edgings, and fastenings; and reveals how to make the most of special fabrics for cushion covers.

CHOOSING A STYLE

ADDING A FEW CUSHIONS TO YOUR ROOM can instantly change its character. When grouped together on a sofa or bed, cushions can provide bright splashes of color, perhaps echoing the style of a picture above them or complementing the scheme of a room by highlighting the dominant color of the wallpaper. Any type of fabric can be used to make up a cushion. Precious lace backed with a colored or plain fabric can create an old-fashioned look. Unique fabrics, such as crewel embroidery or small scraps of a kilim, can supplement the overall design theme and stand out as centerpieces.

EFFECTIVE CONTRASTS

Scatter cushions of various sizes and in contrasting fabric designs can be used to complement the pattern on the cover of a large, fitted seat cushion. Chair cushions provide welcome comfort, and serve as attractive accessories.

Seat cushion stuffed with thick foam forces cover to stretch tightly, ensuring that fabric design is well displayed

COORDINATED DESIGNS

Cushions made in fabrics that match disparate elements within a room help to unify a design scheme. Here, one scatter cushion is made from the same material as the curtain, while the other coordinates attractively with the tablecloth.

Cushion cover matches tablecloth, creating visual harmony

ETHNIC INFLUENCES

In a room where the design scheme is quite specific, scatter cushions can be used to provide a variety in shape, while complementing the overall decoration. Ethnic textiles, such as dhurries, kilims, and Native American flat weaves like the ones shown here, can be used to make cushions of different sizes and shapes. Careful consideration is required when determining how and where particularly delicate fabrics are to be used. Large scatter cushions and box seat cushions should always be covered with heavy, durable fabrics.

Fragments from old, handmade rugs or other decorative textiles make original cushion covers

Geometric patterns echo design of wall hanging

Gray and earth tones of cushion fabric blend well with color of sofas

SOFT AND LUXURIOUS
Cushions of various sizes propped against large, coordinating pillows add to the sheer comfort of a bed. A group of scatter cushions in a similar style can be used to form a decorative focal point on a large bed.

Cushions with lace frills give a pronounced feminine effect

Square cushions with piped edgings provide a contrast to dominant, frill-trimmed cushions

SIMPLE AND FUNCTIONAL
When padded seat cushions are secured to the struts or legs of a chair with matching or contrasting fabric ties, the chair becomes an integrated decorative piece in the room, without losing its functional qualities.

DECORATIVE EDGINGS
Edgings can be used to provide additional color, texture, and pattern to cushions. They can be made in fabrics that either match or contrast with the cushions. Here, a sofa serves as a display for square floral cushions with matching frills.

PLAIN AND PATTERNED
Cushions made from unpatterned fine silk or dress fabric can be used to counterbalance furniture that is covered in highly textured or patterned material, particularly one with a strong contemporary design. Here, the rich blue of the cushions highlights the blue stripes of the sofa fabric and tempers the dominant yellow of the wallpaper and tablecloth.

Simple fabric design contrasts well with wide-striped pattern design of sofa fabric

Rich blue of cushion covers coordinates with color of fringed edging around sofa base

CUSHION FILLINGS

TODAY, FINDING READY-MADE INNER PADS for cushions is a simple task. If, however, you would rather make your own, you must consider which filling is most suitable for the pad. This choice depends on the desired decorative effect and on the type of cushion you are planning to make. In the past, feathers and down, animal hair, and plant fibers such as cotton and kapok were the only stuffing used for cushions and upholstery. Nowadays there is a wide range of material available. Polyester and cotton batting, as well as foam blocks and chips, can all be used to fill cushions.

CHOOSING FILLINGS

Fillings are available as loose material and are usually sold by weight. For comfort and durability, choose natural-fiber fillings, such as cotton. Feathers and down give real luxury, but they are messy to work with. Synthetic fillings are not as soft as natural ones and tend to lose their shape over time. They are easy to work with, however, and are hypoallergenic.

POLYSTYRENE BEADS
These tiny balls of polystyrene provide lightweight but firm fillings for cushion pads. They are best used for stuffing cushions that are unusually shaped, or for large floor cushions, such as bean bags.

FIBER FILL
This form of filling, made of acrylic or polyester, is fully washable once inside a fabric casing. Loose filling must be packed tightly to prevent clumps from forming, but it is a popular choice for making cushion pads, especially those of an unusual shape.

FEATHERS AND DOWN
Down is small, fluffy feathers of birds and is the softest, lightest, and most resilient filling. Feather-and-down mixtures are less expensive than pure down. They are also not as soft, but provide more body for a firmer cushion. When working with down or feathers, use a down-proof casing fabric such as ticking, and sew it with French seams.

KAPOK
This vegetable fiber filling has long been used for quilting, upholstery padding, and seat cushions. Kapok is not washable, and it tends to become lumpy over time.

FOAM
Foam is available in sheets, blocks, and chips, and in a variety of qualities. Foam blocks are easy to cut to a defined shape and are ideal for seat-cushion padding. Foam should always be enclosed in an inner lining, because it tends to crumble with age. Make sure the foam label states that it is flame retardant.

TEASING

If you use polyester or acrylic padding, it may be necessary to tease out the fibers before filling a cushion pad, in order to separate the fibers and break up any lumps and clumps. Hold each portion of padding in one hand, and gently tease the clumps of fibers apart between the fingers and heel of your other hand.

MAKING A SQUARE INNER PAD

Cushion pads can be made in all shapes and sizes, which means that you do not need to be restricted to the shapes of ready-made pads. Make the inner pad ⅝ in (1.5 cm) larger all around than the cushion cover for a plump effect. You can choose among various casing fabrics, such as ticking for feathers, or heavy muslin, lining material, or even old sheeting *(see page 10)*. To make a cushion pad, you will need a suitable filling, the casing fabric, and the basic sewing kit.

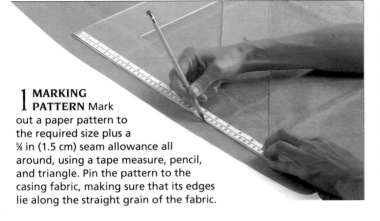

1 MARKING PATTERN Mark out a paper pattern to the required size plus a ⅝ in (1.5 cm) seam allowance all around, using a tape measure, pencil, and triangle. Pin the pattern to the casing fabric, making sure that its edges lie along the straight grain of the fabric.

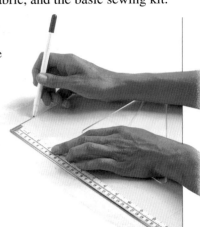

CUTTING WITHOUT A PATTERN
If you wish, you can measure up and mark the measurements for the inner pad directly onto the casing fabric, using a tape measure, triangle, and vanishing-ink pen or tailor's chalk. Again, allow ⅝ in (1.5 cm) for seams, and draw the cutting lines on the straight grain of the fabric. A triangle is useful for marking both paper patterns and fabrics.

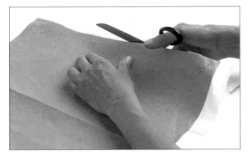

2 CUTTING OUT Use a pair of sharp dressmaker's scissors to cut out the fabric, following the paper pattern pinned to the material or the outline drawn onto the fabric. Cut out two identical pieces of fabric for the front and back panels of the casing.

3 SEWING TOGETHER Place the panels of fabric for the casing right sides together. Pin, tack, and sew the panels together ⅝ in (1.5 cm) from the edge along three sides only. On the fourth side, sew seams 2 in (5 cm) from each corner.

4 CLIPPING CORNERS Clip the corners of the seam allowance to ¼ in (6 mm) from the seam. On a round pad, you will have to clip the allowances as appropriate *(see page 16)*.

5 STUFFING PAD Turn the casing right side out and lay it on a flat surface. Stuff the chosen filling through the opening in the fourth side seam. Make sure that the filling is pushed well into each corner and distributed evenly across the whole pad.

THE FINISHED PAD

6 FINISHING OFF When the casing has been filled to the required thickness and weight, slipstitch the opening closed. If more filling or a change of filling is required at a later date, unpick this slipstitched seam, and when the pad has been restuffed slipstitch it closed again.

OTHER PAD SHAPES

The instructions for making the square cushion pad can be applied to cushions of various designs – such as bolsters or round cushions – to fit in with your decorative scheme.

BOLSTER PAD   ROUND PAD

SQUARE CUSHIONS

*P*ERHAPS THE MOST USEFUL AND VERSATILE soft furnishing, square cushions offer instant comfort as well as an elegant highlight to chairs and sofas. When covered in patterned, brightly colored fabric, a group of square cushions of different sizes can be an attractive decorative contrast to plain furniture upholstery. A variety of edging treatments, such as piping, flange, and frills, can add texture and detail, particularly to simple-patterned fabric. Fastening choices vary, from visible and attractive fine buttons and fabric ties to concealed zippers, snaps, and slipstitches.

SLIPSTITCHED FASTENING

A simple square cushion can be used almost anywhere. Square cushion pads are available ready-made in numerous sizes. Alternatively, they can be easily made at home using a range of stuffings *(see page 106)*. Unless the cover needs to be cleaned frequently, the simplest fastening is a slipstitch. To make a simple square scatter cushion with a slipstitched fastening, you will need the cushion fabric, an inner pad, and the basic sewing kit.

Cover should be made smaller than pad to ensure close fit

1 CUTTING OUT PANELS Using a tape measure and drafting triangle, make a paper pattern to the same size as the pad. Lay pattern piece on a double layer of cushion fabric. If the fabric that you are using has a pattern with large designs, or a nap, check that they are aligned correctly. Pin the paper pattern in place, and cut out the fabric pieces.

Tack ⅝ in (1.5 cm) from edge along three sides

2 TACKING PANELS Lay the fabric pieces right sides together. Ensure that the grains of both pieces align. Pin the panels together along all four sides. Tack ⅝ in (1.5 cm) from the edge along three sides of the square. On the fourth side, stitch only 2 in (5 cm) from both ends, leaving an opening in the center.

3 SEWING TOGETHER Machine sew the panels along the edges of the cushion next to the tacking stitches. Take care not to stitch into the ends of the opening by accident. Fasten off securely at the end, and remove the tacking stitches.

Clip each corner diagonally to reduce fabric bulk when cover is turned out

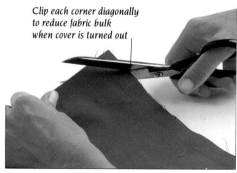

4 CLIPPING CORNERS Within the seam allowance, clip each corner to ensure that the cushion corners will be straight and pointed when turned out. Cut away the seam allowance to within ¼ in (6 mm) of the stitching. This will reduce the bulk and prevent tucking and wrinkling.

Making cover slightly smaller than inner pad ensures a tight fit

5 SLIPSTITCHING CLOSED Turn the cushion cover right side out. With your fingers, push out the corners of the cushion. Press the cover as flat as possible. Insert the inner pad through the cover opening, and push it well into the corners. Slipstitch together the sides of the opening *(see page 14)*.

THE FINISHED CUSHION

SIDE OPENING WITH SNAPS

For a cushion without an edge trimming, such as piping or cording, a side zipper may prove too bulky at the seam, but snaps or a simple slipstitched seam will conceal the opening almost completely. Snaps along the edges of the opening will facilitate the removal of the cushion pad when the cover needs to be cleaned. To make up this cushion cover, you will need the cushion fabric and an inner pad, snaps, and the basic sewing kit.

1 CUTTING OUT PANELS Make up a paper pattern *(see opposite)*. When cutting out the pieces of fabric, add an extra 1¼ in (3 cm) seam allowance on one edge of both panels, for the side opening.

2 TURNING EDGES On each of the two fabric panels, turn the edge that has the extra seam allowance to the wrong side once by ⅝ in (1.5 cm) and press. Turn the edge under again by the same amount. Pin, tack, and slipstitch along the edge of the fold, then remove the tacking stitches.

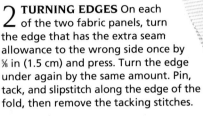

3 SEWING UP Place the panels right sides together, aligning the turned sides. Pin, tack, and sew 2 in (5 cm) at both ends of these sides, and remove the tacking stitches. Pin, tack, and sew the other sides, with a ⅝ in (1.5 cm) allowance. Remove the tacking stitches.

Use as many snaps as are necessary to secure opening

4 ATTACHING SNAPS Sew pairs of snaps at intervals along the right sides of the opening edges *(see page 26)*. Clip the corners and trim the seam allowance. Turn the cover right side out through the opening. Press the cover flat, then insert the pad, pushing it well into the corners.

THE FINISHED CUSHION

BUTTON FASTENING

A central fastening at the back of a cushion is one of the most secure means of closing an opening. A variety of fasteners can be used, including zippers, Velcro tabs or strips, and buttons. All types of fastener can be hidden behind a flange of fabric, but simple, elegant buttons can also be attractively displayed along the center back. To make up this cushion, you will need the cushion fabric and an inner pad, buttons, and the basic sewing kit.

BUTTONS IN CENTER BACK

FRONT VIEW

1 CUTTING OUT Cut the cushion front using a pattern *(see opposite)*. Cut the paper in half. Pin it to a double layer of fabric. Adding 2 in (5 cm) for a center opening, cut two panels.

2 TURNING EDGES Turn the center edges of the backs under by ⅜ in (1 cm), then 1 in (2.5 cm). Pin, tack, and sew the edge. Make buttonholes *(see page 28)* on one turning.

3 SEWING UP Lay the panels right sides together. Overlap the backs by 1 in (2.5 cm), the holed one underneath. Pin, tack, and sew as opposite. Attach the buttons *(see page 28)*.

ROUND CUSHIONS

ROUND CUSHIONS ARE PERHAPS more of a decorative accessory than their square counterparts, and their circular shapes lend themselves to all manner of fanciful and creative edgings. Small round cushions, perhaps with frills or flanges around their edges, mix well among groups of other cushion shapes, especially on a large sofa or at the head of a bed. These round cushions and inner pads are easy to make and you can use a circular paper pattern as a guide to help you cut out the front and back panels of fabric; suitable commercially made inner pads of all diameters and thicknesses are also readily available.

SIMPLE ROUND CUSHION

To make a circular pattern for a round cushion, you will need either a plate of the appropriate size or a simple compass made from a length of string, a pencil, and a drawing pin, as used here. For the cushion, you will need fabric, an inner pad, and the basic sewing kit (see page 12). Because a side-mounted zipper is difficult to hide and can distort the cover fabric, either slipstitch an opening at the side of the cover or fix fastenings into the center of the back panel.

1 MAKING PATTERN Fold a piece of paper larger than the cushion size into quarters. Knot one end of a piece of string and cut it to half the cushion diameter in length. Hold or pin the knotted end at the inner corner of the folded paper and tie a pencil to the other end. Draw an arc. Carefully cut along this curve, then unfold the pattern.

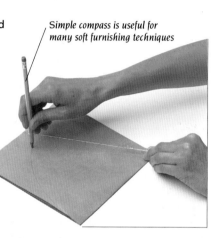

Simple compass is useful for many soft furnishing techniques

2 CUTTING FABRIC Pin the paper on the fabric, and check that any patterns are correctly aligned. Cut out the front and the back panels of the cushion and place the pieces of fabric right sides together, being careful to match the weave and any pattern. Pin and tack the two panels together, ⅝ in (1.5 cm) from the edge. Leave a gap in the seam large enough to allow the inner pad to be inserted.

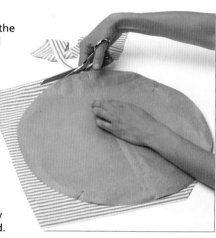

3 JOINING PANELS Machine sew along the tacking on the seam line. Take care not to sew across the opening. Remove the tacking stitches.

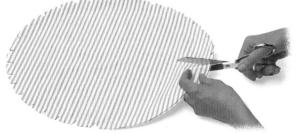

4 NOTCHING Cut notches around the seam allowance (see page 16). Pull the cover right side out and press it. Insert the inner pad through the gap, distributing its bulk around the rim.

Use slipstitches to close opening because they are easy to remove when it is necessary to clean cover

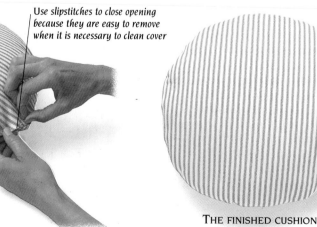

5 STITCHING CLOSED Slipstitch the opening closed (see page 14). When it becomes necessary to clean the cushion, carefully remove the slipstitches, using a seam ripper or a pair of small, sharp scissors, and take out the inner pad. After washing the cover, reinsert the pad and slipstitch the opening closed again.

THE FINISHED CUSHION

ZIPPER AT CENTER BACK

Zippers cannot be used in the side seams of round cushions, because they are too inflexible and would spoil the line. They can, however, be used in an opening running across the back of a round cushion, where they provide a strong and flat fastening. The zipper should be 5 in (13 cm) shorter than the diameter of the cushion and suited to the weight of the fabric.

1 MARKING UP Using a paper pattern *(see opposite)*, cut out the front cushion panel. Remove the pattern and cut it in half to make the back panel template. Pin this to a square piece of fabric, aligning the straight edge of the pattern with the straight grain of the fabric. Mark a cutting line ⅝ in (1.5 cm) from the edge of the pattern for the seam allowance.

2 CUTTING BACKS Cut out two back panels. Pin, tack, and sew the straight edges and the zipper to make a central seam with a zippered opening *(see page 29)*. Open the zipper, and lay the front and the completed back right sides together.

3 JOINING PANELS Pin, tack, and sew fabric pieces ⅝ in (1.5 cm) from the edge. Remove tacking stitches and cut notches around the seam allowance *(see opposite)*. Pull cover right side out through the zipper opening. Press, and insert the pad.

FRONT VIEW

THE FINISHED CUSHION

VELCRO TABS AT CENTER BACK

Velcro is ideal for center-back openings, although it should not be used on lightweight fabrics. Tabs will give a more flexible closure than a strip would. This technique can also be used for buttons and snaps.

1 MARKING UP Cut out the two back-panel halves *(see above)*, but allow 2 in (5 cm) for the turnings on the straight edges. Remove the paper pattern, and turn under the straight edges of both panels once by ⅜ in (1 cm), and then by 1 in (2.5 cm), pressing each time.

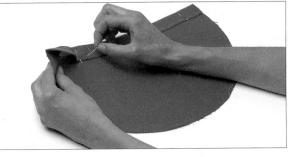

2 STITCHING TURNINGS Pin the turning in place. Secure it by machine sewing or slipstitching along the inner edge. If using buttons, make appropriately sized buttonholes in one of the turnings at this point *(see page 28)*. Lay the pieces right side up and overlap the turnings by 1 in (2.5 cm). If you have made buttonholes, place the edge with the holes in it on top.

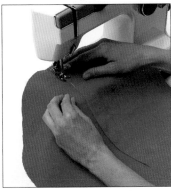

3 SEWING THE CENTER Pin, tack, and sew the back-panel pieces together along the overlapping straight edges. Sew inward from each end, leaving an opening for the pad.

4 SPOTS AND SEAMS Attach the spots, buttons, or snaps *(see page 26)*. Lay the front and back right sides together. Pin, tack, and sew 1.5 cm (⅝ in) from the edge: notch this allowance. Remove the tacking stitches. Pull right sides out and press.

THE FINISHED CUSHION

FRONT VIEW

BOLSTERS

*L*ESS WIDELY USED THAN SQUARE AND ROUND scatter cushions, the bolster cushion is a furnishing accessory that can add character as well as comfort to a sofa, window seat, and, in particular, a chaise longue. Elsewhere in the home, a long and thin bolster may be used in place of pillows on a bed. A bolster cushion of narrow diameter can be laid against the foot of a door for keeping out drafts. Bolsters can be made to match all manner of tastes by simply adding any one of a variety of decorations – from formal piping and buttons to extravagant frills and tassels.

SIMPLE BOLSTER

Almost any type of fabric can be used for a bolster. However, simple bolsters are ideally suited to plain or striped fabrics. Frilled bolsters, on the other hand, look particularly attractive when made up in a patterned fabric, such as a floral print.

Bolster inner pads are available ready made, but you might choose to make your own *(see page 107)*. To make a simple bolster, you will need cushion fabric, an inner pad, simple compass *(see page 110)*, and the basic sewing kit.

1 CUTTING OUT ENDS
Make a pattern for the ends *(see page 110)*. Mark the seam line on the paper pattern ⅝ in (1.5 cm) from the edge, and measure around it to find the circumference of the end panel. Cut out the circular fabric pieces for the end panels.

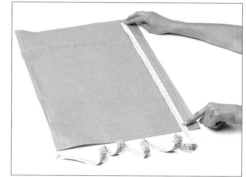

2 THE BODY
The main body width equals the circumference of end panel. Mark the width and length of bolster, plus a ⅝ in (1.5 cm) seam allowance, on paper. Use a drafting triangle to draw corners, then cut out the pattern piece.

3 SEWING THE BODY Pin the body pattern to the fabric, ensuring that any fabric motifs are correctly placed. Cut out the body. Fold it right sides facing, aligning the edges for the central seam. Pin, tack, and sew the seam, leaving an opening for the pad. Press the seam open.

4 ATTACHING ENDS
The end pieces need to be carefully aligned to the main body to avoid bunching. To do this, measure and mark quarters around both ends and the body with tailor's tacks *(see page 14)*. Align the tacks and pin the ends, right sides inward, to the body.

6 SLIPSTITCHING CLOSED Pull the fabric right side out through the central opening in the main body. Press the bolster and insert the inner pad. Slipstitch the opening closed.

Notch seam allowance around ends of cover to reduce fabric bulk

5 NOTCHING ALLOWANCE
Tack end pieces to the main body and make snips of ⅜ in (1 cm) into the seam allowance to ease the fit. Sew the ends to the body. Remove tacking stitches, and notch the allowance around the ends to reduce fabric bulk *(see page 110)*.

THE FINISHED BOLSTER

PIPED AND FRILLED BOLSTER

Simple frills, piping, gathered end panels, and contrasting or matching buttons or tassels are among the many decorative trimmings and treatments that can be used to transform a plain bolster into an unusual and attractive cushion. To make this bolster, you will need enough fabric for the panels and trimmings (the gathered ends will, of course, require more fabric than plain ends), an inner pad, simple compass *(see page 110)*, and the basic sewing kit.

1 MEASURING FOR WIDTH Make paper patterns for an end piece and the body *(see opposite)*. Measure the radius of the end pattern to find the width of fabric needed for gathered ends. Mark width on paper, adding 1¼ in (3 cm) for seam allowances. Check the measurements of this piece against the end-piece pattern.

2 MEASURING FOR LENGTH Measure around the pattern for the end panel as in step 1 opposite. Add 1¼ in (3 cm) for seam allowances, and mark this on the paper. Cut out this pattern piece, pin it to the cushion fabric, and cut out two end pieces around it.

3 SEWING END PIECE On one long edge of a piece for the gathered end, make a ⅝ in (1.5 cm) turning to the wrong side and press it. Bring the short edges of the panel together, the right sides facing. Pin, tack, and sew along these short edges, leaving a ⅝ in (1.5 cm) seam allowance. Remove the tacking stitches. Repeat for the other end panel.

Sew frill to seam allowance of main body piece

4 ATTACHING PIPED FRILL Make up the main body *(see opposite)*. The piping and frill *(see pages 22 and 24)* should be the same length as the fabric for the gathered end. Mark quarters on the frill and the body ends with tailor's tacks. Pin and tack the frills to each end of the main body, then pin and tack the piping to the frill seam line.

5 ATTACHING ENDS Pin, tack, and sew the unturned edges of the ends to piped and frilled body ends. Notch the allowances *(see page 110)*. Turn right side out through opening, then press.

6 GATHERING ENDS Using strong thread, hand sew even gathering stitches *(see page 24)* close to the turned edge of each end. Pull up the gathering thread and distribute the folds evenly. Stitch over the ends of the thread to secure.

END
VIEW

7 ATTACHING BUTTON The gathered ends should be tightly closed, so that buttons will cover the holes. Sew on the buttons *(see page 28)* at the centres of the gathered ends. Insert the pad through the opening in the body seam, then slipstitch it closed.

Sew button to gathered end of bolster

THE FINISHED BOLSTER

EDGINGS

EDGINGS FRAME AND HIGHLIGHT CUSHIONS and add an informal elegance to your furniture. All sorts of cushion trimmings can easily be made or bought, and the techniques for applying them to any shape of plain cushion are straightforward. Cording, the easiest edging to apply, is simply sewn to the outside of the finished cushion cover. Other edgings, such as piping and frills, are machine sewn to the front panel of the cushion during assembly. Some trimmings, such as piping, not only look decorative but also strengthen the edges of a cushion, giving it a longer life.

SIMPLE PIPING WITH ZIPPER

A piped trim around the edge of a cushion, either of the same fabric or in a contrasting color, pattern, or texture, produces a more tailored effect than other trimmings. The following technique can be applied to both square and round cushions.

You will need the cushion panels cut to the size that you desire, an inner pad, piping cord and bias strip for the piping, a zipper 4 in (10 cm) shorter than the side of the cushion, and the basic sewing kit.

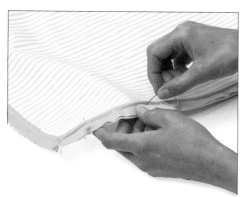

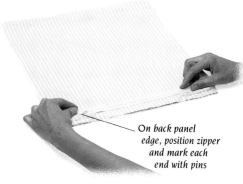

On back panel edge, position zipper and mark each end with pins

1 ATTACHING PIPING To find the length of piping needed, measure around the seam line of the cushion front panel and add 2 in (5 cm) for joining. Make piping to this length *(see page 22)*. Pin and tack the piping at the seam line along the four edges of the right side of the front panel.

2 JOINING PIPING ENDS Leave the overlapping ends of the piping free. Join the ends of the piping cord by thinning and binding them, and the ends of the bias strip either straight across or diagonally *(see page 23)*. Tack the piping to the cushion panel across the joined ends.

3 PLACING ZIPPER Place the front and back pieces of the cushion right sides together. Align the edges and any patterns on the fabric. On the back panel edge for the side opening, mark the length of the zipper with a pin at each end. Pin, tack, and sew in from the ends to these marks.

4 SEWING IN ZIPPER Press seam allowances open. Open the zipper and lay one side of it right side down on the piped seam allowance, on top of piping. Pin, tack, and sew zipper to seam allowance *(see page 29)*, using the zipper attachment on a sewing machine to get close to the piping.

5 SEWING SIDES Lay the panels flat, right sides up, and close the zipper. Pin, tack, and sew the free edge of the zipper to the second panel. Open the zipper. Fold the panels right sides together and pin, tack, and sew the other three sides. Trim the allowance at the corners, turn right side out, and press.

THE FINISHED CUSHION

THICK PIPING

Because thick piping is stuffed with wadding, it makes one of the most comfortable scatter-cushion edgings. A softer, more informal edging than simple piping, thick piping can be made in a fabric the same as, or complementary to, the cushion.

You will need cushion panels cut to the size you desire, medium-weight wadding, a bias strip 3½ in (9 cm) wide for the piping *(see page 22)*, the fasteners you are using, an inner pad, and the basic sewing kit.

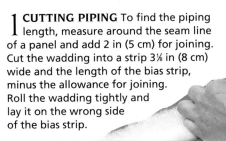

1 CUTTING PIPING To find the piping length, measure around the seam line of a panel and add 2 in (5 cm) for joining. Cut the wadding into a strip 3⅛ in (8 cm) wide and the length of the bias strip, minus the allowance for joining. Roll the wadding tightly and lay it on the wrong side of the bias strip.

2 WRAPPING WADDING Fold the bias strip for the piping over the roll of wadding. Pin and tack along the length of the piping to form a filled tube, then stitch as close to the rolled-up wadding as possible without going through it.

Wadding should be length of bias strip minus diagonal ends

3 SEWING IN PLACE Lay the front panel of the cushion right side up. Pin and tack the piping around the edge of the panel, snipping into the seam allowance at corners to ease the fabric. Trim the seam allowance at the ends of the piping to within 1/16 in (2 mm) of the wadding. Join the piping ends *(see page 23)*. Sew the cushion as appropriate to the fastening.

THE FINISHED CUSHION

CORDED EDGING

Corded edging is simple to attach and, because of its stiffness, strengthens the edges of a cushion. The ends are secured inside the opening of a finished cushion, so this technique is eminently suitable for a cushion with a slipstitched fastening. With any other kind of fastening, use a seam ripper to make a seam opening ¾ in (2 cm) long on one side of the cushion. For this technique, you will need a completed cushion cover, cord or similar trimming, inner pad, and the basic sewing kit.

1 STITCHING IN CORD To find the length of cord needed, measure around the cushion, adding 2 in (5 cm) for securing and the length of the corner loops. Fill the cushion and leave a ¾ in (2 cm) gap in a seam. Tuck 1 in (2.5 cm) of one end of the cord into the gap and oversew to secure. Slipstitch the cord to the cushion edge.

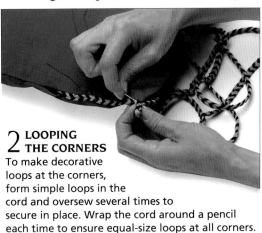

2 LOOPING THE CORNERS To make decorative loops at the corners, form simple loops in the cord and oversew several times to secure in place. Wrap the cord around a pencil each time to ensure equal-size loops at all corners.

3 FINISHING OFF When you have completed stitching the cording around the edge, tuck the end of the cord in the opening so that folded edges of the two ends meet. Overstitch them together, then slipstitch the opening closed.

THE FINISHED CUSHION

SIMPLE FRILL

Frills can be used to highlight a color or a pattern in a cushion fabric, or for their structural effect; of all the edgings for soft furnishings, they produce the softest appearance. To make this cushion, you will need two cushion panels cut to the size you desire, fabric for the frill, a zipper, if you are using one, an inner pad, and the basic sewing kit.

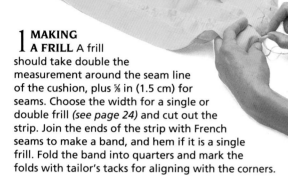

1 MAKING A FRILL A frill should take double the measurement around the seam line of the cushion, plus ⅜ in (1.5 cm) for seams. Choose the width for a single or double frill *(see page 24)* and cut out the strip. Join the ends of the strip with French seams to make a band, and hem if it is a single frill. Fold the band into quarters and mark the folds with tailor's tacks for aligning with the corners.

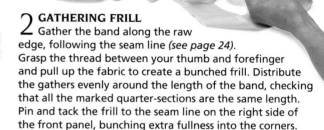

2 GATHERING FRILL Gather the band along the raw edge, following the seam line *(see page 24)*. Grasp the thread between your thumb and forefinger and pull up the fabric to create a bunched frill. Distribute the gathers evenly around the length of the band, checking that all the marked quarter-sections are the same length. Pin and tack the frill to the seam line on the right side of the front panel, bunching extra fullness into the corners.

3 ATTACHING FRILL Sew the frill to the front panel on the seam line, and remove the tacking stitches. Place the cushion panels right sides together, edges aligned. Pin, tack, and sew the panels together as appropriate for the chosen fastening. Trim the corners and remove the tacking stitches. Turn the cover right side out and press it.

THE FINISHED CUSHION

BOUND FRILL

For a smarter effect than a simple frill, a plain frill can be trimmed with a strip, or bias, of fabric in a contrasting or complementary color or pattern. If the frill contrasts with the cushion, it could be bound in the fabric used for the cushion.

To make up a cushion with a bound frill, you will need two cushion panels cut to the size you require, a strip of fabric for the frill *(see above)* and another for the trimming, the fastener you have chosen, an inner pad, and the basic sewing kit.

1 SEWING ON Cut frill and bias strip to the same length, adding ⅜ in (1 cm) seam allowance to the frill and ¼ in (6 mm) to the bias. Join the frill ends to make a band. Press the bias strip's long edges to the middle. Sew the bias to the frill *(see page 16)*.

2 BINDING FRILL Fold the bias strip over the edge of the frill. Pin and tack in place, then slipstitch to the frill band. Remove the tacking stitches. Gather the frill and make up the cushion as for a cushion with a simple frill *(see above)*.

THE FINISHED CUSHION

PIPED AND PLEATED FRILL

For a formal effect, piping works very well with a pleated frill, particularly on a round cushion. To make up this cushion, you will need cushion panels cut to size, the front one with piping sewn around the edge *(see page 114)*, fabric for the pleated frill, the fastener you have chosen to use, an inner pad, and the basic sewing kit.

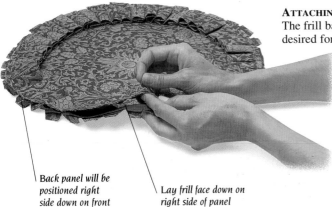

Back panel will be positioned right side down on front panel and frill

Lay frill face down on right side of panel

ATTACHING THE FRILL
The frill band should be double the depth desired for the frill, plus 1¼ in (3 cm) for seams. To find the length needed, measure around the seam line of the front panel and calculate as detailed on page 24, allowing for joins as necessary. Sew the ends to form a band, fold it lengthwise wrong sides together, press, and pleat. Mark the cushion front and fold and mark the band into quarters with tailor's tacks, to help align them. Pin and tack the frill to the front panel, and make up the cover as appropriate for the fastening.

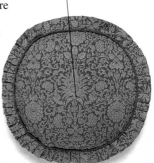

Try to place any prominent motifs centrally on cushion

THE FINISHED CUSHION

GATHERED CORNERS AND TIES

This technique gently rounds the corners of a square cushion, providing a softer and more informal alternative to a plain square. A piped edge in contrasting fabric and matching decorative tie fastenings will both add to the appeal of this style of cover, although you could use almost any of the other edgings and fastenings shown in these pages, such as thick piping or even a frill. In order to make up this cushion, you will need cushion fabric for the front and back panels, cut to the size you desire as for a plain square cushion, bias strip for the rouleau ties, piping cord and bias strip for the piped edging, an inner pad, and the basic sewing kit.

1 MARKING CURVES On the wrong side of each panel, draw a quarter circle to round off the corners, using a round object or a compass. The bigger the curve, the rounder the corners will be. Trim the corners.

2 GATHERING CORNERS Hand sew gathering at the corners, ⅝ in (1.5 cm) out from the arc. Pull the threads to gather, then oversew the ends. Measure along the seam line to find the length of piping required, and add 2 in (5 cm) for joining. Pin, tack, and sew the piping to the panel *(see page 23)*.

3 TURNING OPENING Measure and mark the opening on the edge of the back panel. Turn the edge to the wrong side, press, and slipstitch. Lay the panels right sides together, edges aligned. Pin, tack, and sew the sides, leaving a gap.

4 ATTACHING TIES Make up fabric ties or rouleau strips *(see page 27)* and sew them along the edges of the opening opposite each other. Turn the cover right side out through the opening, and press it before inserting the inner pad.

THE FINISHED CUSHION

FLANGE EDGING

Flanges are often used as decorative edgings for pillowcases, but they are equally suitable for an elegant border on a cushion. In this technique, which is the simplest way of making a flanged edge, the flange is part of the same piece of fabric as that used for the cushion panels. This makes the assembly of the cushion very easy. Using a flange edging on a cushion rules out the possibility of having a fastening in one of the side seams, so the cushion cover has to fasten in the back panel, either with buttons *(see page 109)* or with a zipper or Velcro *(see pages 26 and 29)*. To make this cushion, you will need fabric for the cushion cover, the fastener you have chosen, an inner pad, and the basic sewing kit.

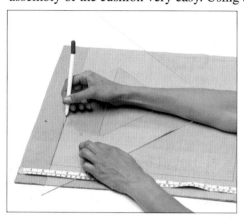

1 MARKING PANEL Cut the panels to size, with 2½ in (6 cm) extra for the flange edging and ⅝ in (1.5 cm) extra for the seam allowance all around. Join the panels as for a square cushion with a center-back fastening. Turn the cover right sides out. On the front, mark a line 2½ in (6 cm) from the edge all around in tailor's chalk, and tack along it.

2 JOINING PANELS Fit a double needle to the sewing machine and sew along the flange line. If your machine does not have a double needle, stitch around the cushion along each side of the tacking stitches; keep the lines parallel and ⅛–³⁄₁₆ in (3–5 mm) apart. Remove the tacking stitches. Press the cushion cover and insert the pad.

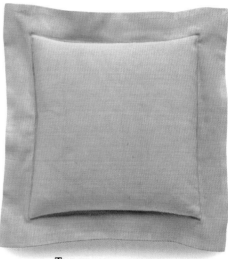

THE FINISHED CUSHION

SCALLOPED FLANGE EDGING

Rounded, serrated, or squared-off cutwork adds decoration to flanges. In this technique, the edging is made from separate pieces of fabric and attached to the cushion panels, so it could be made from fabric that contrasts with the cushion.

To make this cushion, you will need fabric for the front and back cushion panels and the front and back edging pieces, an inner pad, fasteners, a simple compass *(see page 110)* or a glass for the scalloped edges, and the basic sewing kit.

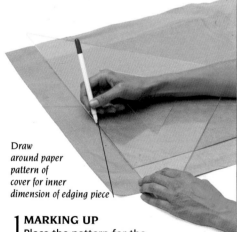

Draw around paper pattern of cover for inner dimension of edging piece

1 MARKING UP Place the pattern for the front panel on the wrong side of the fabric for the edging pieces. On the fabric, draw a line the depth of your frill, plus a ⅜ in (1 cm) seam allowance, from the pattern edge. Cut along this line. Draw a line around the pattern, remove it, and repeat for the second edging piece.

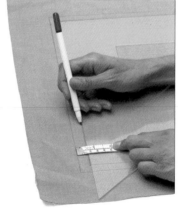

2 MARKING EDGING SEAM Using a tape measure and a drafting triangle as a guide, draw a second line on the edging pieces parallel to, and ⅝ in (1.5 cm) inside, the line you drew around the pattern. Draw the line right around the four sides of both pieces of fabric.

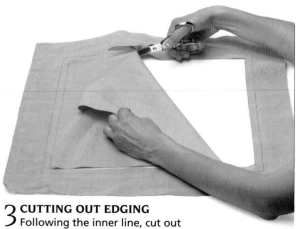

3 CUTTING OUT EDGING Following the inner line, cut out the fabric at the center of each edging piece, which can be used for a smaller cushion. When a center piece is laid on a cushion panel, it should be ⅝ in (1.5 cm) smaller all around than the seam line on the panel. If you are short of fabric and do not mind seams in the flange, you could use strips of fabric mitered at the corners *(see mitering lace, page 25)* for the edging.

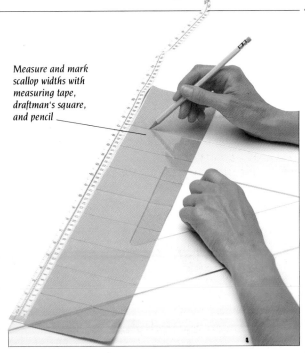

Measure and mark scallop widths with measuring tape, draftman's square, and pencil

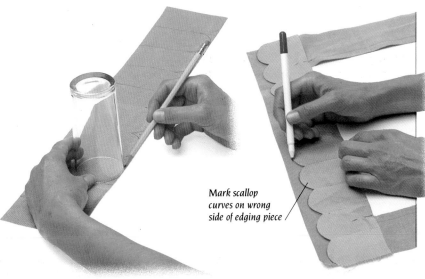

Mark scallop curves on wrong side of edging piece

4 MARKING EDGE Cut a strip of paper to the length and width of one side of an edging piece. Mark the paper strip into equal sections the width of a scallop. The edge should begin and end with a full scallop – adjust the width of the scallops if necessary.

5 MARKING CURVES On one edge of the paper pattern, mark a series of curves between the dividing lines, using either the rim of a glass or a simple compass as a guide. The curves should not be too deep: draw around only about a third of the glass. Carefully cut out the pattern along the curves.

6 MARKING FABRIC Lay edging fabric wrong side up. Align straight edge of pattern with internal edge. Pin in place. Mark up curves with a vanishing-ink pen. Repeat around other three sides and other edging piece.

7 SEWING EDGE Place the two edging pieces right sides together with their edges aligning. Pin, tack, and sew the edging pieces together, stitching ³⁄₁₆ in (5 mm) from, and parallel to, the marked line of the curves on all four sides. Remove the tacking stitches.

8 CLIPPING ALLOWANCE Cut and trim around the curves, and clip into the edges. This will reduce the fabric bulk so the edging is not strained when turned right side out.

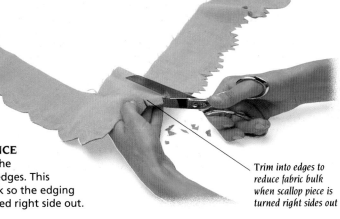

Trim into edges to reduce fabric bulk when scallop piece is turned right sides out

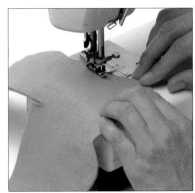

9 TOPSTITCHING EDGE Turn the edging piece right side out and press it. To flatten the edge, topstitch *(see page 17)* along the curved edge in three parallel rows, ¼ in (6 mm) apart, and starting ¼ in (6 mm) in from the curved edge.

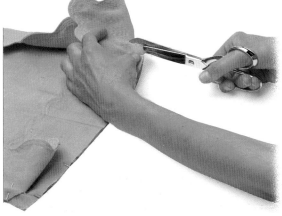

10 ATTACHING EDGING Lay the edging on the right side of the cushion front, edges aligned, and pin, tack, and sew in place. Remove the tacking stitches and clip the corners. Make up the cushion.

THE FINISHED CUSHION

USING SPECIAL FABRICS

MAKING A CUSHION COVER PROVIDES the ideal opportunity to give new life to a small fragment of an old or unusual fabric. The choice of fabrics extends from the relatively well known, such as antique lace or European needlepoint, to the unfamiliar, like the panel of a Central African raffia skirt or part of a kilim. Many such fabrics are delicate, either intrinsically or through age, and they should be reinforced by being mounted on a strong backing cloth. It is also advisable to make up a cushion that can safely be dismantled later, leaving a precious textile intact for framing or further use.

RIBBON-AND-LACEWORK CUSHION

There are many examples of lacework, such as trimmings on garments, tablecloths, napkins, bedspreads, pillows, and sheets. When used as a decorative edging on cushions, lacework or fine linen can transform a simple cover into a fancy antique furnishing. The size of the cushion is determined by the amount of lace or linen available. The cushion below has been trimmed with ribbons and buttons. In addition to lace and adornments, to make this cushion you will need cushion fabric, an inner pad, and the basic sewing kit. Avoid using side zipper fastenings with lace edgings.

1 MARKING PANEL Lay the front panel for the cushion cover (*see page 108*) right-side up, tack the seam line ⅝ in (1.5 cm) from the panel edge, and mark the placement for the outer ribbon parallel to the seam line. Tack in place. Draw the positions for the inner ribbon, decorative bows, and the buttons, using a drafting triangle and a vanishing-ink pen or tailor's chalk.

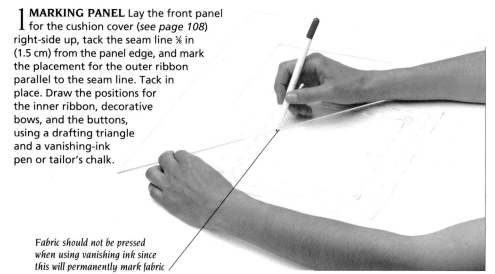

Fabric should not be pressed when using vanishing ink since this will permanently mark fabric

2 ATTACHING RIBBON Following the marked line, pin and tack the ribbon bordering the pattern in place on the face of the front panel. Attach the ribbon by slipstitching it along the edges, mitering at the corners and hiding the necessary joins (*see page 25*). Remove the tacking stitches.

3 ATTACHING DECORATIONS Stitch the buttons and bows in place and make up the cover (*see page 108*). Lay the lace along the edge and mark the position of the corners on it. Miter the lace at corners, and join the ends at one corner (*see page 25*).

4 ATTACHING LACE EDGING Stitch the lace to the cushion edge by hand. Use small, even slipstitches; bad stitching may be camouflaged by the lace, but it will be weak. Wash the cover if you used vanishing ink, then press it carefully and insert the pad.

THE FINISHED CUSHION

TAPESTRY CUSHION

Many densely woven and needleworked textiles – such as kilims and tapestries – make colorfully patterned cushion covers. However, such delicate textiles need backing for added strength. The backing also prevents the inner pad from showing through any gaps in the weave of the fragment. In addition to the chosen textile and the backing material, to make this cushion you will need an inner pad, the fastener you have chosen, and the basic sewing kit.

1 CUTTING OUT PANELS Needleworked textiles, such as this Swedish tapestry, are seldom square, so it is important to mimic the original by using it as a pattern. Lay the tapestry on the piece of backing fabric and secure it with pins. Working carefully, cut out the backing fabric, closely following the edge of the tapestry. Cut out the fabric for the back of the cushion using this same technique.

2 ATTACHING BACKING Lay the tapestry face up on the right side of the backing. Pin and tack together. Place the tapestry and back panel right sides facing. Pin and tack along the edge, leaving a ⅝ in (1.5 cm) allowance.

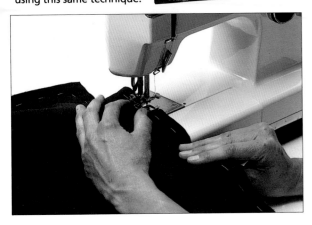

3 JOINING PANELS Following the tacking stitches, sew the front tapestry panel and the back panels together as appropriate for the fastening method you are using. Remove the tacking stitches and clip the seam allowance at the corners, taking care to avoid cutting through the old fabric. Turn the cover right side out, press, and insert the inner pad.

THE FINISHED CUSHION

FABRIC OPTIONS

Cushion covers can be made from a variety of fabrics, provided that the fabric is suited to the decorative or the functional use of the cushion. For color and delicacy, there are fine dress materials, such as muslin, which may have to be strengthened by backing with a stronger cloth. Because it is a light yet durable fabric, silk is ideal for use in making cushion covers, although the finest weaves need to be lined.

In a more exotic vein, the richly varied hand-woven and printed or embroidered tribal and folk textiles of Africa and India make ideal complements, and contrasts in pattern and texture, to ordinary furnishing fabrics. When seeking a more hard-wearing material, look out for densely woven rug fragments from well-worn oriental carpets or kilims, or a piece of closely worked old needlepoint.

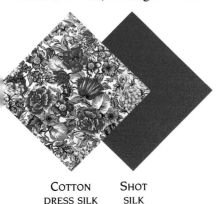

COTTON DRESS SILK	SHOT SILK

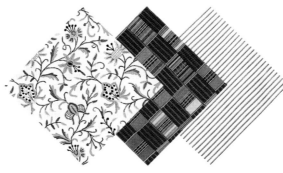

INDIAN CREWELWORK · COTTON AFRICAN CHIEF'S ROBE · COTTON TICKING

PERSIAN KILIM PIECE · MODERN NEEDLEPOINT

SLIPSTITCHING A LIGHTWEIGHT FABRIC

When using a sheer fabric, such as an old and thin textile fragment or a lightweight piece of exotic dress material, for the front panel of a cushion, it is best to find a backing fabric that is compatible with the fabric not only in weight and density but also in color. Here, for example, a piece of skirt material from West Africa with a batik pattern is prepared and carefully slipstitched by hand to the front panel for a cushion cover, cut from similarly colored fabric. To make this cushion, you will need the fabric for the back panel and the backing of the front panel, an inner pad, the fastening you have chosen, and the basic sewing kit.

1 MARKING UP
Lay the piece of decorative fabric right side up. Mark lines around all four sides ⅜ in (1 cm) from the edges. Mark the lines with tailor's chalk, and use a drafting triangle to make the shape as regular as possible – mark farther from the edge if necessary to achieve a true square or rectangle.

2 TURNING AND TACKING Turn the fabric over so that the wrong side faces upward. Fold the fabric edge over to the ⅜ in (1 cm) mark, and press the turning in place. Tack down all the sides of this turning and press the edges flat again. Turning under the border of the fabric in this way ensures that you have a straight edge to work with if the edges of the fabric piece are uneven.

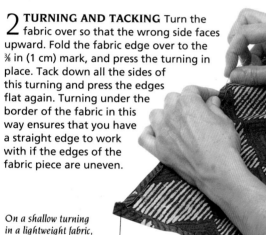

On a shallow turning in a lightweight fabric, corners will not need mitering

3 CUTTING OUT FABRIC Place the patterned fabric right side up on the face of the backing fabric. Use the decorative fabric as a template, adding a seam allowance of ⅝–¾ in (1.5–2 cm) around it, and mark this line. Cut the front backing fabric to this size. Cut the fabric for the back panel of the cushion to this size, taking in any adjustments for your fastening.

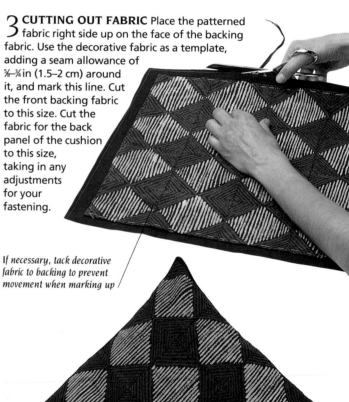

If necessary, tack decorative fabric to backing to prevent movement when marking up

4 ATTACHING TO CUSHION
Make up the cushion cover as appropriate to the fastening used. Pin and tack the patterned fabric to the cushion front. Sew it in place by hand, using small, even slipstitches around the folded edge. Remove the tacking stitches and insert the inner pad.

THE FINISHED CUSHION

BACKING AND BORDERING

One way to hide the slight irregularities that are often found in the shape of an old or unusual fabric fragment is to make up a mount with a border. By varying the depth of the border, or by giving a generous perimeter of plain cloth, the shape of the patterned front panel will be accommodated on a perfectly square cushion cover. As well as the decorative fabric, you will need suitable backing fabric, fabric for the back of the cushion cover, if different from the backing for the old textile, an inner pad, the fastening you are using (a side closure is unsuitable for this kind of cushion) and the basic sewing kit.

1 CUTTING OUT BACKING Place decorative fabric on backing fabric and decide on width required for border – you will need a deeper border to conceal an uneven edge. Add a ⅜ in (1 cm) allowance all around. Use a drafting triangle to mark size required and cut out backing fabric.

2 BORDERING FRONT Place the fabric right side up on the wrong side of the backing. Turn the edge of the backing to the wrong side by ⅜ in (1 cm), then fold it over the decorative fabric to the desired depth. Miter the corners *(see page 21)* and press. Pin, tack, and slipstitch or machine sew in place.

3 CUTTING OUT BACK PANEL If you want a slipstitched closure, cut the back panel using the front panel as a template and adding a ⅝ in (1.5 cm) seam allowance all around. If you want a center-back fastening, adjust your method accordingly *(see pages 109 and 111).*

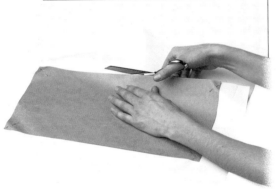

4 TURNING IN Lay the front and back panels wrong sides together. Mark around the front panel on the back one. Place the back panel face down, and turn the edges to the wrong side along marked lines. Clip the corners, press the turning, and tack it in place.

5 JOINING PANELS Place the front and back panels wrong sides together, aligning all the edges. Pin and tack the panels together, then topstitch around them, about 1/16–⅛ in (2–3 mm) from the edges. Any strain will be taken by the cushion back and the border of the front, not by the decorative fabric panel. Remove the tacking stitches, press the completed cover, and insert the inner pad.

Border will hide uneven shape of fabric and give a straight edge

THE FINISHED CUSHION

SIMPLE SEAT CUSHIONS

$\mathcal{M}$OST HOMES CONTAIN A VARIETY of wooden seats – in the kitchen, dining room, study, or playroom – that are hard and uncomfortable. Making simple removable cushions for such chairs is easy. Seat cushions not only add comfort but also bring pattern and color to a room, and can make the furniture a part of the overall decorative scheme. You can choose from a variety of fastenings to anchor seat cushions to chairs. These range from simple fabric ties to elasticated tapes or Velcro strips, depending on the effect you want to achieve. Decorative embellishments include buttons and tufts.

SEAT CUSHION WITH TIES

When making up seat cushions, consider the location of the chair: for a busy area of the home, for example, choose a covering fabric that is easy to clean. Calculate the amount of material needed by measuring the base of the seat, and add an extra quantity for the ties as well as for the piping trim. To establish the length of piping required, measure around the edge of the seat. To make a pattern for cutting out the fabric for the cushion, you will need tracing paper and a felt-tip pen. You will also need 1½ in (4 cm) thick upholstery foam for the padding, and the basic sewing kit.

Tracing paper is easier to use than pattern paper for this technique

1 TRACING A PATTERN Make a pattern of the chair seat with a sheet of tracing paper. First, cut tracing paper slightly larger than the seat area. Lay the paper on the seat and crease it over the edge. On the paper, pencil around the perimeter of the seat. Where the seat meets the back, form the pattern around this obstruction by creasing, marking, and cutting out carefully.

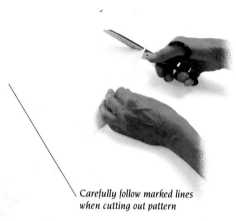

Carefully follow marked lines when cutting out pattern

2 CUTTING PATTERN Remove the paper from the chair seat and fold it in half along the back to front axis of the seat. Make sure that the pattern is symmetrical from side to side, adjust if necessary, then cut it out. Check the fit on the seat, particularly around the uprights, and adjust if necessary.

3 CUTTING FOAM Lay the pattern on the foam. Mark the shape with a felt-tip pen and cut it out of the foam using large shears. Pin the pattern to the fabric, and cut out two panels with a ⅝ in (1.5 cm) allowance all around. Measure the seam line of the cover to find the piping length, adding 2 in (5 cm) for the join.

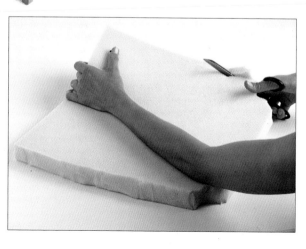

4 JOINING PANELS Make up the piping (*see page 22*). Attach the piping to the right side of the cushion front. Lay the right sides of the front and back panels together, aligning the edges, and pin, tack, and sew, leaving a gap at the back for inserting the pad. Trim and clip the seams and corners. Pull the cushion cover right side out through the opening.

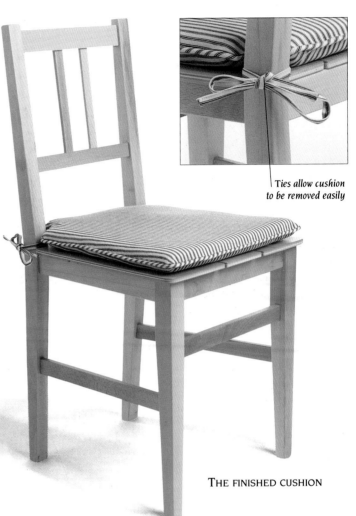

5 ATTACHING TIES Lay the cushion cover on the chair base and mark the positions for the ties. Cut two fabric pieces 24 x 1¼ in (60 x 3 cm) to make the ties *(see page 27)*. Fold the ties in half, pin in place, and oversew each to the inside of the piping on the lower cushion panel. For a more decorative effect, you could make wider ties, which would make larger bows.

Ties allow cushion to be removed easily

6 CLOSING THE OPENING Press the seat-cushion cover and insert the foam pad through the opening. Ensure that the pad is pushed into the corners and curves of the cushion cover. Turn in the seam allowances of the opening, align the edges, and slipstitch closed. When the cushion cover needs to be cleaned, simply cut through the slipstitches to remove the pad.

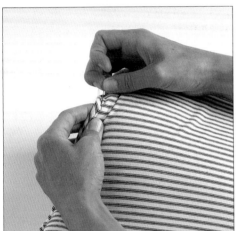

THE FINISHED CUSHION

BUTTONED CUSHION

Buttoning is an upholstery technique that provides quick and easy decoration to furniture coverings, and it is particularly effective on a simple furnishing, such as a removable seat cushion or a box cushion *(see page 128)*. Fabric-covered buttons are used: they can be covered in a fabric with a contrasting color and pattern to the cushion, in which case you can use ready-made buttons, or you may want them covered in the fabric used for the cushion itself, in which case you will probably cover them yourself *(see page 28)*. In addition to the basic sewing kit, you will need a large upholstery needle and strong thread or twine.

THE FINISHED CUSHION

1 THREADING BUTTONS Mark button positions on the cover. Thread the needle with twine and push it into a mark, through the cushion, leaving 4–6 in (10–15 cm) of twine on the top side of cushion. Thread a button onto the needle. Return the needle, through the same hole, to the top side.

2 SECURING BUTTONS Thread onto the twine the second of the first pair of buttons, remove the needle, and fasten it to the cushion with a slipknot. Pull hard on both ends of twine until buttons sink well into the cushion. Securely tie off the ends around the shank of the button and snip off the surplus twine.

SEAT CUSHION WITH ELASTIC STRIP

An elasticized band around the uprights of a chair back will hold a seat cushion in place and give it a somewhat formal finish. Such a band is simple to make up and fit. To remove the cushion for cleaning, or to exchange it for another one in a different color or pattern, just slide the elasticized fabric strip up over the back of the chair. As well as the fabric for the band, you will need a length of elastic some 1¼ in (3 cm) wide and the basic sewing kit.

1 FINDING BAND LENGTH
Measure across the back of the seat and around the sides of the uprights. Cut the elastic to this length. Cut out a strip of the band fabric 3½ in (9 cm) wide and the length of the elastic at its full extension.

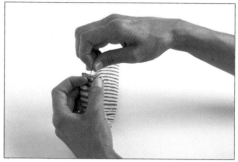

2 MAKING BAND Fold the strip of fabric in half lengthwise, with the right sides together. Using a needle and thread or a sewing machine, sew a seam along the edge to form a narrow tube. Turn this band of fabric right side out. Adjust the the tube so that the seam runs along the center of one side, not the edge. Press in position.

3 THREADING ELASTIC
Secure one end of the elastic to one end of the tube. Attach a safety pin to the other and, using it as a guide, thread the elastic through the tube. Sew in place at the other end. Place the cushion on the seat and mark the positions for fixing the band. Tuck in the raw ends of the tube and sew it onto the cushion.

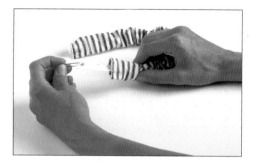

TIES WITH VELCRO FASTENINGS

A discreet method of securing a cushion pad to a chair involves using a pair of simple fabric straps fastened by tabs of "touch-and-close" tape, commonly known by the trade name of Velcro. Measure the distance around the chair uprights that will be used as anchoring points, allowing for a 1 in (2.5 cm) overlap, and cut out two strips of fabric 3½ in (9 cm) wide to this length. For these ties, you will need fabric, Velcro strip, and the basic sewing kit.

MAKING VELCRO TIES

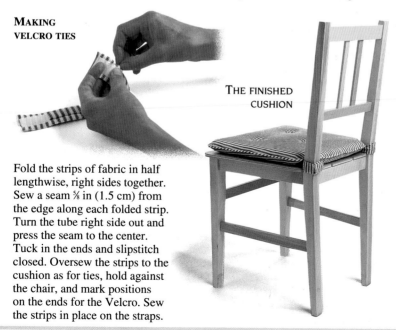

THE FINISHED CUSHION

Fold the strips of fabric in half lengthwise, right sides together. Sew a seam ⅝ in (1.5 cm) from the edge along each folded strip. Turn the tube right side out and press the seam to the center. Tuck in the ends and slipstitch closed. Oversew the strips to the cushion as for ties, hold against the chair, and mark positions on the ends for the Velcro. Sew the strips in place on the straps.

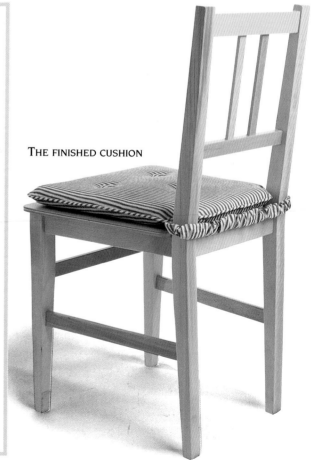

THE FINISHED CUSHION

TUFTED SEAT CUSHION

Tufting is less well known than buttoning but has long been used as a furnishing embellishment. It has a softer effect than buttoning and gives an opportunity to use either matching or contrasting threads, in dense clumps or loose tendrils. Tufts are applied to a finished cushion, here a simple seat pad with matching ties. As well as the seat pad, you will need some thick cotton thread or yarn, a large upholstery needle, twine or strong thread, and the basic sewing kit.

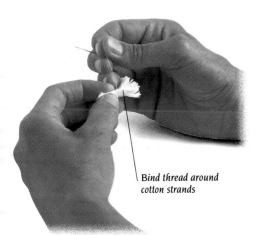

Bind thread around cotton strands

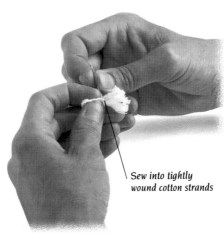

Sew into tightly wound cotton strands

Use your fingers to fray ends of bound strands

1 BINDING TUFTS Mark the places for the tufts on the cushion. Make up each tuft by cutting strands of thick cotton to the same length. Roll the strands together and bind the middle with a needle and thread.

2 SECURING To finish binding the strands, push the needle through the center of the bound clump. You may need to go through the center several times until the strands are secured firmly together.

3 FRAYING END Once the clump of thick threads is securely bound together, use your fingertips to fray out both ends of the bunched strands to give a pronounced tufted effect.

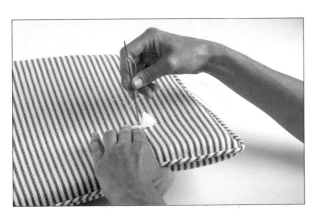

4 ATTACHING TUFT Thread the upholstery needle with the twine or thick thread. Push the needle through the center of a tuft, leaving a tail of 4–6 in (10–15 cm) of twine. Place the tuft on the cushion and drive the threaded needle vertically straight through the pad in the marked position.

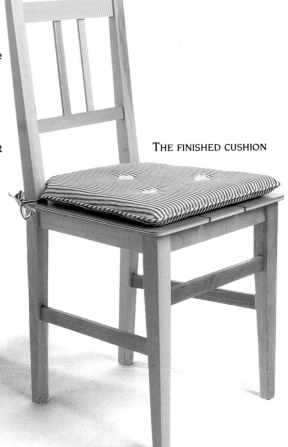

THE FINISHED CUSHION

5 ATTACHING TUFT TO BACK Position a tuft on the back of the cushion cover and secure it in place with the thread. Pass the needle back through the original hole, returning it to the top of the cushion.

6 SECURING TUFTS Remove the needle and fasten the twine ends in a slipknot. Pull on the ends of the twine until both tufts sink into the cushion, then tie off around the base of the tuft and snip off the surplus.

BOX SEAT CUSHIONS

*B*OX SEAT CUSHIONS PADDED with deep foam make comfortable and easy-to-clean accessories for wicker, metal, or wooden chairs, or for benches and garden seats that are used outside the home or in a greenhouse. Use a sturdy fabric, such as a heavy-duty cotton, for the cover. This will keep its shape and be simple to clean. To make it easy to remove the inner pad for cleaning, fit a full-length zipper in a welt along one side of the cushion.

SIMPLE BOX CUSHION

When making a box cushion, give added strength and a neat edging to the chosen furnishing fabric by piping the seams *(see page 22)*. Depending on the nature of the chair, it may also be a good idea to help secure the cushion in place with same-fabric ties *(see page 27)*. When measuring up, allow sufficient fabric for the top and bottom panels, the wide welt, and the piping, as well as any ties. You will also need piping cord, a zipper, tracing paper for pattern making, a felt-tip pen, a sharp, long-bladed kitchen knife for cutting out the foam pad, and the basic sewing kit.

1 **TRACING PATTERN** Trace the seat area for the box seat cushion *(see page 124)*. Transfer the traced pattern onto a sheet of white paper.

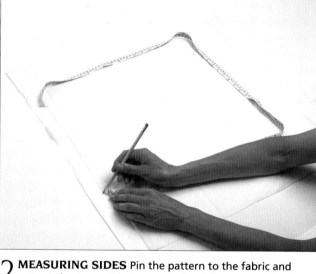

2 **MEASURING SIDES** Pin the pattern to the fabric and cut out the top and bottom panels of the cover with a ⅝ in (1.5 cm) seam allowance. Measure around the edge of the seat cushion pattern to find the length of piping and fabric needed for the welt. Make two lengths of piping *(see page 22)*, adding 2 in (5 cm) for joins.

3 **CUTTING FOAM** Lay the seat pattern on the foam and draw its outline on the pad with a felt-tip pen. Cut the foam to size with a sharp kitchen knife or an electric carving knife.

4 **FITTING WELT** Cut fabric to the length of three cushion sides plus 1¼ in (3 cm), and the depth plus 1¼ in (3 cm). For the fourth side, where the zipper will be, cut two pieces of fabric to the length of the side plus 1¼ in (3 cm), and half the depth plus 1¼ in (3 cm). Fix a zipper between these pieces in a seam *(see page 29)*. If you can get a long zipper, extending the zipped panel around the cushion corners makes it easy to insert and remove the pad. Pin together the welt sections. Check that the welt fits snugly around the pad.

5 **SEWING WELT TO TOP PANEL** Attach the piping to the top and bottom cushion panels *(see page 23)*. Place the welt and the top panel of the cover right sides together, edges aligning. Pin, tack, and sew the welt to the panel. Remove the tacking stitches.

6 ATTACHING BASE With the zipper open, pin, tack, and sew the welt and the bottom panel right sides together. Remove the tacking stitches and clip the corners. Turn the cover right side out and press it. Insert the pad, pushing it firmly into the corners.

THE FINISHED CUSHION

OTHER FILLINGS AND DECORATIONS

When they are made for use exclusively inside the home, for example on a sofa or a window seat, box seat cushions stuffed with a polyester or feather-filled padding prove more comfortable than if stuffed with foam. For feather fillings, an inner pad cover of a feather-proof fabric *(see page 10)* is necessary. Box cushions can be attractively finished with buttoning or tufting on the top and bottom panels, or by quilting the welt.

FEATHER-FILLED CUSHION

QUILTING THE WELT

You can give a deep-sided box seat cushion a decorative finish by quilting the welt when making up the cushion cover. To make up the quilted sides, you will need the fabric itself, plus wadding to pad the quilting, and muslin to back the welt. For this technique, you will also need the basic sewing kit. For the cushion filling, you can choose between foam, feathers, or polyester. To make a box seat cushion with a quilted welt, construct the cushion cover as opposite, but when you come to making up the welt, substitute the following technique.

1 PINNING WELT PIECES Cut out wadding and muslin to the same size as the fabric for the welt; if this will make the seams too bulky, cut wadding without a seam allowance, as here. Lay the fabric and the muslin right sides together with the wadding between them.

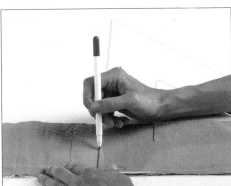

2 MARKING QUILTING LINES Pin and tack around the edges of the wadded welt and across it if necessary to prevent the fabric from slipping. Mark positioning lines for the quilting, using a drafting triangle and tailor's chalk or a vanishing-ink pen.

3 QUILTING Tack along the quilting marks, then machine sew along the tacking stitches. Remove the tacking stitches. Continue to assemble the cushion as detailed opposite and above, replacing the welt with the quilted side panel.

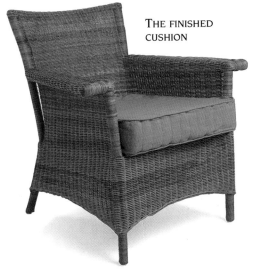

THE FINISHED CUSHION

SIMPLE UPHOLSTERY

JUST AS A CURTAIN OR SHADE CAN ENHANCE a window,
a fabric covering will transform a chair, old or new. Unlike
a fitted cover, which is securely stitched and tacked to the
frame and padding of a chair, a loose cover is made from cut
panels of fabric that are sewn together to form a tailored
assembly, which is slipped into place on the seat. While
possessing many of the tailored qualities of a fitted cover,
a loose cover is also eminently practical, since it can easily
be removed for cleaning or changed to suit your preference.
Whatever your requirements – decorative or practical – in
this chapter you will find all the information you need to
make up elegant loose and fitted covers for armchairs
and sofas. Also included are simple instructions for
upholstering a footstool or ottoman with a fitted cover.

CHOOSING A STYLE

SIMPLE FABRIC COVERS CAN BE USED to provide color, pattern, and texture to almost any form of seating – hard or soft, upright or reclining. The most popular and effective way of benefiting from covers, however, is to use them on living-room sofas and armchairs. A loose cover can give a new lease on life to an old, worn chair or sofa, while even the most ordinary, workaday piece of furniture can be transformed if covered with special fabric. Choose sturdy fabrics that offer protection and complement the scheme of decoration by working in combination with the other fabrics and furnishings in the room.

ETHNIC TEXTILES
It is possible to upholster an item of furniture with almost any heavyweight fabric, as long as it will stand up to the wear and tear it will receive, but the style of fabric that you choose can have a marked impact on the room. Here, a stool has been covered with a fragment of a Turkish rug, imparting an exotic, ethnic feel to the room's overall decorative scheme.

Vividly patterned fabric introduces focus of color

Rug's colors harmonize with colors of curtain and carpet

Matching fabric used for curtains as well as furniture creates visual theme within room

Frilled skirt emphasizes shape of furniture

MATCHING FABRICS
There are numerous ways of coordinating the soft furnishings within a room; matching the window dressing to the upholstery fabric is one popular means of harmonizing a room's decorative style. Fabric coverings can be made in many different styles. Here, an armchair and footstool have been fitted with covers incorporating piped edges and flounced skirts to provide a high degree of sophistication.

FORMAL AND TAILORED

This patterned sofa cover brightens up the traditional setting of the room, and at the same time maintains a formal tone through its tailored design. When assembling loose covers to fit sofas, you will need to join fabric widths. If the fabric has a large pattern, always center the pattern repeat over the length of the sofa to ensure an overall visual balance.

CASUAL AND HOMEY

For an instant result, blankets or rugs can be casually draped over armchairs to provide simple, stylish covers. Make sure that the fabric you use for a throw cover is large enough to drape well over the back of the armchair.

Blanket offers rich color and pattern, enriching warm feel of room

MODERN AND LINEAR

Loose covers can be designed to enhance the shape of furniture. These slip-covers form a dramatic alteration in the proportions and character of a set of dining-room chairs, since they have been made to cover not only the backs and seats of the chairs but also the legs.

CONTRASTING FABRICS

Using covers made from various different fabrics is often the most appropriate method of upholstering disparate items of furniture that do not match in size or shape. Scatter cushions placed on each piece of furniture help to link the different colors and patterns.

MIXING STYLES

Different styles of fabric cover in complementary colors and designs can work well together when combined in the same room. Here, the single seats have fitted covers that accentuate their flowing lines, in contrast to the slip-cover of the informal-looking sofa. Armchairs and sofas often benefit from fabric valances – either flat or frilled – that conceal unsightly casters or exposed wooden legs.

Light-colored and indistinctly patterned fabrics combine easily with other fabrics in room

Fabric valance conceals legs of armchair and provides a soft effect

SIMPLE FITTED COVER

*M*AKING A SIMPLE FITTED COVER FOR AN ARMCHAIR is straightforward, as long as you measure carefully. Before cutting out the fabric, make a plan on graph paper of the dimensions of each section. Label each section as you cut it out. Pin, fit, and cut the sections in place on the chair before sewing the cover together. Choose a durable fabric that is suitable for upholstery, such as heavy cotton, damask, or cotton-linen blend, and check that it is fire retardant – if it is not, you will need to use a flame-resistant interlining. Make sure that the fabric can be either washed by hand or dry cleaned.

MEASURING

The piping for the simple fitted cover should be attached to the seam lines around the outside back piece and to each front arm piece, and along the skirt's top seam. Measure these seam lines, and cut bias strips and piping cord, allowing for ⅝ in (1.5 cm) joins where necessary *(see page 22)*. Remove the seat cushion, and measure and make the cover *(see page 128)*.

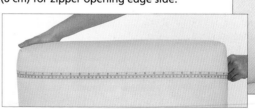

Outside back

Inside back

Inside arm

Seat (cushion)

Front arm

Outside arm seam

Outside arm

As a general rule, a zipper should run along a back corner from bottom edge to approximately 4 in (10 cm) above arm

Apron

Bottom edge

1 OUTSIDE BACK Measure back width across widest part. Add 1 in (2.5 cm) for seams on each edge, plus 2½ in (6 cm) for opening at lower edge of back piece and an outside arm piece. Measure bottom to top. Add 6 in (15 cm) for bottom tuck-under, and 1 in (2.5 cm) for top seam.

2 INSIDE BACK Measure from the inside back top edge to the seat level. Add 1 in (2.5 cm) for the top seam, and 6 in (15 cm) for the tuck-in at the back of the seat. Measure across the inside back from side to side at the widest point, going around the corners to the back edges. Add 1 in (2.5 cm) for one side seam, and 2½ in (6 cm) for zipper opening edge side.

3 SEAT Measure the seat of the chair from the back to the front edge. Add 1 in (2.5 cm) for seam allowance at the front and 6 in (15 cm) for the tuck-in at the back. Measure the width of the seat between the arms of the chair, and add 12 in (30 cm) to this measurement to allow for the tuck-in at each side.

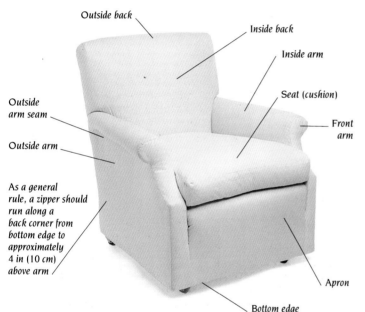

4 APRON Measure the apron from the top to the bottom edge. Add 1 in (2.5 cm) for the seam at the seat front, plus 6 in (15 cm) for the tuck-under along the bottom edge. Measure width of the apron between front arms, adding 1 in (2.5 cm) for each side seam.

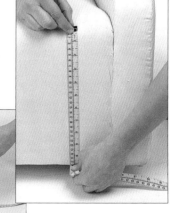

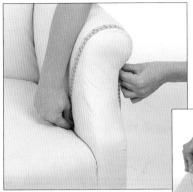

5 **INSIDE ARM** Measure the arm of the chair from the seat over the arm top, and down to the outer arm seam. Add 7 in (18 cm) for the tuck-in at the side of the seat and the outside arm-piece seam. Measure the length of the arm from front to back at the longest point. Add 2 in (5 cm) for the front arm piece and outside and inside back-piece seams.

6 **OUTSIDE ARM** Measure the length of the arm from front to back at the longest point. Add 2 in (5 cm) for the front arm and outside back seams. Measure from the outside arm seam to the bottom edge. Add 1 in (2.5 cm) for the inside arm seam, and 6 in (15 cm) for bottom tuck-under.

7 **FRONT ARM** Measure the front arm at the widest and longest parts. Add 2 in (5 cm) to each of these measurements for the apron, outside arm, and inside arm seams. You will also need to add 6 in (15 cm) lengthwise for the bottom tuck-under.

SKIRT

If you are adding a tailored skirt with corner pleats, remember that the skirt should be lined. When making the length of skirt, join widths of fabric to the total length required, and make the joins so that they are hidden either at corners or inside a pleat or fold.

1 **SKIRT DEPTH** Measure skirt depth, and add 1¼ in (3 cm) for seam allowances. Measure the lining to the same dimensions as the skirt fabric.

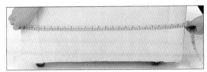

2 **SKIRT SEAM** Measure each side, across skirt seam level, 7 in (18 cm) from floor. Add 5 in (12.5 cm) to each side length for three pleat folds, and 2½ in (6 cm) to ends for zipper opening.

MAKING A CUTTING PLAN

Plain fabrics and fabrics with small patterns are easy to use, while large patterns require more fabric for matching design motifs. Place any motif to the center of each fabric section. Make up a cutting plan. In the plan for the slipcover (see technique, page 140), arrows indicate the straight grain. Draw the dimensions of each fabric piece to scale on paper to enable you to estimate the amount of fabric and assist you in cutting it out. Cut the fabric into rectangles initially, and trim each piece to size as you fit it around the chair. Make a cutting list using the following guideline: outside back: 1; outside arms: 2; front arms: 2; inside back: 1; seat: 1; skirt: cut as required; apron: 1; cushion: cut as required; inside arms: 2; bias strip for piping: cut as required. When cutting out individual pieces, avoid confusion by pinning paper labels to each piece of fabric.

CUTTING PLAN FOR SIMPLE FITTED COVER

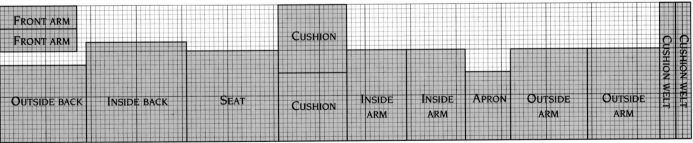

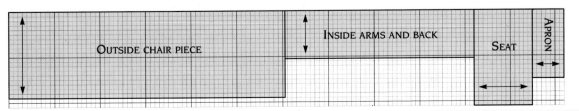

CUTTING PLAN FOR SLIPCOVER (page 140)

FITTING THE COVER

Before fitting the cover, decide whether to fit it right side or wrong side out. Here, the cover is fitted right side out, which facilitates the placement of pattern motifs. However, if it is fitted wrong side out, marking seams is easier. Fit each fabric piece to the chair according to its label (see page 135), and trim to size. You will need the basic sewing kit.

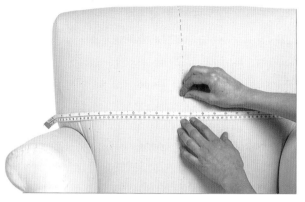

1 MARKING INSIDE BACK Measure the halfway point of the inside back. Using pins or tailor's chalk, mark a vertical line down the center line of the inside back panel on the chair.

2 PINNING FABRIC Place the fabric against the inside back, and center any pattern motif. Mark a line halfway down the fabric piece. Match this line with the line on the chair, and pin the fabric in place down the center.

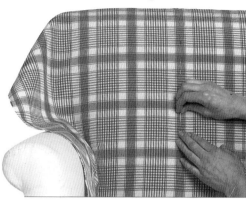

3 PINNING TOP AND SIDES Smooth the inside back fabric piece in place, and pin the top and sides of the fabric piece to the outside back of the chair. Cut away any surplus fabric at the corners.

4 WORKING AROUND ARMS Smooth and pin the fabric around the arms, then trim and clip the fabric to leave a 1 in (2.5 cm) seam allowance. Leave a 6 in (15 cm) allowance for tuck-in at the back of the seat, then trim away any excess fabric.

Pull and pin fabric around shape of chair to ensure a close fit

Cut away bulk of excess fabric at corners

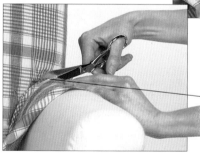

Clip to fit when working around a curve, and always leave a 1 in (2.5 cm) seam allowance

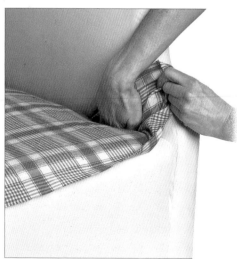

5 MARKING SEAT Measure the halfway point on the seat. Mark a vertical line down the center of the seat and along the center of the fabric seat piece. Place the fabric on the seat and match the two lines.

6 TUCKING IN FABRIC Center and pin the seat fabric along the front edge of the seat, and overlap the inside back piece. Smooth the 6 in (15 cm) tuck-ins in place at the back and sides. Pin the fabric at the sides.

7 PLACING APRON Center and pin the apron fabric piece near the top edge of the apron. Make sure the piece is positioned so that you have 1 in (2.5 cm) for the seams at the seat front, as well as at the arm fronts.

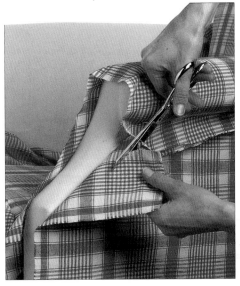

8 TRIMMING INSIDE ARMS Pin the inside arm pieces in place. Trim to shape, leaving 1 in (2.5 cm) for seams. Smooth the tuck-in allowance between the arm and seat.

9 SHAPING OUTSIDE ARMS Pin the outside arm fabric in place. Trim to shape as necessary, allowing 1 in (2.5 cm) for front arm, inside arm, and outside back seams.

10 CUTTING FRONT ARMS Pin the pair of front-arm fabric pieces to the front arms. Cut the fabric to the shape of the front arms, then clip the seam allowances.

11 PINNING OUTSIDE BACK
Mark the center line of the outside back of the chair. Position the outside back piece on the chair, then mark halfway. Allow an extra 2½ in (6 cm) for a zipper at the opening edge. Pin fabric near seam, then trim to shape. Allow 1 in (2.5 cm) for all seams, and 2½ in (6 cm) at zipper opening edge.

12 PINNING SEAMS Work around the chair, and pin the fabric together at all the seams. Be sure to remember every seam line.

Pin close to all seam lines

MARKING ON WRONG SIDE

If the cover has been pinned to the chair with the wrong side out, you can use a vanishing-ink pen to mark the seam lines on the wrong side of the fabric as shown. You might also want to mark some matching points on adjoining pieces to help you align them when the cover has been removed from the chair.

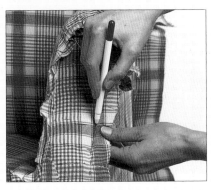

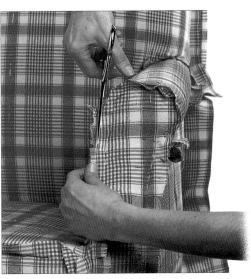

13 DRAWING ACROSS SEAM ALLOWANCES Open the seam allowances in short lengths at a time, and run a vanishing-ink pen or tailor's chalk along the seam lines on the wrong side of the fabric. Mark the matching points for the seams by drawing across the seam allowances. On the straight seams these marks should be 6–8 in (15–20 cm) apart, and on the curved seams they should be every 2 in (5 cm) to ensure accuracy of fit.

14 TRIMMING SEAMS Trim all seams to ⅝ in (1.5 cm), but leave the 2½ in (6 cm) allowance at the zipper opening edge. Remove all pins and fabric pieces from the chair, and relabel the pieces if necessary.

SEWING THE COVER

Before assembling the pieces right sides together by pinning, tacking, and sewing, make the piping *(see page 22)* with medium-weight piping cord to the length required *(see page 134).* Also select cord for the drawstring that secures the corners of the cover underneath the chair, and choose the fastening, such as a zipper, for the opening at the bottom of the join of the outside back and an outside arm piece. To sew the fabric pieces together, you will need the basic sewing kit. Once you begin, check the fit of the cover and adjust it if necessary. Neaten raw seams as you go, and press them open.

1 SEWING CORNERS Pin, tack, and sew the corners on the top edge of the inside back piece to the outside back piece.

2 SEAT AND APRON Pin, tack, and sew the front edge of the seat piece to the top edge of the apron piece.

3 INSIDE ARMS TO BACK AND SEAT Sew one side of the seat to the inside arm. Continue around the seat seam, and attach the lower edge of the inside back piece to the back edge of the seat piece. Attach the other inside arm piece to the seat piece. Sew the inside arms to the inside back piece.

4 PINNING TUCK-INS
Chairs are rarely perfectly square, so your fabric tuck-ins will often not match exactly. To square off the tuck-in, fold the excess fabric of the longer piece over the edge of the shorter piece near to an inside back corner. Next, pin, tack, and sew the outside arms to the inside arms.

Stitch piping to front arm piece along seam line

5 APPLYING PIPING TO FRONT ARM Pin, tack, and sew the piping to the seam line of the front arm pieces. Take care not to stretch the piping when applying it to the curve.

6 CHECKING FIT Pin and tack the outside and inside arm, and the apron, to the edge of the front arm piece, following the seam line. Place these pieces on the chair to check for fit before sewing. When sewing them together, use the zipper-foot attachment on the sewing machine. Repeat for other arm.

Check fit around front arm before sewing

Use a zipper-foot attachment to sew close to piping

Tack cover pieces to outside back piece following seam lines

7 ATTACHING BACK PIECE Pin, tack, and sew the piping to the outside back piece at the seam line. Sew the rest of the cover to the back piece. Leave a 2½ in (6 cm) allowance for the opening at the lower edge of the back and outside arm pieces.

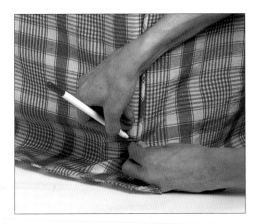

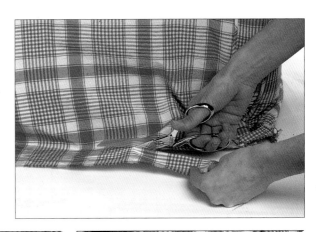

8 MARKING FASTENING
Put the cover on the chair, and mark the bottom edge of the chair on the fabric. This is the position for the bottom end of the fastening. Remove the cover and insert the zipper (see page 29) to the cover opening.

9 TRIMMING SURPLUS
Again, fit the cover onto the chair. Check that the surplus fabric at the bottom edge is the same dimension all around the chair, and trim if necessary.

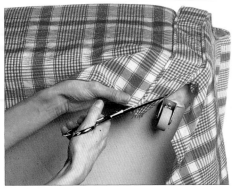

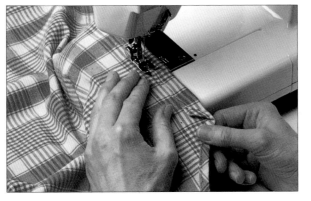

Trim cords to ease securing ends of piping to cover

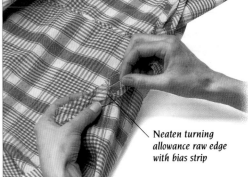

Neaten turning allowance raw edge with bias strip

10 TRIMMING AROUND LEGS
Lay the chair on its back, and unpick the corner seams to the level of the bottom edge of the chair. Trim the fabric to fit around the legs, leaving a ⅜ in (1 cm) allowance for the turnings.

11 SNIPPING CORD
Because sewing through the ends of piping cord can be difficult, it is easiest to trim the piping cord at the ends by pulling it from the bias covering and snipping off ¾ in (2 cm).

12 ATTACHING BIAS STRIP
Neaten the lower edge of the turning allowance around the leg by using a bias strip (see page 22) or by turning a 3/16 in (5 mm) double hem. Repeat this step for the remaining legs of the chair.

13 SEWING DRAWSTRING CASING
Make the drawstring casings by turning the raw edge of each bottom tuck-under section ⅜ in (1 cm) and then ¾ in (2 cm) to the wrong side, and pin, tack, and sew to secure.

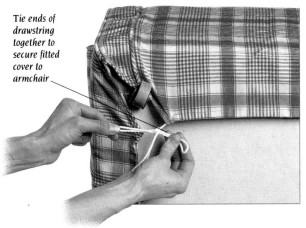

Tie ends of drawstring together to secure fitted cover to armchair

14 SECURING DRAWSTRING ENDS
Place the cover on the chair, thread the drawstrings through the casings, and tie the ends with bows to secure. Smooth out any wrinkles in the chair cover, push down the tuck-ins, and check that the piping is lying straight.

THE COVERED ARMCHAIR

MAKING AND FITTING A SKIRT

Mark the position of the skirt's top edge with a line of pins around the cover. Here, the top edge of the skirt is 7 in (18 cm) from the floor. Check that the line is level, then remove the cover. Cut the fabric to the length and depth required *(see page 135)*. Join fabric to make length with plain flat seams *(see page 16)*. Cut the lining to the size of the skirt. Make any joins with plain flat seams. Press open seams. Place the skirt and lining pieces right sides together. Sew a plain flat seam ⅝ in (1.5 cm) from the lower edge. Turn the pieces right side out and press. The seam between lining and skirt should lie on lining side, ⅛–³⁄₁₆ in (3–5 mm) from edge.

1 ATTACHING PIPING Pin and tack the piping to the cover along the pinned line, with the piped edge facing away from the bottom edge of the cover. At each edge of the cover opening, trim ¾ in (2 cm) from each end of the piping cord. Turn the ends of the bias strip ¾ in (2 cm) to the wrong side, and slipstitch the ends of the bias strip to neaten and close.

2 TRIMMING LINING Trim the top edge of the lining so that it is level with the skirt fabric. Tack the fabrics together ⅝ in (1.5 cm) along the top edge. Finish the raw side edges of the skirt piece with zigzag stitches.

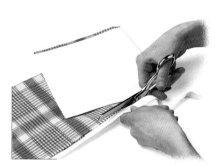

3 SKIRT TO COVER Pin and tack skirt pieces to piped seam line of cover. Fold the three pleats so that the folded edges meet at the corners. Make 2½ in (6 cm) turnings at each side of the opening. Check that bottom edges of skirt match around chair. Sew in place on piped seam line.

THE FINISHED SKIRT

SLIPCOVER

A SLIPCOVER FOR a simply shaped chair or sofa is easy to make and requires only a limited number of fabric pieces. Although the fit of a slipcover will not be quite as snug as that of a simple fitted cover, it is much quicker to make. Use the cutting plan on page 135 to help you visualize the pieces required before you begin measuring the chair.

MAKING THE COVER

A slipcover can be made with ties secured to the underside of the chair, in which case the legs will be visible, or without ties, so that the fabric reaches the floor. To make a cover with ties, allow extra fabric for flaps at all the lower edges. These flaps are folded under the chair at the sides and tied around the legs at each corner. If ties are not required, add a hem allowance of 2 in (5 cm) instead of the extra fabric. You will need cover fabric and the basic sewing kit.

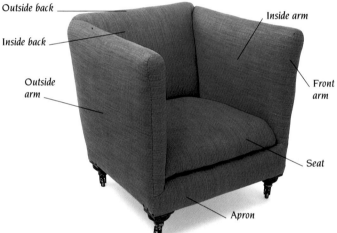

Outside back

Inside back

Outside arm

Inside arm

Front arm

Seat

Apron

MEASURING

Outside of chair: Measure around outside of the chair sides, and chair back at the longest point, from the center of one front arm to the other. Add 1 in (2.5 cm) for each outside arm-piece seam. Measure from the floor to the center of the top of an arm. Add 1 in (2.5 cm) for the top edge seam, and 5 in (12.5 cm) for the tie-under flap.

Inside arms and back: Measure from the seat level to the center of the top of the inside arms. Add 1 in (2.5 cm) for the top edge seam, and 6 in (15 cm) for the tuck-in. Make the inside back piece to this height by the same length as the outside back piece.

Seat: Measure the seat from the back edge to the front edge, adding 6 in (15 cm) for the back tuck-in, and 1 in (2.5 cm) for the apron seam. Measure the seat widthwise from the base of one inside arm to the other at the widest point, plus 6 in (15 cm) to each side for the tuck-ins.

Apron: Measure the apron piece as the width of the seat, plus 2 in (5 cm), by the drop from the seat edge to the floor. Add 1 in (2.5 cm) for the top seam and 2 in (5 cm) for the lower hem allowance. For tie-up flaps, add 1 in (2.5 cm) for seams and 5 in (12.5 cm) for the tie-under flap at the front. Decide on length and width of ties, and cut them out.

Cutting out: Make a cutting plan *(see page 135)*. When cutting out the fabric widths to make the inside and outside back pieces, consider the design motifs of the fabric, as well as the seam positions. Cut out the fabric along the straight grain.

1 MARKING CENTRAL POINTS Mark the central point on the back edge of the seat piece, and the central point on the inside back piece, using a vanishing-ink pen.

Make all seams 1 in (2.5 cm) from raw edges

2 MATCHING CENTRAL PANELS Match the central points of the inside seat pieces. Lay the two panels of fabric right sides together.

3 SEAT TO INSIDE BACK Sew seat piece to inside back piece. Trim the inside back allowance at corners, and neaten seam edges separately with zigzag stitch. Mark central point of front edge of the seat piece, and central point of the top edge of the apron piece.

4 SEAT TO APRON Match the central points of seat front edge and the apron top edge, then sew the seat piece to the apron piece right sides together. Stop at the edge of the seat seam, and snip into the seat seam allowance to turn the corners at the top of the apron.

5 OUTSIDE TO INSIDE CHAIR Pin, tack, and sew the outside back piece to the inside back piece, with the right sides together. The seams should be 1 in (2.5 cm) from the edges. Do not sew front edges of the arms.

6 SEWING ARM EDGES At the front edges of the arms, pin, tack, and sew the outside back piece to the inside back piece, with the right sides together. Stop at the edge of the seat seam.

7 OUTSIDE CHAIR TO APRON Pin, tack, and sew the outside back piece to the apron piece, with the right sides together. Make sure that the seat piece seam is turned back out of the way.

Keep seat-piece seam allowance away from apron and back-piece seam line

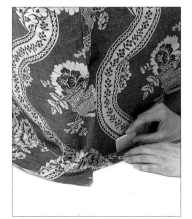

8 MARKING LENGTH Put the cover on the chair and check the length. Trim the cover to reduce the bulk if necessary, but leave a 2 in (5 cm) seam allowance. Mark the required length with tailor's chalk or pins. Remove the cover, and turn and sew a double 1 in (2.5 cm) hem. Press and refit the cover.

THE COVERED ARMCHAIR

TIE-ON COVER

Lay the chair on its back, and trim excess fabric at corners to fit around the legs. Leave a 1 in (2.5 cm) hem allowance for the edges. Turn ⅜ in (1 cm) double hems at side edges of the flaps, and ⅜ in (1 cm) double hems on the longer edges. Make four pairs of fabric ties *(see page 27)*. Sew ties to the flap corners. Fit the cover. Secure ties around the chair legs.

FOOTSTOOLS

*M*AKING A CLOSE-FITTING COVER for a footstool is the simplest form of upholstery, requiring few tools and involving no complicated stitchwork. To decorate a large footstool, you might want to attach buttons to the seat – you can cover the buttons with a fabric that matches or contrasts with the upholstery fabric. If you have an old footstool that is in need of new upholstery, consider having the seat restuffed with fireproof padding materials by a professional before you begin making the new cover.

SMALL FOOTSTOOL

Furniture suppliers have stocks of undecorated cover fabric or muslin ready for upholstery. For a patterned fabric, lay the material over the stool to confirm that the scale of the design is suitable. Measure the dimension of the old cover, adding a 6 in (15 cm) allowance when cutting out. To make the cover, you will need fabric, a length of braid to cover fittings around the base, upholstery skewers, fabric glue, a staple gun or upholstery tacks, a small hammer, and the basic sewing kit.

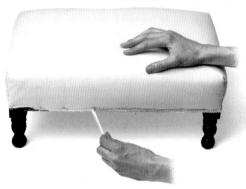

1 REMOVING OLD BRAID Place the footstool on a raised, flat surface, such as a kitchen table or workbench, and remove the old braid from around the edge of the muslin or old cover. If damaged or worn out, you may need to remove the old cover completely.

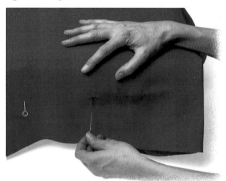

2 FITTING FABRIC Lay fabric over the footstool. Secure fabric in place by pinning it to the muslin or old cover, using the upholstery skewers. Pull fabric down tightly. Continue tightening and securing fabric as you move around the stool, folding the fabric neatly at the corners.

3 TRIMMING EXCESS Make sure that the cover fabric is centered and aligned on the stool. Trim the excess fabric from around the perimeter of the stool to the base of the seat.

4 SECURING FABRIC Lay the stool on its side and, using a staple gun or small tacks and hammer, fasten the fabric onto the wooden frame. Secure the fabric around the frame. Remove the upholstery skewers.

5 NEATENING CORNERS Neaten and secure the overlap of fabric at the corners by hand sewing, using a ladder stitch *(see page 15).* Use thread that complements the fabric.

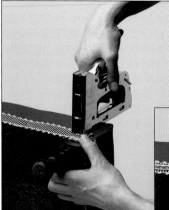

6 ATTACHING BRAID With more than one braid layer, staple or tack first length in place. Apply second using glue. A single edging strip should be glued over the staples or tacks. Where the braid ends meet, glue the overlap.

THE COVERED FOOTSTOOL

LARGE FOOTSTOOL WITH BUTTONS

Measure the old cover, adding 16 in (40 cm) to the length and width. Lay the covering fabric over the footstool to center any pattern and to align the grain. Cut out the fabric to the required dimensions. You will need covering fabric, two-part buttons, upholstery skewers, fabric glue, braid, tacks, a hammer or staple gun, upholstery twine, spare muslin, and the basic sewing kit.

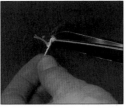 

1 POSITIONING BUTTON Position cut fabric over stool. If stool has buttons, press into each button crevice and mark button placements. If there are no buttons, mark positions equidistantly on fabric and muslin in line with edges of stool. Cut through muslin at button positions. Remove enough padding to push your finger through to the frame.

2 REMOVING OLD TWINE Remove any old buttons by cutting through the upholstery twine that is secured to the underside of the seat of the footstool.

3 COVERING BUTTONS Cover buttons with fabric *(see page 28).* Lay fabric on stool, aligning button marks. Press your finger into central button position to fit fabric into hole. Secure fabric over stool with upholstery skewers, allowing slack for attaching buttons.

4 INSERTING TWINE Thread an upholstery needle with a long piece of strong twine. Starting with central button, push the eye end of needle up from the underside of the stool through to the top of the seat at the corresponding button position.

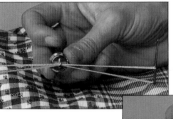

5 THREADING BUTTON At the surface of the fabric, pull twine through, leaving needle and remainder of twine inserted in the seat. Fasten a button onto twine by looping thread through and over the button. Return the needle to underside through same hole.

6 SECURING BUTTON Roll a 1½ in (4 cm) square piece of muslin. Slip this between cords and against underside of stool. Slipknot cords together around muslin piece. Pull on center button to take up fabric slack, and tie off on stool underside. On upper side of stool, fabric will pleat into central buttonhole.

Pull looped thread through and around button shank

Adjust pleats before securing buttons underneath footstool

8 FINISHING BUTTONS When pleats are evenly gathered, turn stool on its side. Make sure slipknots securing each button are well fastened. You can also staple ties against the stool underside. Snip off the excess twine.

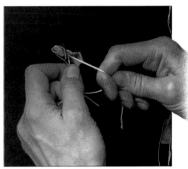

7 ADJUSTING PLEATING Repeat threading, tightening, and tying off process for other buttons. From center outward, unpin and ease fabric across stool to make pleats between buttons. Adjust pleating as necessary.

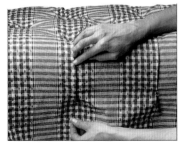

9 SECURING COVER Stretch fabric over seat, securing tucks created by excess fabric around button by pinning in place with skewers. Pull down and pin in between pleats. Fold corners neatly. Stretch, tuck, and pin the fabric in place around the stool.

10 REMOVING EXCESS Cut off excess fabric to the base of the seat. Staple or tack fabric in place. Remove skewers. Using thread that matches or contrasts with the fabric, secure corners with a ladder stitch. Cut a length of braid to the required dimension and glue or sew in place, covering staples or tacks and raw edges of the fabric.

THE COVERED FOOTSTOOL

TABLE LINEN

$\mathcal{M}$ORE THAN SIMPLY PROTECTING A TABLETOP, table linen also provides a convenient way of introducing an element of color, pattern, and texture to a room. Pieces of fabric have long been used not only as practical coverings for protecting the tops of fine-quality tables, but also as a means of dressing up everyday furniture in order to turn it into something special. Historically, textiles of exotic origins, such as small Turkish carpets or shawls from Kashmir, were often used for this purpose. When the table was in use, the fine textile was protected by an easily washable tablecloth, such as a square of white cotton. Tablecloths and napkins are quick to make and require only the simplest of stitches. They can be produced from an enormous range of suitable fabrics, from delicate nets and silks to heavyweight velvet. This chapter demonstrates how to make plain and decorative tablecloths and napkins in a variety of styles and shapes.

CHOOSING A STYLE

*T*ABLE LINEN DOES NOT NEED TO BE RESTRICTED to the dining room: it can be used to set a style for all types of table. Plain linen or cotton tablecloths are practical and elegant and can be enhanced with trimmings, while patterned fabrics can be chosen to coordinate with a room's style. The shape to which you make up a tablecloth is a matter of personal taste. Dining-room and kitchen tablecloths are, however, a comfortable length when they rest on the knees of diners. A dressing table looks good if covered with a long piece of fabric, while display tables can be dressed with two or more layers of contrasting materials in different lengths.

EASY ELEGANCE
The most smoothly elegant way of dressing up a dining-room table is to use a starched, pure white linen or cotton tablecloth, complete with a set of coordinating napkins. Position the tablecloth so that the drop is equal on all four sides above the chairs, and, if possible, allow any decorative features of the table to be seen below the drop of the tablecloth. If you need to protect a table surface, use an underlay in the form of a second, smaller tablecloth.

Crisp white table linen lends itself to stylish formal arrangement

Ironed or starched white napkins coordinate elegantly with tablecloth

CHEERFUL AND INFORMAL
One of life's great pleasures is eating al fresco. Garden furniture can be made to look welcoming with loose-fitting tablecloths and cheerful napkins. Choose fabrics in bright colors and bold patterns for a lively effect outdoors. Ensure that the fabrics you use are washable, and do not leave them out in the sun for prolonged periods, since they will fade.

Informal fabric adds to casual, relaxed atmosphere of eating outdoors

Mixing fabric designs for different furnishings helps create informal atmosphere

SIMPLE AND RESTRAINED

For a tablecloth that is informal and smart, gingham check is an ideal fabric choice. Woven in lightweight cotton, it gives a country look and is effective when used in kitchens as well as in informal dining rooms.

Napkins made up from plain green fabric complement checked tablecloth

LAYERED EFFECTS

When dressing a round table with layers of fabric, it is often best to use a flounced underlying fabric with a rich texture and dark color, in conjunction with a contrasting square of white fabric. For a fully fitted effect, particularly appropriate to display tables, you can make piping around the circumference to create a recess for a glass cover.

PRACTICAL AND STRIKING

Since the kitchen can be one of the most heavily used rooms in the home, the kitchen table may benefit from a sturdy, practical tablecloth. Durable and easy to wipe down, plasticized tablecloths can look vivid and graphic and provide splashes of color and pattern.

Tablecloth fabric has been cut on the round so that it does not interfere with chairs

DECORATIVE AND DISTINCTIVE

When laid over an unused table, a tablecloth can assume a purely decorative character and can provide a welcome splash of color and texture to an otherwise austere room. Here, clean, white-painted walls and hard, plain-tiled floors are lifted by a simple checked tablecloth that is coolly decorative. The rectangular cut and neat pattern of the fabric create an uncluttered effect, and the open weave adds softness.

Simple fabric design of tablecloth complements geometric pattern of wall hanging

Placement of tablecloth allows glimpse of interesting furniture underneath

TABLECLOTHS

*T*HE FABRIC USED FOR TABLECLOTHS should be durable and easy to clean. Your choice of the shape and style of a tablecloth should depend on its use. Full-length tablecloths function well as coverings for display tables, while kitchen or dining tables should have coverings that drop no farther than the seat level of surrounding chairs. Calculate the amount of fabric required, based on accurate measurements of the table. For large tables, avoid making fabric joins that will be visible on the top of the tablecloth by placing a full width of fabric at the center, and adding extra widths at the sides. Join widths with flat fell seams *(see page 17)*.

MEASURING

For all shapes of tablecloth, you will need to know the dimension of the tabletop and the required drop before cutting out the fabric. To determine the required drop for a tablecloth that will cover a kitchen or dining table, measure from the edge of the tabletop to the seat level of a surrounding chair. Find the dimensions for a full-length, decorative tablecloth that will be used on a small display table by measuring from the edge of the tabletop to the floor. To measure and cut out a circular tablecloth for a round tabletop, follow the instructions in steps 1–3 below.

ROUND AND OVAL TABLES

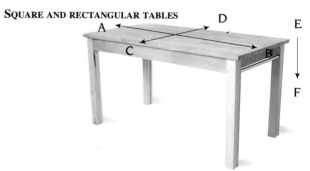

For a square cloth for a round table, measure table's diameter (A–B), and add twice the drop (E–F), plus a 1 in (2.5 cm) hem allowance. This will be the measurement for both sides of the cloth. For a rectangular cloth for an oval table, measure the table's length, and add twice the drop, plus a 1 in (2.5 cm) hem allowance. Measure up in the same way along the width. For an oval cloth for an oval table, pin a paper template of the tabletop to fabric, and add drop (E–F), plus a 1 in (2.5 cm) hem allowance.

SQUARE AND RECTANGULAR TABLES

For a square tablecloth for a square table, or a rectangular tablecloth for a rectangular table, measure the tabletop width (C–D), and add twice the required drop (E–F), plus a 1 in (2.5 cm) hem allowance. Measure the tabletop length (A–B), and add twice the required drop (E–F), plus a 1 in (2.5 cm) hem allowance.

CUTTING OUT A CIRCULAR TABLECLOTH

A circular tablecloth will need to have an equal drop all around. Make an arc-shaped template and use this as a guide to cutting out the fabric to the correct shape. For this technique, you will need a marker, a length of string, and the basic sewing kit. Make a compass by knotting one end of the string around a thumbtack and tying the other end to the marker. You will need to adjust the distance of the string depending on the radius of the tablecloth.

1 FOLDING FABRIC Cut out a fabric square so that each side is equal to the diameter of the tablecloth. This length is twice the drop, plus the table's diameter. Fold the fabric right side together into quarters.

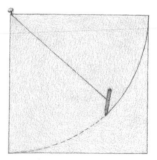

2 MARKING PATTERN Cut a square pattern to the size of the folded fabric. Pin the simple compass at one corner of the pattern. Draw an arc across the paper. Cut out the pattern along the marked line.

3 CUTTING FABRIC Pin the pattern corner to the top of folded fabric corner. Trace arc across folded fabric. Cut fabric along arc. If a hem is required, add necesssary allowance to arc before cutting out the fabric.

OILCLOTH TABLECLOTH WITH BOUND EDGE

When you wish to make a tablecloth for everyday use, you will need to select a fabric that is not only durable, but also easy to keep clean. Cotton fabric is simple to wash but can become stained. A plastic-coated fabric or an oilcloth wipes down easily and is stain resistant. For this technique, you will need the oilcloth fabric and the basic sewing kit.

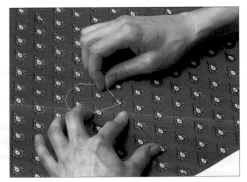

1 JOINING WIDTHS Measure the table and calculate the dimension of the fabric you will need *(see opposite)*. Join fabric widths with flat fell seams *(see page 17)*. First, match the pattern and temporarily secure joins with ladder stitch *(see page 15)*.

2 SEWING WIDTHS Fold the fabric widths right sides together. Pin, tack, and sew along the join ⅝ in (1.5 cm) from the raw edge of each fabric width. Trim one seam allowance to ¼ in (6 mm). Repeat this, if necessary, for any other joins.

3 FINISHING SEAM Fold the wider seam allowance over the shorter one. Press the fold flat. Pin and tack near the raw edge of the wider seam. Turn the fabric right side up and machine sew along the tacked line. Press the seam flat.

Fold long edges of bias strip to right side

4 MAKING BINDING Make a bias strip to the length of the tablecloth's perimeter by twice the desired edging width, plus ¾ in (2 cm) for folds *(see page 22)*. Fold and press the long edges ⅜ in (1 cm) to the right side.

5 ATTACHING BINDING STRIP Open out the binding strip. Place the right side of the binding strip and the right side of the tablecloth fabric together, matching the raw edges. Pin, tack, and sew along the fold line of the binding strip.

6 FOLDING CORNERS At the corners, pinch the binding strip and continue sewing up to, but not over, the fold. Turn the fabric and continue stitching the binding strip to the fabric.

Pin folded edge of binding to wrong side of tablecloth

7 MITERING BINDING Miter the binding at the corners *(see page 21)*. Turn the binding over the raw edge of the fabric, and pin, tack, and sew its folded edge to secure it to the wrong side of the fabric *(see page 16)*. Wrinkles will disappear with use.

THE FINISHED TABLECLOTH

TABLECLOTH WITH KNOTTED FRINGE EDGING

To make up this square tablecloth, you will need a loosely woven fabric that matches the overall design scheme of the room, plus the basic sewing kit. Bear in mind that if you are using a fabric with a woven pattern rather than a printed one, the warp and weft threads may be of different colors, resulting in edging that is not the same color on all sides.

1 SEPARATING THREADS
Measure the round table and cut out a square of fabric *(see page 148)*. Lay the fabric on a flat surface. Use a long needle to tease away threads from one of the raw edges. Carefully separate and remove one thread at a time.

Separate cross-threads with a long needle

2 REMOVING THREADS
Remove the threads by pulling each strand away from the fabric. Continue separating and removing threads all around until you reach the desired fringe depth. The fringe should be long enough for knotting. Here, it is 3 in (7.5 cm) long.

Pull away cross-threads from fabric to leave fringe edging

3 GROUPING FRINGE Working along one edge at a time, divide the fringe into small groups of an equal size. Separate each group into two.

4 KNOTTING FRINGE Make a knot with each of the smaller groups of fringe. Push it toward the edge of the cloth to prevent the fabric from unraveling. Repeat knotting all around the cloth.

THE FINISHED TABLECLOTH

LINEN TABLECLOTH WITH LACE EDGING

A linen tablecloth with a lace edging creates a traditional effect. If you have an old tablecloth with a lace edging, consider removing the edging and attaching it to new fabric. For this technique, you will need linen fabric, lace from an old tablecloth, and the basic sewing kit. Wash the old lace, cover it with a damp cloth, and press. Cut the fabric so that it fits within the lace edging, adding 4 in (10 cm) all around for hems. Join widths with flat fell seams *(see page 17)*.

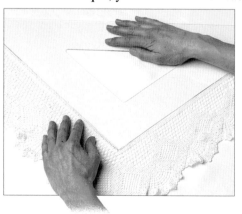

1 ALIGNING CORNER Lay the linen fabric on a flat surface and place the edging around it, aligning the corners. Use a try square to make sure that the corners of the edging are as square as possible. Measure the edges to ensure they are of equal length.

2 POSITIONING EDGING Use a vanishing-ink pen, tailor's chalk, or pushpins to mark the inner edge of the lace on the linen fabric. Remove the edging.

For a professional finish, always use a try square when marking fabric

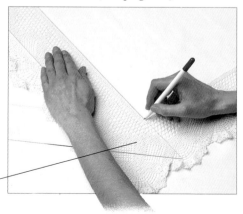

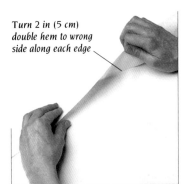

3 MARKING FABRIC You will need a large, double hem for antique lace to give it extra support. Here, a 2 in (5 cm) double hem is required. Mark a line 4 in (10 cm) – twice the double hem – from the first line. Cut fabric around this outer line.

Turn 2 in (5 cm) double hem to wrong side along each edge

4 TURNING HEM Working along each of the four edges at a time, fold a 2 in (5 cm) double hem, and press.

Trim along mitered corner fold to remove excess fabric

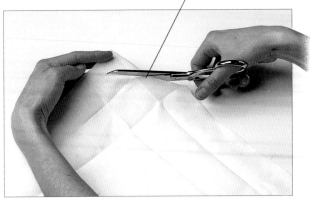

5 TRIMMING CORNER To form corners, unfold the two layers of fabric at each corner, then fold the first turning into a miter *(see page 21)*, and press. Unfold the mitered corner and trim along the fold. Refold the double hem and miter each corner.

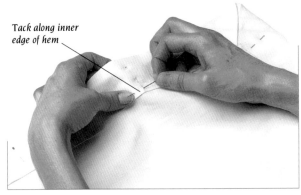

Tack along inner edge of hem

6 TACKING HEM Pin and tack ⅜ in (1 cm) from the inner edge of the hem. Use slipstitch or topstitch to secure the hem.

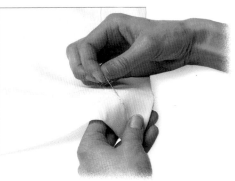

7 STITCHING CORNER At the four mitered corners, neaten the miters by slipstitching the folded edges together.

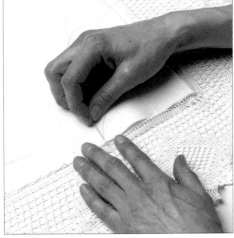

8 ATTACHING EDGING Lay the fabric on a flat surface and carefully position the edging around it. Tack the edging to the fabric, using large slipstitches – do not use pins, which could damage the fragile lace.

9 SECURING LACE Secure the lace edging carefully to the fabric, using slipstitch or shallow zigzag stitch *(see page 16)*. Press the finished tablecloth.

THE FINISHED TABLECLOTH

FRINGED TABLECLOTH

When choosing the material for this tablecloth, bear in mind that loosely woven, medium-weight fabric lends itself best to a fringed edging. For this technique, you will need the fabric and the basic sewing kit. Measure your table *(see page 148)*, then cut out the fabric to the required size, adding extra for the fringe allowance and for any seams.

1 FRAYING EDGE Lay out the fabric on a flat surface. Using a long needle, separate and remove a thread at a time from one edge of the fabric. Continue fraying the edge until the fringe reaches the depth you desire. Fray the remaining edges until you have created the same depth of fringe on all four sides.

2 SECURING EDGE To prevent the fabric from unraveling further, secure the unfrayed edge of the fabric with zigzag stitch *(see page 16)*. Press the tablecloth before use.

THE FINISHED TABLECLOTH

FRINGED TABLECLOTH WITH SCALLOPED EDGE

Ready-made trimmings can be used to decorate the edges of tablecloths, adding character to these furnishings. The fabric you choose for a tablecloth should depend on the nature of its use; a plastic-coated fabric is ideal for a kitchen table. You can create scallops along the edges of the fabric – this is a simple task, since this fabric does not fray and therefore does not require hemming. For this technique, you will need a plastic-coated fabric, fringe, saucer, and the basic sewing kit.

1 MARKING FABRIC Measure your table and add the desired drop of the tablecloth *(see page 148)*. Mark this dimension on the wrong side of the fabric, using a try square, tape measure, and vanishing-ink pen.

2 POSITIONING SCALLOP On the wrong side of the fabric, mark the scallop positions along the line. Try to fit an equal number of scallops on each side, and one complete scallop around each corner. This might take a few attempts.

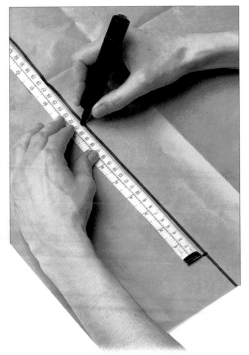

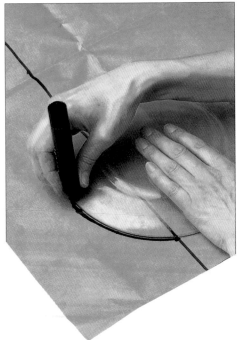

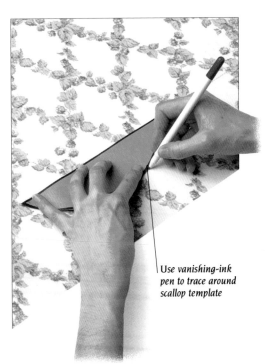

Use vanishing-ink pen to trace around scallop template

3 MARKING PATTERN On a piece of paper, mark a line longer than the length of one scallop. Measure and mark the exact length of one scallop on this line.

4 DRAWING SCALLOP Use a saucer or other circular object as a guide for drawing a suitable curve between the scallop marks on the paper.

5 TRACING PATTERN Cut out the pattern, and place the straight edge against the marked line on the wrong side of the fabric. Trace around the template.

6 CUTTING OUT SCALLOP Following the marked scallop positions along the line, carefully cut out the scallops around the fabric.

Plastic-coated material is self-neatening and does not require hemming

7 ATTACHING FRINGE Plastic-coated material is self-neatening and therefore does not require a hem. Tack the ready-made fringe to the scalloped edge of the fabric. When you have attached the fringe along all four sides, machine sew it in place.

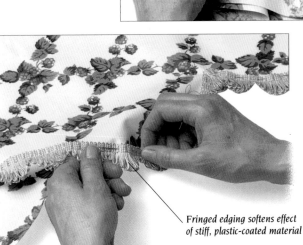

Fringed edging softens effect of stiff, plastic-coated material

THE FINISHED TABLECLOTH

FULL-LENGTH TABLECLOTH WITH TASSELED EDGING

A full-length tablecloth is ideal for dressing a small table or stand. It can also be used as an undercloth when dressing a table with layers of contrasting fabric, acting as a skirt under smaller fabrics. To make this full-length tablecloth with edging, you will need heavyweight fabric for the tablecloth, edging, a length of string, marker, and the basic sewing kit.

1 JOINING FABRIC Measure the table and drop, minus the depth of the edging *(see page 148)*. Join sections of fabric, if necessary, with flat fell seams *(see page 17)* to make a large square of cloth that is equal to the dimensions of the table and drop. Fold the fabric right sides together into quarters.

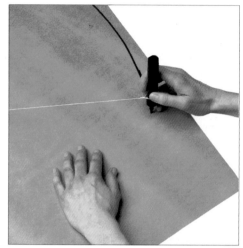

2 MAKING PATTERN Make a square template to the size of the fabric when folded. Using a simple compass pinned to a corner of the template, draw an arc across the paper from one corner to the other *(see page 148)*.

3 MARKING FABRIC Cut out the paper pattern along the arc. Pin the pattern to the folded fabric, aligning the arc with the open edges of the folded fabric. On the wrong side of the fabric, trace around the pattern, adding ¾ in (2 cm) for a single turned hem. Cut out the fabric along the marked line.

4 STITCHING HEM Open out the fabric. Neaten the raw edge of the fabric by turning a ¾ in (2 cm) hem all around. Pin, tack, and sew the hem, then remove the tacking stitches.

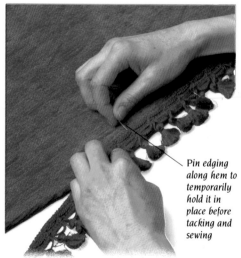

Pin edging along hem to temporarily hold it in place before tacking and sewing

5 PINNING EDGING Measure the circumference of the tablecloth. Cut the edging to the same length as the tablecloth's circumference. Pin the edging along the hem, keeping a straight line.

6 JOINING ENDS Tack and sew the edging to the tablecloth. Where the ends of the edging meet, oversew to make a neat join. Press the fabric carefully before fitting it on the table.

THE FINISHED TABLECLOTH

TABLECLOTH WITH GATHERED SKIRT

To make this two-piece tablecloth, you will need fabric for the tablecloth and piping, piping cord, a length of strong twine, and the basic sewing kit. Measure the tabletop *(see page 148)*. Make a square of fabric to this dimension, joining fabric widths as necessary with flat fell seams *(see page 17)*. Fold the fabric right sides together into quarters.

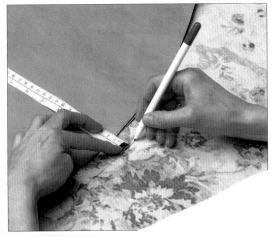

1 MARKING FABRIC Make pattern to size of folded fabric. Cut out a quarter circle *(see page 148)*. Pin pattern to wrong side of fabric. Trace around it, adding ¾ in (2 cm) for seams. Cut fabric along marked line. Make piping to length of table's circumference. Add 4 in (10 cm) for joining *(see page 22)*. Cut out fabric widths for skirt to depth required, plus 2 in (5 cm) for seams and hems by one-and-a-half times piping length.

2 ATTACHING PIPING Pin, tack, and sew the piping to the right side of the top panel, with the piping seam allowance to the outside edge. Join the ends of the piping together.

Attach piping to right side of top panel

3 MAKING SKIRT To make one length of fabric, pin the widths of the skirt together, matching any motifs *(see page 18)*. Make joins with plain flat seams *(see page 16)*.

4 HEMMING SKIRT Neaten the lower edge of the skirt with a row of zigzag stitches *(see page 16)*. Turn a ¾ in (2 cm) hem to the wrong side along the lower edge, and herringbone stitch or machine sew to secure.

5 ATTACHING TWINE Cut twine to the table's circumference. Place it ¾ in (2 cm) from skirt's top edge. Sew zigzag stitches over twine to secure *(see page 24)*. Mark quarter intervals around edge of top panel. Make matching marks on skirt's top edge.

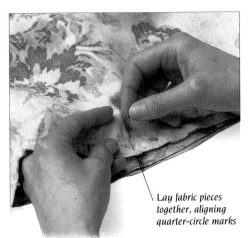

Lay fabric pieces together, aligning quarter-circle marks

6 ALIGNING FABRICS Place top panel and skirt right sides together. Align the quarter-circle marks. At the marks, pin the skirt to the top panel along the piped edge.

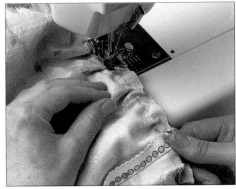

7 SECURING SKIRT Pull the twine to gather skirt, working first from one end and then the other, so that half of the skirt is gathered at a time. Once the gathers are evenly distributed, pin, tack, and sew the skirt to the top panel ⅝ in (1.5 cm) from the raw edges. Press the tablecloth on the right side.

THE FINISHED TABLECLOTH

NAPKINS

NAPKINS ARE THE MOST FREQUENTLY USED TABLE LINEN, and should therefore be made from durable and easy-to-clean fabric. Although there are no hard-and-fast rules, you should try to match the size of the napkin with its intended use – a small napkin is adequate for informal occasions and light meals, while a large napkin is more suitable for dinner parties and formal events. There are plenty of sturdy, colorful fabrics to choose from, and you can make napkins to either match or contrast with your other table linen. Napkins can also be edged with decorative trimmings such as binding or scallops.

PLAIN NAPKIN

When choosing fabric for small napkins, consider using scraps from other soft furnishings. Napkins can be made to any size, but should be no smaller than 12 in (30 cm) square.

When cutting out, make sure to match the grain of the fabric and cut the corners perfectly square. To make this simple napkin, use suitable fabric and the basic sewing kit.

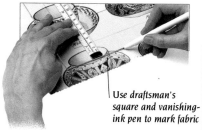

Use draftsman's square and vanishing-ink pen to mark fabric

Refold edges and miter cut corners

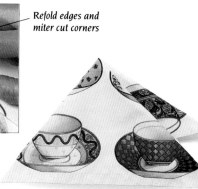

THE FINISHED NAPKIN

1 MARKING FABRIC Mark the fabric to the required size, adding an extra 1¼ in (3 cm) to each side for turning double hems. Make sure that you achieve a perfect square.

2 TRIMMING CORNER Fold a ⅝ in (1.5 cm) double hem on all sides, and press. Unfold edges. Miter corners *(see page 21)* along first fold line, and press. Unfold corners. Cut across each corner.

3 FOLDING MITER Refold edges and finish mitering corners. Slipstitch hems and miters, or topstitch using a sewing machine *(see page 17)*. Press the napkin before use.

NAPKIN WITH BOUND EDGE

For this technique, you will need napkin fabric, edging fabric, and the basic sewing kit. Cut a square piece of fabric to the size required. Cut two binding strips to the length of the napkin, adding ¾ in (2 cm) for turnings, by double the depth

of the edging required. Cut two more binding strips to the length of the napkin, plus 1½ in (4 cm), by double the edging depth required. Fold and press ⅜ in (1 cm) turnings to the wrong side along the long edges of the binding strips.

Trim inner ends of binding to reduce fabric bulk

THE FINISHED NAPKIN

1 ATTACHING BINDING Open out the binding strips. Place the shorter binding strips on two opposing napkin edges, right sides together. Match the raw edges. Pin, tack, and sew along fold line of binding seam allowance. Press seams open.

2 TRIMMING BINDING ENDS To reduce the binding fabric bulk, trim the ¾ in (2 cm) overhangs at the ends of the longer strips to blunt points.

3 PINNING BINDING Place the longer binding strips on the remaining opposing sides of the napkin, right sides together. Sew them along the binding fold line. Fold the corners inward and trim the seam allowances. Fold all strips over the raw edges of the napkin. Pin and tack in place. Slipstitch the binding to the fabric along the binding's folded edge.

SHEER NAPKIN WITH SCALLOPS

This type of scalloped edging is produced using a simple hand-sewn technique. It works best with lightweight and sheer fabrics. For this technique, you will need lightweight or sheer fabric and the basic sewing kit. Cut out the fabric to the size required, adding ⅝ in (1.5 cm) all around for the scalloped hems.

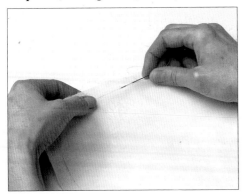

1 TACKING HEM LINE On the wrong side of the fabric, use a vanishing-ink pen to mark the hem line ⅝ in (1.5 cm) from the edges. Tack along the line. Fold each edge twice to meet the tacking line, and press.

2 SECURING CORNER Starting at one corner, oversew across the corner, securing it to the wrong side of the fabric with four or five stitches (see page 16).

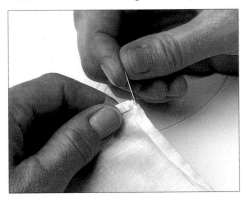

3 BEGINNING SCALLOP Insert the needle at the outer edge of the hem near the corner. Push the needle diagonally to the inside of the hem – the wider the diagonal, the larger the scallops will be.

4 STITCHING HEM Oversew the hem and insert the needle perpendicularly to the edge. Push the needle through to the inside of the hem so that it emerges at the same exit point as in step 3.

5 FINISHING SCALLOP Oversew the hem again, exiting from the same inside point, to form a scallop. Make one blanket stitch to lock in thread (see page 15). Continue the handsewing process along the edge of the napkin and the remaining sides. Oversew each corner with four or five stitches.

THE FINISHED NAPKIN

CUT SCALLOPS

You will need medium-weight fabric and the basic sewing kit. Cut the fabric to size, allowing ¾ in (2 cm) extra for the edging. Make a paper strip 2 in (5 cm) wide by the napkin length. Fold the paper into sections equal to each scallop length (see page 152). Draw a curve on the paper perpendicular to the folded edge. Cut along the curve and unfold pattern. Pin the pattern to one edge of the fabric. Draw the outlines of the scallops. Mark the outlines on the remaining three sides of the fabric.

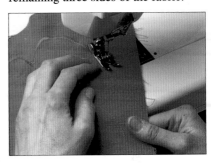

1 STITCHING SCALLOPS Topstitch along the scallop lines to prevent the fabric from stretching (see page 17). Machine sew a close zigzag (see page 16) along the marked lines to border the edges of the scallops.

2 TRIMMING EXCESS Carefully cut away the excess fabric close to the zigzag stitching line. Press the napkin before use.

THE FINISHED NAPKIN

LAMPSHADES

*I*MPORTANT FURNISHING ACCESSORIES, lampshades not only reduce the glow from artificial light sources but also direct and color the light in a room. Making your own lampshades to harmonize with the style of individual rooms is a rewarding task, since you can design shades specifically to match the colors and complement the decor in each room. Fabric lampshades can be made from a variety of different materials, including scraps from the main soft furnishings in a room. For a pleated effect, make up a gathered-fabric lampshade with an optional frill. A lined, tailored lampshade has an elegant shape and can be accessorized with a trim of braid or ribbon. Paper or cardboard lampshades will give a modern dimension to your decorative scheme. Pleated paper lampshades can be assembled from remnants of the wallpaper used in a room, and plain-sided cardboard shades have the advantage of being suitable for many types of lighting.

CHOOSING A STYLE

*A*LTHOUGH THEY ARE OFTEN CONSIDERED to be peripheral accessories, lampshades can play a key role in a decorative scheme. The size and shape of a lampshade are important design considerations; a shade will look best when it is in proportion to the lamp base and in style with the room. The color and texture of the material used for the shade will directly affect the appearance of the lampshade and the quality of the light. A translucent cover of silk, lightweight cotton, or paper casts a soft glow of light, whereas dark cardboard or completely opaque fabric directs the light above and below the lampshade.

Small candle shades combine to create a subdued glow

Dark-colored cardboard throws light above and below lampshade

SMALL AND ELEGANT
Small cardboard lampshades are versatile and easy to assemble. To increase their decorative impact, you can add stenciled designs or apply simple lines of color around their top and bottom circumferences. There are special frames available for making small, neat candle shades. These look ideal grouped on a chandelier or placed on candlestick lamp bases.

MODERN AND PRACTICAL
At a table, where you will probably need general-purpose, overhead illumination, a conical shade made from semitranslucent paper or cardboard is the most suitable design. If you need to raise and lower the light source, use an adjustable fixture.

Conical shape is designed to cast most of the light downward

SOPHISTICATED PLEATS
Making pleated lampshades allows you to experiment with a range of plain or patterned papers. It is easy to create shades in all shapes and sizes – from straight-sided drums to heavily graduated cones – to suit the style of a room.

Patterned cardboard harmonizes with room's decorative scheme

CHARACTERFUL SHAPES

When used on lampshades, knife-pleats bring out the texture of the fabric and the shape of the shade. A popular style for tall lamp bases, these pleated, sophisticated lampshades produce a gentle glow that is ideal for bedrooms.

ORNAMENTAL TRIMMINGS

Pleated lampshades are popular choices for ceramic lamp bases as well as for pendant fixtures. You can use a length of ribbon to gather and hold the pleats around the ring to the required shape, and to act as a decorative accessory.

FORMAL EFFECTS

You can use almost any kind of lightweight to medium-weight furnishing fabric for lampshade covers. It is always beneficial, however, to choose a style of fabric that works well with the surrounding furnishings. Amid desk clutter and against richly colored curtains, a plain fabric lampshade in pale cotton will serve as a discreet and efficient means of directing light over a work area. The lining fabric should meet your lighting needs. White silk tends to reflect the light outward from within the frame; translucent cotton diffuses a warm glow from the center of the lampshade.

Pleats are stretched and flattened between top and bottom rings, producing a formal character with plain fabric

Flat, vertical pleats complement neoclassical decorative scheme of study

SLIM AND TUBULAR

Craft cardboard or heavyweight paper is the perfect medium for unorthodox shapes of lampshade. Here, a length of cardboard has been cut and secured to two rings, forming a tube that makes a visually striking lampshade when set on a tall candlestick lamp base.

EFFICIENT AND MODERN

If you need a light source that will cast a good light over a seating area, use a conical-shaped lampshade. The broad circumference of the lampshade base is designed for dispersing a pool of light over a wide surface area.

LAMPSHADE FRAMES

RIGID LAMPSHADE FRAMES, WHICH ARE MADE of lightweight metal, are needed to provide support, structure, and shape for many types of lampshades. The frames are available from specialist suppliers in a wide variety of shapes and sizes. Lampshades made from self-supporting stiff paper or lightweight cardboard can be supported by specially made lower and upper rings, which are obtainable in different diameters. When choosing a suitable frame, you will need to decide on the size and shape of the finished lampshade, and take into account the material for the cover and any trimmings that you might wish to add.

CHOOSING A FRAME

The exact shape of a lampshade is determined by the size and style of the frame, or – in the case of a ring-mounted lampshade – by the diameter of the upper and lower support rings and the distance between them. Fabric lampshades always need the support of a rigid frame; cardboard and paper are best suited to being supported on specially made rings.

FRAMES
Lampshade frames are available in an extraordinary variety of shapes and sizes to suit every decorative style. They are designed to fit lamp bases, pendant light fixtures, and even candles. Lightbulb clips are used for supporting very small lampshades. The metallic frames are sold either unfinished or coated in white enamel paint.

DUPLEX FRAME

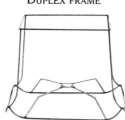

SINGLE-SIDED LAMP-BASE FRAME

SQUARE LAMP-BASE FRAME

LIGHTBULB CLIPS

FRAMES WITH GIMBAL FITTINGS
For versatility, choose a frame that has a swiveling gimbal, since this will allow you to fit the lampshade either to a lamp base or to a pendant light.

BOWED OVAL FRAME

BOX FRAME

DRUM-SHAPED FRAME

CONICAL FRAME

LAMPSHADE RINGS
Pleated and small shades made from stiff paper or cardboard need only an upper ring fitted with a mounting ring, or gimbal. Shades made from light paper require a lower ring for extra support. Ensure that rings form a circle and that the struts are aligned before you assemble the lampshade.

LOWER SUPPORT RINGS

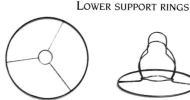

GIMBAL RING FITTING

PENDANT RING FITTING

BULB-CLIP RING FITTING

PAINTING LAMPSHADE FRAMES
Paint bare metal frames and support rings to prevent the covering material from being stained by rust and to stop the binding tape from slipping when you bind the uprights and rings. You will need medium-grade sandpaper, a small paintbrush, enamel paint, and a paint solvent for diluting it.

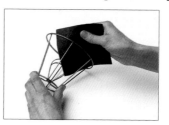 

1 PREPPING SURFACE
Prep the surface of the frame or support ring by rubbing it down evenly and smoothly with a piece of medium-grade sandpaper.

2 APPLYING PAINT
Carefully paint the frame or support ring, using a small paintbrush. Avoid the surfaces that will be in direct contact with a light bulb.

TOOLS AND EQUIPMENT

Making a shade does not require special tools; since accuracy in cutting out and assembly is important, however, ensure that the equipment is in excellent working order. The tools required for making fabric and paper shades are basically the same, with the few exceptions noted below. Additionally, you will need some equipment from the household tool kit, the basic sewing kit, and a specific lampshade frame or support ring.

FABRIC AND PAPER LAMPSHADES

You will need medium-grade sandpaper, enamel paint, solvent, and a small brush for painting the frame. To bind the frame, you will need lampshade binding tape and clear glue that will not stain fabric or paper. Use clean clothespins to hold the shade material in position on the frame while the glue is drying.

LAMPSHADE BINDING TAPE

CLEAR GLUE

CLOTHESPINS

SANDPAPER   ENAMEL PAINT   SMALL PAINTBRUSH

PAPER LAMPSHADES

Use paper scissors for cutting. When gluing paper, position a weight on the join until the glue sets. For measuring, use a compass made from a strip of cardboard; pivot it with a thumbtack secured to a cutting board. Attach the cover to the rings using masking tape. Score creases with a knife edge. Use a hole punch for pleated shades.

KNIFE

THUMBTACKS

PAPER SCISSORS

CUTTING BOARD

WEIGHT

HOLE PUNCH   MASKING TAPE

TAPING A LAMPSHADE FRAME

After painting the frame or rings, apply the binding tape. Loosely woven tape designed for the purpose is bound to the frame or rings, presenting a surface to which you can either sew a fabric or glue a paper shade cover. Estimate how much tape you will need by measuring the circumference of the rings and the lengths of the vertical struts, and double this measurement. Do not bind the internal wires that hold the shade to the light fixture. You will also need the basic sewing kit.

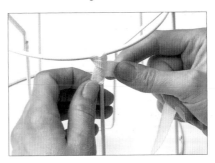

1 SECURING TAPE Tape the vertical struts, starting and finishing in each case at a top or bottom support ring. Secure the binding tape in place by folding one end under the top ring and down the outside of the strut to a length of approximately 1 in (2.5 cm).

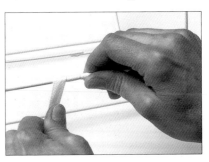

2 TAPING STRUT Wind the tape in a spiral along each strut, covering over the initial fold and making ⅛ in (3 mm) overlaps. Wind the tape as smoothly and as tightly as possible to avoid unsightly ridges and to prevent the possibility of the tape slipping.

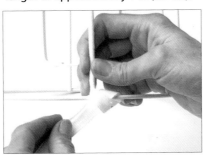

3 KNOTTING END At the other end of the strut, wind the tape over the outside of the lower ring to the back, and pass the end through the loop to form a half-knot. Pull the knot tight and cut the tape. Tape all but one of the remaining struts in this way.

4 TAPING TOP RING Start at the upper end of the untaped strut. Place the tape end on the outside of the ring. Wrap the tape around it and the strut to hold the end in place. Tape around the ring, making figure eights at the tops of the struts.

5 TAPING STRUT Wind the binding tape down the untaped strut and around the lower support ring, again securing it in place at each strut with a figure eight.

6 STITCHING END To finish binding the frame, fold under about ¼ in (6 mm) of the tape end and stitch it neatly to the outside of a bound ring. Check the fit of the tape on the wire. If it twists over the wire, it will need to be unwound and reapplied.

FABRIC LAMPSHADES

$\mathcal{M}$ADE FROM FABRIC THAT IS GATHERED, stretched, or pleated over a frame, fabric lampshades provide the opportunity to create original, personal accessories to add to your furnishings. For the external fabric, use furnishing or dress material that is reasonably pliable. This is an essential quality, since the fabric needs to be stretched over the lampshade frame to ensure a tight fit. If a fabric is suitable, you can use scraps to coordinate with larger soft furnishings in a room. You will also need an inner fabric lining to conceal the frame; this should be pale in color to reflect the light outward from the shade.

GATHERED LAMPSHADE

Choose a lampshade frame and paint it, if necessary. Bind the upper and lower rings, where the fabric will be attached, using specially made tape *(see page 163)*. Allow enough outer fabric for binding strips and a gathered frill. You will also need lining fabric, clear fabric glue, and the basic sewing kit. Cut out the fabric and lining on the straight grain to twice the circumference of the lower ring, by the height of the frame, and add 2 in (5 cm) all around for seams.

1 **SEWING EDGES** With the right sides together, tack and sew the two short edges of the outer fabric, ⅝ in (1.5 cm) from the edges, to form a circular shape. Turn right side out.

2 **SEWING GATHERING STITCHES** To enable you to make folds in the fabric, sew a line of gathering stitches *(see page 24)* ⅝ in (1.5 cm) from the top and bottom edges.

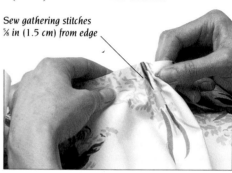
Sew gathering stitches ⅝ in (1.5 cm) from edge

3 **GATHERING FABRIC** Place the fabric over the frame, and fit it to the shape of the frame by pulling up the gathering stitches around the top edge. Arrange the gathers so that they are neat, plus spaced and sized equally, and pin the fabric to the tape binding the upper ring.

Pin lining to tape binding frame's rings, adjusting gathers as you go

4 **PINNING FABRIC** Pull up the gathers around the lower ring. Pin the fabric to the tape binding the lower ring. The gathers should be tighter around the upper ring than around the lower ring. Unpin to adjust the gathered fabric. Stretch the fabric between the rings, form the gathers into folds, and repin the fabric to the tape binding the rings. Trim the surplus fabric from the rings.

5 **PINNING LINING** Slipstitch the gathered fabric to the tape binding the rings. Prepare the lining with gathering stitches ⅝ in (1.5 cm) from top and bottom edges. Pin the lining to the bound rings, adjusting the gathers, as above.

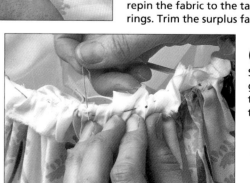

6 **SEWING LINING** Slipstitch the gathered lining to the tape binding the upper ring.

7 FITTING LINING As you work around the upper ring, you will encounter the frame's inner supporting struts. Cut the lining to fit it around these, using a pair of scissors.

Cut snips in lining to fit it around struts

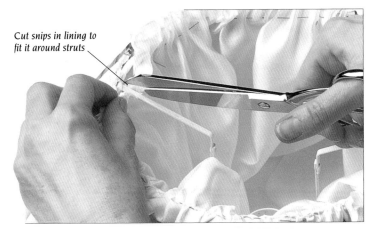

8 TRIMMING LINING Trim the surplus lining fabric around the top ring, cutting as close as possible to the stitching so that there is a minimum of fabric bulk.

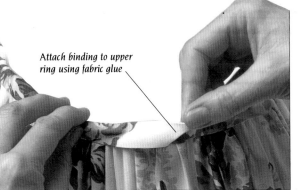

Attach binding to upper ring using fabric glue

9 ATTACHING BINDING Make a bias strip from the outer fabric (*see page 22*) to use as a trim for top edge of shade to hide raw edges and stitching. Attach binding with fabric glue. Slipstitch lining to tape binding lower ring. Trim surplus fabric.

SECURING BINDING

To make a neat join in the binding, press the turned ends of the bias strip, overlap them, then use fabric glue to attach the binding to the ring. Clean clothespins are very useful for holding the bias strip firmly in place around the ring while the fabric glue is drying.

10 ATTACHING FRILL Cut out a length of outer fabric to twice the circumference of the lower ring, by two and a half times the required depth of the finished frill. Fold the strip lengthwise, right sides together. Press, then sew gathering stitches ³⁄₁₆ in (5 mm) from the raw edges. Pull up the gathering stitches so that the frill fits the lower ring. Pin and slipstitch the frill through the edge of the main fabric to the lower ring.

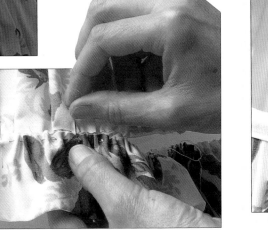

Glue binding in place once frill has been attached

11 ATTACHING LOWER BINDING Complete the lampshade by making a second bias strip that is equal to the circumference of the lower ring. Glue the binding to the top of the frill so that it conceals the raw edges and stitching.

THE FINISHED LAMPSHADE

TAILORED LAMPSHADE

A tailored, fabric-covered lampshade can be made to fit most frame shapes. Choose a frame, paint it if necessary, and bind the top and base rings, as well as an opposite pair of uprights, with binding tape *(see page 163)*. Select the outer and lining fabrics. A white silk lining will reflect the light outward from the interior of the shade. Measure the circumference of the lampshade at its widest point, and add 6 in (15 cm). Measure the shade height, and add 3 in (7.5 cm). Cut out the outer fabric along the bias to these dimensions. You will also need the basic sewing kit and clear fabric glue.

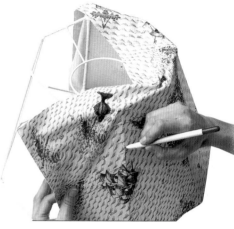

1 PINNING FABRIC TO UPRIGHTS Cut the outer panel of fabric in half. Pin one piece of the fabric to the frame. First, pin the fabric to the taped uprights, stretching the fullness around the frame, then pin it to the taped rings.

2 PINNING FABRIC TO RING Work around frame, pinning fabric to top and base rings between the pair of taped uprights. Pull fabric taut to remove any creases, and apply the pins inward.

3 MARKING FABRIC As long as the fabric is stretched taut, you will have a clear outline of one half of the frame. Draw the shape of this outline on the fabric, using a vanishing-ink pen or tailor's chalk. Draw between the pins, following the lines of the rings and the two uprights.

4 CUTTING OUT FABRIC Unpin fabric from frame. Cut out, following drawn line, adding ¾ in (2 cm) all around. Cut out an identical panel on the bias. Cut out two panels of lining, using a panel of outer fabric as a pattern.

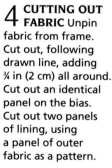

5 SEWING OUTER PANELS Lay the two outer fabric panels right sides together, and pin, tack, and sew them along the two short sides to form a tube of fabric. Do the same with the lining fabric. Press the fabrics, and turn the outer fabric to the right side.

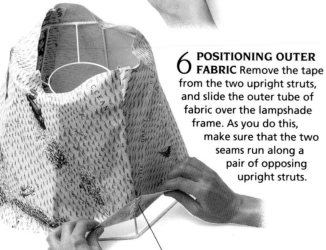

6 POSITIONING OUTER FABRIC Remove the tape from the two upright struts, and slide the outer tube of fabric over the lampshade frame. As you do this, make sure that the two seams run along a pair of opposing upright struts.

7 PINNING FABRIC Pin the fabric to the top and base rings. As you pin it, pull and snip the fabric allowance to avoid any creasing. Make sure that the side seams do not move out of line with the two upright struts.

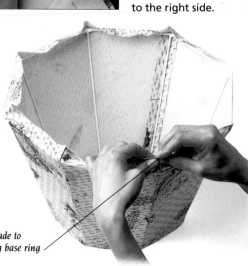

Match fabric seam to strut when pulling lampshade over frame

Pin lampshade to tape binding base ring

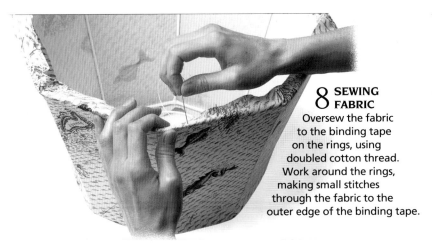

8 SEWING FABRIC

Oversew the fabric to the binding tape on the rings, using doubled cotton thread. Work around the rings, making small stitches through the fabric to the outer edge of the binding tape.

9 TRIMMING FABRIC
Use a sharp pair of scissors to trim the excess fabric around the ring by cutting as close as possible to the stitching.

10 PINNING LINING

Place the lining fabric inside the frame, right sides to the inside of the frame. Match the seams with those of the outer fabric before stretching and pinning the lining to the top and base rings.

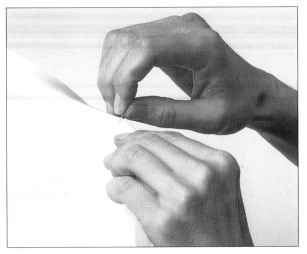

11 CUTTING INCISIONS
Make short incisions in the lining, so that it fits neatly in place around the gimbal supports. Adjust and pin the lining fabric, keeping it taut. Oversew the lining all around, making sure that the stitches are on the outer edge of the shade, so that the edging will conceal them.

12 TRIMMING FABRIC

Trim the excess lining fabric around the top and base rings. Neaten the points where the gimbal supports meet the top ring by covering each join with a piece of lining fabric. Cut out strips of lining on the bias – each should measure 1¼ x 2 in (3 x 5 cm). Fold under the long edges of each strip by 6 mm (¼ in), and press.

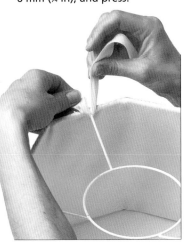

13 ATTACHING STRIPS
Wrap the lining strips around and over the tops of the gimbal supports and top ring, and glue them in place. When dry, trim them to match the outer edge of the shade. Make up edging by cutting two bias strips of fabric to the same lengths as the circumferences of the rings, by 1¾ in (4.5 cm) wide. Turn the long edges under by ⅜ in (1 cm), and press. Glue edging to top and base rings. Work in 6 in (15 cm) lengths at a time. Fold the ends under by ¼ in (6 mm), and overlap the turnings by ¾ in (2 cm). Use clothespins to secure the strips while they are drying.

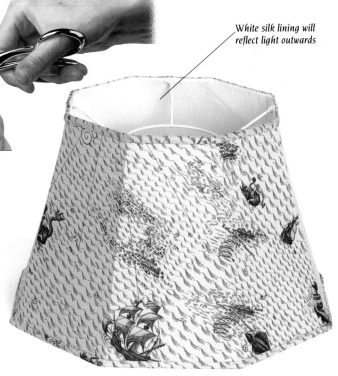

White silk lining will reflect light outwards

THE FINISHED LAMPSHADE

PAPER LAMPSHADES

$\mathcal{M}$AKING YOUR OWN PAPER or cardboard lampshades can be one of the most satisfying and rewarding home decorating projects. You can construct a variety of lampshades for lamp bases or pendant fittings, using plain or patterned paper. The sides, which are supported by a standard lampshade ring with a gimbal, can be either pleated or flat. Self-reinforced by its own folds, a pleated paper lampshade can be made from a variety of weights of paper, ranging from cartridge to light cardboard. A flat-sided shade must, however, be made with substantial cardboard, or paper reinforced with a commercial lampshade lamination.

PLEATED PAPER LAMPSHADE

Choose the paper or cardboard, and decide on the height of the finished shade. Select an appropriately sized painted wire ring to support the lampshade at the top, and a length of ribbon. You will also need a hole puncher, ruler, try square, craft knife, pencil, scissors, table knife, and glue. Calculate the circumference of the completed lower edge of the lampshade. Decide how deep you wish the pleats to be – here they are ¾ in (2 cm) from the point to the trough. Depending on how deep the pleats are, multiply the circumference by approximately two to give the total length of paper required.

Calculate dimension of lampshade and mark length and width on thick paper or cardboard

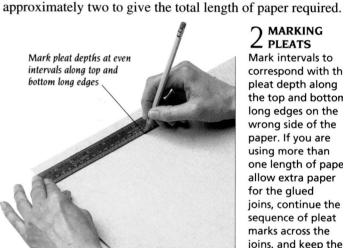

Mark pleat depths at even intervals along top and bottom long edges

1 MEASURING Divide the circumference by size of one pleat – in this case, 1½ in (4 cm) – and round up to an even number for the total of pleats needed. Using a ruler, try square, and sharp craft knife, cut the paper into one or more strips to the total length calculated above, by the height of the finished shade.

2 MARKING PLEATS Mark intervals to correspond with the pleat depth along the top and bottom long edges on the wrong side of the paper. If you are using more than one length of paper, allow extra paper for the glued joins, continue the sequence of pleat marks across the joins, and keep the marks on the inside.

3 FOLDING PLEATS To make crisp pleats, press down and draw a crease line between the marks, using the blunt edge of a table knife or dressmaker's scissors; guide the blade with a metal ruler. Fold the creases into alternate pleats over the edge of a table. If joining strips to make up a complete length, glue the strips within a pleat.

4 MAKING TEMPLATE Cut out a piece of cardboard measuring ¾ x 2 in (2 x 5 cm). Draw a central line down the length of this template, and make two holes with a hole puncher, one for the gathering ribbon, 1 in (2.5 cm) from the top edge, and the second a little over 1 in (2.5 cm) below this, for the supporting ring. Place the template on one side of each fold, and accurately mark the punch holes with a pencil.

5 PUNCHING HOLES Grip each double pleat between the jaws of the punch at the marks, and punch through the paper. In this way, punch pairs of holes in the pleats. At each end of the paper, leave the final pleat unpunched ready for gluing.

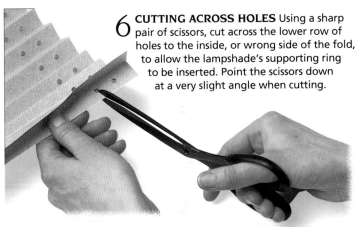

6 **CUTTING ACROSS HOLES** Using a sharp pair of scissors, cut across the lower row of holes to the inside, or wrong side of the fold, to allow the lampshade's supporting ring to be inserted. Point the scissors down at a very slight angle when cutting.

7 **GLUING ENDS** Secure the ends of the paper by applying glue to the surface of each end fold. Join the two ends to make a complete pleat. Allow the glue to dry thoroughly.

8 **SECURING ENDS** Hold the ends together until the glue has dried. Using the template, mark a pair of holes through the overlap. Punch the holes. Using the scissors, cut through the lower holes to the inside.

Punch two holes in glued pleat

9 **THREADING RIBBON** Cut a piece of ribbon to fit through the top set of holes – here, approximately 1 yd (1 m) has been cut. Wind tape around the leading end, and thread the ribbon through the holes.

SEALING ENDS OF RIBBON

To prevent the ribbon from fraying when it is threaded through the holes, seal the leading end with tape after you have cut the ribbon. Knot the other end of the ribbon to prevent it from slipping out of place.

10 **INSERTING RING** Ease open the top of the shade, and insert the ring. Carefully fit half of the ring through the lower set of punched, cut holes. Fit the other half of the ring.

Fit frame ring through lower row of punched holes

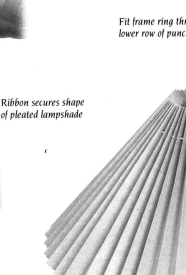

Ribbon secures shape of pleated lampshade

11 **TYING RIBBON** Form the shade into its final shape by drawing together the ends of the ribbon. At the same time, spread the lower edge of the shade to the required circumference. Tie the ribbon, and trim it to size, if necessary. Once you have mounted the shade on the lamp, you can turn it to hide the knotted ribbon.

THE FINISHED LAMPSHADE

PLAIN-SIDED CONICAL LAMPSHADE

You can construct a paper lampshade using either paper stiffened with a commercial laminate, or heavy cardboard supported by two rings, one with a lamp-fitting gimbal. Decide on the proportions of the lampshade, and select and paint the rings. You will also need a tape measure, try square, ruler, pencil, glue, hole puncher, scissors, craft knife, clothespins, masking tape, and a weight. In order to glue the cardboard to the rings, prepare the rings by taping them.

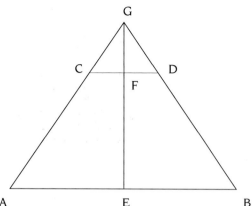

1 MEASURING Use a try square, ruler, and pencil to draw a diagram of the cross section of the lampshade. Measure the rings' diameter (A to B and C to D), and the shade height from the center of the bottom ring to the center of the top ring (E to F). The measuring, drawing, and cutting out must be accurate in order for the lampshade to fit well.

2 MAKING COMPASS Construct a simple compass, using a strip of cardboard about ¾ in (2 cm) wide, and slightly longer than the line G to B. Draw a central line down the compass, lay it on the diagram, and mark on the line the points G, D, and B.

Mark points corresponding with ring positions on card compass

3 PUNCHING HOLES Using the smallest setting on the punch, make two holes in the cardboard compass along the line, slightly above points B and D. Align the bottom edges of the holes you punch – the position of the pencil point – with points B and D.

4 DRAWING ARCS Tape the lampshade cardboard, right side down, to a piece of board. Affix the compass firmly to the board with a pin at point G. Draw an arc with the pencil in hole D, followed by another with the pencil in hole B. These arcs give the shape of the cardboard needed to cut it out.

5 MEASURING LOWER RING Measure the circumference of the lower lampshade ring with a tape measure. Add 2 in (5 cm) for the seam overlap to the circumference. Mark this dimension on the longer arc, using a tape measure set on its edge. Work in 4 in (10 cm) stages for accuracy.

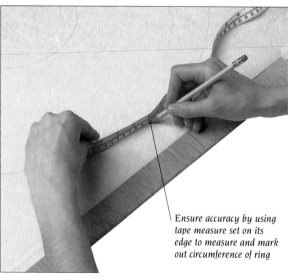

Ensure accuracy by using tape measure set on its edge to measure and mark out circumference of ring

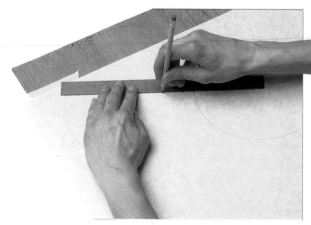

6 DRAWING END MARKS Remove the compass, and rule two lines from point G, across the shorter arc, to the end points of the measured circumference of the lower ring that are marked on the longer arc.

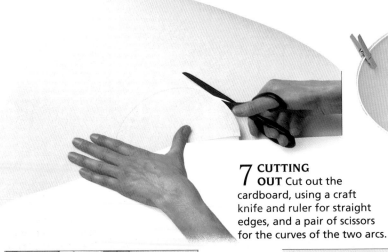

7 CUTTING OUT Cut out the cardboard, using a craft knife and ruler for straight edges, and a pair of scissors for the curves of the two arcs.

Use clothespins to hold cardboard in place

8 POSITIONING RINGS Bend the cardboard around the top gimbal and ring, using clothespins to hold the cardboard in place. Insert the lower ring, and pin it to hold it temporarily in position. Take time to position the cardboard tautly over the rings, all the while adjusting it and the clothespins, so that the rings lie flush with the edge of the cardboard, and the overlap is even all around.

9 MARKING OVERLAP When you are certain that you have a snug fit, mark the overlap made by the extra cardboard at the top and bottom on the inside of the cardboard, using a sharp, soft pencil.

10 TRIMMING OVERLAP Detach the lampshade cardboard from the rings, and add a ½ in (12 mm) seam overlap parallel to your marks, using a pencil and ruler. Cut off the excess overlap with the scissors.

11 WEIGHTING CARDBOARD Apply glue to the tongue of the overlap, align it with the marks, and join cardboard. Avoid smearing glue on the surface. Press the join flat with a ruler and weight. Let stand for at least 30 minutes for the glue to set.

12 TAPING RINGS Once the glue is dry, fit the rings again, using the clothespins to hold them in place. Make sure that the support wire of the gimbal is perpendicular to the seam. Use masking tape to secure rings. Apply tape to the outside surface in 4 in (10 cm) sections, with a ¼ in (6 mm) overlap. Reposition tape as you work around shade, and smooth it into place on the cardboard's surface.

Use sharp craft knife to trim excess tape

13 TRIMMING TAPE Push the tape over to the inside surface, and press it in place. Trim the tape so that the inside edge is parallel to the ring, using a very sharp craft knife – make sure you do not cut through the cardboard. Glue a piece of fabric trim over the tape if desired, then mount the finished shade on the light fixture.

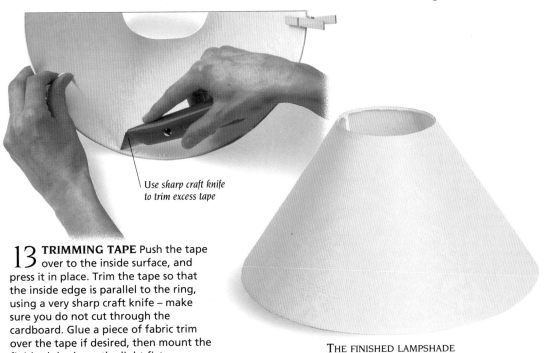

THE FINISHED LAMPSHADE

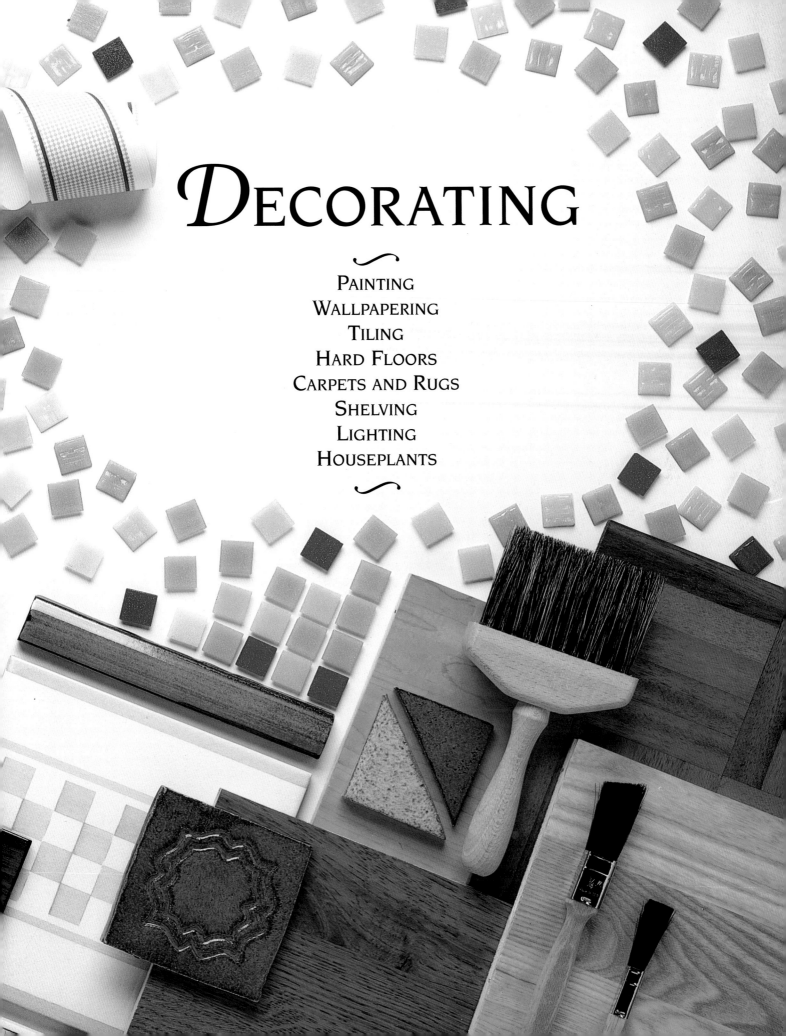

DECORATING

PAINTING
WALLPAPERING
TILING
HARD FLOORS
CARPETS AND RUGS
SHELVING
LIGHTING
HOUSEPLANTS

HOUSEHOLD TOOL KIT

*A*LWAYS TRY TO BUY AND USE HIGH-QUALITY TOOLS when carrying out home improvements. Good tools will greatly ease the task of decorating your home, so it is always best to purchase a few well-made tools rather than many poor-quality ones. You do not need to acquire your whole tool kit at once – collect the requisite tools when needed as you tackle different decorating tasks. A comprehensive range of hand and power tools is a good investment, so clean and store all your tools carefully after use to keep them in good condition. More specialized tools can be rented from a home-improvement center.

STEPLADDER
A stepladder is essential for many home tasks. To work close to ceilings, use a stepladder 6½ ft (2 m) tall. When choosing a stepladder, consider the safety and comfort aspects first. Stability and wide, sturdy treads with a non-slip surface are essential, and a platform at the top is useful for resting tools and materials.

PORTABLE WORKBENCH
A rigid, portable workbench that folds flat for storage is a key appliance. A basic portable bench will clamp materials to be cut, painted, or worked on in some other way and serves as a useful platform for cans of paint. More comprehensive benches include a marked edge for measuring, parallel lines for guiding materials to be cut, and a circle marked in degrees to help when mitering corners.

MARKERS
A good general-pupose marker is a carpenter's pencil. A fine pencil is useful for delicate assignments, and a china marker is best for marking tiles and glass.

CHINA MARKER

CARPENTER'S PENCIL

FINE PENCIL

LEVELING
For true verticals, use a plumb line or a large carpenter's level. A small level will also be useful. A combination square is a versatile tool for measuring angles and short lengths. Right angles can be checked with a try square. A steel tape measure, ruler, and straightedge are vital for most work.

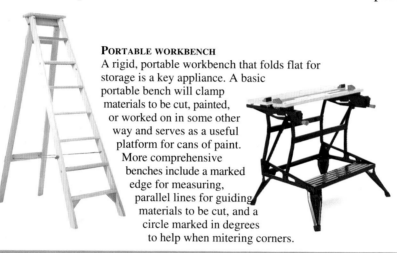

TRY SQUARE

COMBINATION SQUARE

SMALL LEVEL

PLUMB LINE

STEEL RULER

STRAIGHTEDGE

STEEL TAPE

LARGE CARPENTER'S LEVEL

DRILLS
When buying a power drill, make sure that the motor is powerful enough for all tasks, and look for features such as hammer action for boring walls, reversible rotation, and variable speeds. Some drills with very low speed settings can be used for putting in screws. Use a selection of general-purpose and masonry drill bits.

POWER DRILL

GENERAL-PURPOSE DRILL BITS

MASONRY DRILL BITS

HAMMERS AND MALLETS
A claw hammer is indispensable for general-purpose tasks and for levering out exposed nails or tacks. Use a tack hammer for delicate applications, and a sledge hammer for heavy work. A mallet is used only to drive wooden-handled tools, such as chisels. Set nails into wood with a punch. Use masonry nails for mounting into solid walls and floors. Finishing nails are best when appearance is important. Flat-head nails should be used when strength is necessary.

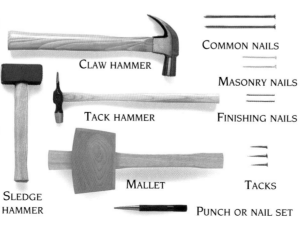

CLAW HAMMER

TACK HAMMER

MALLET

SLEDGE HAMMER

COMMON NAILS

MASONRY NAILS

FINISHING NAILS

TACKS

PUNCH OR NAIL SET

GRIPPERS
Have a selection of pliers and grippers available for tasks where you need a good grip. Gripping pliers will remove nails and tacks with ease from wood. A plier-wrench is designed for clamping onto and turning. For general-purpose work, you should use a strong pair of lineman's pliers with curved toothed jaws and cutting blades.

GRIPPING PLIERS

PLIER-WRENCH

LINEMAN'S PLIERS

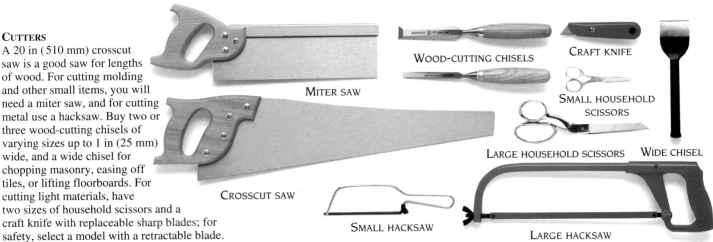

CUTTERS

A 20 in (510 mm) crosscut saw is a good saw for lengths of wood. For cutting molding and other small items, you will need a miter saw, and for cutting metal use a hacksaw. Buy two or three wood-cutting chisels of varying sizes up to 1 in (25 mm) wide, and a wide chisel for chopping masonry, easing off tiles, or lifting floorboards. For cutting light materials, have two sizes of household scissors and a craft knife with replaceable sharp blades; for safety, select a model with a retractable blade.

WOOD-CUTTING CHISELS

CRAFT KNIFE

MITER SAW

SMALL HOUSEHOLD SCISSORS

LARGE HOUSEHOLD SCISSORS WIDE CHISEL

CROSSCUT SAW

SMALL HACKSAW

LARGE HACKSAW

SCRAPING AND FILLING

Putty knives are used to smooth filler into cracks and holes. Scrapers are indispensable for removing old paint and wallpaper. Prior to scraping, perforate wallpaper with a spiker or scraper. A steam stripper is useful for removing large areas of wallpaper. A decorator's sponge has a host of uses when painting and wallpapering. Clean metal with a wire brush. Abrade surfaces with steel wool, or sandpaper wrapped around a cork block.

SCREWDRIVERS

There are various screwdrivers for slotted and Phillips head screws. General screws and woodscrews are available in different finishes and shapes. Mark a pilot drilling hole with an awl. Use a solid or hollow wall anchor that matches the screw size when making a wall attachment. For handling electricity, use an insulated screwdriver.

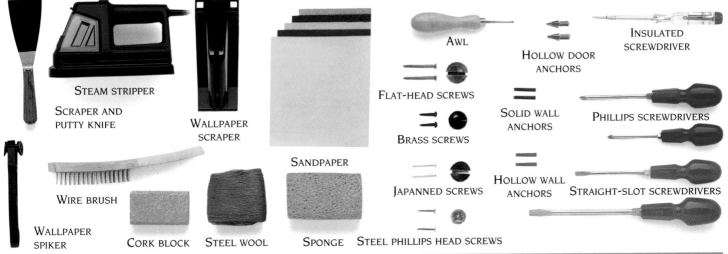

STEAM STRIPPER

SCRAPER AND PUTTY KNIFE

WALLPAPER SCRAPER

SANDPAPER

WIRE BRUSH

WALLPAPER SPIKER

CORK BLOCK STEEL WOOL SPONGE

AWL

HOLLOW DOOR ANCHORS

INSULATED SCREWDRIVER

FLAT-HEAD SCREWS

SOLID WALL ANCHORS

PHILLIPS SCREWDRIVERS

BRASS SCREWS

JAPANNED SCREWS

HOLLOW WALL ANCHORS

STRAIGHT-SLOT SCREWDRIVERS

STEEL PHILLIPS HEAD SCREWS

MISCELLANEOUS

Before drilling, use a metal detector to locate objects hidden within a wall. For protecting clothing and to provide a useful pocket for tools, wear a carpenter's apron. When handling caustic materials, protect your hands with rubber gloves. Fabric gloves are useful for general decorating tasks. Cover furniture with drop cloths. Safety goggles will protect your eyes. Use a mask when working in a dusty area. Masking tape is available in several widths and strengths. String and a staple gun are useful for many tasks. Use a heavy-duty pail.

METAL DETECTOR SAFETY GOGGLES

STAPLE GUN

DUST MASK

STRING

CLOTH-AND-LEATHER GLOVES

DROP CLOTH

CARPENTER'S APRON

PAIL

MASKING TAPE RUBBER GLOVES

PAINTING

*A*PPLYING A COAT OF PAINT is the simplest, quickest, and most economical means of changing the character of a room. Yet paintwork provides much more than just decoration, since it also protects the underlying plaster, wood, or metal from surface abrasion and damage caused by moisture. New materials are continuously being developed to make paint easier to apply and longer lasting. Paint will not, however, adhere properly to unsuitable surfaces, and for the best results, surfaces must be thoroughly prepared and then coated with the recommended primary coats and undercoats. This chapter includes an examination of paint types, explains how to prepare surfaces, and demonstrates the different methods of applying paint to produce good-quality, hard-wearing finishes. Finally, for those who wish to create special decorative effects, there are comprehensive instructions for painting techniques such as sponging, dragging, and stenciling.

CHOOSING A STYLE

COLORED PAINTS CAN BE USED TO CREATE all manner of visual effects, and your choice of paint color should depend on the size, position, and function of the room. Pale colors will expand and brighten a small, dimly lit room; warm, dark tones can make a large, cold room appear cozy. Paint can even influence the perceived size and shape of a room, bringing space to a small room or foreshortening a spacious room. When choosing a color scheme, you will need to decide whether you wish to create a strong visual impact, using vivid, primary colors, or to form a neutral, natural-toned backdrop.

LIGHT AND BRIGHT
Pale colors produce a visual impression of bright, airy spaciousness. Whether a ceiling is high or low, a coat of white paint will appear to raise the height of a room. When applied to walls, off-white presents a pristine surface that is ideal for displaying paintings and wall hangings in sharp outline.

Pale pastel color warms room without diminishing sense of space

Dark, cool color emphasizes small room with low, sloping ceiling, especially when the space is well lit by natural or artificial light

SOOTHING AND COZY
To impart a strong character to your decor and to reduce the scale of a room, select rich, dark colors for the walls and ceiling. Deep shades of primary and secondary colors, particularly blue, red, and orange, can create a relaxed atmosphere of warmth and coziness perfectly suited to personal or private rooms, such as bedrooms and studies.

MATTE EFFECTS
It is an established practice to paint woodwork such as doors, baseboards, and chair rails in durable white gloss. For a coating that is not as shiny as gloss, but equally tough, use oil-based eggshell paint, which dries to give a subtle sheen.

Cool, pale color clearly defines woodwork in contrast to warm-colored walls and adds character to room

NATURAL TEXTURES
Special paint effects bring not only the benefits of color but also great visual character to painted surfaces. One of the simplest techniques to apply is sponging. A final paint color is dabbed onto a properly prepared, painted surface with a natural sponge, producing mottled, overlapping patterns.

Sealing bare surface of woodwork with varnish, oil, or wax, rather than paint, allows natural texture of wood to show through

White-painted upper wall gives impression of height and enhances natural light in small-proportioned kitchen

Bright color emphasizes structure of room and helps highlight style of furnishings

BOLD PRIMARY COLORS
When applied to walls, a primary color such as yellow infuses a room with a bright, cheerful glow, best suited to much-used areas of the home, such as kitchens or bathrooms. Rooms such as these are subject to the greatest wear and tear and benefit from a durable, washable, oil-based paint on the walls. For a delicate, unobtrusive sheen, use eggshell paint.

SURFACES AND EQUIPMENT

CHANGING THE CHARACTER OF A ROOM WITH PAINT requires more than simply applying the color. Paint is useful for disguising surface faults, as well as altering the proportions of the room. Achieving a professional finish starts with careful preparation and planning. A smooth, clean surface makes the task easier, whether applying a simple coat of latex or a special paint effect such as dragging, stippling, or sponging. There are numerous easy-to-use tools and materials available to aid every stage of painting – from smoothing wood to varnishing a finished surface, and from painting bare wood to recoating a damaged surface.

WHAT TO DO WHERE

Different types of surface demand different preparatory treatments before applying the paint: for instance, bare wood should be sanded and cracks in plaster filled. To achieve a durable finish, you first must choose the appropriate painting and decorating equipment for each surface. When deciding on the style for the room, you should take time to examine the character and texture of the surface, and consider matching the new with the old. While it may be desirable to achieve the smoothest finish in a modern home, rough layers of paint can add to the character of an older home.

UNCOATED SURFACES

PLASTER

BRICK

BARE WOOD

COPPER PIPES

Once plaster is dry, brush, prime, and seal with diluted latex or undercoat. Consider painting bathroom walls using a water-resistant coating. Brush over brickwork and coat it with masonry paint. On bare wood apply knotting to knots to prevent resin seepage. Hide all but very large cracks in wood with wood filler. Sand bare wood, then varnish or prime, undercoat, and oil paint. Use coarse-grade sandpaper to remove rust from iron; prime before oil painting. Clean new copper pipes with mineral spirits and then coat with oil paint.

COATED SURFACES: WALLS AND CEILINGS

TEMPERA

PAINT

WALLPAPER

CERAMIC TILES

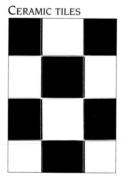

Wipe surfaces with damp cloth. If color comes off, the paint may be tempera. Smooth and recoat. To cover a tempera surface with latex, scrape and seal before painting with surface conditioner. Use filler in cracks, and sand before repainting. Wash latex surfaces with TSP (trisodium phosphate). You can also create a smooth surface by first hanging lining paper *(see page 211)*. Nonvinyl wallpaper can be painted over, and ceramic tiles can be coated with gloss or enamel paints. Strip both tiled and wallpapered surfaces before painting.

COATED SURFACES

PAINT

WAX

STAIN

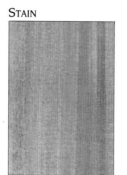

VARNISH

Old painted wood should be washed with TSP and repainted with oil-based paint. Repair damaged wood with interior filler, and sand before priming and painting. To remove paint, use liquid paint stripper, blow torch, or heat gun. Sand in the direction of the grain, and dust varnished wood before recoating. To prime and paint varnished or waxed wood, remove topcoat with chemical stripper and neutralize with 1:20 mixture of vinegar and water. Sand and prime stained wood before painting. Remove stain with wood bleach before applying clear sealant.

EQUIPMENT

The effort needed to paint a room can be eased by using quality tools and equipment, particularly brushes and rollers, for the appropriate task. If necessary, rent or borrow the more expensive specialized tools to achieve the best finish. Use a scaffold or stepladders and wooden planks (see page 208) to make a sound and safe working platform when painting high walls and ceilings. Follow the manufacturer's or dealer's instructions for proper and safe use of all equipment.

BRUSHES
Use 4–6 in (100–150 mm) brushes for painting walls and ceilings, and narrower brushes for details. Oval-head brushes should be used for applying varnish. For painting window frames, use an angled-head brush. A radiator brush is made for reaching into crevices and behind radiators. Artist's brushes should be used for painting details on surfaces.

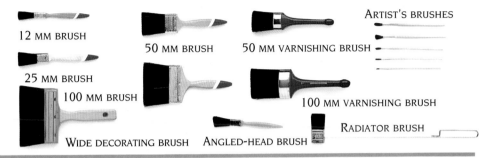
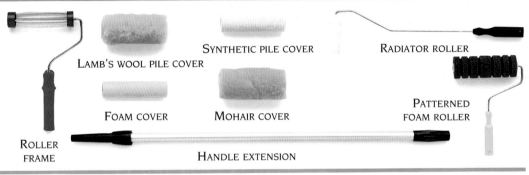

12 MM BRUSH

50 MM BRUSH   50 MM VARNISHING BRUSH

ARTIST'S BRUSHES

25 MM BRUSH

100 MM BRUSH

100 MM VARNISHING BRUSH

WIDE DECORATING BRUSH   ANGLED-HEAD BRUSH

RADIATOR BRUSH

ROLLERS
The best rollers have a soft pile. A roller frame and removable cover allow for easy cleaning and reuse. Paint ceilings and high walls using a handle extension, and reach awkward areas with a radiator roller. Create texture on a surface using a patterned foam roller and suitable paint.

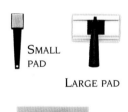

SYNTHETIC PILE COVER   RADIATOR ROLLER

LAMB'S WOOL PILE COVER

FOAM COVER   MOHAIR COVER

PATTERNED FOAM ROLLER

ROLLER FRAME   HANDLE EXTENSION

PADS
Paint pads are made of mohair bonded to a foam backing. They are available in various sizes and often come with hollow handles for use with long-handle extensions to reach ceilings and high walls. Like rollers, pads are best used with water-based paints.

SMALL PAD

LARGE PAD

SPARE PAD

CONTAINERS
Your choice of a paint container depends on what applicator you are using. Metal or plastic is usually best for paintbrushes. Trays should be used with rollers and paint pads.

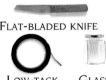

METAL PAINT CAN   PLASTIC TRAY   METAL TRAY

OTHER TOOLS AND MATERIALS
Mineral spirits are solvent for oil-based paint. Use a maulstick to steady your hand when painting details. Stir paint with wooden doweling. Use lint-free cloth for wiping and sandpaper wrapped around cork block for smoothing. Store small amounts of paint in glass jars. Open cans with a flat-bladed knife. Use low-tack masking tape to mask surfaces.

MAULSTICK

WOODEN DOWELING

FLAT-BLADED KNIFE

MINERAL SPIRITS   LOW-TACK MASKING TAPE   GLASS JAR   LINT-FREE RAG   CORK BLOCK   SANDPAPER

BATTERY-POWERED PAINTBRUSH
Paint is pumped from a reservoir to the brush for convenient usage.

BATTERY-POWERED PAINT ROLLER
Avoids the need for a paint tray and therefore can save you time when coating large, flat surfaces.

SPRAY GUN AND FACE MASK
A spray gun covers large areas very quickly. Wear a face mask for protection when using a spray gun.

PLANNING AHEAD

A PROFESSIONAL PAINT JOB BEGINS with thorough planning. Start by isolating the
room and its contents. The surface you are going to paint should be as smooth as possible.
Before sanding and scraping to make a surface smooth, seal the edges of the exit door
with masking tape to prevent dust and dirt from spreading throughout the house. Remove
all pictures and furniture from the room, or place them in the center of the room and
cover with drop cloths. Take down movable light fittings and protect electrical
fixtures with plastic bags. Cover the floor with plastic or drop cloths.

PREPARING SURFACES

Wear old clothing, a decorator's apron, or overalls
when preparing a surface, and use a paper face mask for
protection against heavy dust. Prepare a surface using a
bucket of water and decorator's sponge to apply TSP, and
wipe it dry with lint-free cloth. Use a cork block wrapped in
sandpaper to smooth a surface. A small, ½ in (12 mm)
brush is ideal for dusting and wetting a crack before filling.
Apply interior filler with a narrow-bladed knife. When the
filler is completely dry, smooth the surface with sandpaper
wrapped around a cork block.

PAINTED SURFACES

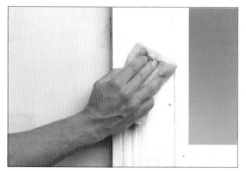

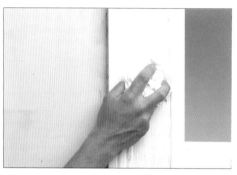

REMOVING FLAKING PAINT

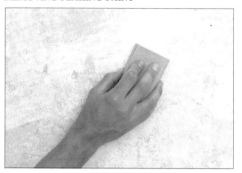

1 PREPARING A SURFACE When a
painted surface is in good and smooth
condition there is no need to strip it before
repainting. Clean off the dust and dirt, and
prepare the existing paint with TSP applied
with a large sponge. This will reveal minor
damage to the surface that needs filling.

2 DRYING A SURFACE Dry off the
painted surface with a lint-free cloth.
If TSP is not available, wash down the
surface of the old paintwork with household
detergent, rub dry, and then abrade lightly
with medium-to-fine sandpaper. Dust off
with a brush or wash down the surface again.

Old paint that is flaking on a wall should
first be scraped off with a wide-bladed
scraper. The surface should then be sanded
smooth using medium-grade sandpaper
wrapped around a cork block. Seal a
tempera surface with a surface conditioner
before applying the first coat of latex.

FILLING HOLES

1 CLEANING HOLES The
secret of filling holes in
plaster is to apply as smooth a
layer of filler as possible. This
reduces the effort needed to
sand the surface. Begin by
brushing out any loose debris
with a small decorating brush.

2 WETTING HOLES Dampen
the holes with water – this
will help to ensure that the filler
is held in place. Using a small
decorating brush, apply water
liberally in and around the hole.

3 FILLING Use a putty knife
to apply the filler, pressing it
well into the hole and cleaning
off any excess. Fill large holes in
layers, allowing each application
to dry thoroughly. Shallow
cracks should be coated with a
skim of filler on a wet blade.

4 SANDING SMOOTH Soon
after applying the filler,
wet the blade of the putty knife
and smooth over the surface to
remove excess material from the
repair and the surrounding wall.
Once the surface is dry, sand it
using a fine-grade sandpaper.

ESTIMATING QUANTITIES

When estimating the amount of paint needed, allow for multiple coatings, particularly over a dark tone. Divide the room into small units of the same color or type of paint. Multiply the height by the width of each unit. Add together the individual unit totals to arrive at an estimate of the amount of paint needed. Follow the paint manufacturer's coverage guide, but be aware of the porousness of the surface. New plasterwork, for example, absorbs paint more easily than old plaster.

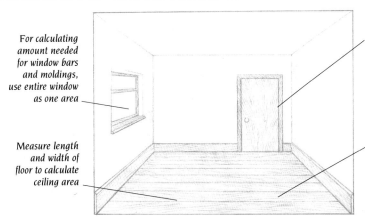

For calculating amount needed for window bars and moldings, use entire window as one area

Measure length and width of floor to calculate ceiling area

Add an extra third to length of molding around doors for estimating total amount of paint needed here

When sealing a floor with varnish or wax, allow for at least two coats

PREPARING PAINT

Unused paint that has been opened can become contaminated or form a top skin. Examine paint carefully and, if necessary, sieve it before application. You will need a small dusting brush, flat-bladed knife, wooden doweling, and a paint can.

1 DUSTING RIM Before opening the paint can, dust around the rim with a small decorating brush. This will keep debris from falling into the paint when opened.

2 OPENING CAN Use the blunt edge of a flat-bladed knife to pry up the lid of the can. Work around the lid of the can, easing up a section at a time until it springs open.

3 STIRRING To ensure that the color remains consistent, stir the paint thoroughly. Using a piece of wooden doweling, stir the paint in wide and narrow circles, simultaneously working it up and down.

4 TRANSFERRING PAINT Pour half of the well-mixed paint into a clean plastic or metal container – this is easier to manage than a full paint can. You can hang the container from a ladder, making reloading brushes easier. If you are using a roller or paint pad, transfer the paint to a paint tray.

SIEVING PAINT

Paint can form skin on the surface once exposed to the air. To avoid this, replace the lid of a can immediately after use, and store the sealed can upside down. If debris has gotten into the unused paint, sieve it before using.

1 CUTTING THE SKIN Clean the lid of an old can of paint before opening it. If a hard top skin has formed, use a knife to cut around it, then remove and discard the skin. Top-skin that is very elastic can be pulled to one side with a knife or removed using a piece of wooden doweling.

2 SIEVING PAINT Stretch and secure a piece of fine cotton muslin or a section of stockings over the paint can rim. Pour the old paint into this sieve to remove any fragments of skin, debris, and dirt. Store the sieved paint in an airtight jar.

How to Paint

BEFORE YOU BEGIN APPLYING COLOR, make sure that all the dust, debris, and dirt is removed from the room, shake out the drop cloths, and vacuum. Replace the drop cloths before painting. Try to have a reliable and strong light source, such as a bare bulb, to illuminate the room. Select a large brush or roller for painting walls or extensive flat surfaces, and a smaller narrow brush for painting small areas or wood moldings. There are basically two types of paint: oil-based and latex. Wood and metal should be coated with oil-based paints. Latex, a water-soluble paint, is ideal for coloring walls and ceilings.

PREPARING A BRUSH

Choose a brush that matches the task. For walls and ceilings, use a 4 in (100 mm) or wider brush. Use a 1–3 in (25–75 mm) brush for doors and windows. Large brushes cover smooth walls quickly and easily; small artist's brushes are best for painting details or intricate woodwork.

1 FLICKING BRISTLES Flick bristles against your hand to shake off debris. New brushes will lose bristles, which embed in fresh paint. Using new brushes for priming should get rid of loose bristles.

2 LOADING BRUSH Dip the brush straight into the paint, covering a third of the bristles. Remove the excess paint by dabbing the bristles against the side of the paint can, rather than scraping it over the rim.

APPLYING LATEX

Latex is easy to use and can be applied with a paintbrush, roller, or paint pad. It provides a water-resistant coating and is available in both matte and silk finishes. Unlike oil-based paints, latex is fast drying, so it is important to apply the paint accurately and quickly to prevent shading. Work so that a wet edge is maintained, allowing one paint area to merge with the next when working across the surface.

1 BEGINNING Dust the surface and begin painting near a natural light source, if possible, either at the top corner of the wall or in a strip on the ceiling near a window. Grip a large brush around the handle. Work in areas approximately 2 ft (60 cm) square.

2 LAYING OFF Smooth the painted area with light, crisscross strokes. Finish on a gentle upward stroke, known as laying off. Move quickly on to an adjacent area. Do not apply paint too thickly. Wait until the paint is dry before applying subsequent coats.

APPLYING OIL-BASED PAINT

Oil-based paints, which come in high-gloss, eggshell, and flat finishes, produce a durable and waterproof coating. They must be applied carefully and in layers, beginning with a primer on wood, followed by an undercoat, before finishing with one or more topcoats. Keep the room well ventilated when using oil-based paints, because the fumes can be very strong and potentially dangerous.

1 APPLYING VERTICAL STROKES Begin by applying vertical, parallel lines of paint, holding a small brush like a pen. Work in areas approximately 1 ft (30 cm) square.

2 JOINING STROKES When the brush is out of paint, do not reload it but work quickly across the vertical lines from the top, creating horizontal bands to cover the area.

3 FINISHING Lightly brush in vertical movements over the wet paint. Immediately reload the brush and move to the next area, adjoining the wet edges for a smooth blending of color.

BEADING

Beading is a technique for making a clearly defined join of different colors – for example, where walls meet a ceiling. The adjacent color must be dry before you apply the second color. Experiment with brush sizes for one that suits the task best.

BEADING AT CEILING
Bring the loaded paintbrush to the surface, parallel to but a short distance from the ceiling edge. Gently press the paintbrush flat against the surface, so that the bristles are slightly splayed. This will create a bead of paint that should be pushed steadily into the edge or corner and moved sideways or downward to make a smooth junction of color.

To ease the cleaning of a paint pan, use aluminum foil to line it. When you have finished painting, carefully remove the foil and dispose of it. Oil-based paints are impossible to remove from containers without using mineral spirits.

CUTTING IN

Cutting in is a technique for painting the edges around a room, such as at a window frame or door frame, before painting the rest of the wall. Use a small brush to paint a band of color, some 1–2 in (2.5–5 cm) wide, from the edges of the joins. A large brush or roller can then be used to paint into the band and blend in the color.

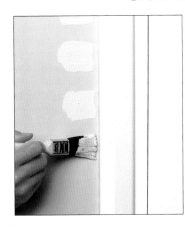

1 PAINTING STRIPS Paint a series of small strips of color on the wall at right angles to the door frame.

2 JOINING STRIPS Over the strips of color, paint one steady line parallel to the frame. Ease the bristles close to the frame to create a well-defined edge. Do this throughout the room before painting large areas and blending them with the strips of color.

SMOOTHING PAINTWORK

Blemishes, such as debris, dust particles, or bristles from the paintbrush, can become embedded in the paint as you work. It may therefore be necessary to lightly sand, dust, and wipe off the surface between coats of paint. You will need fine sandpaper, an old paintbrush, and lint-free cloth to remove unwanted glitches and obtain a smooth finished surface.

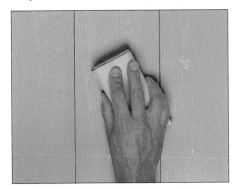

1 SANDING PAINTED SURFACE When the coat of paint has dried, use fine sandpaper wrapped around a cork block to smooth lightly over the problem area.

2 DUSTING OFF Rub the palm of your hand over the surface to check that the rough patches have been smoothed. Sweep away the dust with an old paintbrush.

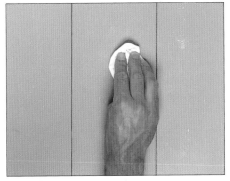

3 WIPING SURFACE Remove the finest dust particles and residue by wiping over the painted surface with a damp, lint-free cloth. Now, paint the surface again.

USING A ROLLER

Roller covers are available in a range of widths, textures, and materials. Foam and mohair pile covers are good for coating large flat areas, while deep-pile synthetic and lamb's wool covers are ideal for applying paint on textured or rough surfaces. Before using a roller on the wall, cut in at the edges around the room *(see page 185)*. Use a roller tray for loading paint onto the roller. To prevent paint from splattering when using a roller, apply thin coats of color.

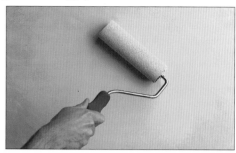

1 FILLING TRAY Make sure that the tray is clean and dry before pouring in paint. Latex is well suited for rollers because it is water soluble. You can use oil-based paint, but it is harder to remove from a roller.

2 LOADING ROLLER Slide the cover onto the frame and rub your hand over it to check that it is clean. Dip the roller into the paint and roll it up and down the incline of the tray, spreading paint over the cover.

3 APPLYING PAINT Push the roller up and down the wall and from side to side, using random strokes and spreading the paint evenly. Try not to let the roller slide on the surface.

4 LAYING OFF Lift off on an upward stroke and reload. Move to an adjacent area, rolling over the wet edges to blend.

TEXTURED PAINT

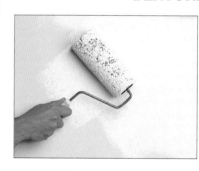

If you wish to achieve textured effects on your walls, there are various cut-foam rollers and specially textured paints available for this purpose. Textured paint is usually white. Roll it onto the wall with overlapping strokes. Once it has dried, a latex paint can be applied over it to add color, if you desire.

USING A PAINT PAD

Paint pads, like rollers, are tools for applying water-based paints to large surface areas. They are available in a range of sizes and can be used on lightly textured surfaces as well as on metalwork and wood. You can use oil-based paints with pads, but the cleaning solvents used for removing the paint could possibly damage the sponge.

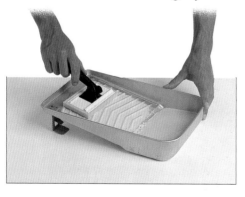

1 LOADING PAD Pour the paint into a paint-pad receptacle or roller tray. Dip the pad flat into the paint so that the tips of the pad pile are loaded, but not submerged. Check that the pad is not overloaded before applying it to the surface.

2 APPLYING PAINT Rub the loaded paint pad in various directions on the wall. Experiment to find the pressure needed to apply the paint without causing it to drip. You will need to reload a paint pad more often than a roller.

ORDER OF WORK

When all of the preparation work has been completed, the surfaces smoothed and dried, and the room thoroughly cleaned of all debris and dust, you are ready to start painting. To prevent the paint from splattering onto newly coated surfaces, begin by working from the ceiling, move down across the walls, and finish by painting the woodwork throughout the room. If you are painting over a dark-colored surface, two undercoats may be needed before applying the topcoat.

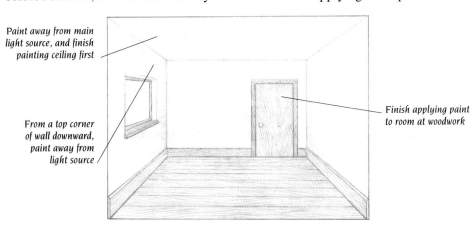

Paint away from main light source, and finish painting ceiling first

From a top corner of wall downward, paint away from light source

Finish applying paint to room at woodwork

TEMPORARY STORAGE

Paint tools will be ruined if left loaded for long periods of time. Store a brush that has oil-based paint on it for a few days by suspending it on the rim of a water-filled jar with the bristles in the water. Drill a hole in the handle and insert wire through the hole. For shorter periods, wrap brushes in aluminum foil, plastic wrap, or a bag.

SUSPENDED BRUSH

WRAPPED BRUSH

PAINTING WALLS AND CEILINGS

After cutting in, paint the wall with a large decorating brush or roller. Use a stepladder, and paint from the top of the wall to the floor. With a paintbrush, work in areas of 2 ft (60 cm) square, starting at a top corner nearest to the light source, if possible. Paint downward in blocks to the floor before moving to the next area across. Rollers should be used in bands 2 ft (60 cm) wide, beginning parallel to the ceiling and working in horizontal strips toward the floor.

PAINTING A CEILING

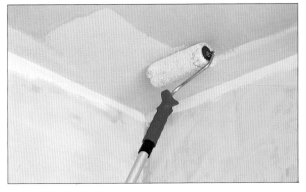

To paint a ceiling, use a roller, large decorating brush, or paint pad. You can work from a stepladder, but it will be more comfortable raising the working height with a ladder-and-board platform (*see page 208*). Aim to leave about 3 in (7.5 cm) between your head and the ceiling. If using a roller or paint pad, you can work from the floor with a long handle extension. Apply the paint in strips 1–1½ ft (30–45 cm) wide, working away from the light source.

PAINTING AROUND ELECTRICAL FITTINGS

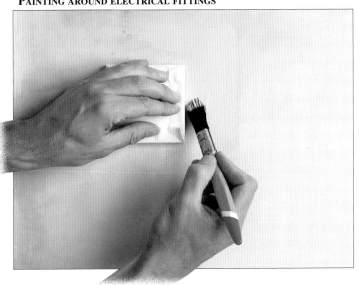

You can remove fittings, but be sure to switch off the electricity first. Remove the electrical face plate from the surface with a screwdriver or gently pry it off with a flat-bladed knife, and paint behind it. Applying masking tape to the edges of an electrical fitting is a safe and simple option. Paint around the electrical fitting. When the paint is completely dry, gently peel away the masking tape to reveal a straight edge.

APPLYING PAINT DETAILS

Many older homes contain original features such as moldings, cornices, and dado or picture rails. These wooden or plaster details should be painted using a small decorating or artist's brush. Apply background color with a 1 in (25 mm) or smaller brush, and paint fine details with an artist's brush. When using an artist's brush to paint details, steady your hand against a maulstick.

PAINTING WOODWORK

ONCE THE FINAL COAT OF PAINT HAS BEEN APPLIED to the ceiling and walls, you can move on to decorate the woodwork in the room. In order to prepare new or painted woodwork properly prior to applying fresh color or finish, you will need to clean and smooth all of the wood *(see page 182)* and apply knotting where necessary. Several layers of oil-based paint will provide the most durable coating for wood. If the woodwork is in good condition, or if an unusual finish is desired, you can choose from a wide range of other coatings, such as whitewashing, staining, varnishing, or waxing.

PAINTING WOOD

Glossy or eggshell oil-based paints should be layered to form a protective coating over a wooden surface. Make sure that each layer has dried before recoating; in low temperatures paint can take several days to dry. Paint the final coat with a well-worn, soft-bristled brush to obtain a smooth finish. When using oil-based paints, always work in a well-ventilated room.

PAINTING BARE WOOD

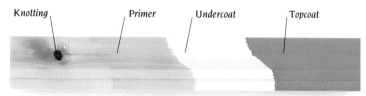

Knotting   Primer   Undercoat   Topcoat

Lightly sand any rough edges or surfaces on new wood. Remove dust by wiping the sanded areas with a lint-free cloth dampened in mineral spirits. Knots in wood can be sealed with shellac or knotting. When the knotting is completely dry, apply a wood primer. Brush the primer well into the wood; when dry, smooth the surface by rubbing lightly with fine sandpaper. Paint on one or two layers of undercoat. When the undercoat is dry, rub down the surface with fine-grade sandpaper. Wipe clean the sanded surface and brush on the topcoat to finish.

REPAINTING WOOD

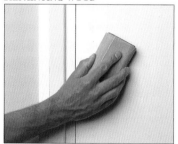

1 **SANDING** Wash surface with TSP. Sand rough finish using medium-to-fine sandpaper. Wipe off dust with a lint-free cloth dampened in mineral spirits.

2 **APPLYING TOPCOAT** Paint the topcoat onto the prepared surface. If a new color is desired, use an undercoat and apply the topcoat to the dry undercoat.

VARNISHING AND STAINING WOOD

Varnishes give coatings as durable as oil-based paints and are available in matte, satin, and gloss finishes. Pigmented varnishes change the color of wood. Staining produces a more effective tone than varnishing. Prepare the wood for varnishing as for oil-based paints: sand and fill to create a smooth surface. Brush away the dust and wipe surfaces with a lint-free cloth dipped in mineral spirits. You will need lint-free cloth, fine sandpaper, and a varnishing brush.

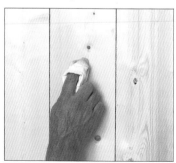

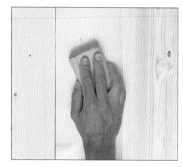

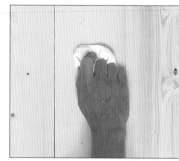

1 **RUBBING IN VARNISH** Pour some of the varnish into a wide-mouthed can, then dab a cloth into the coating. Rub the varnish into the surface, working in the direction of the grain.

2 **SANDING FIRST COAT** Once the first coat of varnish has dried – up to 12 hours, depending on the temperature and type of coating – lightly rub the surface with fine sandpaper.

3 **REMOVING DUST** Clean the particles off the surface with a dusting brush or old decorating brush. Remove last traces of dust by wiping with a lint-free cloth dampened in mineral spirits.

4 **APPLYING FINAL VARNISH** Following the manufacturer's instructions, apply each coat with a clean brush. Rub the surface lightly after each coat of varnish has dried.

ORDER OF WORK

Painting woodwork usually takes a good deal longer than imagined. Applying the paint, waiting for it to dry, and smoothing the finished surface, particularly if you are using several coats of oil-based paint, requires patience. Minimize the painting time and ensure fine results on woodwork by following a preplanned sequence of work. Paint the highest surfaces in the room, such as a picture rail, first, then work downward, finishing off at the baseboard.

FLUSH DOORS

Follow numbered sequence and paint frame last, applying coating from top downward

Start painting from the top of the door and work downward in narrow horizontal bands, using a 2 or 3 in (50 or 75 mm) brush. Make sure that the adjoining edge of the horizontal band is wet, so that the paint sections blend well together. Paint the frame of the door at the end, using a smaller brush.

PANELED DOORS

You will need two sizes of brushes for painting a paneled door. Use the smaller brush for painting the moldings, and the larger brush for rapid coverage of the wood frame and panels. To keep the oil-based paint off any door panels decorated in a special paint effect, cover them with masking tape or a paint shield.

PAINTING IN TWO COLORS

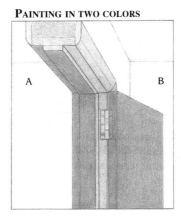

To paint a door and frame between rooms in different colors, stand in one room (A) and open the door to the inside of the other room (B). Paint in one color the lock edge, the adjacent edge of the frame, the doorstop, and the door front. Move through the opening to the next room (B). Open the door wide, so that its hinge edge is visible. Paint the hinge edge, the flat of the doorstop, the frame, and the door front on the inner side in the second color.

BASEBOARD

A baseboard needs a durable finish to protect it from hard wear. Use a 2 in (50 mm) brush to paint baseboards. Slide a cardboard mask or a paint shield under the baseboard, or cover the edge of the floor with masking tape. The cardboard, paint shield, or masking tape will keep the paint off the floor, as well as preventing dust particles and debris from sticking to the brush.

SASH WINDOWS

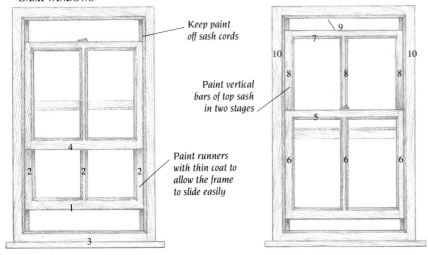

Keep paint off sash cords

Paint vertical bars of top sash in two stages

Paint runners with thin coat to allow the frame to slide easily

Mask the edges of the glass with tape. Leave a 1/32–1/16 in (1–2 mm) gap between the frame and window. The paint will overlap slightly onto the glass, helping to protect the frame against water damage. Slide open the sashes to reverse the top and bottom frames. Paint as follows: meeting rail (1), vertical bars (2), lower runners and frame (3), crossrail and its underside (4). Once the paint is dry, return the window to its normal position and paint a crossrail (5), vertical bars (6), other crossrail (7), remainder (8). Finally, paint the undersurface of an architrave, known as the soffit, the upper runners, and behind the cords (9), frame (10).

CASEMENT WINDOWS

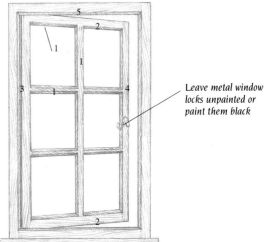

Leave metal window locks unpainted or paint them black

Plan on painting windows as early as possible in the day, so that you do not have to leave them open at night to dry. Remember that in cold weather, oil-based paints can take several hours to dry. To paint a casement window, mask the glass carefully, prop open the window, and paint in the following order: rebates and crossbars (1), top and bottom crossrails (2), hinge edge and hanging stile (3), meeting stile (4), frame (5).

CLEANING UP

*B*RUSHES, PADS, AND ROLLERS SHOULD BE CLEANED immediately after use to ensure long life. Brushes actually improve over time and give a smoother finish if they are cleaned and stored properly. For short intervals, for example during a meal break or overnight, it is possible to store some painting tools without cleaning them *(see page 187)*. When applying chemicals such as paint stripper or wood bleach to surfaces, use inexpensive brushes that can either be cleaned and kept solely for such tasks or thrown away when finished.

CLEANING PAINTING TOOLS

When buying paint, refer to the manufacturer's cleaning instructions and purchase the appropriate solvent at the same time. Oil-based paints can be removed from brushes and rollers with mineral spirits, turpentine, or kerosene. Water-based paints can be rinsed away from tools with water. Other paints have to be removed from tools with specific solvents, such as thinners or commercial brush cleaners. Finish cleaning all brushes, pads, and rollers by using a detergent, such as dishwashing liquid, to remove the last traces of the paint before storing the tools.

LATEX

1 SCRAPING OFF PAINT Clean a brush on several layers of newspaper, gently squeezing the bristles flat and scraping off the paint with the blunt edge of a flat-bladed knife.

2 RINSING BRUSH Splay bristles under warm water, making sure no paint remains in the heel of the brush, add some detergent, and rinse well. Vigorously shake out the water.

OIL-BASED PAINTS

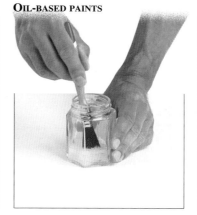

1 REMOVING PAINT Squeeze out the paint onto layers of newspaper, scraping it off with the blunt edge of a flat-bladed knife. Dip the brush in a jar of mineral spirits and stir rapidly.

2 WASHING BRUSH Wash the solvent out of the brush with detergent and lukewarm water. Rinse the brush thoroughly and shake dry. Take care not to damage the shape of the brush.

PAINT SAFETY

Refer to the manufacturer's instructions, and make sure that the room you are working in is well ventilated. Do not eat, drink, or smoke when painting, and keep open containers out of reach of pets and children. Use goggles when painting overhead, and wear gloves, if necessary, to minimize the risk of skin irritation. Wear a dust mask when handling powder colors or using a paint spray gun, and be careful of the fumes and dust released during heat stripping and sanding of old paint.

ROLLERS AND PADS

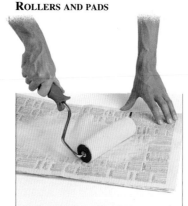

1 REMOVING PAINT Firmly roll the remainder of the paint onto several layers of newspaper. Replace and dispose of the newspaper regularly to prevent the roller or pad from getting reloaded with paint.

2 RINSING If possible, remove the cover from the roller frame and clean with the necessary solvent. Wash the roller or pad with detergent and lukewarm water. Rinse the roller or pad thoroughly and shake dry.

WORKING WITH CHEMICALS

If necessary, wear the recommended protective clothing such as gloves, goggles, and a face mask. When cleaning brushes or thinning paint, be aware of the dangers of solvents. Denatured alcohol, mineral spirits, and turpentine, are highly dangerous, whether inhaled, swallowed, or allowed to come in contact with the skin. Use and store chemicals well away from children and pets. Always follow manufacturer's instructions when using any type of chemical.

STORING PAINTING TOOLS

Brushes, rollers, and paint pads will last longer if they are cleaned, dried, and stored correctly when you have finished painting. A can of used paint will be easier to open if the lid was not damaged when you last closed the can. For storing your equipment, you will need rubber bands, paper or lint-free cloth, hammer and piece of wood, and airtight glass jars.

Wrap elastic band around bristles while brush is drying

STORING BRUSHES
Shake as much water from the brush as possible. Secure the bristles in position with an elastic band (*far left*) and lay the brush on its side to dry. Wrap brushes, paint pads, and rollers in lint-free cloth or paper (*left*), and store in a dry place.

CLOSING A PAINT CAN
Place a piece of flat wood on the rim of the lid and gently tap the wood with a hammer.

STORING PAINTS
Paints have a limited shelf life. Mark the date of use on the container and follow manufacturer's instructions for storage. Small quantities of paint should be stored in airtight glass jars, labeled with paint type, color, and batch code.

PAINT FAULTS

Paint faults can be avoided if surfaces, paint, and tools are well prepared. Surfaces should be clean, dry, and dust free (*see page 182*). Use paint that is freshly manufactured or sieved, and apply it to a compatible undercoat. Your equipment should be clean and in good condition, and should be used as appropriate for the task.

DARKENED AREAS

Shellac or knotting on wood will prevent resin from seeping through the paint. Scrape off the paint from the affected area with a sharp scraper, sand smooth, apply knotting, and recoat when dry.

TEARS AND RUNS

Caused by applying too much paint at once or by brushing a coat once it has begun to set. Do not recoat, but let the paint dry. Once dry, rub lightly with fine sandpaper, clean off the dust, and recoat.

WRINKLING

Wrinkling occurs when oil-based paint is applied before the first coat has dried. Most paints are so stable that wrinkling is a rare problem. Remove the paint and recoat after an adequate drying period.

GRIT

It is impossible to prevent dust, grit, and dirt from finding their way onto painted surfaces. To remove particles from dry paint, sand lightly, brush, and wipe off the surface when dry.

BLISTERING

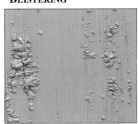

Blistering is caused by trapped moisture or air expanding underneath a coating of oil-based paint. Strip off the paint, fill open-grained wood if necessary, and prime, undercoat, and repaint.

POOR COVERAGE

If the color of the undercoat shows through the topcoat, apply at least one more layer of paint. Latex paint in particular needs many coatings to cover a dark background or undercoat color.

FLAKING

Paint flakes when surfaces have not been prepared correctly. Latex tends to peel and flake when applied to tempera, or to a high-gloss finish. Strip the flaking surface, prepare properly, and repaint.

STAINING

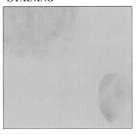

Staining affects latex. Water in paint can react with surface impurities such as salts, iron fixings, or residues from a chimney flue. Coat with aluminum primer sealer and repaint when dry.

ALLIGATORING

Occurs when a painted surface is coated with an incompatible paint, or as a result of using two or more paint coats with different drying times. Strip and prepare surface. Paint with appropriate coating.

INSECTS

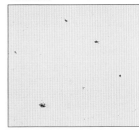

Remove insects from wet paint by brushing them off and then touching up the area. For insects found in dry paint, sand and then recoat the spot with matching paint, from the same batch if possible.

SPECIAL PAINT EFFECTS

IN RECENT YEARS, PAINT MANUFACTURERS and decorators have perfected methods of applying an even coating of color to a smooth surface. Just as they have done so, however, there has been a revival of interest in providing variety of texture and tone in painted decoration. These effects are known as distressing, and they involve the application of a matching or delicately contrasting tone to a white or pastel-colored background. Once the preserve of specialists, many distressed finishes are easily achieved by using simple techniques and materials. You can use ordinary latex paints for distressing, but because the process requires the coloring to be manipulated once applied, slower-drying oil-based paints are more suitable. Time can be saved if you enroll the help of an assistant who can apply the paint ahead, while you do the distressing. To gain confidence and to experiment, first practice the effect you wish to achieve on sheets of oil-painted hardboard.

MAKING A TINTED OIL GLAZE

Tinted oil glaze is the easiest coloring material to work with for special effects. Depending on the room temperature, it possesses a 30-minute to one-hour workable time. A tinted oil-glaze finish should be applied to a matte oil-painted surface, and protected with a coat or two of matte varnish when fully dry. Transparent oil glaze is sold ready-mixed in specialty paint stores as glaze coat or glazing liquid. It can be colored with artist's oil paints, universal tints, or powder colors. Commercial glazes are generally easiest to use when thinned with mineral spirits to resemble a maple-syrup consistency.

MAKING TRANSPARENT OIL GLAZE

Make a liter of homemade transparent oil glaze by whisking together 1 pint (.473 liter) turpentine, ½ pint (.236 liter) boiled linseed oil, ⅓ pint (.158 liter) drier, and a tablespoon of whiting in a paint can. When the glaze is stored in an airtight container, it has a shelf life of approximately one year.

TINTING THE GLAZE

Dissolve a small amount of the chosen coloring in a jar one-third full of mineral spirits. Add color and/or mineral spirits until you reach the desired tone. Mix in a tablespoon of glaze. Stir in the remaining glaze for the project. Add more color and mineral spirits mix to obtain the desired tone.

MASKING TECHNIQUES

There are many occasions when one area of coloring must be masked from another area to ensure a clearly defined line, for example where latex on the wall meets a light switch, or the wooden molding around doors and windows. Use low-tack masking tape to create a division between different colors on the wall. This will help to ensure that the tape adhesive will not pull away any paint when peeled off. Remove the tape once the paint is completely dry.

1 **MARKING LINE** Establish a vertical or horizontal line (see page 229) for the division between the colors. Mark this line with a soft pencil.

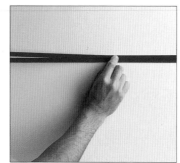

2 **APPLYING TAPE** Apply strips of masking tape to run parallel to, and above, the pencil line. Make sure that the pencil mark remains visible.

3 **APPLYING PAINT** Using a small decorating brush and starting from the middle of the masking-tape strips, apply paint downwards to the wall.

4 **REMOVING TAPE** Complete the remaining area of wall with a larger decorating brush, pad, or roller. When the paint is dry, slowly pull away the tape.

TOOLS AND EQUIPMENT

The variety of equipment and raw materials associated with the application of a distressed finish ranges from the specialized softener brush to the everyday plastic bag used as a simple tool. To purchase or rent specialist equipment, you will need to find outlets such as professional decorators' suppliers, craft and printing-supply shops, and art-supply stores. The majority of these specialist suppliers publish catalogs of their stock and will usually send tools and raw materials by mail. You can obtain everyday tools from a hardware store or home-improvement center.

BRUSHES

Large decorating brushes are used for applying color quickly to large areas, while short-haired ones are used for its distribution. A horsehair flogger is most suitable for dragging. To soften a paint effect, use either a dusting brush or, for the most subtle result, a gentle softener. A stippler is used to fleck a surface. Stenciling brushes are used with a stabbing action.

LARGE DECORATING BRUSH

SHORT-HAIRED DECORATING BRUSH

STIPPLER

FLOGGER

SOFTENER

STENCILING BRUSH

OTHER EQUIPMENT

A variety of other equipment can be used to create distressed effects, particularly on easy-to-work, tinted oil glaze. For a sponged effect, changing the pressure of application and the grip on a natural sponge will result in an endless variety of mottled patterns. A synthetic sponge will leave a more regular pattern. A crinkle pattern, known as bagging, is produced with a plastic bag loaded with a rag, while lint-free cloths are used to create a ragging and rag-rolling finish.

LINT-FREE CLOTH

PLASTIC BAG

SPONGE

PIGMENTS

Pigments in the form of powder or artist's oil color are used to give color to transparent oil glaze. Regardless of the constituents, you should make up enough tinted oil glaze of one formula to complete a room or piece of furniture, because matching subsequent tints can be very difficult.

POWDER COLORS

ARTIST'S OIL COLOR

LINOLEUM CUTTING AND STAMPING

This method involves making prints from blocks cut from linoleum flooring material. The blocks are used to stamp walls with decorative patterns. The tools and materials required for this effect can be obtained from a printer's supplier or a good craft shop.

PRINTER'S INK

ROLLER

BEVELED-EDGED GLASS

CUTTING TOOLS AND KNIFE

LINOLEUM TILE

CARBON PAPER

WHITEWASHING WOOD

To open the grain, use a bronze-wire hand brush obtainable from specialist suppliers. Apply wax or paste with fine-grade steel wool.

WHITEWASHING WAX

BRONZE-WIRE HAND BRUSH

TRANSPARENT OIL GLAZE INGREDIENTS

To increase the working time of glaze (*see opposite*) add more boiled linseed oil. Whiting gives body to a glaze, and driers hasten the speed at which it hardens. Add mineral spirits or turpentine to a transparent oil glaze to ease its application.

POWDERED WHITING

DRIER

TURPENTINE

LINSEED OIL

SOFTENED GLAZEWORK

The simplest of the special paint effects, a tinted oil glaze adds a subtle tinge and a softening hue to complement the underlying color on the surface. The walls should be prepared for as smooth a surface as possible *(see page 182)* and then evenly coated with two layers of eggshell paint. To apply, spread, and finish the tinted oil glaze, you will need a decorating brush, a wide, short-bristled decorating brush, and a softener brush. The tinted oil glaze is created by coloring transparent oil glaze, which is available ready-made or you can mix it at home, with artist's oil paint. When dry, the softened glazework can be made durable by applying a coat of matte varnish.

1 APPLYING GLAZE Load the decorating brush with the tinted oil glaze and apply with random strokes over an area of 1 sq yd (1 sq m) at a time. Tinted oil glaze is quick drying, so it is important to work rapidly.

2 SPREADING GLAZEWORK A wide, short-bristled decorating brush should be used to spread the tinted oil glaze. Begin by erasing the most obvious brush marks. Work to achieve an even coating of tinted glaze.

3 SMOOTHING GLAZE To smooth tinted oil glaze and disperse brush marks, stroke the paint in all directions with the tips of the softening brush. To avoid paint buildup, occasionally wipe the bristles on lint-free cloth.

SPONGING ON

Using a sponge to apply glaze is a straightforward decorative process. The tools are simple – all that is needed is a tray to hold the glaze and a quality natural sponge. Tinted oil glaze is the most versatile paint for sponging and should be applied to a surface covered with two coats of matte (flat) oil-based paint, such as eggshell. Depending on the desired effect, you can apply two or three colors that complement the matte (flat) oil-based coat.

1 LOADING SPONGE A roller tray is an ideal container for tinted glaze. In a paint can, mix up the tinted glaze and pour it into the tray reservoir. Dab the sponge in the tinted glaze and press the excess paint onto the slope of the tray.

2 DABBING TINTED GLAZE Grip the sponge lightly and dab it in a haphazard pecking manner across the surface to create a dappling of background and applied tones. If the sponge becomes overloaded with tinted oil glaze and the paint begins to run, squeeze the excess onto a lint-free cloth. When dry, seal the surface with a coat of matte (flat) varnish.

SPONGING OFF

Sponging off creates a regular, one-color, near-opaque effect. For the application and selective removal of the tinted oil glaze, you will need a decorating brush, a natural sponge soaked in mineral spirits and squeezed out, and tinted oil glaze. The surface of the wall must be sealed with two coats of eggshell or other matte (flat) oil-based paint. To protect and seal the tinted oil glaze at the finish, paint on one or more layers of a matte (flat) varnish once the glaze is dry.

1 APPLYING GLAZE Mix tinted oil glaze in a paint can to the consistency of thick cream and apply to the surface with a decorating brush. Work rapidly over small areas of the wall, since glaze dries quickly.

2 DABBING OFF PAINT Wring out the sponge in mineral spirits. Dab it onto the tinted oil glaze to create a cloudy effect. The more glaze is removed, the lighter the finish will be.

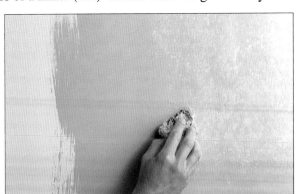

RAGGING

Ragging a surface that has been coated with a tinted oil glaze will produce a subtle effect that can be softened further if you use fresh lint-free cloths soaked in mineral spirits and wrung out. Before brushing on the tinted oil glaze with a decorating brush, prepare the wall with one layer of matte (flat) oil-based paint.

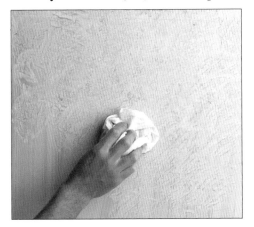

DABBING OFF GLAZE
Bunch the cloth in one hand and dab the tinted oil glaze off the surface to create patterns. Vary your grip on the cloth to create different effects. To soften the pattern, go over the glaze with the tip of a softening brush approximately half an hour after application.

BAGGING TINTED OIL GLAZE
Place a bunched-up cloth in a plastic bag. Use a flattened edge of this handmade tool to imprint the tinted glaze with different overlapping patterns. From time to time, wipe the excess glaze from the bag with a cloth. When dry, coat the surface with a layer of matte (flat) varnish.

RAG-ROLLING

Rag-rolling produces a randomly distressed effect. For the rolling process, you will need either many fresh lint-free cloths or a piece of chamois leather, both of which must be soaked in mineral spirits and wrung out, as well as a wide decorating brush.

ROLLING OFF PAINT
Apply one coat of the tinted oil glaze to a small area of the wall at a time. Work or roll the fresh rag or chamois in various directions.

BAGGING

Surfaces coated with tinted oil glaze can be distressed using various equipment. One of the simplest tools is a plastic bag and a bunched-up cloth. Prepare the surfaces with a layer of matte (flat) oil-based paint. Use a wide decorating brush and paint the tinted oil glaze onto an area of 2 sq yd (2 sq m).

STIPPLING

Stippling is one of the more subtle and sophisticated paint effects using a tinted oil glaze. First, apply the tinted oil glaze to a smooth surface with a decorating brush. Then use a large, firm-bristled brush to pounce a multitip pattern onto the glaze. Although a stiff broom-head will produce a similar stippling effect, there is no real substitute for a stippling brush, which is available from specialty paint suppliers.

1 STIPPLING
Mix the glaze, mineral spirits, and oil color to a thick consistency and apply to the wall over an area of approximately 1 sq yd (1 sq m). Grip the stippling brush securely and stab it at the wall. This stabbing action on the thick glaze coat will create a fine mottle. Control the dotted effect by keeping the same rhythm and force of the stabbing action.

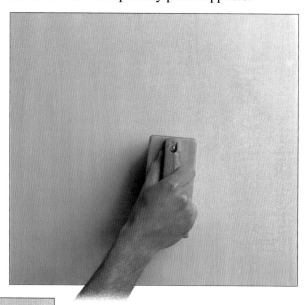

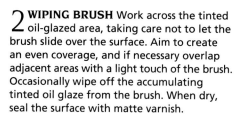

2 WIPING BRUSH Work across the tinted oil-glazed area, taking care not to let the brush slide over the surface. Aim to create an even coverage, and if necessary overlap adjacent areas with a light touch of the brush. Occasionally wipe off the accumulating tinted oil glaze from the brush. When dry, seal the surface with matte varnish.

DRAGGING

This decorative technique demands a particularly smooth surface *(see page 182)*, which must be sealed with two coats of a matte oil-based paint. You will need a decorating brush to apply the tinted oil glaze. This should be painted on in vertical strips 2 ft (60 cm) wide from ceiling to floor. Carefully drag a dry flogger brush in smooth, vertical strokes through the tinted oil glaze. In this special paint effect, the shade of the background surface will show through as fine, uneven stripes of color.

USING THE FLOGGER
Drag the flogger from ceiling to floor. Brush the wet glaze in a steady motion, carefully avoiding jolts and stop-start marks. Hold the flogger to the wall with a light, even pressure, dragging from the middle of the bristles. After each pass, wipe off excess glaze from the brush with a lint-free cloth.

LIMING WOOD

Liming pastes and waxes give a soft-white tint and are easy to apply to bare wood. Furniture is ideally suited to the subtle coloring. Floorboards also look good when limed, although this is not a durable finish. You will need a wire brush, the finest steel wool, and lint-free cloths for this technique.

1 OPENING WOOD GRAIN
Open the wood grain by stroking with a wire brush. Prevent scratches by working in the direction of the wood grain.

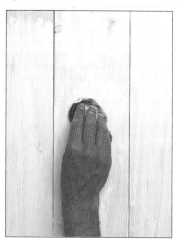

2 RUBBING LIME
Apply liming paste or wax with the fine steel wool, working to fill the grain. Rub in a circular motion and complete an area of ½ sq yd (½ sq m) at one time, allowing the liming wax or paste to dry for a few minutes. Remove the excess liming by rubbing the surface with a fine, clear paste wax.

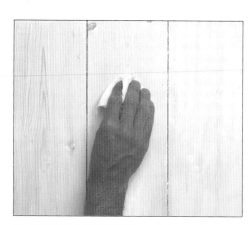

3 BUFFING SURFACE Buff the surface thoroughly with a fine, clear paste wax, using a soft, lint-free cloth to give a dull sheen to the finish.

GLAZING

Before the introduction of opaque and easy-to-apply latex paints, walls were routinely colored with water-based coatings such as tempera. These paints were economical to use but usually left a watery dappling of colors and a dusty finish when dry. These properties are now appreciated as decorative effects. Tempera may sometimes be found at specialty paint suppliers. Alternatively, thinned latex paint applied with a large decorating brush will produce a similar effect on walls. For glazing, or colorwashing, wooden surfaces such as floorboards and doors, you will need a large decorating brush, a supply of lint-free cloths, fine-grade sandpaper, and a clear paste wax.

GLAZING WALLS

1 APPLYING GLAZE Seal the surface of a smooth wall with an opaque coating of latex paint. Thin the glazing latex with water to a ratio of between 4:1 and 9:1, depending on the nature of the paint. Apply the watery color to an area of 1 sq yd (1 sq m). Immediately go over the entire painted surface with a damp brush to soften the brush marks.

2 APPLYING SECOND COAT Leave the first coat of color, which will often appear messy, to dry overnight. Paint on another wash with a wide decorating brush. As before, work in one small area at a time, and be prepared for runs and splattering of the watery paint. If desired, apply a coat of matte varnish to protect the finished effect.

GLAZING WOOD

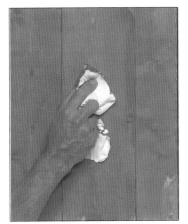

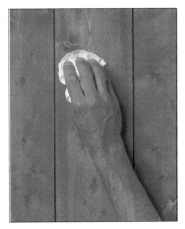

1 APPLYING GLAZE Strip and sand the wood. Dilute the latex to penetrate the surface, and then test on a small area. Following the direction of the grain, slop on glaze with a wide decorating brush.

2 REMOVING EXCESS Brush on the glaze over a small area. When nearly dry, wipe off the excess paint with a lint-free cloth to expose the grain. Apply and wipe the paint in sections across the surface.

3 SANDING After wiping, leave the glaze to dry overnight. If the resulting color effect is too weak, apply another coat and wipe. To finish, smooth the surface by sanding lightly with fine-grade sandpaper.

4 SEALING Clean off the wood by stroking the surface with a dry decorating brush. Remove all traces of dust with a damp cloth. Surfaces such as floorboards should then be sealed with clear paste wax.

STENCILING

Until recently, stencils for repeating patterns onto walls and furniture were made of thin metal sheets. These days, stencil cardboard or a thin sheet of acetate is more commonly used. To copy a design, you will need tracing paper, a medium-hard pencil, and a soft pencil. A craft knife will enable you to cut the cardboard or acetate. A cutting mat is useful, and you will invariably need a metal ruler. A small level will help you to position the stencil on the surface. Fix the stencil to the surface with low-tack tape, and use a stencil brush to apply the paint.

1 TRACING DESIGN Draw or copy a design onto a sheet of tracing paper, using a soft pencil. Stencils look best when used as friezes or borders, so design an interconnecting pattern, using registration marks on the cardboard as a guide. If different colors are being used, then a separate stencil needs to be made for each one.

2 TRANSFERRING Turn over the tracing paper. Secure it to the cardboard with masking tape. Using a medium-hard pencil, draw or rub over the reverse of the pattern. Remove the tracing paper.

3 MAKING TEMPLATE Draw a system of "bridges" to secure any "islands" in the design. With the craft knife, pierce the cardboard. Turn and pull the pattern toward the blade.

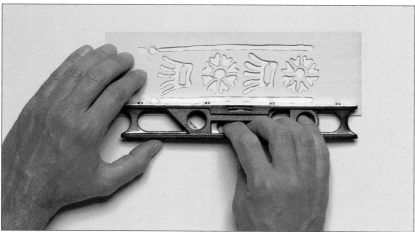

4 POSITIONING STENCIL Decide where to run the stencil pattern and mark the position of the first piece of the frieze with a light pencil. For each application of the stencil, find the horizontal or vertical with a level and secure the cardboard to the wall with low-tack tape.

DESIGN INSPIRATION

There exists a wealth of inspirations for highly decorative stencils and stamps. The geometric beauty of tribal and folk textiles from areas such as Indonesia, Latin America, Africa, and India provide excellent sources for designs. A photocopier is useful for sizing patterns. For the stamp design opposite, a pattern was photocopied from an Indian cloth and the print enlarged for easy tracing.

5 PAINTING DESIGN A stencil brush makes an ideal applicator for the paint, but a stiff decorating brush also works well. Latex is the most adaptable paint for stenciling on the wall. Load the brush lightly and wipe off the excess onto scrap paper before pouncing the color onto the stencil.

THE FINISHED EFFECT

STAMPING

The art and craft of making and applying a patterned stamp to walls or furniture can be creative and challenging. A stamp can either be copied from a scale drawing onto a manufactured rubber block or made at home from linoleum. Linoleum-cutting materials are easy to use, and the techniques allow for great expression. From an art supply or crafts shop, you will need linoleum, linoleum-cutting tools, glass with beveled edges, an inking roller, printer's color, tracing paper and carbon paper, pencil, ballpoint and felt-tip pens, as well as a piece of ¾ in (2 cm) plywood, paper, mineral spirits, and some lint-free cloth.

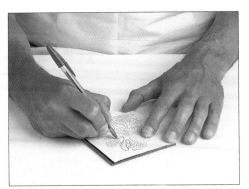

1 IMPRINTING DESIGN Use a photocopier to find the best dimension for the pattern. Cut the linoleum to size. Imprint the design by drawing with a ballpoint pen over the outline through a sheet of carbon paper onto the stamp.

2 CUTTING LINOLEUM Go over the outline with a fine, indelible felt-tip pen, and fill in areas that are to be cut away. Test the cutting tools on a spare piece until you can confidently cut away both large and small areas. Linoleum cuts easily when warm.

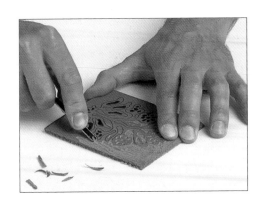

3 ROLLING INK Prepare the printing ink. Squeeze a blob of the color onto the center of the glass and distribute the ink with the roller. Coat the surface of the roller evenly with the glutinous ink, adding color and rolling again.

4 INKING Raise the linoleum onto plywood, then run the inked roller over the design. Areas above the design that "take" ink will appear when printed. Clean the stamp with mineral spirits and cut away unwanted elevated areas.

5 TESTING STAMP When satisfied that the design is isolated on the stamp, roll it with ink and test the linoleum cut on a piece of paper. Make a clear imprint by pressing hard with steady hands, and pull the block away in one confident movement.

6 STAMPING WALL Ink the design and press the stamp steadily onto the painted surface, using a firm rocking motion. Hold tightly so that the stamp does not slide on the surface. When finished with the job, clean the ink off all tools with mineral spirits.

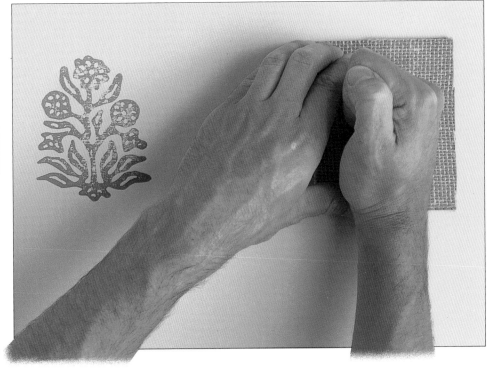

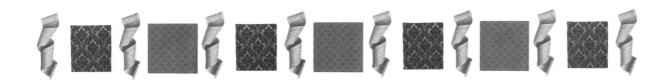

WALLPAPERING

WALLPAPER PROVIDES AN EFFICIENT MEANS of applying a regularly colored and patterned finish to a wall or ceiling in a single layer. There is an enormous range of styles and materials available, and you can obtain a covering for virtually any surface and decorative scheme. Additionally, there are various types of wallpaper borders that can be used to complement papered or painted walls. As well as having a decorative function, wallpaper provides a means of covering surfaces that are less than perfect prior to painting or papering. Certain types of wallpaper, such as lining paper and woodchip paper, are particularly strong and durable, and specifically designed for this purpose. Applying paper to a room is easy once you have mastered a few simple techniques. In this chapter, you will find information on the types of wallpaper available, preparation techniques, and the sequence and method of hanging wallpaper on ceilings and walls.

CHOOSING A STYLE

WALLPAPER IS BY NO MEANS LIMITED TO PAPER. There is a great variety of modern materials available, both natural and synthetic, that can be used for covering walls and ceilings in every room. The ever-increasing range of contemporary designs provides an almost limitless choice of decorative possibilities. Hand- or machine-printed wallpapers, however, offer the most comprehensive selection of patterns, colors, and finishes. Recent advancements in manufacturing have produced wallpapers in improved designs and colors that are quick to apply, washable, and easy to strip.

PERFECT PATTERNS
One of the most valuable decorative features of wallpaper is its ability to convey repeating patterns with regularity and precision. The horizontal pattern repeat is restricted by the width of the rolls. For this reason, the most popular wallpaper patterns are designed with appropriately proportioned patterns, such as these floral motifs. When the wallpaper is in place, the regularly patterned composition can be interpreted not only horizontally and vertically but also diagonally. Wallpapers with linear patterns have found great popularity in bedrooms, since they are informal and communicate a special, personal atmosphere.

Wallpaper on sloping ceiling provides continuity of design throughout the room

White background of wallpaper harmonizes with furnishings

Conspicuous pattern on walls counterbalances plain, white-painted window frame and white curtain

REGENCY STRIPES
Broad stripes in two shades of the same color give a formal room a grand atmosphere. When using wallpapers with predominantly dark tones, avoid shade variations by ensuring that all the rolls have the same batch number.

Stenciled border in gold paint adds detail and breaks up simple stripes

ORNAMENTAL FRAMES
Wallpaper manufacturers produce a range of complementary borders to match their paper patterns. When used in combination with a corner section, strips of wallpaper border can be hung horizontally and vertically to create a distinctive frame on appropriate surfaces such as chimney pieces. Borders can also be applied as chair rails to form boundaries between wallpaper above and paintwork below.

Colors of border complement main wallpaper

DUAL STYLES
In a period home complete with original wooden molding, take advantage of these decorative features with the judicious application of wallpaper. Here, the wallpaper serves to inspire the rich tones of the paintwork below the rail.

PAINT EFFECTS
Decorating all the walls of a room in a uniform color and in a special paint effect is a painstaking and time-consuming task. As an alternative, use patterned wallpapers that mimic paint finishes such as dragging, stippling, and sponging.

PRACTICAL AND MODERN
Wallpaper used to be vulnerable to damage from everyday wear and tear. For this reason, wallpapering tended to be restricted to reception rooms and bedrooms. In recent years, however, washable and durable wallpapers in modern, stylish designs have been developed that are suitable for even the most heavily used rooms, including bathrooms, kitchens, and dining rooms.

Striped wallpaper in light tones gives impression of brightness and space

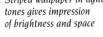

Washable wallpaper is ideally suited for much-used dining area

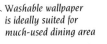

WALLPAPER MATERIALS

*A*PPLYING PAPER TO WALLS was originally devised as an inexpensive method of decorating the formal rooms in a home, which received relatively little wear and tear. Nowadays, wallpapers are made to be more durable and washable than in the past, enabling them to be utilized in even the most heavily used rooms, such as kitchens and bathrooms. Wallpapers are available in a wide variety of colors, patterns, and textures to suit almost every decorative style. The equipment and materials required for applying wallpaper are readily available from your local hardware store.

WALLPAPER CHOICES

Undecorated wallpaper, such as lining paper, is widely used to cover walls that are in poor and unsightly condition. Various grades of lining paper are available for making surfaces smooth before you begin painting or hanging wallpaper. Wallpapers are also made of more unusual materials, ranging from the exotic, such as silks, burlap, and grass cloth, to the highly durable, such as textured vinyl, which is heat treated *(see page 219)*. Recently, however, manufacturers have concentrated on making wallpapers resembling "standard" paper, but are much easier to hang and simpler to clean than in the past.

WOODCHIP PAPER
This heavy-duty, textured paper is ideal for disguising walls that have small cracks and surface imperfections. You can paint woodchip wallpaper after hanging, but once glued to the wall this paper is very difficult to remove.

BORDERS
Many manufacturers produce borders to complement their wallpaper collections. Easy to hang, borders are normally applied at the tops of walls or as horizontal decorative divisions between different colors of paint.

VINYL PAPER
Made of a layer of vinyl with a paper backing, this wallpaper is easy to hang, can be washed down or scrubbed clean, and is simple to remove. Also available prepasted *(see page 219)*, vinyl is an ideal hard-wearing surface.

DECORATED PAPER
Decorated paper is made in a range of patterns and qualities. Vinyl-coated decorated paper is wipeable, but varieties without a coating cannot be washed and therefore require special maintenance.

LINING PAPER
This plain paper is readily available in a variety of grades. It is applied before painting and papering ceilings and walls, particularly when the surfaces are in poor condition.

EQUIPMENT

For applying wallpaper, you will need a sturdy stepladder to reach the top of the wall or the ceiling. In addition to the tools listed below, you will also need a tape measure, carpenter's pencil, 1 yd (1 m) ruler, straightedge, craft knife with replaceable blades, carpenter's level or chalk line, and sponge or damp cloth to wipe excess paste or size from surfaces. Keep a few trash bags handy for disposal of trimmed pieces of paste-coated wallpaper.

BRUSHES
Apply adhesive with an easy-to-clean, synthetic-bristled pasting brush. A smoothing brush is essential for smoothing paper in place after hanging. Use a radiator roller for applying and smoothing paper behind a radiator. A broom is ideal for holding up folded pasted paper when working at the ceiling.

PASTING BRUSH

RADIATOR ROLLER

SMOOTHING BRUSH

HOUSEHOLD BROOM

ADHESIVES AND SIZES
The manufacturer's instructions that accompany the paper should specify the type of adhesive. You should also use the size that is recommended by the maker of the suggested adhesive. When overlapping vinyl wallpaper, you will need to glue the surfaces together with specially made vinyl adhesive.

SIZE

ADHESIVE

VINYL ADHESIVE

WATER TRAY

CONTAINERS
Mix the size and paste in a clean bucket with a handle. When applying prepasted papers, you will need to soak the cut lengths of wallpaper in a water tray before hanging them.

BUCKET WITH HANDLE

OTHER TOOLS AND EQUIPMENT
When pasting paper, work at a level platform of a suitable height; a folding pasting table is ideal. Press the paper seams in place with a seam roller, and use small scissors and wallpaper scissors to cut and crease paper. Use doweling to stir paste or size, and matchsticks to mark positions of fixtures in the wall.

PASTING TABLE

SEAM ROLLER

WALLPAPER SCISSORS

MATCHSTICKS

WOODEN DOWELING

CALCULATING THE NUMBER OF ROLLS

Measure the whole of the surface to be covered. Take these measurements to the supplier, choose the wallpaper, and consult the manufacturer's charts for the number of rolls required, allowing extra for trimming. Always select rolls of wallpaper bearing the same batch number. The following charts apply for standard rolls of wallpaper only – these are approximately 33 ft (10 m) long and 21 in (530 mm) wide.

ROLL REQUIREMENTS FOR CEILINGS

Distance around room						
Feet Metres	30–40 9–12	42–50 13–15	55–60 17–18	65–70 20–21	75–80 23–24	85–90 26–27	95–100 29–30
Number of rolls	2	3	4	6	7	9	10

ROLL REQUIREMENTS FOR WALLS

Wall height	Distance around room (including doors and windows)							
	33 ft 10 m	39 ft 12 m	46 ft 14 m	52 ft 16 m	59 ft 18 m	66 ft 20 m	72 ft 22 m	79 ft 24 m
7 ft–7 ft 6 in 2.1–2.3 m	5	5	6	7	8	9	10	11
7 ft 6 in–8 ft 2.3–2.4 m	5	6	7	8	9	10	10	11
8 ft–8 ft 6 in 2.4–2.6 m	5	6	7	9	10	11	12	13
8 ft 6 in–9 ft 2.6–2.7 m	5	6	7	9	10	11	12	13
9 ft–9 ft 6 in 2.7–2.9 m	6	7	8	9	10	12	12	14

PREPARATION

BEFORE HANGING YOUR WALLPAPER, remove as much furniture as possible from the room. Take down the curtains or blinds, shelving, if possible, and all loose wall decorations, including pictures and mirrors, but leave the hooks and electrical fittings in place. Group any remaining furniture in the center of the room and cover this, and the floor, with drop cloths. Do not cover the floor with plastic sheets, because they are slippery when wet.

PREPARING SURFACES

When starting to hang wallpaper, always begin with a smooth surface. Most old wallpaper in good condition can be papered over, but you should remove relief, washable, and metallic papers. Surfaces that have been newly plastered must be completely dry (drying may take several weeks) before applying size and wallpaper. Fill all cracks and holes (see page 182). Wash painted surfaces down with trisodium phosphate (TSP) or, if shiny, abrade with sandpaper. Seal flaking paint with an oil-based primer sealer. Apply size before the wallpaper. For the best finish, hang lining paper first.

REMOVING OLD WALLPAPER

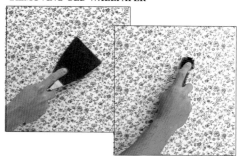

1 SCORING PAPER Use the sharp edge of a scraper or a wallpaper spiker to score the old wallpaper diagonally. Take care not to mark or dig into the underlying wall when you are scoring.

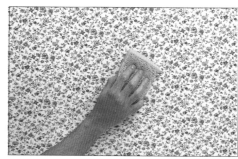

2 SPONGING PAPER Fill a bucket with warm water and liberally sponge the scored wallpaper. Press the wet sponge onto the old paper. Soak the paper in sections across the wall so that as one area of old wallpaper is being removed, other sections will be loosening.

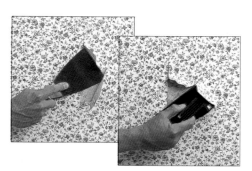

3 SCRAPING OFF PAPER Once the old paper and paste are soaked, remove them with a scraper or wallpaper remover. Be careful not to dig into the wall, because plaster is fragile when wet. After all the paper has been removed, wipe and lightly scrape the surface again to remove all of the old glue.

STEAM STRIPPER

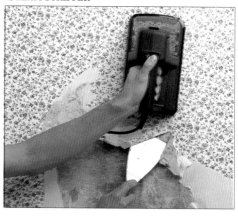

A steam stripper is useful for removing large areas of old wallpaper. Steam strippers are available in several sizes and can be rented locally. Score the old wallpaper with the sharp edge of a scraper or a wallpaper spiker (see above). Hold the steam stripper against the surface. Scrape off the paper as it becomes loose, then move the steam stripper to an adjacent area.

REMOVING VINYL WALLPAPER

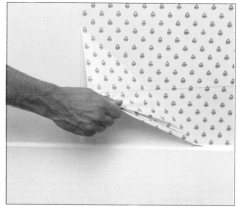

Old vinyl and washable wallpaper must be removed from a surface before hanging new wallpaper. Mounted on special backing paper, vinyl wallpaper is simple and straightforward to remove. Pry up a corner of the vinyl and peel it away from the wall, leaving the backing paper. Apply a wet sponge to the backing paper (see above) and remove it from the wall.

SIZING SURFACES

Apply size to a clean, smooth, and dry surface before hanging the wallpaper. Size will reduce the absorbency of the surface and make hanging paper much easier. Consult the paper or adhesive manufacturer's instructions, and apply the recommended size with a large decorating or pasting brush. Wipe off splashes of size immediately from any woodwork, using a damp cloth.

ORDER OF WORK

MIXING PASTE

After the preparation work, consider what painting is required in the room. When papering walls, paint the ceiling and the woodwork first, because any splashes of paste can easily be wiped off a finished surface. If coating all surfaces with paper, apply lining paper to the ceiling and paint it, then apply the lining paper to the walls and hang the wallpaper. Start on the most important wall, and hang the lengths working away from the main light source. Finish at the least noticeable corner of the room, which is usually adjacent to the door.

Use the paste recommended by the lining or wallpaper manufacturer. Follow the instructions for mixing the paste – you will need to fill a bucket with cold water and add the powder. Stir the mixture with a long piece of wooden doweling and, if specified, leave to stand before using.

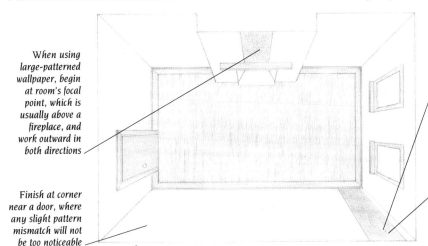

When using large-patterned wallpaper, begin at room's focal point, which is usually above a fireplace, and work outward in both directions

Finish at corner near a door, where any slight pattern mismatch will not be too noticeable

For small-patterned, striped, or plain wallpapers, begin on longest wall nearest light source and work away from it

Mark vertical line from ceiling to floor as guide for aligning first length of wallpaper

LINING PAPER

Lining paper is available in five different grades of thickness and is usually used to create a smooth surface prior to painting or hanging wallpaper. When a surface, and particularly an old ceiling, has several small cracks across it, you can cover it with lining paper. Use medium-weight lining or decorative paper on walls and thicker lining paper, which is less likely to tear, on ceilings. When hanging lining paper, always use a size and paste that is compatible with the manufacturer's recommended adhesive for the decorative wallpaper. You should wait until the lining paper is completely dry and secured to the wall before applying the decorative wallpaper. When preparing to wallpaper, plan ahead for drying time, because once applied it can take up to 12 hours for lining paper to dry on the wall.

CEILINGS

On a ceiling, hang lining paper parallel to a window, and work away from it

Hang lining paper on the ceiling parallel to the window or main light source, and work away from it. Ceilings with poor plasterwork may need to be lined again at right angles to the first layer in order to cover all cracks and create a surface as smooth as possible.

HANGING PAPER HORIZONTALLY

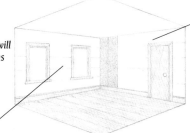

Applying lining paper horizontally will prevent seams of decorative covering and lining paper falling in same places

When hanging lining paper horizontally, begin at ceiling and work downward

Decorative wallpaper is usually hung vertically. Lining paper can be applied horizontally on the walls so that it is at right angles to the direction of the final wall covering *(see page 211)*. This will prevent the joins from coinciding.

HANGING PAPER VERTICALLY

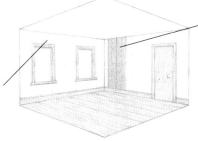

Starting from ceiling and working down, smooth each section of paper as you go

Decide where first length of decorative paper is to go, then hang a half width of lining paper in that place

Start with a half width of lining paper, working from a vertical line, and continue with full widths along the wall. Hang full widths of decorative wallpaper from the same vertical line to ensure that the joins of the lining paper and wallpaper never coincide.

PAPERING A CEILING

CEILINGS ARE USUALLY DECORATED WITH PAINT rather than wallpaper, but if a ceiling has small cracks, lining paper will provide a smooth surface to paint on. Use medium- or heavy-grade lining paper to cover a ceiling, because thicker-grade paper is less likely to tear than thin lining paper when being applied. Hang the decorative paper at right angles to the lining paper, so that the seams of both layers of paper do not run along the same lines. Papering a ceiling is awkward because you are working against gravity. To ease the task, enroll the help of an assistant or assemble a safe and convenient platform to work from.

PLATFORMS

Assemble a platform in the room to raise your work level. The ceiling should be approximately 3 in (7.5 cm) above your head when you are working for you to hang the paper properly.

WORK PLATFORM

Build a platform that is safe and comfortable to work from. Lay strong scaffold planks between the secure rungs of two stepladders or on top of trestles. Build the scaffold to the same length as the hanging paper, so that you can work easily and without stepping down. If the ladders are more than 5 ft (1.5 m) apart, position two planks stacked on top of each other in between the ladders – this will strengthen the support of the platform.

MEASURING AND CUTTING

Take accurate measurements of both the ceiling and the paper, and cut the paper precisely in order to minimize room for error. You will need the wallpaper, a tape measure, chalk line, pencil, wallpaper scissors, and straightedge. Assemble the equipment on the pasting table for easy access.

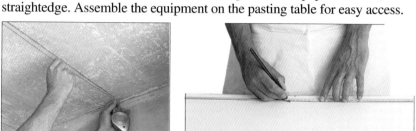

1 MARKING GUIDELINE Measure the paper width and subtract ⅜ in (1 cm). Mark this on the ceiling at opposite ends. String the chalk line taut between the two marks. Snap it against the ceiling to obtain a colored guideline.

2 MARKING PAPER Measure the distance across the ceiling, following the guideline. Near one long edge of the paper, mark the length of the ceiling, adding 2 in (5 cm) to each end for the paper overhang. Mark the same distance, including the overhang, on the opposite long edge of the paper.

3 MARKING A CUTTING LINE Using a straightedge and pencil, draw a line from edge to edge that joins the two length marks across the width of the paper.

4 CUTTING OUT FIRST LENGTH Following the marked line, cut out the first length of paper with long-bladed wallpaper scissors. This length of wallpaper should equal the length of the ceiling, with 2 in (5 cm) at each end for the overhang.

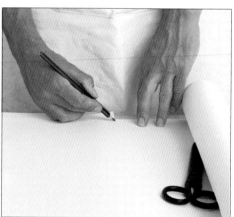

5 MARKING LENGTHS If the ceiling is true, use the first length of paper as a guide to cut out the remaining number of lengths required. Otherwise, take separate measurements and number each length of paper for positioning across the ceiling.

PASTING AND FOLDING

Work on a pasting table covered with a strip of old lining paper. For applying the paste, you will need a bucket and a pasting brush. Unravel a section of the paper length and lay the cut end and the far edge slightly over the side of the table. Push the rest of the paper to the right side. Place a tape measure or scissors against the roll of paper to stop it rolling back on itself.

1 **APPLYING PASTE** Load the brush with paste and apply it along the center of the paper. Apply the paste to sections approximately 3 ft (1 m) long at a time. Make sure that the edges of the paper are well coated, but in order to avoid getting paste on the table, apply the paste to the paper only when the edges overhang the sides.

USEFUL TIPS

PASTE BRUSH REST
Tie a piece of string across the rim of a bucket, from one end of the handle to the other, to serve as a rest for the brush.

2 **SPREADING PASTE** Generously spread the paste from the center toward the far edge, coating half the width of the paper. Reload the brush with paste and move the paper toward you so that the edge overhangs the near side of the table. Apply paste to the remaining half of the paper, coating the edge completely.

LAYERING PAPER
Instead of having loose rolls about the room, layer them on the pasting table ready for pasting. Tie loops of string around the table legs at each end. Tuck the cut ends of the lengths between the loops of string to secure the paper.

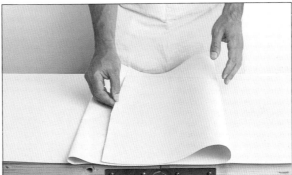

3 **FOLDING ACCORDION** Pick up the pasted cut end of the paper and fold it loosely, pasted side to pasted side, accordion style, about 1 ft (30 cm) wide. When making up the stack, be careful not to crease the folds.

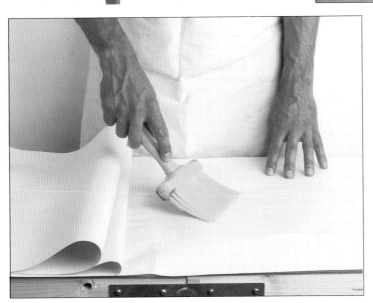

4 **COVERING WITH PASTE** Keep the pasted folds to one side, and apply the adhesive to the next section of the length of paper. Continue to reload the brush with paste and to cover the entire width of the paper, including the edges, working from the center outward.

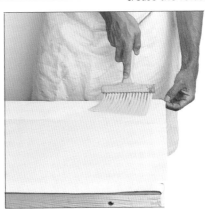

5 **PASTING ENDS** Work across the length of paper until you end up with a prepared pasted "accordion" on one end of the table and a short length of paper lying flat to one side. Cover this last section with paste. Begin to hang the paper from this section.

HANGING THE CEILING PAPER

Position the work platform or stepladder directly underneath the chalk-line guide mark on the ceiling *(see page 208)*. Brush the area of the ceiling for the first strip of paper with a coat of size. As you are papering, hold the folded paper in your left hand and apply the tongue of the paper with your right hand to the right corner. For papering the ceiling, you will need a paper-hanging brush, wallpaper scissors, small scissors, and seam roller. Keep these tools within easy reach.

1 ALIGNING PAPER Hold the folded paper to the ceiling corner. Here, an unopened roll of lining paper and a long-handled broom have been used to hold up the paper. Align the long edge of the paper with the chalk mark and press the tongue into the corner. Leave an overhang of 2 in (5 cm) on the sides next to the walls.

2 APPLYING PAPER Smooth the paper against the ceiling. Release another fold, align it against the chalk mark, and smooth from the center outward. Press the overhang to the side wall. Using the chalk line as a guide, work across the ceiling.

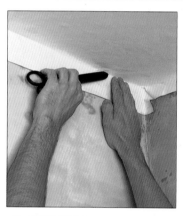

3 CREASING PAPER Run the rounded tip of the wallpaper scissors along the overhang to form a crease in the paper at the join of the ceiling and walls.

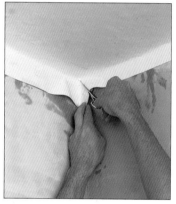

4 CUTTING TO FIT Using small scissors, carefully make one diagonal cut into the overhang toward the ceiling corner. Overlap the loose ends to fit the overhang into the corner.

5 MARKING CREASE If you are using heavy decorative or lining paper, which usually does not crease easily, mark the crease in the overhang of the paper with a pencil.

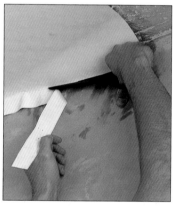

6 REMOVING OVERHANG Gently pull the overhang away from the wall and ceiling. Following the pencil mark, cut off the overhang with the wallpaper scissors.

7 FITTING INTO PLACE Smooth the paper back. Cut off the overhang along the remaining sides and smooth the paper into place. Apply sizing to the adjacent width of ceiling ready for the second length of paper.

8 SMOOTHING JOINS Butt the long side edge of the second length against the side edge of the first. Run a seam roller over the join between the two lengths. Continue papering the rest of the ceiling.

FILLING GAPS IN THE SEAM

Flexible filler can be used to hide gaps between the lengths of lining paper on a ceiling. After you have finished papering, use a wide-bladed putty knife to apply a small, smooth amount of filler within the seam line.

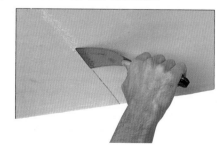

WORKING AROUND OBSTRUCTIONS

When papering a ceiling, you will need to maneuver around fixed objects and difficult corners. Electrical fixtures and corners of alcoves or a fireplace are the most common obstructions. The paper must be cut to make it fit into, or over, the problem area. Use sharp cutting tools such as small scissors, wallpaper scissors, or a craft knife to make the task easier. Make sure you turn off the electricity before applying size around a light fixtures or switch. Remove the bulb and lamp, and cover the fixtures with insulating tape or masking tape.

LINING WALLS

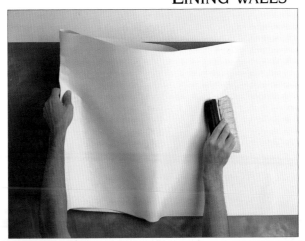

If you are going to hang decorative wallpaper over lining paper, hang the lining paper horizontally (*see page 207*), then hang the wallpaper vertically. Measure the walls and cut out, paste, and accordion fold manageable lengths of paper. Apply size to the walls and position the first length of paper adjacent to the ceiling. Carefully unfold one section of the "accordion" at a time, sliding the paper into place.

ALCOVE

1 **SMOOTHING CORNER** Smooth the paper to the outside of the external corner. Tap the bristles of a paper-hanging brush into the junction of the ceiling and wall, and over the external corner, to make a crease line in the paper.

2 **CUTTING TO FIT** Pull the paper away from the ceiling and wall. Using small scissors, make a diagonal cut toward the point where the external corner of the wall meets the ceiling. Make sure that the scissors are clean of wallpaper paste before cutting.

3 **BRUSHING INTO CORNER** Brush the paper into the internal corner. Crease the overhang and cut diagonally into the corner. Overlap loose ends of overhang from each wall and fit the paper in the corner. Crease and cut away overhang of the corners.

ELECTRICAL FIXTURES

1 **CUTTING PAPER** Paper over the fitting. Enlist the help of an assistant to hold up the remaining paper with a long-handled broom. Directly under the fixture, cut a cross in the paper large enough for the pendant to be pulled through.

2 **REVEALING PENDANT** Pull the pendant through the hole in the paper and wipe the excess paste from around the fixture. Using the paper-hanging brush, smooth the paper toward the fixture.

3 **SNIPPING OVERHANG** Make a series of small, V-shaped cuts into the paper overhang around the electrical fixture. Use a paper-hanging brush to form a well-defined crease in the paper overhang around the fixture.

4 **REMOVING OVERHANG** Use a craft knife to carefully cut around the fixture and remove the overhang. Wipe off the excess paste on the fixture with a damp cloth.

PAPERING WALLS

$\mathcal{P}$APERING WALLS IS A MUCH SIMPLER task than papering ceilings. Many decorative wallpapers are expensive, so it is important to plan ahead carefully and always take accurate measurements of the walls to avoid wasting paper. To guarantee uniformity of pattern and color, always use paper from the same batch for the whole job. Read the manufacturer's instructions to find the recommended adhesive. Clear as large a working area as possible, and make sure that you have good lighting when papering. Set up the pasting table, and protect its surface by taping a sheet of old lining paper onto it.

MEASURING AND PASTING

Measure the distance from ceiling to baseboard or floor, where the first length of paper will be hung, adding 4 in (10 cm) for the paper overhang. The overhang will allow you to crease and cut the ends of the paper to fit it into corners and edgings around the room. Follow the manufacturer's instructions for mixing the paste. For measuring and pasting wallpaper, you will need wallpaper scissors, a pencil, straightedge, tape measure, pasting brush, wooden doweling, and bucket.

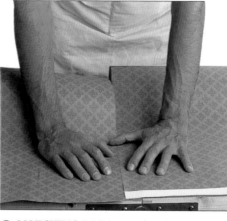

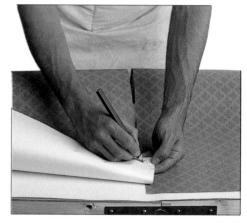

1 **CUTTING FIRST LENGTH** Unravel and mark up a length of wallpaper. Cut out the first length, using wallpaper scissors. If the walls in the room are evenly shaped, consider cutting out several paper lengths at once, matching patterns when necessary.

2 **MATCHING PATTERN** If you are using patterned wallpaper, turn the cut paper so that the pattern faces upward. Match the pattern in the adjoining lengths, ensuring that it aligns and that there is enough paper for the overhang.

3 **NUMBERING LENGTHS** On the top corner of the wrong side of each length of paper, number it and mark the direction in which it will hang. Put the cut lengths aside. Spread out the first length on the pasting table, right side down, and apply the paste.

KEEPING SCISSORS CLEAN

To loosen the paste that can accumulate on wallpaper scissors, occasionally immerse the scissors in a jar filled with warm water.

4 **FOLDING** Paste and accordion-fold the length of paper in 3 ft (1 m) sections. Loosely fold the length so that the pasted areas of the paper lie adjacent to each other. Be particularly careful not to crease the pasted paper when you are folding it.

5 **FINISHING FOLD** Leave a 2 ft 4 in (70 cm) tongue of paper at the end for the length's bottom section. Fold the tongue, pasted sides together, to prevent it from sticking to the wall as you are working down it.

HANGING THE PAPER

Mark a vertical line on the wall to use as a guide for the first length by holding a chalk line against the wall near the floor or baseboard and snapping a guideline. Apply the size to the wall, covering slightly more than the width of the strip of paper. You will need wallpaper scissors, paper-hanging brush, damp sponge, seam roller, stepladder, and waste basket.

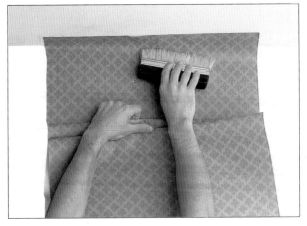

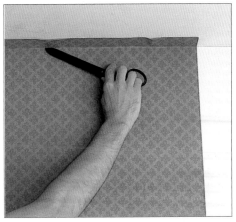

1 POSITIONING PAPER Standing on the stepladder, guide the top edge of the pasted, folded paper to the ceiling, allowing for a 2 in (5 cm) overhang. Brush the first unfolded section of paper from the center outward, smoothing it well against the wall.

2 SMOOTHING PAPER Unravel the paper down the wall, aligning the edge with the vertical line, and smooth each section as you unfold it. Let the length hang down without sticking the bottom in place.

3 CREASING OVERHANG At the junction of the wall and the ceiling, run the rounded tip of the scissors along the overhang to crease it. If necessary, make the crease line more visible by marking it with a pencil.

4 REMOVING OVERHANG Carefully pull the top part of the paper away from the ceiling and wall, and cut off the overhang following the crease mark. Keep a waste basket nearby to dispose of scraps.

5 FITTING CUT EDGE Use the paper-hanging brush to smooth the top cut edge back into place against the ceiling.

6 CLEANING SURFACE Excess paste can be removed from washable surfaces with a damp sponge. On a ceiling with nonwashable finish, use a smaller overhang and keep the top edge away when creasing and trimming.

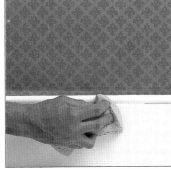

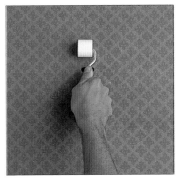

7 PAPERING NEAR FLOOR At the foot of the wall, unravel the folded tongue of paper. Carefully align the bottom edge of the paper with the top edge of the baseboard or the floor.

8 CREASING OVERHANG Push the paper into the edge between the wall and baseboard. Crease the overhang. Ease paper away from the wall and cut along crease. Replace paper and brush it into place.

9 REMOVING PASTE Wipe excess paste off the woodwork with a damp sponge. Continue to hang the rest of the lengths. Where necessary, slide the paper into place to match the decorative pattern.

10 SECURING EDGES Secure the edges by running a seam roller up and down along the edge or over the seam line. Do not press hard when using a seam roller on delicate wallpapers.

COPING WITH CORNERS

Corners should not pose a problem, even with patterned paper. Fitting wallpaper into internal and external corners involves hanging the paper slightly beyond the corner and pasting a scrap over the overhang. When using vinyl, apply vinyl adhesive to the face of the overhang so that the scrap will adhere. To paper around corners, you will need a craft knife, straightedge, wallpaper scissors, tape measure, paper-hanging brush, pencil, seam roller, and carpenter's level or chalk line.

EXTERNAL CORNER

1 SMOOTHING AROUND CORNER
Smooth the paper toward the external corner. Ease it around the corner, using a brush. Do not brush the flap of paper in place on the internal wall.

2 CREASING PAPER
Rub your thumb and forefinger along the external corner to crease the paper. Use a straight-edge and pencil to mark a vertical line from ceiling to floor, about 1 in (2.5 cm) in from the external corner.

3 CUTTING STRIP Run
a craft knife against a straightedge to cut through the paper along the vertical line. Reduce the risk of tearing the paper by fitting the craft knife with a new blade.

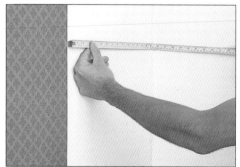

4 REMOVING SCRAP
Carefully ease away from the wall the width of paper leading to the internal corner. Place the scrap on the pasting table. Apply sizing to the wall and apply extra paste to the scrap, if necessary.

5 SMOOTHING OVERHANG
Run a seam roller up and down the edge of the overhang to ensure that the paper adheres firmly to the wall.

6 REPLACING SCRAP Return the scrap
to the wall and paste it onto the overhang near the edge, matching the pattern as closely as possible. Smooth down and run a seam roller along the overlap of paper.

INTERNAL CORNER

1 MEASURING INTO CORNER Measure
from the edge of the last full width of wallpaper into the internal corner. Add an extra 1 in (2.5 cm) for the overhang. Cut out a length of paper to this width. Place this scrap on the pasting table.

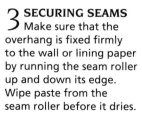

2 SMOOTHING PAPER
Hang the cut length in place, butting it to the edge of the last full width and aligning the pattern if necessary. Use a paper-hanging brush to smooth the paper into the internal corner.

3 SECURING SEAMS
Make sure that the overhang is fixed firmly to the wall or lining paper by running the seam roller up and down its edge. Wipe paste from the seam roller before it dries.

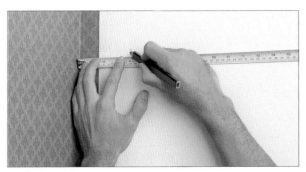

4 MARKING SCRAP From the internal corner, mark the scrap width, adding ³⁄₁₆ in (5 mm). Mark this distance from the internal corner at points up and down the wall.

5 MARKING VERTICAL Align a large level with the scrap width-marks on the wall to establish a true vertical line. On the pasting table, apply paste to the scrap.

6 BRUSHING IN PLACE Position the scrap against the inside of the internal corner. Continue papering the room using the vertical line as the starting point.

ELECTRICAL FIXTURES

Turn off the electricity when working around a light switch or outlet. Papering over and around wall fixtures is similar to negotiating light fixtures on a ceiling *(see page 211)*. You will need a paper-hanging brush and craft knife to work with switches and socket plates. Cover the fixtures with masking tape or insulating tape before sizing the wall.

1 OUTLINING FIXTURE Use a paper-hanging brush to make a clear impression of the switch plate through the wallpaper.

2 CUTTING PAPER From the center of the fixture to its corners, cut diagonals with a craft knife. Peel back the flaps of paper. Ease the paper over the switch plate.

3 REMOVING EXCESS Cut off the excess paper. Smooth the paper around the switch plate. Wipe off the paste from the fixture before turning on the electricity.

PAPERING BEHIND A FIXTURE

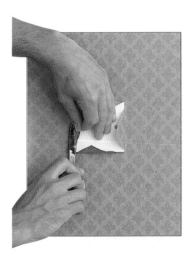

1 REMOVING CUTS Repeat steps 1 and 2 above. Cut away the excess triangular strips of paper around the face plate, using small scissors. Unscrew and ease away the face plate. Leave a gap of about ¼ in (6 mm) between the wall and the face plate.

2 PUSHING BEHIND Ease the paper behind the electrical face plate and smooth it into place with the bristles of the paper-hanging brush. Reposition the face plate and tighten the screws. Turn on the electricity. Do not use this method with wallpaper that contains metal.

WINDOW AND DOOR FRAMES

Between full lengths of wallpaper, and openings such as windows and doorways, hang lengths of paper that are cut to fill the space, matching the pattern where necessary. Allow for an overhang of at least 1¼ in (3 cm) when cutting out the paper to fit around the frame. You will need a paper-hanging brush, wallpaper scissors, small scissors, and a craft knife.

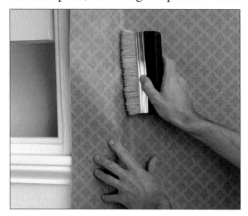

1 SMOOTHING EDGE On the sized surface, smooth a length of pasted paper toward the frame. Push the paper into the junction between the wall and the frame with a paper-hanging brush. Mark the outline of the molding by smoothing the wallpaper over the wood with the tips of your fingers.

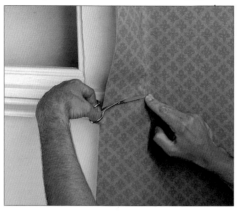

2 CUTTING TO FIT Following the marked outline of the molding, use small scissors to make a diagonal cut in the paper toward the edge of the frame. Peel away, snip, and reposition the paper on the wall. Repeat this process until you have fitted the paper around the corner of the frame.

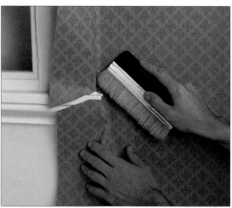

3 PRESSING INTO PLACE Once you have cut the decorative paper around the first rung of the molding, gently press it into place with the paper-hanging brush. Immediately wipe the excess paste from the frame with a cloth or sponge.

4 MAKING SMALL CUTS Make several close cuts in the paper toward the next rung of the molding. Continue snipping around the corner of the frame.

5 OUTLINING MOLDING Form an outline in the paper again by using your fingers to press the paper well into and around the corner of the frame.

6 CUTTING TO FIT Peel the paper away from the wall, and cut along the outline. If the paste on the paper begins to dry, reapply adhesive.

7 SMOOTHING IN PLACE Brush the paper into place, using the tips of the bristles to push the paper into the edge of the frame.

RADIATORS

Many homes are heated with wall-mounted radiators or heating units connected to either a central system or an individual electrical power supply. Removing radiators can be difficult; it is easier to hang wallpaper behind the unit. You can hang a single ceiling-to-floor length of paper and cut a slit near the bottom to fit over the radiator wall bracket. Alternatively, apply one length from the ceiling to just above the wall bracket and a shorter length from the bracket to the baseboard or floor.

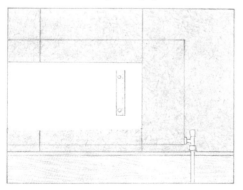

TWO LENGTHS
Cut a length to hang from the ceiling to the bracket that secures the radiator to the wall. Cut a second length to fit between the wall bracket and the baseboard. Hang the short length to fit well to the baseboard *(see page 213)*.

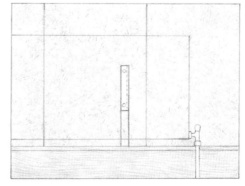

SINGLE LENGTH
Measure from the top of the baseboard to the top of the wall bracket. At the bottom of the length, cut out a vertical slit to fit around the bracket. Push the cut ends over the wall bracket, using a radiator roller to smooth the paper.

STAIRWELLS AND LANDINGS

Hanging decorative paper on walls surrounding a stairwell requires a scaffold or other safe support. Rent scaffolding that will fit conveniently on the stairs. Alternatively, you can use a combination of sturdy stepladders, scaffold planks, and ladders to assemble your own platform. Place a stepladder on the landing, safely back from the top step, and lean a straight ladder against the head wall. Slide the planks between the two ladders. Make a sandwich of two boards when the span exceeds 5 ft (1.5 m). Enlist the help of an assistant to hold the extended lengths, and use heavy-grade lining and decorative papers for the walls to avoid tearing. If you are using a platform, do not risk overbalancing when reaching difficult areas; always move the platform to make the task safer. Hang the top paper while standing on the platform, and enroll the help of an assistant to fix the lower part in place.

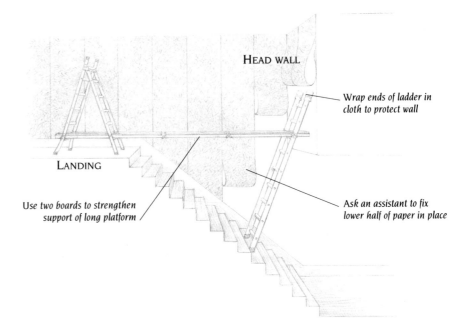

HEAD WALL

Wrap ends of ladder in cloth to protect wall

LANDING

Use two boards to strengthen support of long platform

Ask an assistant to fix lower half of paper in place

BORDERS

Many paper manufacturers make borders to complement their wallpapers. Borders can be applied on wallpaper or painted surfaces to produce decorative frames, to create a dado and picture rail effect, or to provide a cornice adjacent to the ceiling.

DADO OR PICTURE RAILS

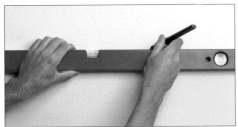

1 MARKING WALL Use a level and pencil to mark a horizontal line that will divide the two colors on a wall. Measure around the room, then cut the border to manageable lengths.

3 HANGING BORDER Apply the border to the wall by releasing an accordion fold at a time, lining up the top edge with the horizontal mark and smoothing it into place with a paper-hanging brush.

2 PASTING BORDER Apply the paste to the back of the border paper, brushing over the edges for complete coverage. Loosely accordion-fold the border, taking care not to crease the folds.

CORNICE

To apply a cornice, follow the junction between wall and ceiling. Release and smooth each accordion fold of the paper as you work along the wall. Wipe excess paste from the ceiling or wall with a cloth.

USING MATCHSTICKS

Before papering, remove wall fixtures. Matchsticks are useful for marking the positions of the fixtures, enabling you to rehang pictures and shelves in the identical positions after decorating.

1 MARKING POSITION Prepare the walls and remove the fixture, then mark its position with a matchstick. Hang the paper and let it fall over the matchstick.

2 PIERCING PAPER Press the paper over the matchstick. Let the matchstick pierce the paper. Remove the matchstick. When the paper is completely dry, insert the fixture.

CLEANING TOOLS

As you are wallpapering, make sure that all the tools that come into frequent contact with wallpaper paste or size – particularly scissors, knives, and the paper-hanging brush – are regularly wiped clean with a cloth. All tools used for hanging wallpaper should be cleaned before storage to ensure long life.

CLEANING TOOLS
Use a damp, clean cloth to remove wallpaper paste from a seam roller, scissors, or paper-hanging brush. Store the tools in a dry place.

WASHING TOOLS
Thoroughly wash out the paste bucket, and use household detergent and warm water to rinse the adhesive from the bristles of the pasting brush. Shake the brush vigorously to remove the excess water, leave to dry, and store flat.

FAULTS AND CURES

Manufacturers of wallpaper are constantly improving their paper and adhesives, making the products more durable and convenient to handle. Because of these improvements, the majority of faults and problems that occur when hanging wallpaper are usually due to poor preparation of the surface, lack of size, or the insufficient application of paste.

BUBBLES

LIFTING SEAMS

SHINY PATCHES

1 PIERCING BUBBLE
To remove an air bubble in decorative or lining paper after the adhesive has dried, make an incision through the bubble with a sharp-bladed craft knife.

2 APPLYING PASTE
Apply a small amount of paste behind the cut opening. If there are too many bubbles in the paper to repair, strip and rehang the whole length of wallpaper.

3 SMOOTHING PAPER Use a paper-hanging brush to smooth the cut area back into position. With a damp cloth, immediately wipe away any excess paste on the wallpaper.

Seams may open up when there has been too little paste applied edge to edge. Lift the seam with a knife and apply some paste under the paper. Press together the seam with a seam roller.

If matte wallpaper has been brushed into place too vigorously or too often, shiny patches may appear on the surface. Dull the shine by rubbing the affected area with a ball of soft white bread.

POOR PATTERN MATCH

CREASES

FLATTENED RELIEF

DAMP PATCHES

BROWN SPOTS

Examine the rolls of paper to see if the pattern is faulty. If it is, return the paper to the dealer. If the rolls are accurate, reapply the paper following the manufacturer's instructions carefully.

Wallpaper may crease as you smooth it across surfaces that are not flat, or at corners that are not true. Cut open the crease with a craft knife or razor blade, apply adhesive, and smooth into place.

Applying too much pressure when rolling the seams of relief paper with a seam roller will flatten the design. Do not use a seam roller; instead, press the edges into place with a damp cloth.

Damp patches in paper that are evident long after the paste has dried could indicate moisture in the wall. When this occurs, take the advice of a specialist and be prepared to strip the wallpaper.

Brown spotting may be due to impurities within the plaster. Strip the paper and treat the affected area with fungicide. Dry out any damp spots and apply the paper using a fungicidal paste.

OTHER WALL COVERINGS

WALLPAPER IS AVAILABLE in a range of textures and materials. Each variety will invariably require a specific and sometimes unique type of adhesive. Refer to the manufacturer's instructions for advice on application and maintenance.

VINYL WALLPAPER

Vinyl and ready-pasted vinyl wallpapers are easy to apply to flat walls. Unlike standard wallpaper, vinyl does not have to be left to stand after pasting. You need a trough slightly larger than the roll that is filled with water, as well as a sponge for smoothing. Keep a small quantity of mixed paste on hand for applying to the wall or to the paper when necessary. You can use vinyl adhesive for adhering together cut overlaps when working around and into corners and obstructions.

1 ROLLING LENGTH
Cut and number the first length, adding 4 in (10 cm) for overhang. Roll the length, pattern facing inward. Place the trough near the wall. Fill it with water and immerse the roll.

2 LIFTING SOAKED VINYL
Pick up the top edge of the well-soaked vinyl paper with both hands and let the surplus water drain into the trough.

3 SPONGING SMOOTH
Apply the first length to the wall. Smooth the vinyl with a sponge. After hanging several lengths, run over the seams with a seam roller. Remove excess paste with a sponge.

4 GLUING OVERLAP Apply vinyl adhesive in between the layers of the overlap with a small paintbrush and press into place. This will create a lasting bond.

VINYL
Vinyl wallpaper is popular and very practical because it is so simple to clean. Mounted on backing paper, vinyl is easy to remove from a wall.

NOVAMURA
Novamura is lightweight wallpaper made of foamed polyethylene. It has a soft and springy texture.

EXPANDED VINYL
Expanded, or blown, vinyl is mounted on a flat backing paper. The vinyl layer of the wallpaper is heated to create a relief pattern.

DUPLEX
Duplex is a strong wall covering that is made of two layers that are bonded together. It is often decorated with a surface relief pattern.

EMBOSSED
Embossed decorative paper is heavyweight and can be painted onto after it has been applied. It is usually hung on ceilings and below dado rails.

SILK
Silk wallpaper is made by backing woven silk with a layer of fine paper. Try to avoid leaving the seams visible when hanging silk wallpaper.

FLOCKED
Flocked wallpaper contains patterns that are cut in velvet pile. It is mounted on backing paper and should be applied like standard decorative wallpaper.

GRASS CLOTH
Grass cloth is manufactured with a thick backing paper for easy hanging. It is difficult to hide the seams when hanging.

TILING

*T*ILES ARE THE BEST MATERIALS for covering a wall in order to attain a hard-wearing surface that is impervious to moisture and heat. As well as being long lasting and easy to clean, tiles can be used to create unusual or striking decorative schemes. Wall tiles are produced in regular shapes as well as in small sizes, which makes it easy both to arrange them in patterns and to cut them to fit around surface obstructions. Of all the wall tiles available, ceramic tiles are manufactured in the greatest range of sizes, colors, and patterns. You may, however, wish to experiment with the textures and design possibilities of tiles made from other materials, such as marble, slate, cork, or mirrored glass. This chapter helps you select the most appropriate tiles and tools, shows you how to prepare and mark up a wall before tiling, and demonstrates the techniques of cementing tiles in place and grouting the joins.

CHOOSING A STYLE

CERAMIC TILES AND WALL MOSAICS are long lasting and versatile, which makes them well suited for covering surfaces that need to be durable and water resistant, such as the walls of kitchens and bathrooms. Wall tiles are available in a wide variety of materials, colors, and shapes, as well as in numerous plain, patterned, and pictorial styles. This extensive choice allows you to coordinate the tiling with a room's decor, and opens up an array of unique decorating possibilities. You can also use border tiles and matching trim to complement the main wall tiles and form a coherent design.

THEMATIC IMAGES
Decorative effects can be achieved by juxtaposing groups of patterned tiles among a background of plain tiles. Just how you arrange decorated tiles is a matter of personal preference. Some look effective grouped together, or regularly interspersed to produce an even pattern; others are better arranged as a random selection over a tiled area. Clearly defined areas of walls, such as the recesses behind stoves, present the perfect opportunity for tiling self-contained panels. Here, a selection of tiles hand painted with rustic imagery serves not only as a lively, decorative backdrop but also protects the wall from the wear and tear that inevitably occurs in the vicinity of the cooking area.

Oven niche provides perfect spot for making decorative arrangement

Pictorial tiles produced in same size and finish as plain background tiles create visual coherence

Specially made heat-resistant tiles are a practical choice for covering surface near stove

CLEAN AND WHITE
White tiles are always a popular choice for bathroom walls. White often matches a bathroom's sanitary ware and looks effective when contrasted with the lines of chrome-plated plumbing fixtures, mirrors, and other accessories.

ELEGANT BORDERS
Even in much-used bathrooms, wall tiles do not need to look utilitarian. Plain wall tiles can be enlivened and divided up by borders of regularly sized tiles. Many manufacturers produce these in colors and designs that coordinate with their larger plain tiles.

INSPIRATIONAL EFFECTS
Tiles can be used to create special design features within a room, rather than simply to cover areas of wall with hard-wearing surfaces. Many modern kitchens are fitted with cupboards that line the wall above the work area, which often leaves an awkward rectangular panel of wall that needs to be decorated with a durable finish. A layer of ceramic tiles arranged in lines of color or pattern is an ideal solution. Here, a colorful frieze has been composed from broken fragments of ceramic tiles and rows of handmade tiles.

Broken tile fragments produce natural, random effect within a very constrained area

Rows of tiles in one color give illusion of extra space

SMART AND PRACTICAL
Rather than covering an extensive area with ceramic tiles, you may prefer to limit the tiling to a part of the wall that is affected by moisture. A functional, plain-tiled splashback can be enlivened by a purely decorative strip of color.

GRAPHIC PATTERNS
If you wish to give a tiled area – such as this bathtub with shower – definition in terms of shape, as well as providing color, choose a range of tiles that are produced with matching border tiles, since with these you can form designs tailor-made to suit your specific needs.

TYPES OF TILE

WALL TILES PROVIDE A SURFACE THAT IS NOT only decorative but also protective and easy to clean. They are available in so many different sizes, colors, finishes, and shapes that it is essential to assess their functional and ornamental qualities before making a choice. In the intensively used areas of the home, such as the bathroom or kitchen, always apply heavy-duty, waterproof tiles, such as those made from strong ceramics or marble, or any of the mosaics. Plain ceramic tiles are usually made to match standard bathroom fixtures and can be used with decorative patterned tiles. Some patterned tiles can be placed randomly within plain tiling, while others are designed to be arranged in groups or as panels. You can also purchase borders and rails that complement plain tiles at surface edges and corners.

CERAMIC TILES

Machine-made ceramic tiles are used with spacers or have angled edges that butt together, and some are decorated. Handmade ceramic tiles give a rustic effect, which can be accentuated by spacing them up to ³⁄₁₆ in (5 mm) apart. Some tiles have unglazed sides – when these are used on a surface with visible edges, special border tiles must be utilized on the edges.

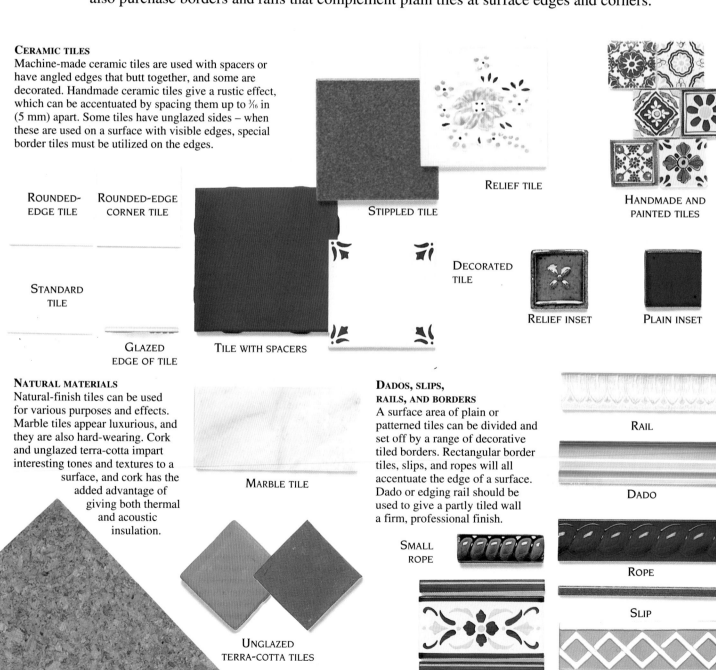

ROUNDED-EDGE TILE

ROUNDED-EDGE CORNER TILE

STANDARD TILE

GLAZED EDGE OF TILE

TILE WITH SPACERS

STIPPLED TILE

RELIEF TILE

DECORATED TILE

HANDMADE AND PAINTED TILES

RELIEF INSET

PLAIN INSET

NATURAL MATERIALS

Natural-finish tiles can be used for various purposes and effects. Marble tiles appear luxurious, and they are also hard-wearing. Cork and unglazed terra-cotta impart interesting tones and textures to a surface, and cork has the added advantage of giving both thermal and acoustic insulation.

MARBLE TILE

UNGLAZED TERRA-COTTA TILES

CORK

DADOS, SLIPS, RAILS, AND BORDERS

A surface area of plain or patterned tiles can be divided and set off by a range of decorative tiled borders. Rectangular border tiles, slips, and ropes will all accentuate the edge of a surface. Dado or edging rail should be used to give a partly tiled wall a firm, professional finish.

SMALL ROPE

RAIL

DADO

ROPE

SLIP

BORDER AND SLIPS

BORDER

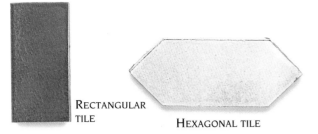

RECTANGULAR
TILE

HEXAGONAL TILE

MOSAICS

Mosaic tiles, also called chips, are available in simple shapes. They may be ceramic, glass, glazed terra-cotta, or marble. The tiles are held together as a sheet prior to application, either by a layer of removable paper or by a backing of netting that is applied to the wall.

MARBLE MOSAIC WITH NET BACKING

UNUSUAL TILE SHAPES

Unusually shaped tiles can be used to create a distinctive interlocking pattern. Simple combinations of rectangles, hexagons, and diamonds, or complicated compositions of triangles and unique shapes, can all be effective. Always plot the pattern on graph paper before starting to tile to make sure that it will work.

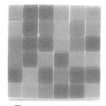

DIAMOND
TILE

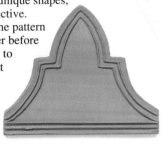

PAPER-COVERED
GLASS MOSAIC

FINISHED-GLASS
MOSAIC

INTERLOCKING TILE

TRIANGULAR TILES

PICTORIAL TILES AND PANELS

Pictorial, patterned, or relief-decorated tiles can be purchased to match plain tiles or other surfaces. Some individual pictorial tiles can be inserted at random or with planned regularity to produce a decorative geometric design across a field of plain tiles. Complete pictorial panels of tiles can be used to colorful effect in a small room or an alcove.

COVING

Where wall tiles meet the edge of a fixture such as a bath, sink, or shower base, it is essential to form a waterproof seal. Strips of ceramic coving are available in a range of sizes and colors, and should be installed with a flexible sealant. If you cannot find suitable coving, cover the join with a bead of silicone caulk.

HAND-COLORED
PICTORIAL PATTERN

MITERED TILE

QUADRANT TILE

BULLNOSE TILE

ARRANGING WALL TILES

Tiles are usually mounted so that they align vertically and horizontally. This is known as contemporary or plain tiling. It is possible to make a variety of different arrangements, such as checkerboard, diamond, or brick bond, that will instantly change the decorative appearance and scale of a tiled wall surface without using decorated borders or unusually shaped tiles.

CONTEMPORARY

CHECKERBOARD

DIAMOND

BRICK BOND

This layout is accepted as the standard pattern for arranging tiles on a wall.

Use tiles in a contrasting color to make a checkerboard pattern on a contemporary layout.

Although it requires tiles to be cut at the edges, this simple pattern creates an eye-catching effect.

Also known as Victorian style, brick bond is most suited to plain, rectangular wall tiles. It gives an old-fashioned feel.

PREPARATION

*T*ILING A WALL IS BASICALLY A SIMPLE TASK, but good preparation is essential. The quality and durability of the finished surface will depend as much on a thorough and thoughtful approach to preparation as on good finishing techniques. Such work may be time consuming, but the time will certainly prove to be well spent. When you are planning the job, bear in mind that the position of the first tile will have an effect on the final result. Allow for grouting space between tiles when determining the tiling area. Choose appropriate adhesives and grouting for the room and type of tile you are using.

PREPARING WALL SURFACES

The surface must be prepared with care, because any imperfection or unevenness will be made more apparent by the glaze of tiles. The surface of the wall must also be sound and dry, so that the adhesive can make a secure bond. When tiling over sheets of interior-grade chipboard or plywood, seal the surface with a dilute solution of PVA adhesive.

PAINT

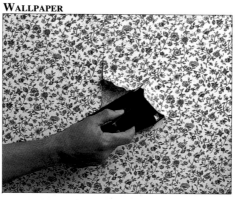

Tiles applied over either oil-based or latex paint will tend to stick to the paint rather than to the wall. To allow the tile adhesive to penetrate through the surface paint to the wall behind, key, or roughen, the paint by rubbing with coarse sandpaper wrapped around a cork block. After sanding down the surface, strip off any flaking paint with a scraper.

WALLPAPER

Always strip off all types of wallpaper before tiling so that the tile adhesive can bond securely with the wall; otherwise, the tiles will be held in place by the wallpaper and wallpaper paste alone. Peel off vinyls, and remove other types of wallpaper by scoring and soaking with water or steaming, before stripping with a suitable scraper.

REMOVING OLD TILES

It is safe to tile over an old tiled surface if it is sound and flat. Rub down the old glazed tiles with silicon carbide paper to prepare them to receive the tile adhesive. If a double layer of tiles will be too thick, remove the old tiles with a wide chisel and sledge hammer – wear goggles to protect your eyes – and replaster the wall before tiling again.

BARE WALLS

Make a bare wall surface as smooth as possible by patching any holes and cracks *(see page 182)*. If a wall is extensively damaged or uneven, it may be necessary to skim the surface with a new coat of plaster. Correct the cause of any damage, such as dampness, before tiling a wall.

MAKING A TILING GAUGE

A simple, homemade tool, the tiling gauge is invaluable when deciding on the vertical and horizontal positioning of the tiles. When you are working from the floor to the ceiling on a flat wall, hold the tiling gauge vertically against the surface to determine the right placement for horizontal rows. You can also use the gauge to plan for working around unavoidable obstructions, such as windows, alcoves, and doorways.

To make a tiling gauge, cut a length of wood longer than any obstruction (an alcove, for example). Lay the gauge alongside the row of tiles, spaced as they will be when positioned on the wall, allowing for grouting space between tiles, and mark their widths along one edge of the gauge.

EQUIPMENT

A variety of specialized equipment is needed for tiling. Most of these tools are small and inexpensive, with the exception of electric disk cutters and manual diamond-tipped cutters. These are used for cutting and shaping thick tiles, and they can be rented from tile stores or certain tool or hardware stores. In addition to specialized equipment, you will need a variety of general-purpose tools (see page 174), such as a level and chalk line, for establishing true horizontal and vertical lines.

PREPARATORY TOOLS
Position tiles with a tiling gauge. Use a length of wood as a batten (a platform support) for tiles. Establish a true horizontal with a try square and a level, and hammer the batten in place with masonry nails.

TRY SQUARE

LENGTH OF WOOD FOR BATTEN

TILING GAUGE

CUTTING TOOLS
The simplest tool is a glass cutter, but hand-held or surface-mounted score-and-snap devices are most effective. Nippers are used for nibbling edges; a tile file smoothes rough edges. Cut curves with a tile saw. For cutting thick tiles, use an electric disk cutter.

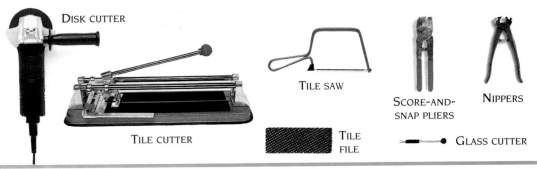

DISK CUTTER

TILE SAW

SCORE-AND-SNAP PLIERS

NIPPERS

TILE CUTTER

TILE FILE

GLASS CUTTER

TILING TOOLS
Use the correct adhesive for both the type of tile and its use – refer to the tile manufacturer's instructions if necessary. Adhesive is best applied to walls with a pointing trowel or a putty knife, and spread into ridges with a notched spreader. Either matchsticks or plastic spacers can be used to make equal gaps between tiles, and the lie of tiles should be checked often with a level.

TILE ADHESIVE

POINTING TROWEL

NOTCHED SPREADER

SMALL-NOTCHED SPREADER

PLASTIC SPACERS   HALF-MATCHSTICKS

FINISHING TOOLS
Fill the gaps between tiles with an appropriate grout – epoxy grout should be used to make a waterproof surface. Ordinary grout is applied with a squeegee or decorating sponge, then smoothed with a dowel before wiping off the excess with a cloth. Joins between tiles and surfaces should be sealed with mastic or silicone caulk.

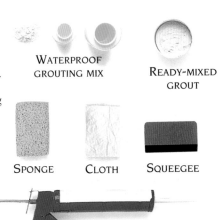

WATERPROOF GROUTING MIX

READY-MIXED GROUT

SPONGE   CLOTH   SQUEEGEE

DOWEL

SILICONE CAULK AND GUN

ESTIMATING QUANTITIES

Calculate the surface area to be tiled. For square tiles, use this chart or the manufacturer's details to find an estimated number of tiles needed. If using unusually shaped tiles, or handmade tiles spaced farther apart than normal (see page 225), use your tiling gauge to determine how many tiles, with spacing included, will be required in each direction. Multiply the figures to give the total number of tiles. When you purchase tiles, always buy a few extra to allow for breakage.

SIZE OF TILE	AREA TO BE TILED IN SQUARE FEET							
	1	2	3	4	5	6	7	8
1 x 1 in	144	288	432	576	720	864	1008	1152
2 x 2 in	36	72	108	144	180	216	252	288
3 x 3 in	16	32	48	64	80	96	112	128
4 x 4 in	9	18	27	36	45	54	63	72
6 x 6 in	4	8	12	16	20	24	28	32
12 x 12 in	1	2	3	4	5	6	7	8

PLANNING

*I*T IS VERY IMPORTANT TO SPEND TIME preparing and carefully planning before beginning to tile, because the position of the first tile will determine the layout of the remaining tiles. If the first row is out of alignment, all the other tiles on the wall will be crooked; you will need a chalk line or plumb line and a carpenter's level to find the true vertical and horizontal lines to use as guides to tile against. Start with a row of whole tiles resting along the top edge of the horizontal batten near the bottom of the wall.

FINDING A LEVEL STARTING POINT

The edges of fixtures, windows, and doorways – and even the floor and baseboard – are rarely level, so you will need a carpenter's level and a plumb line to establish the true horizontal and vertical. You will also need a claw hammer, tape measure, tiling gauge, and one of the tiles. When you have marked the true horizontal, you can mount straight lengths of wooden batten to the wall with masonry nails to make a horizontal edge to tile against. Hammer nails into the batten at intervals of about 4 in (10 cm) before attaching to the wall. This batten will support the tiles while the adhesive dries. Use a level to check that the edge is horizontal and to confirm that the battens are straight before starting.

1 ESTIMATING BATTEN LEVEL Hold one of the tiles in position against the bottom of the wall. Allowing for the gaps for grout, lightly nail a batten in place. If possible, secure the batten with one nail for pivoting when establishing a true horizontal.

2 LEVELING BATTEN Hold the level against the batten, and make sure that it is horizontal. Hammer alternate nails lightly into the wall to fix in position. If tiling over an existing layer of tiles, you will have to mount the batten in place with screws.

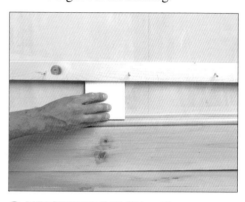

3 MEASURING GAP Slide a tile between batten and bottom of wall to establish the minimum distance to the skirting or the floor. Using a pencil, mark this point on the wall at the bottom edge of the batten. Remove the batten.

4 CALCULATING ROWS Use the tiling gauge to find how many rows of whole tiles are required to fit the height of the wall *(see page 226).* Place the gauge on the mark and work up the wall. If you will have to cut a very awkward, narrow horizontal row at the top of the wall, adjust the position of the mark near the bottom of the wall to make the gap at the top larger. From the mark, draw a true horizontal.

5 FIXING BATTEN The horizontal mark is the starting position for the first row of whole tiles. Hold and level horizontally the upper edge of batten against this mark. Mount batten in place, leaving the nail heads protruding for easy removal later. When the rest of the wall is tiled, remove the batten. Cut tiles as necessary to fill the gap.

PREPARING TO TILE A PLAIN WALL

It is unlikely that whole tiles will fit the space exactly, so you will have to cut tiles to fit. Try to ensure that the tiles at each end will be cut to the same size, ideally about half a tile wide. Use a carpenter's level or chalk line to establish a true line for the vertical battens. You will also need a hammer, masonry nails, pencil, tape measure, and tiles.

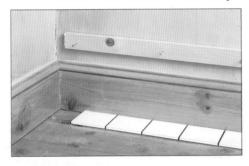

1 POSITIONING TILES Lay a row of tiles on the floor along the bottom of the wall. Allow even gaps between each tile for the grout. When no more tiles will fit, move the row to give an equal space at each end.

PARTLY TILED WALLS

When a wall is to be partly tiled, the top row should be made up of whole tiles. Using a pencil, mark on the wall where the tiling will stop. Work downward with the tiling gauge and mark the bottom edge of the last whole tile. Align the top edge of the batten with this mark, and level the batten horizontally.

2 FINDING VERTICAL EDGE Mark the edge of the first tile on the top surface of the batten attached to the wall. This is the point at which the tiling will begin. Establish a true vertical to the mark with a level or a chalk line, and mark it with a pencil or snap a colored line.

3 PLACING VERTICAL BATTEN Take a straight batten and hammer masonry nails into position at 4 in (10 cm) intervals along its length. Hold the batten to the wall so that the inside edge aligns with the vertical line and the mark on the horizontal batten. Hammer the nails into the wall, leaving the heads protruding from wood for easy removal when finished.

PREPARING TO TILE AROUND OBSTRUCTIONS

Cut tiles of equal size should fit around a centerpiece such as a recess. Getting the whole and cut tiles right around an obstruction will often, however, put the edging tiles at the side walls out of balance. For tiling around obstructions, you will need a tiling gauge, a pencil, hammer, masonry nails, batten, tape measure, chalk line, and carpenter's level.

1 EQUALIZING AT SIDES Mount a horizontal batten at the bottom of the wall. Aim to have cut tiles of equal heights above and below obstruction. Hold a tiling gauge up to the obstruction horizontally, and position it so that an equal width of cut tile will be needed on each side. Mark the outer edge of the cut end tiles.

2 MARKING VERTICALS Use a chalk line to snap a vertical line through the mark nearest the side wall and down to the horizontal batten at the bottom of the wall.

3 POSITIONING Mark on the batten where the vertical falls. Lay the gauge against the batten and align the vertical line with a tile mark. Work from the obstruction toward the side wall, and mark the position of the last whole tile. Follow steps 2 and 3 above.

TILING TECHNIQUES

ONCE THE PREPARATION AND PLANNING have been completed, you can begin to attach the tiles to the wall. The horizontal and vertical battens will provide a position guide for placing the tiles, as well as support for the tiles. After you have put up all the complete tiles and when the grout has fully dried, the battens can be removed from the wall. With the main ground in place, you can begin to cut and shape tiles to fit around the perimeter.

APPLYING WHOLE TILES

Inspect each tile, and set aside faulty tiles to be cut for corners and edges or returned to the manufacturer. Ensure that the boxes of tiles have the same batch number. There can be slight color and tone differences, so if applying plain tiles, shuffle them together to mix up the variations. Consult the manufacturer's instructions and choose the appropriate adhesive. Apply adhesive with a pointing trowel and notched spreader. Space the tiles using either plastic spacers or matchsticks. Keep a damp cloth at hand for wiping excess adhesive from the tiles.

1 CHECKING CORNER Make sure that the horizontal and vertical battens are placed securely in position. Using a try square or a whole tile, confirm that the corner from which you will begin to tile is perfectly square. If it is not, check and adjust the position of the battens, using a level.

2 APPLYING ADHESIVE Use a pointing trowel to spread adhesive on the wall, beginning at the corner where the horizontal and vertical battens meet. Spread the adhesive as evenly as possible to a thickness of about ⅛ in (3 mm). Do not cover more than 1 sq yd (1 sq m) at a time.

3 SPREADING ADHESIVE Hold a notched spreader at an angle of 45 degrees to the surface and pull it across the area to distribute the adhesive evenly. The ridges will create suction, securing the tiles to the wall.

4 APPLYING TILES Starting in the corner, rest the bottom edge of the first tile on the horizontal support. Press it firmly into place. Apply the bottom row, putting in spacers to separate the tiles.

5 CHECKING LEVEL Apply tiles across one coated area at a time. Check that each row is horizontal. Lay all the whole tiles and wait 12 hours before removing battens and matchsticks. Grout over plastic spacers.

CUTTING TILES

To cut and apply edging tiles, you will need a try square and a china marker. If you have space for a number of identical cut tiles, cut out all tiles in one batch before application. If you have to cut a variety of sizes, number the backs and the corresponding spaces on the wall. Cut straight lines with a tile cutter or score-and-snap pliers. Use a diamond-tipped or disk cutter for thick tiles. Nibble out corners and curves with nippers, and smooth all edges with a tile file.

SCORE-AND-SNAP PLIERS

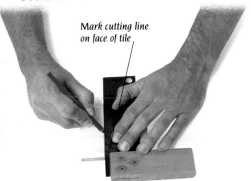

Mark cutting line on face of tile

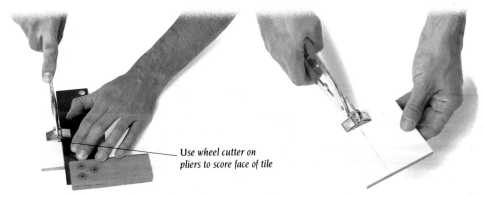

Use wheel cutter on pliers to score face of tile

1 MARKING A TILE Measure the gap on the wall to be filled and mark this on the face of the tile. Using a try square or steel ruler, draw a straight line across the face of the tile with a china marker. China marker on tiles will wipe off easily.

2 SCORING LINE Holding a try square or ruler in place against the marked line, score along the line with the wheel cutter of the score-and-snap pliers. It is important to apply sufficient downward pressure to break through the glaze in one stroke.

3 BREAKING TILE Place the scored tile between the jaws of the pliers, aligning the mark with the center of the pinching plate. Hold the pliers and tile just above the table or workbench, and gently squeeze the handles of the pliers together.

TILE SCORER AND MATCHSTICKS

1 SCORING TILE Measure the gap on the wall, and mark it on the face of the tile, using a china marker and try square. Hold the try square firmly against this mark and score across the face of the tile with the tip of the scorer. Carefully score through the glaze with one firm stroke.

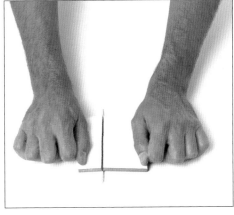

2 BREAKING TILE Lay the scored tile on a smooth, hard surface. Position two matchsticks under the tile, directly beneath each end of the mark. Press down firmly and evenly on the side edges of the tile until it snaps in two.

TILE NIPPER
The sharp-edged jaws of a tile nipper are designed for removing thin slivers from the edge of a tile. Measure the gap, and mark it on the face of the tile with a china marker. Penetrate the glaze along this line with a scoring tool and a try square as a guide. Use the nipper to snip away small portions of the tile up to the scored line.

TILE FILE
A tile file is an essential tool for achieving a clean finish on the rough edges of tiles once they have been cut or nibbled. Lay the tile file on a flat surface, and rub the cut edge of the tile over its abrasive surface. This action will smooth both the glaze and the ceramic. From time to time, lift the file and shake away the dust from the mesh.

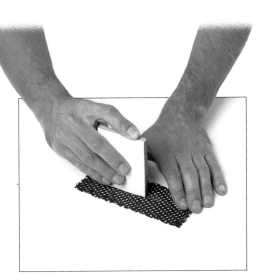

CUTTING AROUND CORNERS

Cutting tiles to fit awkward shapes is a relatively simple task if you methodically examine each space and plan how to mark and cut the tiles. To avoid confusing different cut tiles, number the tiles and their corresponding spaces on the wall. For applying your measurements to the tiles, you will need a try square, a china marker, and a carpenter's pencil. If you have to make a template, you will also need scissors, some paper, and a fine pencil. Once the tiles have been marked, the excess can be cut away by scoring and snipping with tile nippers, or accurately cut with a tile saw.

CORNERS WITH SQUARED-OFF EDGES

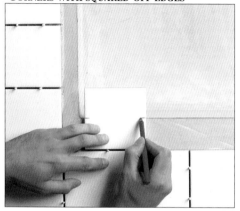

1 MARKING TILE Hold the tile to the wall, resting it on the spacers on the edge of the last row of whole tiles. Use a china marker to mark the wall edge on the side edges of the tile. Shift the tile across to the vertical edge of the wall, and make marks on the top and bottom edges of the tile.

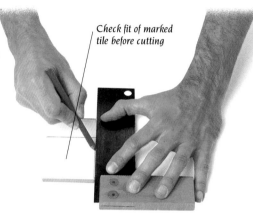

Check fit of marked tile before cutting

2 JOINING MARKS Using the try square and china marker, draw lines between the vertical and horizontal marks to show the area of tile to be cut away. Hold the tile against the wall corner to check the marks. Score the lines and nibble away the excess. File cut edges before mounting.

CORNERS WITH NON-SQUARED EDGES

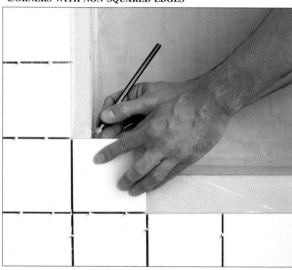

1 MARKING TILE Hold the tile in the required position, remembering to use spacers. With a carpenter's pencil, mark the vertical and horizontal edges, as well as the corner of the opening, on the back of the tile.

Use a fine pencil to mark reverse of tile

2 JOINING MARKS Using a try square or a ruler, join up the pencil marks on the back of the tile. To be certain of the orientation of the tile, draw and label pencil arrows pointing to the top and side exterior edges on the back of the tile.

3 MARKING TEMPLATE Take a piece of thin white paper or tracing paper, and align its edges with the markings on the back of the tile. If the lines do not make a right angle, trace them and trim the paper along them. Hold the paper in place, and trace the edges of the tile. Draw and label arrows on the paper, matching those on the tile, as a guide.

Draw arrows on paper to help align template

4 MARKING FRONT Cut out the template along the edge lines, and place it face down on the front of the tile. Make sure that the arrows on the paper and the reverse of the tile run in the same directions. Draw along the edges of the template with a china marker to transfer the shape of the corner to the face of the tile. Score along this mark, nibble away the corner, and file the cut edges before mounting.

CUTTING OUT CURVES

You may have to cut a curved edge into tiles that fit around fixtures that cannot be easily removed, such as pipes and basins. Use a pair of small scissors, fine pencil, and china marker to make up a simple paper template to transfer the curved shape onto the face of the tile. Curves can be cut with a special tile saw, with the tile held steady in a vise.

  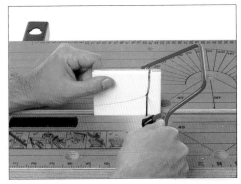

1 MARKING TEMPLATE Cut a paper template to the size of the tile. Make a series of cuts in the paper to fit it well against the curve. Mark the line of the curve along the bottom of the cut flaps of paper.

2 MARKING TILE Cut along the marked line of the curve, and place the template on the tile's glazed face. Use a china marker to trace the curve onto the tile. Carefully score along this curve.

3 CUTTING OUT Clamp the tile in a vise, taking care not to damage the glaze. Cut along the scored curve with a tile saw, using gentle pressure to avoid chipping the glaze. Smooth the cut edge with a small tile file.

TILING CORNERS

If you are tiling a wall with a recess, you will have to deal with the internal and external corners. At these corners, it is important to cut tile edges for a neat finish. Tiles can be marked with a try square and china marker, and straight lines cut by one of several methods *(see page 231)*. For thicker tiles, you will need a tile cutter.

EXTERNAL CORNERS

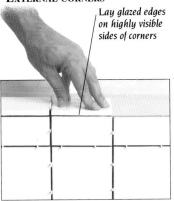

Lay glazed edges on highly visible sides of corners

Decide which side of the corner is least prominent. Tile this side, cutting the tiles to lie flush with the other surface. Tile the more visible surface, laying corner tiles, round-edged tiles, or the glazed edges of tiles over the cut tile edges. Alternatively, cover the corner with a plastic, wooden, or metal edging.

APPLYING SMALL CUT TILES

It can be difficult applying tile adhesive into a small space without spreading it onto the surface of the surrounding tiles. To avoid this, use a small notched spreader to apply the adhesive to the back of the tile.

INTERNAL CORNERS

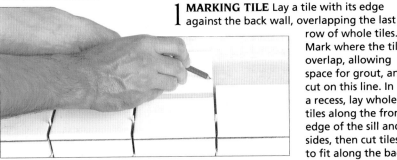

1 MARKING TILE Lay a tile with its edge against the back wall, overlapping the last row of whole tiles. Mark where the tiles overlap, allowing space for grout, and cut on this line. In a recess, lay whole tiles along the front edge of the sill and sides, then cut tiles to fit along the back.

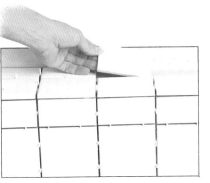 

2 LAYING TILES Cut tiles to fit the space, and file cut edges smooth. Place tiles so that cut edges lie in the corner to give a neat appearance. In a recess, tile the sill first, then sides and top. Tiles at the top will have to be supported with a batten until set.

3 COMPLETING CORNER When tiling walls into an internal corner, repeat steps 1 and 2 for the second surface. When tiling a recess, lay tiles on all the sides first, then calculate the area of the back wall and tile it as for a plain wall *(see page 230)*.

GROUTING

Once the adhesive has dried, spaces between the tiles must be filled with an appropriate grout. For an intermittently wet area, a water-resistant product is sufficient, but when grouting a shower area, use a waterproof grout. Epoxy grout should also be used on tiled work surfaces, to keep them germ-free.

Ready-made grout is available in various colors. Powdered grout can be colored with pigments before adding water. After grouting, seal gaps between tiles and a work surface or fixture with silicone caulk. For simple grouting, you will need a squeegee and sponge, dowel, and a soft, dry cloth.

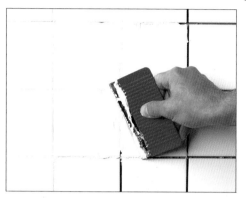

1 APPLYING GROUT Powdered grout should be mixed with water in small amounts. Ready-made grout comes in small tubs. Scoop up grout with the squeegee and apply it to the gaps between the tiles, working it deep into the joints.

2 WIPING SURFACE Apply grout over about 1 sq yd (1 sq m) at a time, using the squeegee to fill the joints so that the grout lies flush with the surface. Use a clean, damp sponge to wipe away the excess grout from the surface of the tiles before it dries.

3 MOLDING GROUT As soon as the grout begins to harden, draw the blunt end of a narrow rod, such as a dowel, along the filled gaps. This removes the excess grout and gives a neat finish. Select a rod slightly wider than the gap for this purpose.

4 POLISHING OFF Wipe any excess grout from the surface of the tiles with a sponge. Remove all traces of grout by polishing the surface with a soft, dry cloth. Allow the grout to set hard, following the manufacturer's guidelines, before letting it get wet.

APPLYING SEALANT

Use silicone sealant, or caulk, to cover gaps found between a tiled area and another surface such as a bath. Silicone sealants are available either transparent or in a range of colors. They are sold in tubes or trigger-action cartridges. Keep a damp cloth at hand for removing any excess.

FLUSH GROUTING

For a slightly different effect than a recessed finish, and for a more durable and completely waterproof joint, wipe over the grout rather than running a piece of wooden dowel over it, so that it lies flush with the surface of the tiles.

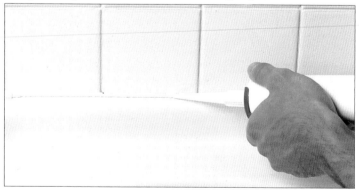

1 INSERTING SEALANT The sealant is applied directly from the nozzle, so it is important to cut the tip of the tapered tube to a diameter that matches the size of the joint. Make sure that the joint is clean and dry before squeezing a bead of sealant into the gap. Try to do this in one continuous, smooth movement.

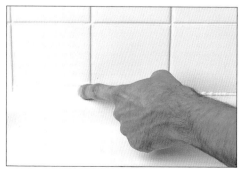

2 SMOOTHING SEALANT Draw over the bead of sealant to make a smooth, rounded, waterproof joint. The tip of a wet finger is the best tool for this task. Immediately wipe off excess sealant with a damp cloth.

ATTACHING FIXTURES

To attach fixtures to a tiled surface with screws, penetrate the layer of tiles and insert a wall anchor into the wall beyond. You will need an electric drill and masonry drill bit, fine pencil or china marker, glass cutter, and masking tape. Ask someone to hold a vacuum cleaner nozzle under the hole as you drill. Make sure that wall anchors are pushed beyond the layer of tiles to rest in place flush with the wall, and be careful not to overtighten screws, because the tile could crack.

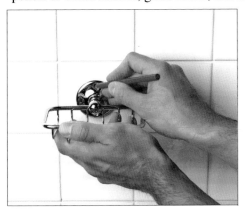

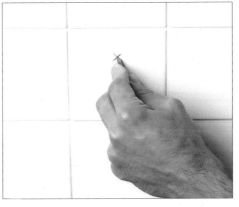

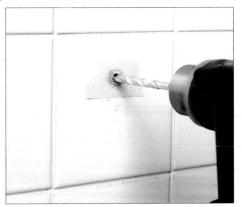

1 MARKING UP Hold the fixture in position on the tiled surface, and use a fine pencil or china marker to mark the top drilling point. If you drill this hole first and hang the fixture on a screw through it, it will be held firm while you check that the fixture is level and mark the other holes.

2 SCORING GLAZE To hold the drill bit in position when drilling through a smooth glazed surface, make a pilot hole or mark through the glaze with a sharp tool such as the tip of a glass cutter. Hold it steady, pressing hard onto the mark, and rotate the tool to make a small round hole.

3 DRILLING HOLE Steady the tip of the drill against the tile by applying a strip of masking tape over the mark. Place the tip of the masonry drill bit on the marked tape and begin to drill at a slow speed. Press lightly against the tile until you have made a clearly defined hole well into the wall.

CLEANING TOOLS

Adhesives, particularly waterproof grout, dry very quickly. The tools used to apply tiling adhesive and grout need to be cleaned as soon as possible after use. Follow the adhesive or grout manufacturer's instructions for cleaning. Most substances can be washed off in water, but avoid blocking your plumbing with residues from the adhesive or grout.

RINSING SPONGE
Rinse adhesive or grouting mixture from a sponge by repeated soakings in clean water. Allow to dry completely before storing, and retain this sponge for tiling purposes only.

WASHING TOOLS
Wash the pointing trowel and the spreading tool in water, removing all of the adhesive or grout. Make sure that the metal blade of the pointing trowel is completely dry before coating it with oil to prevent rust.

USING LEFTOVER TILES

After the wall tiling has been completed, there may be a number of unused whole tiles remaining. The majority of these should be stored as replacement tiles, in case of later breakages. A heavy, decorative tile, however, can easily be made into a sturdy trivet. Place the leftover tile on a thin layer of cork sheeting; a section cut from a cork wall tile is ideal. Mark out and cut the cork so that it is ⅛ in (3 mm) smaller all around than the tile, and stick it to the underside of the tile with a heatproof glue.

Hard Floors

$\mathcal{A}$ MAJOR DECORATING PROJECT, laying a new hard floor can be time consuming and costly, but the end result has a tremendous impact on the character of a room. Moreover, whether you use wood, tiles, flagstones, or bricks, there is no doubt that, at a practical level, all hard flooring is functional and can be extremely long lasting. Indeed, a good-quality hard floor often outlasts many of the other changes that inevitably take place to the design of a room. A carefully made hard floor also provides a perfect background for displaying other furnishings, such as decorative rugs. In this chapter, the full range of materials that can be used for hard flooring is presented. All of the surfaces shown – ceramic, stone, wooden, and synthetic – are highly functional and possess a decorative finish in their own right.

FLOOR TILES

*A*VAILABLE IN A WIDE VARIETY OF MATERIALS, including ceramic, marble, stone, cork, rubber, and vinyl, as well as in an extensive range of designs, floor tiles provide the decorator with endless style options. If chosen and laid carefully, floor tiles can have an immense impact on the look and atmosphere of a room, generating color and warmth, and even giving the illusion of extra space. Choosing the type of flooring depends, in part, on the function of a room – wooden floors work well in living rooms, but floor tiles are more suitable for areas that are subjected to heavy daily wear, such as kitchens.

NATURAL EFFECTS
The bold character of a stone floor, combined with its hard-wearing nature, more than make up for its coldness underfoot. Flagstones are laid on a leveled cement or sand bed, and their weight restricts their use to ground and basement floors. If they are unavailable, you can achieve a similar effect using stone tiles, which are made in several sizes and finishes.

STRIKING PATTERNS
Unglazed floor tiles, also known as quarry tiles, are ideal for creating patterns, since they are produced in a range of natural shades, like earth reds, dark grays, and browns. Their natural rough finish makes for characterful and practical flooring, ideal for kitchens and utility rooms.

Graphic checkerboard pattern emphasizes floor space, particularly when tiles are laid diagonally

WARM AND RUSTIC
Floor bricks are perhaps the least-known material for hard-floor surfaces. Also known as pavers, floor bricks are very durable and are available in a range of colors, including the warm, natural tones of red, brown, and yellow, but also green, purple, and blue. They are ideal for the floors of rooms that lead to the outside, such as kitchens or hallways. To achieve a similar effect, you can use rectangular unglazed floor tiles.

Raw bricks coated with specially made floor sealant provide smooth, matte-finish flooring

Brick floor produces natural, irregular effect that is ideally suited to a rustic interior

TYPES OF FLOOR TILE

When choosing floor tiles, you will need to consider a number of factors, such as the wear and tear the floor surface will be subjected to and whether the floor can withstand the weight of the material. Once you have decided which type of floor tile is best suited to your needs, consult the manufacturer's instructions for the preparation of the floor.

CERAMIC TILES

Ceramic floor tiles are fired at very high temperatures to make them virtually unbreakable. This type of tile has the advantage of being available in many shapes, sizes, and colors. You can create a patterned floor by laying small, square inset tiles made of glazed or unglazed ceramic or stone. Glazed tiles tend to be slippery underfoot when wet.

INSET TILES

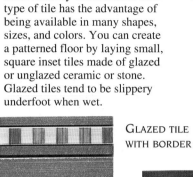

GLAZED TILE WITH BORDER

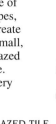

GLAZED TILE WITH INSETS

GLAZED TILES

UNGLAZED TILE WITH BORDER

BORDER TILES

Border tiles are available in a wide range of styles, including plain or patterned, and as rectangles or interlocking shapes. They are designed to fit around the perimeter of a tiled area, forming a natural boundary to a tiled floor, and complementing plain floor tiles.

CORK TILE

VINYL TILE

CORK, RUBBER, AND VINYL FLOOR TILES

Providing a warm surface, cork tiles are quiet and comfortable underfoot. Make sure that you use floor-grade cork tiles, and seal them if you require a water-resistant finish. Vinyl, rubber, and linoleum tiles are durable and easy to cut and lay.

RUBBER TILE

MARBLE BORDER TILES

MOSAIC FLOOR TILES

Most mosaic tiling for walls, whether made of glass, marble, or ceramic, can also be used to create interesting floor surfaces. If you need a particularly durable finish, use large-scale floor mosaics.

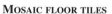

MATTE-FINISH, VITREOUS MOSAIC TILES

GLAZED MOSAIC TILES

MARBLE TILE WITH INSET

DECORATIVE CERAMIC FLOOR TILES

Hand-painted decorative floor tiles can be used to create interesting effects when they are interspersed within a plain tiled floor. You will need to set the thicker varieties in a bed of cement, rather than using floor-tile adhesive.

SLATE TILE

STONE TILES

Marble tiles come in a range of beautiful natural colors and a variety of shapes, which can be combined with contrasting insets. Durable and waterproof, slate tiles are available in dusty tones of gray, green, and blue. Porous limestone tiles need to be sealed once laid. Earthy terra-cotta tiles wear well and have a Mediterranean look.

HAND-PAINTED CERAMIC TILES

TERRA-COTTA TILE

LIMESTONE TILE

WOODEN FLOORS

WOODEN FLOORING HAS A CHARACTER that is without match. Wood adds a natural style to any room, and as long as it is not laid in areas where there is excessive dampness, it provides a warm, smooth surface and a variety of subtle colors, patterns, and textures. Wooden floors may be hard underfoot, but they are less noisy than ceramic tiles, easy to maintain, and durable. There are various styles of wooden flooring. These include existing floorboards, which can be painted, stained, or sealed; interlocking parquet wood pieces; long wood strips that slot together; and precomposed "tiles" of mosaic panels.

HARMONIOUS COLORS
If you are fortunate enough to have sound wooden floorboards in your home, you can renovate and paint them to great effect. You can consider using more than one color to make a pattern; here, the color theme that runs throughout the room is echoed in the painted floor.

Painted floorboards present ideal surface for rugs

NATURAL TONES
Wooden floor surfaces can be sealed in a great variety of finishes. If you are satisfied with the existing natural color of the wood, seal the surface with layers of clear wax or a commercial transparent sealer in either a matte or a gloss finish.

PAINTED PATTERNS
A stenciled motif is easy to apply and enlivens a room by breaking up the rigid uniformity of the floorboards. Seal the floor with transparent sealer after the paint has dried completely.

POLISHED AND LUXURIOUS
Ready-made parquet produces a floor with a timeless elegance that lends itself to modern and period homes alike. Parquet is produced in a variety of hardwoods and can be arranged into many different patterns, including herringbone and brick patterns. It gives an unsurpassably flat, solid surface.

Parquet offers versatile means for creating patterned surfaces

TYPES OF WOODEN FLOORING

Prepared wooden flooring consists of pieces of hardwood timber laid over a prepared subfloor. This type of flooring, whether it is laid as parquet, wood strips, or mosaic parquet, is available in different colors and grains, allowing you to choose a finish to suit your needs. Follow the manufacturer's instructions when laying wooden floors; certain components, such as parquets, should be left to acclimatize in the room for a few days before they are installed.

PARQUET FLOORING
Parquet consists of shallow wood strips or pieces that interlock or juxtapose to form solid panels. Prepared parquet is manufactured in a range of durable hardwoods. Select the color of wood and style of grain most appropriate for the room. All parquet flooring should be laid on a prepared solid floor surface; the pieces are secured by glue, and some are fitted together with tongue-and-groove joints.

MAHOGANY

LIGHT MAHOGANY

MAPLE

MERBAU

LIGHT MAPLE

OAK MOSAIC PARQUET

MOSAIC PARQUET
Mosaic panels are made from short strips glued together into small squares. These squares are then assembled with a backing into larger panels arranged in a basketweave pattern. The panels are glued to a prepared sub-floor, and require sanding and sealing after laying.

STANDARD HARDWOOD FLOORING
Available in a wide range of hardwoods in random lengths, wood strips are laid parallel to each other in straight rows, giving a finished appearance of short, narrow floorboards. They can be laid using a variety of techniques, depending on the manufacture. These include gluing, hidden nailing, and tongue-and-groove joints.

ASH

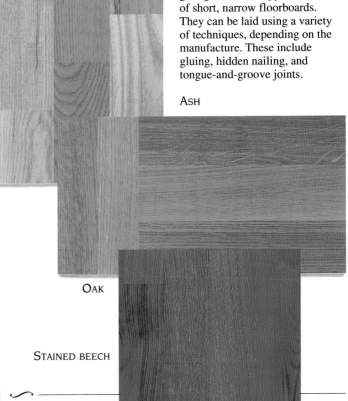

OAK

STAINED BEECH

PROTECTING HARDWOOD SOURCES

Many types of hardwood flooring that we value for their decorative qualities and durability originate from the slow-growing trees of tropical forests. Wherever possible, you should try to select timber from plantations that are properly ecologically managed. If you are careful to purchase hardwood from approved sources – and the wood should be clearly labeled as plantation grown – then you will be encouraging the continued production of slow-growing hardwood trees on managed plantations, thereby helping to protect natural forests.

CARPETS AND RUGS

*A*MONG THE MOST STRIKING decorative enhancements,
carpets and rugs have long provided elegant ways of softening
cold and unyielding floor surfaces, making them warm
and luxurious to walk over or sit upon. A soft floor,
composed of a fitted carpet, rugs, or matting, performs a
decorative role, simultaneously improving the comfort of a
surface. Wall-to-wall carpeting is the most commonly used
soft flooring, since it is available in various materials,
textures, and colors. Decorative matting, made of natural
vegetable fibers, is becoming increasingly popular. If you
possess a floor that has an even texture and color, you may
want to enhance the surface with rugs – they can be used
to introduce disparate pools of color and pattern to your
decorative scheme. As well as examining the quality and
style of the different types of soft flooring, this chapter
shows you how to display rugs by mounting them on walls.

FITTED CARPETS AND MATTING

WALL-TO-WALL CARPETING IS ONE of the most popular household floorings for decorative and practical reasons. Fitted carpets are produced in so many styles, and in such a wide range of materials, that a suitable carpet can always be found to provide a perfect background in terms of color, texture, and pattern for almost any style of room. Wall-to-wall carpeting has important practical qualities, providing thermal and acoustic insulation, and comfort underfoot. Carpeting also plays an important role in helping to unify the style of a room by providing a background that integrates walls, furnishings, and accessories.

HARMONIZING BACKGROUND
Stairway carpeting should always be durable enough to withstand the heavy wear and tear it will receive. Plain colors generally provide the best medium for setting off furnishings and accessories in stairwells.

Rich red color of carpet provides warmth to area dominated by pale cream paintwork

COORDINATED LUXURY
Bedrooms are usually subjected to less wear and tear than the other rooms in a home, so they lend themselves well to pale colors. Here, the carpet blends subtly with the other furnishings.

RICH AND TRADITIONAL
One of the primary concerns when carpeting bedrooms is to create a comfortable and relaxing atmosphere. A good-quality carpet in a restrained color provides a dignified surface for dark furniture.

NATURAL AND RUGGED
Matting woven from plant fibers provides a light, natural covering with a rustic touch and is very durable. A recently awakened interest in natural-fiber matting has led to the introduction of a tremendous range of patterned, colored, and textured floor coverings, which are valued for their unusual decorative qualities.

Rug introduces bright splash of color to neutral-toned matting

Plant-fiber matting gives natural base and enhances color and quality of exposed wood

TYPES OF CARPET AND MATTING

There is a bewildering choice of carpets available in a variety of materials and styles. If selected with care, fitted carpeting presents a durable surface that is easy to maintain. Quality carpets are made from a mixture of natural and artificial fibers, and the most long-lasting have a densely woven, secure pile. Plant-fiber matting is available in various designs and can provide a useful alternative to carpets; its comfort underfoot can be improved by using padding.

WILTON

Wilton is a type of high-quality woven carpet, manufactured by closely interweaving the pile and backing in one continuous length to provide a particularly strong, dense, flattened surface. Wilton carpets are generally produced in plain colors.

AXMINSTER

Woven one row of tufts at a time, Axminster carpets are made with a high wool content and burlap backings. Unlike the predominantly plain weaves of Wilton carpets, Axminster carpets tend to be patterned and present a looser, taller pile than Wilton weaves.

BERBER

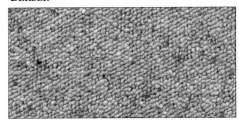

Berber carpets are manufactured with a looped pile and have a smooth surface. Produced in a range of soft, natural colors and in a variety of materials ranging from a high wool content to entirely synthetic fibers, Berber carpets have either a burlap or a foam backing.

TUFTED

Unlike woven Wilton and Axminster carpets, tufted carpets are made by pushing, rather than weaving, the strands of fiber into the backing. The tufts are secured by an adhesive backing. For a coarse texture, you should choose a tufted carpet with a twisted pile.

CORD

Cord carpets are durable and have a flat appearance. They are constructed by pulling loops of yarn tight to the backing to form a succession of well-defined ridges. Once made entirely of animal fibers, cord carpets are nowadays available in synthetic yarns.

CARPET TILES

Well known for their heavy-duty, durable qualities, carpet tiles are very easy to install as well as to replace, when necessary. They are available in a relatively limited

range of colors, patterns, and sizes, and are constructed with either a cord or a pile finish.

PADDING

Padding increases the longevity of a carpet, provides it with a softer tread, and improves its insulating properties. Traditionally made of felt, padding is now composed of rubber as well as other synthetic materials. You should use rug padding to prevent rugs from slipping underfoot.

PADDING FOR SCATTER RUGS

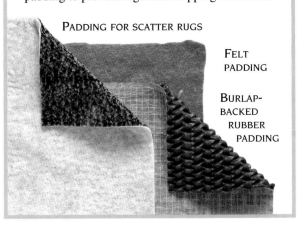

FELT PADDING

BURLAP-BACKED RUBBER PADDING

SISAL
Made from the agave plant, sisal is used to produce long-lasting matting woven in a range of textures.

COIR
Coir matting is woven from coconut fibers and is produced in a range of colors, textures, and weaves.

JUTE
Jute is a finely textured fiber that is most suitable for lightweight matting with detailed surface patterning.

SEAGRASS
This natural fiber has a smooth, shiny finish, which when twisted and woven as matting gives a ridged surface.

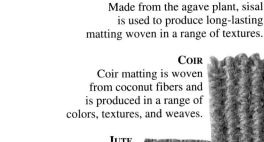

RUGS

*E*XOTIC ETHNIC RUGS HAVE LONG BEEN AMONG the most highly valued and decorative types of soft flooring in the home. Intricately patterned and often richly colored, ethnic textiles such as dhurries and Native American blankets are becoming increasingly popular, since they can be matched with all styles of decor, adding touches of comfort, luxury, and interest to a plain room without completely obscuring the floor. Rugs can also be used to make splendid wall hangings; wall mounting presents an ideal opportunity to display rugs that are either too delicate to use on the floor or simply look best when viewed at eye level.

ETHNIC STYLES
Strongly patterned rugs such as flat-weave kilims can be wall mounted to great effect and provide stunning backdrops to a room's furnishings. Brightly colored rugs are ideal for placing over parquet flooring, without creating disharmony in a room.

Restrained colors of kilim blend subtly with contents of room

DOMINANT PATTERNS
Large, richly colored and patterned rugs always present a natural focus of attention, especially when they are laid over plain carpets. Rugs always introduce an element of luxury into bedrooms.

HARD AND SOFT
Rugs look effective and neat when laid over hard floors. In this room, a small rug has been positioned carefully to allow the natural stone floor to remain visible.

TRANQUIL COLORS
Large rugs are highly versatile floor coverings. As well as being furnishings in their own right, plain, monochrome rugs make ideal islands for arranging furniture, and at the same time protect floor surfaces.

Plain rug emphasizes shapes and colors of furniture

Unpatterned rug allows polished wooden floor to be highlighted

TYPES OF RUG

Choosing a rug can be a formidable task, since there is such a large variety of styles available. The merit and value vary according to a number of factors, including the fiber content, the intricacy of the design, and the rug's age, but the choice should ultimately depend on your personal taste and the style of room where the rug is to be placed. Old and fragile rugs can be very expensive and difficult to maintain, but there are many well-made modern reproductions available.

PERSIAN RUG

Knotted rugs have long been made in the Orient for export. This antique Persian carpet was woven in a palette of colors to suit a European decor.

TRADITIONAL VILLAGE RUG

The villagers of Iran and Turkey have been weaving rugs for their own use for generations. These rugs are identified by their rich colors and expressive patterns.

REPRODUCTION RUG

This modern rug was made using natural dyes and was inspired by Turkish designs. Such copies need some wear before acquiring the desirable patina of age.

MODERN VILLAGE RUG

As in the past, Middle Eastern villagers continue to make rugs that are colorful and patterned with idiosyncratic designs that reflect the heritage of the weavers.

TRADITIONAL KILIM

A kilim is a flat-woven rug from the Middle East or the Orient. Often made from wool and typified by bold colors, they were originally made for family use.

MODERN KILIM

Kilims are used as floor rugs and wall hangings alike. They are now made in large quantities, and in sizes, colors, and patterns to suit many decors.

TRADITIONAL DHURRIE

A dhurrie is a flat-woven cotton rug from India. Some of the finest and largest traditional dhurries were commissioned for the palaces of the subcontinent.

MODERN DHURRIE

Nowadays, dhurries are produced in a wide range of sizes, colors, and patterns to suit contemporary decorative styles and can be specially made to order.

TRADITIONAL NATIVE AMERICAN RUG

Flat-weave textiles were traditionally made by Native Americans to wear as blankets and wraps. This rug would have been produced for trading purposes.

REPRODUCTION NATIVE AMERICAN RUG

Like kilims, Native American rugs have attracted a wide following of collectors. Nowadays, new rugs are often copies of traditional designs.

MODERN DESIGNER RUG

Today, rug merchants work with artists seeking to emulate the skills of traditional rug weavers, in order to produce colorful and expressive rugs with a modern look.

PADDING

When you lay a rug on a floor surface, particularly polished wooden or tiled flooring, test it to make sure that it does not create a hazard underfoot by slipping or creeping. To prevent accidents, use the rug manufacturer's or dealer's recommended padding for the type of flooring that the rug is to lie on (see page 245). Padding is also useful for preventing an old rug from abrading when lying on a much-used hard floor.

HANGING RUGS ON WALLS

MANY FLOOR RUGS, SUCH AS ORIENTALS, kilims, and dhurries, can be used as attention-getting wall hangings. Some collectors hang rugs on walls in order to preserve the condition of the textile; in other cases, a rug hung on a wall can act as a decorative centerpiece and add considerable interest to a room. All but the very largest of rugs can be hung with ease, and there are two basic methods of securing them to walls. For a concealed hanging system, use a tack strip. Alternatively, you can suspend your rug by a simple hanging system that includes a pole, a fabric sleeve, and hooks.

EQUIPMENT

Attach tack strip to the wall with anchors and screws. Alternatively, use a pole attached to hooks and secured with anchors and screws. Use heavyweight cotton to make a sleeve to fit the pole. Hang mothballs behind the rug in a muslin bag. You will also need a pencil, saw, power drill with a selection of drill bits, carpenter's level, screwdriver, and needle and thread.

TACK STRIP

WOODEN DOWELING

HEAVYWEIGHT COTTON

CUP HOOKS

MOTHBALLS

MUSLIN BAG

HANGING A RUG WITH A TACK STRIP

Tack strip is used for securing wall-to-wall carpet to the perimeter of a room. Available in precut lengths, it is armed with rows of sharp spikes, which make it ideal for hanging a rug. When using tack strip, you will need to buy a strip at least as wide as the rug. If you are hanging a very wide rug, you may have to butt different lengths end to end.

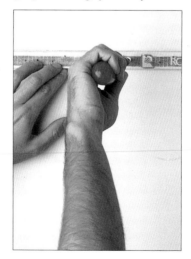

Mark gripper so it is ½ in (12 mm) shorter than rug

1 MARKING STRIP Remove the floor nails from the strip. Lay the top edge of the rug next to the strip. Measure, mark, and saw a length of strip ½ in (12 mm) shorter than the width of the rug. Using a level and a carpenter's pencil, draw a horizontal line on the wall, the same length as the strip.

2 SECURING STRIP Mark positions for screw holes on the strip and on the horizontal line. Drill holes through strip. Drill and insert anchor. Make sure tacks point upward. Screw the strip to the wall.

Tuck fringe to wrong side when fixing rug to gripper

3 ATTACHING RUG Beginning at one side, press the edge of the rug onto the tacks – if the rug has a fringe, you may wish to tuck this behind the rug at the top to conceal it. As you work along the tack strip, make sure that the weave thoroughly catches on the tacks. You can remove and reposition the rug as necessary, to ensure that it hangs straight.

THE DISPLAYED RUG

HANGING A RUG FROM A POLE AND HOOKS

You can suspend a rug from a wall by means of a pole that is held in a sleeve, which is sewn behind the rug. For a decorative effect, use a curtain pole or rod of a suitable length, with finials *(see page 34)*. Alternatively, cut plain wooden doweling slightly wider than the rug. The pole is suspended between two carefully positioned cup hooks.

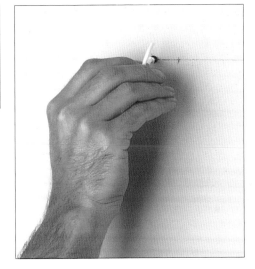

1 **MARKING HANGING LEVEL** Using a level and carpenter's pencil, mark a horizontal line on the wall at the level at which you wish to hang the rug. Draw the horizontal line to the same dimension as the top edge of the rug, adding ⅜ in (1 cm). At each end of the line, pierce the surface of the wall with an awl.

2 **INSERTING HOOKS** Drill holes, and fit wall anchors to the correct gauge for the screw thread on the cup hooks. Insert hooks, and screw them in. Make up a sleeve of heavyweight cotton to the same width as the rug, and slightly larger than the pole's diameter. Press double ³⁄₁₆ in (5 mm) hems along both long edges of the sleeve fabric.

PROTECTION AGAINST MOTHS

The household moth is the scourge of textiles. The larvae of the moth devour fabric, and since moths will seek to lay their eggs in undisturbed cloth, the back of a hanging rug is an ideal target. You can, however, protect a rug against moth damage. Shake it out twice yearly, and renew the mothproofing at the same time.

MOTHPROOFING SPRAY

Lay the rug on a smooth, flat surface in a well-ventilated area. Spray both sides of the rug with a specially made mothproofing compound, recommended by the manufacturer for use on textiles. Renew this treatment twice yearly.

MOTHBALLS

Make up a small square muslin bag with a drawstring – use more than one bag if you need to mothproof a large rug. Fill the bag with mothballs, and carefully slipstitch it to the back of the rug. Renew the contents of the bag twice yearly.

Slipstitch sleeve to top edge of rug

3 **ATTACHING SLEEVE** Slipstitch the top edge of the sleeve securely ³⁄₁₆–⅜ in (5–10 mm) below the top edge of the wrong side of the rug. Slipstitch the lower edge in place. Measure between the cup hooks, and cut the doweling to this length, adding a total of 1½ in (4 cm) at each end for the overhangs.

4 **INSERTING POLE** With the rug on a flat surface, slide the cut length of doweling into the sleeve. Adjust the position so that there is an overhang of ¾ in (2 cm) on each side. Hang the doweling from the hooks. If necessary, cut the doweling to a minimum possible overhang.

THE DISPLAYED RUG

SHELVING

SHELVING PROVIDES ONE of the most efficient methods of maximizing storage space. Shelving systems vary, from simple, single shelves supported by fixed brackets to fully adjustable units. You can construct shelves with the raw materials of your choice, or you may prefer to purchase ready-made shelves and assemble them according to your requirements. Either way, first consider the strength and rigidity of the shelves, and estimate the load that you intend to place on them. You can obtain shelves in a large range of woods of different thicknesses and in a variety of finishes, as well as in certain types of glass. There are essentially two categories of shelving support: brackets for supporting fixed shelves, and track systems, which are used for height-adjustable shelving. This chapter examines the range of materials available, provides advice on choosing a support system, and demonstrates how to put up long-lasting shelving.

CHOOSING A STYLE

*T*HE STYLE OF SHELVING THAT YOU OPT FOR depends not only on such considerations as the space available and the use to which the shelves will be put, but also on the construction of the shelving materials, the type of shelving unit, and where you position it. Shelving does not have to be purely utilitarian; it can be designed to blend in with the style, character, and shape of a room, or even to function as a decorative feature. Always make sure that the materials you use are strong enough to bear the load; if you wish to display a collection of small, delicate objects, however, you can construct lightweight shelving for the purpose.

DECORATIVE AND ORIGINAL
Making a set of shelves entirely for display purposes gives the opportunity to design a tailor-made, highly decorative unit. The lighter the load, the more decorative and unorthodox the materials and supports can be. These short pieces of white painted wood spanning pairs of terra-cotta pots form an arrangement that has great visual impact and originality.

Exceptionally thick boards create an imposing visual effect

Decorative terra-cotta pots complement objects displayed on shelves

FLEXIBLE AND PRACTICAL
The most flexible type of shelving – and one that is ideal for storing objects of various sizes, such as books – is a track system. The upright tracks are available in a range of gauges to support loads that vary from the lightest display objects to the heaviest books.

STYLISH AND EFFICIENT
In the kitchen, there is invariably a need for extensive – and easily accessible – storage space, and this can be provided by well-designed shelving. Storage jars and cooking utensils tend to be heavy, so make sure that you choose a style of shelving that fits the task and is secure and sturdy.

SUSPENDED SPACE-SAVERS
When you need to position shelving in front of a window, you may need to resort to a secondary hanging system. Here, lightweight brackets are attached to the window uprights. To enable the shelves to sustain the heavy weight of pots and pans, steel wires attached to the ceiling and shelves have been used to provide additional support, without being obtrusive.

Delicate wires support leading edges of shelves while allowing full access

Rigid composite wood, such as particle board, is ideal for shelves that are to be painted

COLOR-MATCHED DISPLAYS
Adjustable track systems are available in wood, which means that you can paint the shelves, uprights, and brackets to match the woodwork in the rest of the room. An attractively painted shelving unit is ideal for displaying china and pottery. If you wish to make shelves from thin pieces of lumber, prevent them from sagging when loaded by positioning the uprights no more than approximately 1 ft (30 cm) apart.

Cup hooks attached to shelf provide design solution to storage problem

Blue paintwork complements overall color scheme

CHOOSING A SHELVING SYSTEM

BEFORE PUTTING UP SHELVING, you will need to consider first and foremost the wall to which you intend to mount the shelves. This is important, since it determines the type and size of hardware that you require. Expect to spend some time selecting from a wide variety of shelf supports and shelving materials. The simplest shelf supports are non-adjustable brackets. For greater versatility in the arrangement of your shelves, use an adjustable track system. When choosing shelves, check that both supports and shelving materials will withstand the intended load for an extended period of time.

FIXED BRACKETS

Right-angled brackets made of wood or metal have long been the most efficient and popular means of supporting lengths of shelving. Once the bracket has been attached to the wall with suitable hardware, the shelving is secured to the bracket by means of small screws. Fixed brackets are manufactured in a great variety of sizes, gauges, and decorative styles.

LIGHTWEIGHT
Manufactured from strips of steel, these lightweight brackets are ideal for supporting thin shelving, specially made for displaying small, decorative objects.

MEDIUM-WEIGHT
Available in steel, solid brass, and painted finishes, these shelf supports can be used for lightweight to medium-weight shelving.

MEDIUM-HEAVY
Medium-strength brackets, made from painted steel, are readily available. Small steel brackets are ideal for heavyweight shelves.

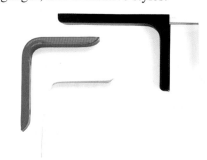

HEAVYWEIGHT
Many heavyweight brackets are produced with one arm longer than the other. Some are made with a clip-on trim that hides the fixed bracket.

ADJUSTABLE SHELF SUPPORTS

An adjustable shelving system is made of metal or wooden tracks that are mounted to the wall. Removable flanged brackets, available in different lengths, are slotted or clipped into these tracks, then locked in place to support the shelving. Adjustable supports are produced in wood and metal and are available in various gauges for different weight requirements.

LIGHTWEIGHT
This aluminum track-and-bracket system is designed to support lightweight shelving. It is unsuitable for supporting heavy loads, such as books.

METAL SUPPORT HOOK

MEDIUM-WEIGHT WOOD
Less common than the metal varieties, wooden track systems are often available complete with shelves in a matching color and finish. In this system, the brackets slot into the track by means of metal support hooks.

MEDIUM-WEIGHT STEEL
Manufactured in pressed steel, this support is strong enough to bear a medium-weight load. The brackets are designed with tongues for securing the shelving. End brackets hold items on shelves in place.

END BRACKET

END BRACKET

HEAVYWEIGHT
Designed to support heavy loads, such as books, the tracks for this system take double-flanged brackets for extra strength.

SHELVING MATERIALS

Once you have chosen a shelf support system, select the appropriate shelving material. Solid woods or composites are the most practical. Glass is useful for lightweight display purposes.

Make sure the shelving material is strong enough for the load it will take, and resistant to sagging. Reduce the distance between the brackets or tracks to increase support.

WALL HARDWARE

Always use hardware that suits the structure of the wall. Secure screws in solid walls with anchors or, for heavy loads, expanding bolts. Metal and plastic screw anchors, as well as toggle bolts, are available for securing screws in cavity walls.

CAVITY WALL HARDWARE

TOGGLE BOLT

METAL SLEEVE AND MATCHING SCREW

PLASTIC WING ANCHORS

PLASTIC DOOR SCREW ANCHORS

A range of metal and plastic anchors, as well as bolts with spring clips, is available for securing screws or a bracket to cavity walls. Only the very lightest shelving can be hung from a cavity wall. The strength of the hardware always relies on the strength of the wall. If possible, locate the studs that support the wall boards, and secure the shelving to these.

SOLID WALL HARDWARE

RAWL PLUGS

PLASTIC SCREW ANCHORS

CINDERBLOCK PLASTIC ANCHORS

WEDGE ANCHOR

When screwing a shelving system to a solid wall, use the appropriate size of screw or bolt, and its matching anchor. Anchors for solid walls are made of metal, compressed fiber, or plastic. Always drill the hole for the anchor to the size stated by the manufacturer. When you need to support very heavy loads, use wedge anchors. These do not require extra anchors.

GLASS AND SOLID WOODS
If you use glass for shelving, make sure that it is at least ¼ in (6 mm) thick and has polished edges. A glass dealer will cut the glass to size. Glass is heavy and requires heavyweight brackets, spaced no more than 16 in (40 cm) apart. Soft and hardwoods have the advantage of being attractive when varnished or waxed. They are more expensive than composite woods, however, and are prone to warping.

COMPOSITE WOODS
The most popular materials for shelving, composite woods are manufactured by gluing together and compressing wood or wood products. Medium-density fiberboard, plywood, and lumber core are inexpensive, easy to cut, and readily available in a variety of thicknesses. Of the three, lumber core is the most rigid.

VENEERED COMPOSITE WOODS
Composite woods are available in a range of decorative veneered finishes, which are produced from hardwood, softwood, melamine, and PVC. Lengths of veneered composite woods are manufactured specifically for shelving. They are also available in various widths; these need to be sawed to the necessary length, after which the cut ends should be faced with a strip of veneer.

GLASS

SOFTWOOD

HARDWOOD

MEDIUM-DENSITY FIBERBOARD (MDF)

PLYWOOD

LUMBER (VENEER) CORE

OAK VENEER ON MDF

OAK VENEER ON PARTICLEBOARD

MELAMINE ON PARTICLEBOARD

FORMICA

MOUNTING SHELVING

ONCE YOU HAVE DECIDED ON THE SHELVING support system that you need and have chosen the most appropriate shelving material, you will be ready to secure the shelves to the wall. Remember that your shelves will need to support objects that may be heavy or valuable over a long period of time. It is therefore important to use the correct equipment and techniques at each stage. Whether you are putting up fixed brackets or an adjustable system, make sure that you secure the shelf supports safely to the wall, and take care to hang the shelves so that they are perfectly level.

MOUNTING SHELVING BRACKETS TO A SOLID WALL

Decide on the position for each bracket. Consult the manufacturer's guidelines, so that you use the correct gauge and length of screws and anchors. Use appropriate anchors for securing screws into solid walls. You will also need a pencil, metal detector, awl, power drill with hammer setting, suitable bit, safety goggles, and screwdriver.

1 MARKING DRILLING POINTS Pass the metal detector over the area to check for hidden pipes and electrical wires. Hold the bracket against the wall, and make sure that it is positioned vertically. Mark drilling points through the screw holes with a pencil.

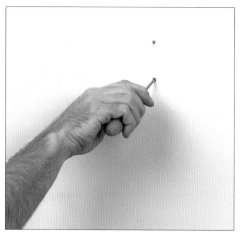

2 PIERCING DRILLING POINTS Use an awl to pierce the wall at the marked drilling points. This serves to guide the tip of the masonry drill bit, preventing it from slipping as you start to drill, and ensures that the holes are accurately centered.

3 DRILLING HOLE Fit the bit to the drill. Switch the drill to a slow speed and to the hammer setting. At the pierced mark, drill a hole to a depth slightly longer than the screw. Repeat at the other drilling points. Wear safety goggles when drilling.

4 FITTING ANCHOR Push an anchor into the drilled hole. The anchor should fit snugly and be slightly recessed, to reduce the risk of cracking the plaster.

5 SCREWING BRACKET Place the bracket in position, and pass a screw through a screw hole into the anchor. Drive the screw home tightly with a screwdriver. Position and secure the second screw.

CAVITY WALLS

When mounting lightweight shelving on a cavity wall, use anchors made of plastic or metal. Most have wings that expand against the wall within the cavity. Select the size of bit recommended by the anchor manufacturer. Mark and drill the holes. Insert an anchor, and drive home the screws.

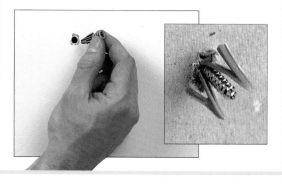

MOUNTING FIXED-POSITION SHELVING

Decide on the position for the brackets and the shelves. Use a metal detector to determine that there are no pipes or electrical wires hidden within the wall. When mounting brackets on a cavity wall, use a metal detector to locate the wooden frames. Use screws that will project at least 1 in (2.5 cm) into the wall. You will also need a pencil, awl, power drill, suitable masonry bit, anchors, carpenter's level, screwdriver, and small screws to secure the shelf to the brackets.

1 POSITIONING FIRST BRACKET
Hold the first bracket to the wall, aligning the top with the point at which the bottom of the shelf will lie. Mark the drilling points with a pencil, and mount the bracket in place as shown opposite.

3 POSITIONING INTERMEDIATE BRACKET
Make sure that the intermediate brackets are attached at the right height and equidistantly between the outside brackets. Lay the shelf on its edge, and align the bracket to this edge. Mark the drilling points with a pencil, and screw the bracket in place.

MOUNTING A SMALL SHELF
When hanging a short length of shelving, attach the brackets to the shelf first. Lay the shelf on its edge on a flat surface. Hold a bracket in place. Mark the shelf through the mounting holes. Pierce the marks with an awl. Drill pilot holes. Screw the bracket into position. Repeat this with the other bracket.

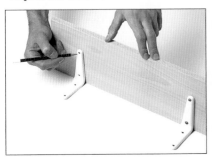

2 POSITIONING SECOND BRACKET
Place the second bracket against the wall. With the shelf in place, use a level to guide the bracket into position. Mark the drilling points with a pencil. Check that the shelf overhang is the same on each side. Drill the holes, and screw the bracket to the wall.

4 SECURING SHELF
Lay the shelf on the mounted brackets. Underneath the shelf, mark the positions with an awl for the screws that pass through the holes in the brackets. Drill pilot holes for screws, but do not pierce the top surface of the shelf. Twist home the screws.

For drilling holes for anchors to equal depths, use a depth indicator. Many power drills are equipped with depth indicators. Alternatively, use tape and a tape measure.

1 MEASURING DEPTH
Lay the support on a flat surface. Pass a screw through a screw hole. Press the screw against the support, and measure the length of screw projecting from the support. This is the depth you will need to drill.

2 MARKING BIT
Mark this measurement on the bit, using colored adhesive tape. Measure from the tip of the bit, and wrap a sleeve of tape around the bit at this point. The hole will be drilled to the required depth when you reach the tape.

THE MOUNTED SHELF

MOUNTING ADJUSTABLE SHELVING

Use a track-and-bracket support system if you wish to have the option of adjusting the levels of the shelves. Select a track system that is strong enough for the weight of the shelving. In addition to the chosen track system, you will need a pencil, metal detector, awl, power drill and a selection of masonry drill bits, suitable screws and anchors, screwdriver, carpenter's level, plumb line, and appropriate small screws for securing the shelves to the brackets.

METAL DETECTOR

Manufactured specifically for the home-decorating market, battery-powered metal detectors are a welcome asset as far as safety is concerned. They possess an audiovisual alert mechanism and a sensitivity control, which can be adjusted for detecting nails, screws, electrical wiring, or heavier metal obstructions embedded in a wall.

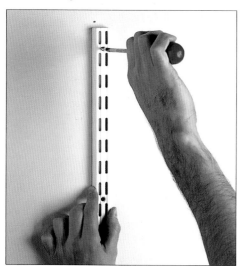

1 **POSITIONING TRACK** Check the area with a metal detector. Position the first length of track. Mark wall through top screw hole. Pierce mark with an awl. Drill a hole and fit an anchor. Attach the track loosely.

2 **ALIGNING TRACK** Make sure that the track can swing from the top mounting. Using a level, align the track vertically. When the track is vertical, mark all the drilling points on the wall with a pencil.

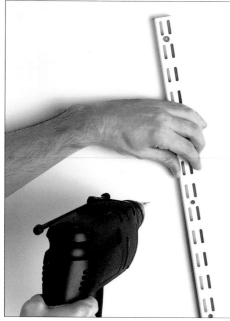

3 **DRILLING HOLES** Swing the track aside to gain access to the drilling points. Pierce them with an awl, and drill holes into the wall at the marked drilling points. Fit anchors in the holes. Return the track to the vertical, and fasten it securely to the wall with a screw in each hole.

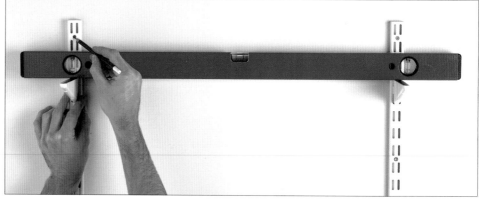

4 **POSITIONING SECOND TRACK** Fit a bracket to the top of the secured track, and another similarly into the second track. Lay a level between the brackets. Make sure the tracks are distanced correctly. Establish a true horizontal. Mark first drilling point on wall. Mount second track as before.

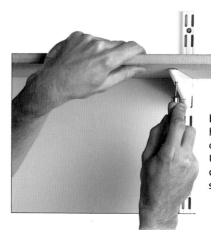

5 **POSITIONING SHELF** Lay a shelf on the brackets at the desired height. Position the shelf centrally over the brackets. Using an awl, mark the drilling points for the small securing screws.

6 DRILLING PILOT HOLES

Once you have marked the drilling points on each shelf, carefully drill pilot holes for the screws with a power drill fitted with a suitable bit. If access is poor, remove the shelf to drill it.

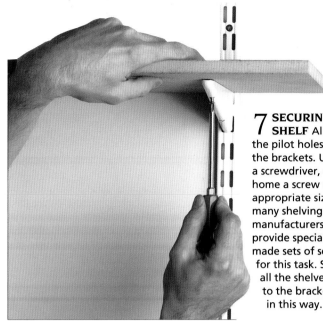

7 SECURING SHELF

Align the pilot holes with the brackets. Using a screwdriver, drive home a screw of the appropriate size – many shelving manufacturers provide specially made sets of screws for this task. Secure all the shelves to the brackets in this way.

8 ALIGNING SHELVES

When erecting a shelving system with several rows of shelves of an identical length, use a plumb line to ensure that the shelves are perfectly aligned at each end. Mount the top shelf in place, and hang a plumb line from it. Position the remaining shelves, using the plumb line as a vertical guide.

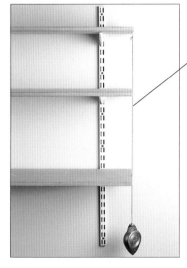

Align stack of shelves accurately, using plumb line

Track-and-bracket system is ideal for adjustable-height shelving

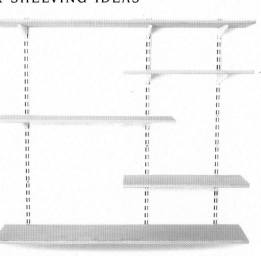

THE MOUNTED SHELF

OTHER SHELVING IDEAS

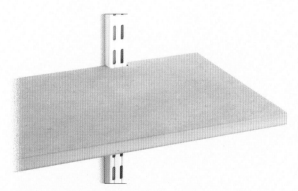

MOUNTING SHELVES FLUSH TO A WALL
A track-and-bracket system will support shelves slightly away from a wall. To make it flush with a wall, cut notches in back edge of each shelf to fit around tracks.

THREE-TRACK FLEXIBILITY
A three-track support system offers several advantages for arranging shelf levels and spacing. You can use shelves of varying dimensions to give a great degree of flexibility when arranging and displaying objects. When securing the shelves, always remember to equalize overhangs at the ends.

LIGHTING

LIGHTING CONTRIBUTES A GREAT DEAL to the atmosphere of a room, and should thus be one of the fundamental elements of any home decorating scheme. Many people are restricted by light sources that are inextricably linked to an existing wiring system and supply basic illumination, rather than providing mood and atmosphere. Despite the limitations of electrical systems, there are many possibilities for enhancing the quality of artificial lighting. Recent technological advances in the manufacture of lightbulbs and fixtures have produced lighting designed to suit the specific character and contents of each room in a home. This chapter includes information on how to use a variety of bulbs and fixtures to produce different effects with light, and shows how you can make the most of fixed and movable light sources to create the quality of light most appropriate to your needs.

CHOOSING A STYLE

*W*HEN PROPERLY USED, LIGHT ENHANCES the character of a room, highlighting specific objects or creating a certain mood. Rooms such as kitchens, which require general illumination, can be lit by various types of fixtures that complement the design scheme, while providing the necessary amount of light. Candlelight is an example of mood lighting – this subdued light produces a relaxed atmosphere. Accent lighting focuses on particular objects: a narrow-beam spotlight directed onto a specific object, such as a wall hanging, will emphasize the textile's design, while adding to the level of illumination. Other types of lighting are more functional – these include table lamps used to illuminate work surfaces.

MOOD LIGHTING
Subdued lighting is conducive to establishing a relaxed mood. An overhead electrical light used in an antique fixture, complemented by the welcoming glow of candlelight, is well suited to the intimacy of a dining room.

MODERN ELEGANCE
There exists a wide range of fixtures suitable for all manner of design schemes. This contemporary pendant directs light onto the kitchen table, as well as providing good general illumination.

Simple style of pendant harmonizes with overall design scheme

Large window allows a gentle flood of sunlight to brighten room

An incandescent bulb emitting light from a desk lamp gives concentrated illumination suitable for reading

BRIGHT AND GENTLE
Work areas such as studies usually require more intense local light than other rooms, although this light should never be harsh. Here, the desk lamp focuses light onto the work surface, while the warm, general glow of sunlight shining through the large windows brightens the room in the daytime. At night, the ceiling lights, which are out of view, provide general illumination.

SUBTLE HIGHLIGHTS
Hidden inside the front edge of a display case, small light fixtures can be used to highlight a collection of objects. The function of this type of lighting is to illuminate the display, not to add secondary brightness to the room.

SOFT GLOW
Dimly lit areas of the home can be made brighter with uplights or other wall fixtures designed to flood the immediate area with light. Here, a half-dome uplight brightens the hallway with a subtle, soft glow.

OLD-FASHIONED EFFECTS
Here, a kerosene lamp provides light that is of little use for a specific task but complements the old-fashioned design scheme of the kitchen. During the day, light pours in through the large window, providing sufficient general illumination. At night, the old-style kerosene lamp emanates a warm and pleasant glow around the table.

FORMAL STYLE
Table lamps are excellent for providing secondary illumination that supplements a room's principal light source. Decorative table lamps in period designs complement antique furniture well, while providing strong areas of incandescent light. Lampshade designs are important, since they provide style as well as giving direction and color to the light.

Opaque shade highlights shape of lampshade when lit, as well as projecting strong patterns of light above and below

Straight-sided cardboard shade complements elegant design of lamp base

SOURCES OF LIGHT

*I*N THE PAST, ARTIFICIAL LIGHTING USUALLY ORIGINATED from restricted, diffuse sources such as candles, hanging lamps, and table lamps. Nowadays, it is much easier to direct and control light for a variety of purposes, because of the wide-scale availability of an enormous range of light fixtures and bulb types. In conjunction with the advancement of lighting technology, a desire to save energy has led to the development of efficient light bulbs that have a long life and use less electricity than previous models.

REFLECTOR BEAM PROFILES

A standard domestic tungsten-filament light bulb gives off diffuse illumination, which is ideal for general lighting. To control the direction of artificial light, choose from a range of reflector bulbs to fit spotlights, downlights, and uplights. A narrow beam, from 3 to 25 degrees, is suitable for illuminating small areas. A medium beam of between 25 and 40 degrees provides a more general-purpose light, whereas a wide beam of over 40 degrees is good for floodlighting a large area.

NARROW BEAM: 3–25 DEGREES

MEDIUM BEAM: 25–40 DEGREES

WIDE BEAM: OVER 40 DEGREES

EFFICIENT BULBS

Over the past decade, a great deal of research has concentrated on making energy-efficient bulbs that give off an attractive light and possess a long life. Halogen bulbs, such as tungsten or quartz, are compact and powerful and emit a white light.

Fluorescent bulbs, by contrast, are known more for their economic efficiency than for their lighting quality. Because of recent technological advances, however, they are now a viable alternative to standard domestic light bulbs.

TUNGSTEN-HALOGEN BULBS
Originally developed for floodlighting large areas, tungsten-halogen bulbs have become popular for domestic use. Low-voltage, miniaturized halogen bulbs, with their special fixtures, are well suited for use in areas where accurate, powerful lighting is required. Recently, halogen bulbs have been used in conventional spotlight fixtures.

MINIATURE, LOW-VOLTAGE TUNGSTEN-HALOGEN REFLECTOR BULB

MINIATURE FLUORESCENT BULBS FOR LAMP FIXTURES
Most of these energy-saving bulbs use one quarter of the electricity of a conventional bulb, and last more than five times longer. Fluorescents require a transformer, which is built into the bulb base.

SCREW BASE

BAYONET CAP BASE

2-D MINIATURE FLUORESCENT BULB
This bulb was designed for use with a specific wall or ceiling fixture, equipped with the appropriate transformer. An adapter is available, however, for attachment to a conventional lamp socket.

TUNGSTEN-HALOGEN REFLECTOR BULB

2-D MINIATURE FLUORESCENT BULB

EFFECTS OF LIGHTING

The startling growth in the range of bulbs and light fixtures for domestic use ensures that you have the opportunity to exercise considerable control over the quality of artificial lighting in every room of the home. What type of light you use and how you manipulate it directly affects the color and shape of a lit area, as well as the character of a room itself.

NATURAL DAYLIGHT

This light is used to judge the naturalness of color. Its variable nature, from bright sunlight to a dull pall, provides inspiration for artificial lighting effects.

FLUORESCENT LIGHTING

Associated with a diffuse, cool-blue or greenish light, fluorescent tubes are available in a wide range of colors, including artificial daylight.

QUARTZ-HALOGEN UPLIGHT

Fitted on a long stem with a semi-opaque shade, the uplight here has a quartz-halogen bulb. The light is diffused by the shade and reflected from the ceiling.

CANDLES

The light emitted by a burning candle possesses a comfortable, atmospheric warmth. Candles should always be used judiciously, and with safety foremost in mind.

TABLE LAMP WITH TUNGSTEN-FILAMENT BULB

The warm and diffuse light from a tungsten-filament bulb is directed across this table by a semi-opaque conical shade fitted to a wooden lamp base.

PENDANT FIXTURE WITH TUNGSTEN-FILAMENT BULB

Suspended overhead, the bright light from a tungsten bulb is cast downward and onto these flowers by a semi-opaque, conical, paper lampshade.

TUNGSTEN SPOTLIGHT FROM OVERHEAD

Positioned overhead, a reflector bulb provides a focused light that retains a warm hue. The bulbs are available with beam profiles of between 12 and 80 degrees.

HALOGEN SPOTLIGHT FROM OVERHEAD

From a low-voltage spotlight positioned overhead, the wide beam from a quartz-halogen reflector bulb provides a white light with strong, clear shadows.

HALOGEN SPOTLIGHT FROM ABOVE AND BEHIND

A medium-beam halogen reflector bulb is the light source from a point above and behind the object. The light beam enhances the outline shape of the flowers.

HALOGEN SPOTLIGHT FROM ABOVE AND IN FRONT

Moving the medium-beam halogen reflector bulb to shine from above and in front of the vase of flowers results in a sharp shadow cast beyond the object.

HALOGEN SPOTLIGHT FROM THE SIDE

Positioned to the side of the object and 15 to 45 degrees above it, a medium-beam halogen reflector bulb produces the effect of daylight coming from a window.

SMALL UPLIGHT FROM BEHIND

If a medium-beam halogen reflector bulb is positioned in a small uplight behind the vase, the outline of the illuminated object will be highlighted.

FIXED LIGHTING

ONCE YOU HAVE DECIDED ON THE NATURE and quality of lighting for a room, you will need to select the fixtures. Fixed lighting is ideal for static and general illumination, and there are various styles of fixtures to choose from. Most fixed lights require hidden electrical wiring, either above the ceiling or behind the plaster in a wall. To replace such fixtures with a different style of unit, consult a professional electrician for guidance and safety information. Do not replace or rewire any part of your home until you understand fully what is required. Installing an electrical system is not difficult as long as you know how to do it safely.

WALL LIGHTS

Wall lights are fixtures, often set at eye level, that provide a subtle and practical light source. Electrical wall lights, complete with shades or glass globes, replaced the candle, oil, or gas lamps that were common in homes up to the early 20th century. More recent designs for wall lights include fixtures that illuminate the wall with a halo effect.

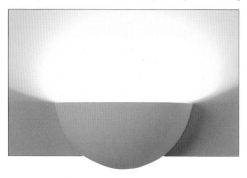

OPAQUE BOWL
This half-dome fixture concentrates the wash of light directly upward across the wall and onto the ceiling. Made of plaster, this type of fixture can be painted to match or contrast with the color of the wall.

PERIOD DESIGN
Wall lights were some of the earliest electrical fixtures invented. Today, there are various period imitations available, ranging from the chrome and smoked glass of an Art Deco fixture, as shown here, to the polished brass bracket and etched glass bowl that is reminiscent of an antique gas lamp.

WALL LIGHT WITH DIFFUSER
Rather than direct the light up the wall, this fixture radiates light around the surface through a stepped, smoked-glass diffuser.

PLUG-IN WALL LIGHT

Most wall lights are designed to be supplied with electricity from hidden wiring, but some are created with the shape of an electrical cord in mind. These lights should be installed above an electrical socket to avoid long electrical cords across your wall.

DOUBLE WALL LIGHT
This double-bracket lamp is an example of a modern design inspired by wrought-iron torch and candle fittings of the past. Small paper shades clip onto candle-shaped bulbs and illuminate the immediate area.

PICTURE LIGHT
This shaded strip light is specially made for illuminating objects that are mounted to the wall. Depending on the size and position of the object, the bracket for mounting the light can be hidden behind, above, or below the object. When you are lighting a textile, old document, or painting, it is very important that you seek professional advice about the light sensitivity of the object before installing a fixture.

CEILING LIGHTS

The most common source of general-purpose, fixed-ceiling lighting comes from pendant fixtures. Pendants used to consist solely of a length of cord, light socket, and paper shade.

Hanging lights are now available in all manner of designs. As an alternative to a suspended or surface-mounted fixture, consider lighting a room with modern recessed downlights.

GLASS-GLOBE PENDANT

This smoked-glass globe is suspended by a chromium-plated rod from a ceiling bracket, and diffuses the light from a standard domestic bulb. Glass-globe pendants are available in a wide range of different sizes and rod lengths.

DOMED FIXTURE
This fixture gives off a diffuse light. Designed for use with a miniature fluorescent bulb, it can be surface mounted or semi-recessed on either the ceiling or the wall.

PENDANT WITH SHADE

Diffusing the light from a hanging bulb with a shade is perhaps the most common means of illuminating a room. The aluminum fixture shown here is a modern alternative to traditional paper and fabric shades.

DISCUS-SHAPED FIXTURE
Discus-shaped fixtures are ideal for high-level lighting. This one consists of a smoked-glass diffuser attached to a circular metal bracket, which is securely mounted onto the ceiling.

CHANDELIER

The old-fashioned shape of a chandelier is well suited to electrical lighting. Chandeliers are manufactured using various materials, from glass to metal. Before installing a chandelier, you should make sure that the ceiling and hardware can support the often considerable weight of the fixture.

CIRCULAR FIXTURE WITH SPOTLIGHTS
Circular fixtures, complete with multiple spotlights, provide an economical and practical alternative to attaching a lighting track and spotlight system to the ceiling. Fitted with a standard tungsten-filament reflector bulb, the beam of each spotlight is easily adjustable.

TUNGSTEN REFLECTOR
The design of this downlight is simple and unobtrusive. Fitted with a tungsten-filament reflector bulb, this downlight is an ideal fixture for general-purpose use.

MINIATURE FLUORESCENT
Containing miniature fluorescent bulbs, this downlight with reflector cone gives efficient usage, making it well suited for continuous operation.

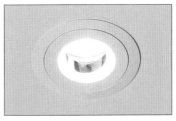

LOW-VOLTAGE HALOGEN
These are the smallest-diameter downlights. Their low-voltage bulbs must be attached to the right electrical transformer. Here, the transformer is above the ceiling.

ADJUSTABLE DOWNLIGHT
Rather than shine a beam of light downward, some downlights are available with a pivoting lamp or a rotating cutout that enables the light to be directed to one side.

MOVABLE LIGHTS

*W*HEN LIGHTING A ROOM, YOU WILL PROBABLY want to use several different types of movable and permanent fixtures. Movable lights are an attractive and easy-to-use alternative to fixed lighting systems, which usually require hidden electrical wiring, and they can be easily adjusted to suit your decorative and practical lighting needs. Although a track system is more permanent than a table or standing lamp, it provides you with the flexibility to change the position of the bulbs in order to redirect the light. Candlelight creates a more atmospheric effect than electrical lighting and can be used in many different ways.

TABLE LIGHTS

There are basically two types of movable lights that are designed to be placed on, or attached to, a table. Desk lights are made for illuminating small work areas and are available in a wide range of shapes and sizes. Table lights provide additional general lighting to a room or local lighting for small areas, such as an armchair or a corner of a room.

LOW-VOLTAGE QUARTZ HALOGEN
A desk light should be easily adjustable and provide suitable illumination. This heavy-based light has pivots and springs – only the slightest touch is needed to change the beam angle.

PERIOD DESK LIGHT
Originally designed in 1930, this classic style remains very popular. Available in chrome or brass finishes, with matching metal shade and base, it is suitable for most uses on a desk.

WOODEN BASE WITH PAPER SHADE
Made of turned hardwood, this simple and elegant table lamp, with a plain paper, conical shade, provides suitable local lighting and a diffuse spread of secondary light within a room.

DESK LIGHT WITH CLAMP
Rather than have a large and often heavy base, some desk lights are available with an adjustable clamp that can be secured to the top of a desk or table. The concept behind this sprung and pivoted light was pioneered in 1933.

CERAMIC BASE WITH FABRIC SHADE
Ceramic lamp bases are available in various shapes and designs. This fabric lampshade is lined with semi-opaque paper and directs most of the light onto the table.

CANDLES

A candlestick is ideal for raising the height of candlelight from a flat surface. A pierced lantern makes a fine decorative hanging. To hang candles on a wall, use a reflecting sconce. Always make sure that you use candles safely and place them well away from flammable objects.

CANDLESTICK

PIERCED LANTERN

REFLECTING SCONCE

FLOOR LIGHTS

Light fixtures that are freestanding on a floor are available in a wide range of shapes and sizes and, like table lights, are very easy to move and set up. Floor lights are well suited for use as sources for general, mood, and local lighting. They are manufactured in a variety of decorative designs. Uplights and spotlights are designed for illuminating specific areas.

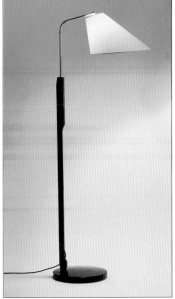

WOOD-AND-METAL STANDARD LAMP WITH PAPER SHADE
This is a modern version of the standard floor lamp. Adjustable in height and fitted with a paper shade that directs the light forward, this light is suitable for illuminating an armchair or other specific area.

SMALL UPLIGHT
The short stem on this fixture conceals a transformer for the low-voltage tungsten-halogen bulb. This uplight can be placed on the floor or on top of a raised surface.

TALL-STEMMED UPLIGHT
This type of uplight, with a tungsten-halogen bulb, is an efficient and newly popular source of indirect light. It is useful for general and decorative lighting.

BRASS STANDARD LAMP WITH PAPER SHADE
Mounted on a sturdy pedestal, this lamp can be adjusted laterally, making it a useful fixture for a living room, where it can provide a balance of light for a specific area and a whole room.

SPOTLIGHT STAND
Designed for use as a portable light to illuminate small areas, this spotlight stand with its transformer base provides an ideal means for shining a localized pool of light.

TRACK LIGHTS

Ceiling-mounted tracks with adjustable spotlight fixtures were originally developed for commercial use, in order to facilitate the frequent changes needed in directing light onto specific areas. Similar systems have become popular for home use. Some systems are available with either square or round profiles, and can be arranged in various configurations.

LOW-VOLTAGE SPOTLIGHT
When you wish to pinpoint an object with a narrow beam of light, or to create a suitably impressive splash of decorative lighting, a fixture with a tungsten-halogen bulb is ideal. This spotlight, with its built-in transformer, is designed to use a low-voltage tungsten-halogen bulb, shining a beam width between 9 and 36 degrees.

SPOTLIGHT WITH COWL
The reflector lamp for this spotlight is hidden within a white aluminum sleeve, or cowl. The cowl is a lighting feature that is designed to be stylish and functional.

SPOTLIGHT WITH NO COWL
This fixture consists of a sleeve into which a reflector bulb is screwed. Depending on the reflector bulb type, you can vary the beam width by between 10 and 30 degrees.

$\mathcal{H}$OUSEPLANTS

$\mathcal{H}$OUSEPLANTS GREATLY ENHANCE the atmosphere of a living space, counterbalancing and softening the shapes of inanimate furnishings and the hard lines of rooms. Just as there are myriad ways of decorating, furnishing, and lighting a room, similarly there is a tremendous variety of plants that can be used in the home to complement or modify the decor. In this chapter, you will find suggestions for selecting plants for your home according to the shape of their foliage and the color and fragrance of their flowers. Also included are ideas for attractive plants whose leaves can, as an added bonus, be used for culinary purposes, as well as advice on choosing the most appropriate containers for different types of plants.

CHOOSING PLANTS

*I*F CHOSEN AND SITED CAREFULLY, houseplants can be actively incorporated into your decorative schemes, creating a fresh, natural, and comfortable atmosphere in every room of the home. The style of a room will help determine the types of plant that you display. Traditional interiors are complemented by bushy foliage and large, colorful flowers, while modern settings generally benefit from bold, architectural, or exotic plants. Always make sure that a living area has adequate light and the right level of humidity, as well as the correct temperature range, to support the type of plant you intend to display.

LEAFY BACKDROPS
It is often the case that the most appropriate method of displaying plants in a garden is in groups of two or three; the same principle applies to houseplants. Small and medium-sized houseplants always look best when clustered together. Here, the Cape leadwort creates a foliage backdrop to the low-growing primrose displayed on the table in the foreground.

ISLANDS OF GREEN
A conservatory is the natural choice of room for growing a large selection of houseplants. When adorned with a variety of plants, hanging from the ceiling, growing in containers, and tumbling out of planters, a conservatory assumes the qualities of a tranquil oasis within a home, and becomes filled with heady fragrances and rich colors.

LUSH AND SHADY
Vigorous, large-leafed plants soften the hard edges of a room and provide welcome shade. Here, a robust grapevine, growing on the outside, has been ingeniously incorporated inside a new conservatory, making a stunning dominant feature.

Cut flowers provide small points of adornment within sea of foliage

Hand-painted ceramic containers soften impact of dramatic grapevine

TALL AND BUSHY
Using tall, substantial plants is an effective and convenient method of altering the appearance of large rooms. When a room has an extensive floor area and severe angles, rows of bushy indoor trees, such as these weeping figs, are ideal for dividing up the living space and providing an inviting look for the room.

Rich masses of foliage on tall stems enhance proportions of modern, high-ceilinged room

TRADITIONAL CENTERPIECE
One of the more useful attributes of small and medium-sized houseplants is their portability – they can be moved from room to room and sited to serve as points of interest in various positions. Houseplants with very dense foliage, such as this Boston fern, make excellent focal points when they are displayed in fireplaces.

Classical lines of formal fireplace are softened by dainty foliage

VARIATIONS ON A THEME
A room can benefit from the decorative unity of an arrangement of a single plant group. Here, for instance, the room has been entirely devoted to the cultivation of colorful and often exotically scented geraniums which provide a distinct theme and mood. The flowers of some houseplants can be short-lived; in order to enhance their impact, furnishings and accessories can be introduced that pick up the flower colors.

Unglazed terra-cotta pots give rustic, traditional note

Geranium theme is echoed in furnishings and accessories

TYPES OF HOUSEPLANT

PLANTS OF EVERY COLOR, SHAPE, SIZE, AND TEXTURE, from a variety of sources
the world over, can be grown with relative ease indoors. You can find something
suitable for every room. In order to decide which plants are most appropriate for your
needs, consider how the decorative qualities of plants can contribute in different ways
to the overall styling of your home. When selecting plants, always consider carefully
not only their decorative features, but also the conditions they require – light,
temperature, and humidity – and choose containers that match the style of plant.

PLANTS FOR FOLIAGE INTEREST

One of the most important decorative features of a plant is the appearance of its foliage. Indoor plants selected for their foliage have a consistent appeal, since they are not entirely dependent on a flowering season. The decorative potential of a foliage plant is derived principally from the plant's form, but also from the size, shape, texture, and color of its leaves.

*Bright red,
leaf-like bracts*

Elongated red fruits

*Central rosette is
tinged deep red*

POINSETTIA
Euphorbia pulcherrima
Well known for its bright red bracts from
autumn to spring, this shrub is popular as a
striking table centerpiece. It is also available
with pink or cream coloration. Place it in a
warm, sunny room and keep the soil moist.

ORNAMENTAL PEPPER
Capsicum annuum
Another plant that can be used to provide
a decorative splash of color in winter, the
ornamental pepper produces elongated fruits
that change from green to yellow to red.
Keep it in a warm, sunny place.

BIRD'S-NEST BROMELIAD
Nidularium innocentii
This evergreen possesses arching leaves.
Its most decorative feature is a central rosette
of dark green foliage, tinged dark red at
flowering. It requires special soil mix, since it
is epiphytic, and a partially shaded, warm site.

*Stiff leaves with
sharp spikes*

*Undersides of
leaves are purple*

*Leaves dappled with
irregular pink spots*

PURPLE PASSION
Gynura aurantiaca
This plant is endowed with velvety, purple
down on ornamental foliage. Initially growing
upright, the stems bend over as they age. The
shrub therefore looks dramatic grown in a
hanging basket suspended in a window.

ROYAL AGAVE
Agave victoriae-reginae
A domed succulent with rosettes of chunky
leaves terminating in sharp spines, this
plant looks best viewed from above, so site
it on a low table. Position it in a sunny spot,
and water it infrequently in winter.

POLKA-DOT PLANT
Hypoestes phyllostachya
Grow this plant in a prominent place for its
unusual coloring – its dark green leaves are
speckled and dappled with pink. Encourage
the plant's bushy habit by pinching out the
growing tips. Grow it in a warm, shaded spot.

Drooping, ivy-shaped leaves

Arching, light green fronds on black stems

PIGGYBACK PLANT
Tolmiea menziesii
Ideal for displaying in a hanging basket, this plant's fully grown, ivy-shaped leaves produce small plantlets on their top surfaces. The plant should be kept in a cool site with partial shade.

MAIDENHAIR FERN
Adiantum capillus-veneris
This fern possesses delightfully delicate fronds on dainty, black stems, making it perfect for adding a soft note to a cluster of houseplants. It needs a humid, warm, shaded place.

LEMON GERANIUM
Pelargonium crispum 'Variegatum'
This variety of geranium is noted for its gold-variegated, aromatic leaves, the fragrance of which is released when the plant is warmed by the sun or touched. Site it in a sunny position.

HERBS

Herbs have been cultivated for ages, primarily for medicinal uses, and more recently as culinary flavorings. Many types of herb will grow indoors, providing appealing colors and aromas, and natural, decorative touches on kitchen windowsills. A well-lit conservatory can also be a home for potted herbs.

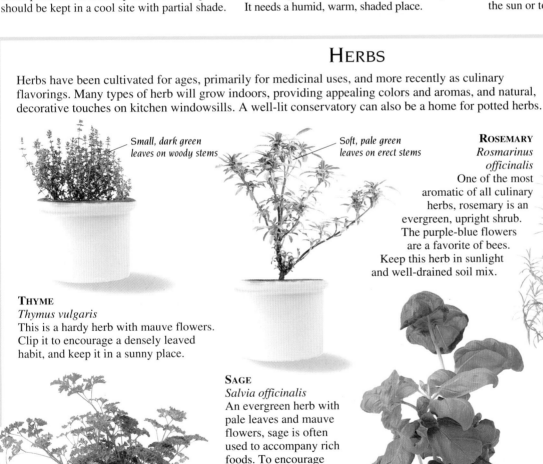

Small, dark green leaves on woody stems

Soft, pale green leaves on erect stems

ROSEMARY
Rosmarinus officinalis
One of the most aromatic of all culinary herbs, rosemary is an evergreen, upright shrub. The purple-blue flowers are a favorite of bees. Keep this herb in sunlight and well-drained soil mix.

THYME
Thymus vulgaris
This is a hardy herb with mauve flowers. Clip it to encourage a densely leaved habit, and keep it in a sunny place.

SAGE
Salvia officinalis
An evergreen herb with pale leaves and mauve flowers, sage is often used to accompany rich foods. To encourage leaf growth, cut it back vigorously in spring. Sage needs dryish soil and full sunlight.

PARSLEY
Petroselinum crispum
Used copiously in cooking, this is a perfect plant for growing on a sunny kitchen windowsill.

BASIL
Ocimum basilicum
A tender annual plant, basil will thrive in the warmth of a kitchen, if placed in a sunny spot. Encourage its bushy foliage by picking out the tip of the main stem when it reaches 6 in (15 cm).

FLOWERING PLANTS

Such is the range of flowering house plants available, and so great is the choice of colors, shapes, sizes, and textures, that suitable plants can be found to enhance all styles of interior.

When creating a decorative arrangement, you can choose to group together plants of the same color for a gentle effect, or mix complementary colors for a stronger statement.

Profuse, long-lasting, yellow-eyed flowers

Plant can be trained around wire

REGAL GERANIUM
Pelargonium domesticum
This plant produces trumpet-shaped flowers that can emerge in different colors. The large blooms are tempered by the plant's short flowering season, which is confined to spring. Place in a cool setting.

PRIMULA
Primula obconica
The primula is a colorful plant with long-lasting clusters of yellow-eyed flowers that can be mauve, white, salmon, or pink. It is best treated as an annual. Keep it in a cool site that is partially shaded, such as a hallway.

PASSION FLOWER
Passiflora caerulea
This plant provides a succession of interesting flowers throughout summer and autumn. It can grow to a height of 33 ft (10 m), making it ideal for a conservatory or large windowsill area. The plant enjoys a warm, sunny situation.

CROCUS
Crocus
The crocus provides welcome color during winter and early spring. Because it grows to only 4¾ in (12 cm) in height, display several plants in a cluster of one variety in a shallow bowl. Crocuses enjoy cool, partial shade.

Large, daisy-like flowers grow in clusters

CINERARIA
Pericallis x *hybrida*
This plant has large flowers and tactile leaves, making a striking display when several specimens are bunched together in one container. Flowering in the spring, the blooms can be pink, magenta, red, orange, blue, or purple. Best grown for one season only, cineraria needs a cool, sunny site.

GRAPE HYACINTH
Muscari
The grape hyacinth has neat spikes of small, blue or white flowers at the heads of tall, narrow stalks. For maximum decorative effect, it is best to cluster several plants together, and to display them in a cool, sunny position, such as a windowsill.

Strong,
upright growth

Rounded, flat flowers with
very dark brown centers

FLOWERING MAPLE
Abutilon hybridum
'Canary Bird'
This shrub looks
dramatic when placed in
front of a tall window. It can
reach a height and spread of
1 yd (1 m). Emerging from
among the maple-shaped leaves
are yellow, red, pink, or white
flowers. Keep it in a sunny site.

**BLACK-EYED
SUSAN VINE**
Thunbergia alata
Named after the
color of the "eye"
at the center of each
flower, this plant
produces brightly colored, round
blooms from spring through to
autumn. It looks attractive
trained to climb up in front of
a sunny, but cool, window.

GLOXINIA
Sinningia speciosa
From the center of a spread of large leaves
rises a cluster of flowers
that can be pink, red, white,
or purple, frequently
bordered with white.
Gloxinias make showy
displays either singly
or grouped together, and
should be kept in a warm spot.

Large, funnel-
shaped flowers

TULIP
Tulipa
Tulips grow in all shapes, sizes, and colors,
providing elegant and welcome displays of
flowers in winter and early spring. For maximum
decorative effect, plant the same variety in one
large container, or in a cluster of pots. Keep
tulips in cool, diffuse sunlight.

Colorful blooms are
produced in clusters

Rounded, fleshy,
dark green leaves

AZALEA
Rhododendron varieties
The azalea is well known for its spring
flowers, which range from pink to bright red.
The flowers form a brilliant contrast to the
small, shiny leaves. Azaleas benefit from
being placed in a cool, shaded position.

KALANCHOE
Kalanchoe blossfeldiana
This succulent produces a profusion of small
flowers at the ends of long stems. The flowers
emerge in many colors, from pink through to
red, orange, and yellow. Treat kalanchoes as
annuals, and place them in a warm, sunny site.

WAX BEGONIA
Begonia semperflorens-cultorum
These small plants are grown for their
long-lasting, red, pink, or white flowers, and
provide excellent displays of color. Group
different-colored wax begonias together
in a light, warm, well-ventilated position.

FRAGRANT PLANTS

A plant's aromas originate in the flowers or the leaves and are released when a flower opens or a leaf is touched – or, in some cases, when a plant is warmed by the sun's rays. Make the most of fragrant plants by siting them in well-used areas of the home, such as the living room, kitchen, or bathroom, where the delicious scents can be enjoyed close-up.

MINIATURE IRIS
Iris reticulata
Early-flowering, bulbous plants with a subtle aroma, these irises make a delightful display in the winter months. Growing to about 6 in (15 cm) in height, and surrounded by slender leaves, the flowers produce a delicate fragrance, best appreciated in close proximity. Place them in a cool spot with shaded sunlight.

Each plant bears a solitary, long-tubed flower

WAX FLOWER
Stephanotis floribunda
The wax flower has been known to grow to a considerable 10 ft (3 m) in height and spread. Its readiness to be trained on any type of support makes it ideal for decorating a conservatory or large windowsill. The waxy, white flowers are wonderfully scented. Site the plant in a warm, sunny position.

DAFFODIL
Narcissus
These handsome bulbs have been extensively hybridized and can produce single to double flowers in various shades, including orange, yellow, pink, cream, and white. Many varieties also have a pleasing fragrance. Display them in a cool place with diffuse sunlight.

Twining, woody stems with dark green leaflets

HYACINTH
Hyacinthus orientalis
Their distinctive fragrance and flower configurations make hyacinths among the most popular plants for brightening up the home in the spring. Keep them in a cool position in diffuse sunlight.

WHITE JASMINE
Jasminum polyanthum
Possessing a vigorous climbing nature, this strongly scented jasmine can be trained to grow both in height and in spread, making it a splendid plant for conservatories. The scented, white flowers emerge during winter and spring. Grow in a cool, but sunny, site, and place outside in summer, if possible.

CHOOSING CONTAINERS

Once you have selected the best houseplants for your home environment, it is important to consider the most suitable containers for them. The type of plant container that you need is subject to various factors. The principal consideration is the proportion of the container in relation to the plant. Moreover, the style of the container should always be in harmony with the style of the room for which it is intended.

WOODEN BARREL
In a simply decorated room, the most appropriate container is often one that has a simple form and a functional appearance. This rustic wooden barrel complements the unusual shape of the cactus.

GLASS BOWL
The advantage of glass is that it has a clean, but unimposing, profile and a smooth, shiny exterior. This style of container is ideal for displaying plants with strong outlines and is particularly suited to an uncluttered, modern interior.

Filigree, bronze-colored foliage contrasts effectively with solid-looking terra-cotta container

CLASSICAL URN
The classical design of this lead urn, in combination with a Boston fern, creates a formal atmosphere and conveys images of the grand style. This type of planting will form an eye-catching centerpiece in any room.

RUSH BASKET
A basket with a hooped handle provides support for small climbing house plants, obviating the need for stakes or trellises. The twiggy texture of basketwork is particularly appropriate for rustic interiors.

GLAZED CERAMIC POT
The glazed finish of this simple ceramic container gives an unassertive, sophisticated look, while its attractive, classic shape and wide rim complement the rising, bare stems of the caladiums.

LARGE TERRA-COTTA POT
The earthy colors and solidity of terra-cotta have ensured its use for many centuries as a material for decorative plant containers. Terra-cotta's natural look makes it ideal for setting off foliage, and its easygoing texture harmonizes with any type of interior.

CARE AND MAINTENANCE

THE LIFE SPAN OF ANY SOFT FURNISHING will be increased if you ensure that the fabric is protected from intensive wear and tear. Direct sunlight fades the colors and patterns of many fabrics and eventually weakens them. Sources of heat also damage fabrics, so do not let soft furnishings come into contact with radiators, heaters, or open fires. The best way of keeping your soft furnishings in good condition is to ensure that they are regularly cleaned. Always use a vacuum cleaner to remove surface dust from upholstered furniture. Animal hairs can become embedded in the fabric weave; dab the area with sticky tape to remove them. To limit the amount of maintenance needed on painted, wallpapered, or tiled surfaces, make sure that you prepare surfaces correctly before decorating them, and follow product manufacturers' instructions for cleaning and repairing.

FABRIC CARE

CLEANING FABRICS

All fabrics will last longer if you keep them in good condition. Most fabrics display their cleaning requirements in the form of international symbols, either printed along the selvage or displayed on a label. Follow manufacturers' recommendations carefully. The safest course of action is to have fabrics dry cleaned if you are in any doubt as to their washing requirements, or about their shrinkage. Make sure that you prewash piping cord before making a soft furnishing that will need to be hand washed, since piping tends to shrink during the first wash.

CURTAINS AND SHADES
If you have curtains fitted with heading tape, remove the hooks and undo the knot that holds the gathers in place. Flatten out the heading tape and shake off the surface dust. If washable, soak curtains or shades in cold water for ten minutes with a small quantity of liquid detergent. Rinse, then wash the curtains as recommended. Sheer and net curtains should be given a delicate wash as often as necessary to keep them looking pristine. If the curtains are not to be rehung immediately after washing, keep them on a clothes hanger so that they maintain their shape. You will find it easier to reestablish the pleats and folds of sheer and net curtains when replacing them if you rehang them while they are still slightly damp.

LOOSE COVERS AND CUSHION COVERS
It is important that loose covers fit the furniture snugly after they have been washed, so you must consider carefully the percentage of possible shrinkage. First, clean the cover with a vacuum cleaner while it is in place on the furniture. This also gives you the chance to examine the fabric and make any necessary small repairs. Remove the cover, and wash by hand, by machine, or dry clean, as recommended by the manufacturer. In the case of cushion covers, secure the fasteners before washing the covers. Hang the covers to dry and, if possible, press with an iron while the fabric is slightly damp. In the case of upholstery, fit the cover over the furniture, and, if necessary, press the fabric again once it is in place with an iron through a layer of clean fabric.

STAIN REMOVAL

Remove any excess immediately. Treat stains by dabbing, rather than rubbing them, and work from the outside toward the center. If possible, treat stains from the underside of the fabric while simultaneously holding a piece of absorbent cloth or paper on the outer surface of the fabric. Apply solvents or commercial stain removers with a piece of clean white cloth. If you are in any doubt as to the most effective treatment, take the fabric to a professional cleaner. Most stain removers and cleansing agents are poisonous, flammable, and dangerous to inhale. Do not drench fabric with cleansing agents. Always take care when applying them, and follow manufacturers' recommendations for their use.

GREASY OR OILY STAINS
Scrape off any residue with a blunt knife, and blot the fabric with absorbent tissue. Treat the area with an appropriate grease solvent. Alternatively, sprinkle talcum powder over the area to absorb the oil or grease, and brush off the powder when it is impregnated. Continue powdering and brushing off until all the oil has been absorbed.

NONGREASY STAINS
Remove as much of the residue as possible with a blunt knife, and blot the area with absorbent paper. Rinse, if possible, or sponge with cold water. If necessary, use a commercial stain remover.

BLOOD
Sponge recent stains with cold, salted water. Soak the fabric, and wash it with an enzymatic detergent. Rinse thoroughly.

CANDLE WAX
Remove excess wax. Sandwich the stained area between two layers of brown paper or blotting paper, and gently pass a warm iron over the paper applied to the surface to melt the wax. Remove any remaining stains with a commercial grease solvent. On a pile fabric do not attempt to pick off the wax, but place paper on the surface of the fabric and iron the reverse side to melt the wax onto the paper.

CHEWING GUM
Solidify the gum by holding a bag of ice cubes over the area. Once the gum has hardened, pick it off the fabric. Commercial chewing gum removers are also available.

COFFEE AND TEA
Mop up any remaining liquid immediately, then soak the area in a warm solution of enzymatic detergent. Use a commercial stain remover, if necessary, once the stain has dried.

INK
Identify the type of ink, and use the correct stain remover, since treating ink incorrectly will set the stain. If in doubt, refer to a professional cleaner. Dab the ink stain with a commercial stain remover or denatured alcohol, and wash the fabric as recommended.

LIPSTICK
Scrape off the excess, and dab eucalyptus oil on the stain. After an hour, rinse the fabric and wash as recommended.

PAINT AND VARNISH
With water-based paint or varnish, dab off any excess and sponge the area with cold water. Wash as recommended, or use a commercial paint-stain remover. With oil-based paint or varnish, scrape away the residue and apply mineral spirits or a commercial paint remover.

WINE
Do not let the stain dry in. Mop up the wine, then soak the area in tepid water. Alternatively, apply some talcum powder, allow it to absorb the wine for 12 hours, and vacuum the powder. Wash the fabric with an enzymatic detergent, or use a commercial stain remover.

SURFACE MAINTENANCE

PAINT

Most painted surfaces can be wiped clean without any difficulty. Make sure, however, that the surface is in good condition before attempting to clean it. If you are in any doubt, it may be worth repainting the surface. Paint manufacturers supply information regarding the appropriate cleaning method for their products. Oil-based paints tend to be more durable than water-based paints, and can usually be washed down or lightly scrubbed to remove surface dirt.

WALLPAPER

Wallpapers are manufactured in many finishes, some of which are so sturdy that they can be scrubbed, while others are susceptible to the slightest surface abrasion. Washable wallpaper is coated with glaze so that the surface is spongeable. Vinyl wallpapers are also washable. Flocked wallpapers should be brushed to remove dust. If you are in doubt about cleaning wallpaper, consult the manufacturer's literature that accompanies each roll. When it is not possible to clean it, apply fresh wallpaper as a patch or a new length, or, if necessary, replace a complete section on a wall.

TILING

Tiles are very durable: a properly tiled surface will last a long time. It is the grout that tends to suffer wear and tear and become discolored. Usually, problems can be solved without having to retile a large area. Tiling grout is prone to decay when it is in prolonged contact with moisture. Always use the appropriate grout when tiling in a damp environment.

DIRTY GROUT
Dirty grouting does not always need to be replaced. It can be renewed with whitener. Remove dirt with a fine scrubbing brush or an old toothbrush and a warm solution of detergent. When the grout has dried, apply grout whitener. If the grout is badly damaged, scrape it out and replace it with fresh grout.

MOLDY GROUT
Mold can flourish on grout in the damp conditions encountered in bathrooms and kitchens. Apply commercial fungicide by following the manufacturer's instructions. If the existing grout has become stained, renovate it with grout whitener. Alternatively, scrape out the old grout and replace it with fresh grout.

CARPETS AND RUGS

Flooring surfaces tend to be subjected to a great deal of wear and tear, and accumulate dirt rapidly unless they are carefully and regularly maintained. Carpets and plant-fiber matting always look better and last longer if they are vacuumed thoroughly once a week. In addition, they should be shampooed occasionally with a commercial carpet shampoo. Clean any individual stains as soon as they occur, taking care not to drench the flooring. If you apply a cleansing agent to a stain, first test its effect in an inconspicuous area, initially using only a very small amount of the cleansing agent. If a carpet or rug becomes stained with mud, wait until the mud has solidified, and brush or lift it off from the pile. Vacuum the area, sponge it with detergent solution, and rinse off the detergent thoroughly. Rugs can be kept in good condition in much the same way as carpets. Deep-pile rugs should also be shaken out occasionally.

GLOSSARY

BACKGROUND LIGHTING Artificial lighting providing general illumination that often imitates natural daylight.

BACKING FABRIC Material sewn to the wrong side of delicate or translucent fabric for added strength or protection from sunlight.

BACKSTITCH Hand stitch used for making permanent seams or for attaching zippers. Also known as imitation machine stitch.

BAGGING Decorative paint effect using a plastic bag filled with a bunched-up cloth. This is dabbed across a surface coated with tinted oil glaze. The technique produces impressions in the wet paint (*see also* TINTED OIL GLAZE).

BASEBOARD Narrow border, usually made of wood, running along the base of a wall at the floor. Sometimes known as skirting board.

BATTEN A narrow strip of wood used as a guide (as in laying wall tiles) or other temporary support.

BIAS A 45-degree diagonal to the direction of the weave in a fabric (*see also* WARP THREADS *and* WEFT THREADS).

BIAS STRIP Strips of material cut from the diagonal of a piece of fabric. Used to cover piping cord and bind raw edges of fabrics (*see also* BINDING *and* PIPING).

BINDING Fabric strip that covers the raw edge of a fabric (*see also* TRIMMINGS).

BLANKET STITCH Used for neatening raw edges, or as a decorative stitch.

BORDER Horizontal decorative band, usually quite wide and running along the upper part of a wall near the ceiling. It is applied with paint or using a strip of specially made wallpaper contrasting with the rest of the wall (*see also* STENCILING *and* STAMPING).

BUCKRAM Thick, stiffened jute cotton or linen. Used to give a lasting shape to cornices and other soft furnishings (*see also* CORNICE).

BURLAP Coarse, plain, woven cloth used for wallpaper, upholstery fabric, and other soft furnishing material.

CASEMENT WINDOW Type of window, usually hinged at the side, typically having a small top pane and a large pane that can be opened, and one stationary pane (*see also* SASH WINDOW).

CASING Made in the same basic way as a cushion cover. Used to enclose cushion stuffing or wadding. Suitable fabrics include ticking, muslin, lining material, and old sheeting.

CASTELLATION Cut shape that resembles a castle wall with alternating turret and battlement patterns (*see also* CORNICE).

CAVITY WALL A wall formed with usually wooden studs, and surfaced with plasterboard (drywall) or paneling.

CHAIR RAIL Horizontal molding usually at waist height along a wall, dividing the lower part of a wall from the upper wall (*see also* MOLDING).

CHALK LINE Cord or string coated in colored chalk and attached to a pointed weight. Used to mark straight, vertical lines (*see also* PLUMB LINE).

CORNICE Decorative wooden or fabric structure used to cover the top edge of a curtain or shade (*see also* VALANCE).

CREWELWORK Embroidery involving bright threads on a pale background.

CURTAIN DROP Length of a curtain from the hanging system to the bottom edge.

DHURRIE Indian flat-weave rug, usually made from cotton, often displaying geometric designs.

DIRECTIONAL LIGHTS Adjustable light fixtures such as spotlights and desk lights that are designed to illuminate selected objects or all or part of a work surface.

DOUBLE HEM Hem in which the fabric is turned over twice, usually by the same amount, so that the raw edge is completely enclosed (*see also* HEM *and* NEATENING).

DOWNLIGHT Ceiling-mounted fixture that emits a beam of light downward.

DRAGGING Paint effect using a flogger brush dragged carefully from ceiling to floor over a coat of tinted oil glaze, leaving fine, vertical stroke marks (*see also* TINTED OIL GLAZE).

ENGLISH EMBROIDERY Fine, embroidered fabric, usually white with a floral design, which can be used as an edging (*see also* TRIMMINGS). Also known as broderie Anglaise.

FINIAL Ornamental projection on a piece of furniture or on the ends of curtain poles.

FLAT FELL SEAM Strong, flat seam, often used on upholstery and soft furnishings that are subjected to hard wear (*see also* SEAM).

FRENCH SEAM Self-neatening strong seam that does not show a stitching line from the right side of the fabric. Ideal for sheer fabric, and used only on straight edges (*see also* SEAM).

GATHER Multiple layers of gathered swag, as on an Austrian shade (*see also* SWAG).

GATHERING STITCH Type of running stitch used for gathering the edge of fabric (*see also* RUNNING STITCH).

GIMBAL Ring-shaped part of a frame, which supports the light fixture inside a lampshade.

GLAZING Paint technique using a large decorating brush and thin, watery emulsion to produce a dappled effect.

GROUT Powder-based, water-resistant paste applied to the gaps between tiles. The technique for the application of grout is known as grouting.

HEADING TAPE Ready-made strip that is sewn to the top of a curtain and attached to the hanging system. Heading tapes are available in various styles and, when gathered by use of built-in drawstrings, determine the shape of the curtain pleats.

HEM Turning under and sewing the raw edge of fabric (*see also* DOUBLE HEM *and* NEATENING).

HERRINGBONE STITCH Used for finishing single hems (*see also* HEM).

HOOK AND EYE Small metal fastener in two parts that fit together.

INTERFACING Iron-on material that gives bulk and stiffness to curtain tiebacks and other soft furnishings.

INTERLINING Thick, soft cotton or synthetic material used to line curtains for insulation (*see also* LOCKSTITCH).

KEY Rough surface suitable for the adhesion of paint or glue. A surface is usually keyed by being rubbed with sandpaper or steel wool. Also known as prepping.

KILIM Flat, woven rug from the Middle East or Central Asia. Usually made of wool and displaying geometric designs.

LADDER STITCH Used for joining two pieces of patterned fabric, ensuring that the pattern matches across the seam (*see also* SEAM).

LATEX PAINT Quick-drying, water-based paint suitable for coating walls and ceiling.

LIMING Treatment for wood using special paste or wax that produces a subtle, bleached effect.

LINING PAPER Plain paper used for creating a smooth surface on walls. Pasted to a wall or ceiling prior to applying paint or wallpaper.

LOCKSTITCH Large stitch used in making curtains to hold the lining and interlining loosely to the curtain fabric. Involves picking up only one or two threads of fabric with each stitch and working the thread over itself to form loops.

MASKING TAPE Adhesive tape having multiple decorating uses, including masking specific areas when painting.

MATTING Woven plant-fiber floor covering often used for informal effects.

MITERING Method of neatly turning a hem at a corner (*see also* HEM).

MOLDING Narrow strip of wood, plaster, or other material, often used as decoration running horizontally along a wall (*see also* BASEBOARD, CHAIR RAIL, *and* PICTURE RAIL).

MUSLIN Strong cotton fabric, usually white, used to make casings for cushion pads and other soft furnishings (*see also* CASING).

NEATENING Stitching, binding, or hemming a raw edge of a piece of fabric to prevent it from fraying or to provide an attractive edge.

OIL-BASED PAINT Suitable for applying to wood and metal surfaces. Available in gloss, eggshell, and flat finishes (*see also* LATEX PAINT).

OVERLOCKING Stitching technique for hiding raw edges. Requires a greater amount of seam allowance than plain flat seam (*see also* NEATENING *and* SEAM ALLOWANCE).

OVERSEWING One technique of neatening an edge. Also used to stitch over the end of a sewing thread in order to secure it (*see also* NEATENING).

PATCHWORK Method of joining same-sized or variously sized pieces of fabric to form larger pieces, which may in turn be joined together to form one large piece. Often done to be quilted (*see also* QUILTING).

PATTERN REPEATS The length of a pattern repeat is the distance between the places where a motif is repeated on fabric or wallpaper. It is important to know this measurement in order to join patterned fabrics or wallpaper, and to match patterns across a pair of closed curtains.

PHILLIPS HEAD Type of screw and matching screwdriver with a cross-shaped head.

PICTURE RAIL Molding along the top of a wall, but well away from the ceiling, and used to take the hooks from which picture frames hang (*see also* MOLDING).

PINKING Neatening technique using pinking shears for removing and neatening the raw edge of fabric. Most suitable for internal seams (*see also* NEATENING).

PINNING AND TACKING Sequence for securing pieces of fabric together prior to sewing. Pins are placed perpendicular to the intended stitching line, then loose tacking stitches are sewn along the seam line. Pins are removed after tacking, and tacking thread is removed after final sewing (*see also* TACKING).

PIPING Edging that can be used on most soft furnishings, including cushions, pillowcases, and bedspreads (*see also* TRIMMINGS).

PLAIN FLAT SEAM Simplest method of joining two lengths of fabric (*see also* SEAM).

PLASTERBOARD Used to line or form the surface of walls or ceilings. Made of plaster sandwiched between thick external paper. Also called drywall or gypsum board.

PLUMB LINE Cord or string that is secured to a pointed weight and used to ensure straight, vertical lines along walls when decorating (*see also* CHALK LINE).

PRIMER Liquid substance that is applied to wood or metal before the undercoat in order to stabilize the surface.

QUILTING Method of sewing together two pieces of fabric that are sandwiching a layer of padding (*see also* PATCHWORK).

RAGGING Paint effect using a clean piece of lint-free cloth dabbed across a surface coated with tinted oil glaze. This technique produces subtle impressions in the wet paint (*see also* TINTED OIL GLAZE).

RAG-ROLLING Paint effect using a clean piece of lint-free cloth or chamois soaked in mineral spirits. By rolling the rag over a coat of tinted oil glaze, random abstract impressions are left in the wet paint (*see also* TINTED OIL GLAZE).

RAW EDGE Unhemmed, frayed, or cut edge of a piece of fabric (*see also* NEATENING).

ROULEAU STRIP Narrow tube of fabric strip that can be made into loops. Often attached to the opening edges of cushions or pillowcases and used in place of buttonholes.

RUNNING STITCH Simple stitch that works in and out of layers of fabric, always moving in the same direction. Tacking and gathering stitches are both known as running stitches (*see also* PINNING AND TACKING).

SASH WINDOW A window with one or two sash cords, which can be slid open vertically (*see also* CASEMENT WINDOW).

SCONCE Reflective candle or light fixture that is attached to a wall.

SEAM Where two pieces or lengths of fabric are sewn together (*see also* SEAM ALLOWANCE).

SEAM ALLOWANCE Extra amount of material used when joining fabric. It is usually trimmed after the seam has been sewn (*see also* SEAM).

SELVAGE Edges of fabric that run down both sides of a length of fabric. These edges are finished off and therefore do not fray (*see also* WARP THREADS).

SIMPLE COMPASS Apparatus made with a piece of string tied to a pencil and a thumbtack. Used for marking circles or arcs on a template or fabric (*see also* TEMPLATE).

SIZE Glutinous solution used for stiffening and mounting wallpaper to a smooth surface.

SKIRT Strips of fabric fitted around the lower edge of a bedspread, bed valance, or upholstered chair (*see also* VALANCE).

SLIPSTITCH Used for hems or where a seam is required along the right side of a fabric, for example when securing closed a cushion cover opening (*see also* SEAM *and* PINNING AND TACKING).

SOFTENED GLAZEWORK Smooth, even coating of tinted oil glaze applied onto a couple of layers of dried eggshell paint. The translucent glaze produces a subtle, complementary tinge to the underlying color on the surface (*see also* TINTED OIL GLAZE).

SPONGING There are two variations on this paint effect. One is where tinted oil glaze is sponged onto a smooth surface. The other technique requires soaking a sponge in mineral spirits and dabbing off freshly applied colored glaze (*see also* TINTED OIL GLAZE).

STAMPING Process of making and applying inked designs to a smooth surface. Used to make decorative borders (*see also* BORDER).

STENCILING Application of paint over a stencil and onto a surface to produce a design that can be isolated or linked (*see also* BORDER).

STIPPLING Paint technique requiring a stippling brush or stiff broom-head. Wet, tinted oil glaze is carefully dabbed on a surface with a brush, leaving a fine impression of the bristles (*see also* TINTED OIL GLAZE).

STRAIGHT GRAIN Direction of the weave in a fabric (*see also* WARP THREADS *and* WEFT THREADS).

SWAG Draping of fabric so that the ends are secured or pulled above the middle, causing it to fall in a curve. Applicable to Austrian and balloon shades, and to the curtain cornice known as swag and cascades.

TACKING Long stitch used to temporarily hold pieces or parts of fabric together before undertaking final sewing. Also known as basting (*see also* PINNING AND TACKING).

TASK LIGHTING Localized lighting used mainly to illuminate a specific work surface or area.

TAILOR'S TACK Loose temporary stitch used to mark fabrics, for example when they need to be joined accurately.

TEMPLATE Shaped pattern used to cut or sew around an object.

TICKING Fine white linen or cotton material, which can be used as casing for a cushion pad. Because of its tight weave it is most suitable for enclosing feathers and down (*see also* CASING).

TINTED OIL GLAZE Mixture of turpentine, linseed oil, dryers, white pigment, mineral spirits, and coloring such as artist's oil paints or powdered pigment. Used for creating special paint effects.

TOPSTITCH Thick, decorative stitch used to highlight a seam line.

TRIMMINGS Adornments such as bindings, piping, frills, and flanges that are attached to soft furnishings. Many are available ready-made, including fringes and decorative cords.

UPLIGHT Floor- or wall-mounted fixture that emits a beam of light upward.

VALANCE Material used to cover part of a soft furnishing. Often attached to cornices above curtains or around the bases of beds (*see also* CORNICE *and* SKIRT).

VARNISH Substance used for sealing a wooden surface. Available in different glossy finishes and colors.

VELCRO Brand name for "touch-and-close" fastener that consists of two pieces of nylon, one with tiny hooks and the other with small loops, which adhere when pressed together.

VENEER Thin wood or other similar material used to cover the surface of coarse wood to provide a smooth surface.

WADDING Light, fleecy material used to stuff upholstery, cushions, pillows, or quilts. Also called batting.

WARP THREADS Lengthwise threads running parallel to a fabric's selvage (*see also* SELVAGE *and* WEFT THREADS).

WEFT THREADS Threads that run across the fabric and over and under the warp threads (*see also* SELVAGE *and* WARP THREADS).

ZIGZAG STITCH Machine stitch commonly used for neatening raw edges (*see also* NEATENING).

INDEX

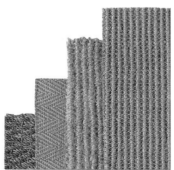

Acknowledgments

Author's Acknowledgments

I dedicate this book to my wife, Julia, whose loving support and patient helpfulness guided me through the assembly of this work.

For the painstaking research, making, and assembly of all the soft furnishings, I owe a considerable debt of gratitude to Alison Kingsbury. At Dorling Kindersley, Lee Stacy and Gurinder Purewall were the models of forbearance and efficiency, and Derek Coombes and Krystyna Mayer were the constant providers of enthusiastic advice. My thanks also to David Lamb for his encouragement. I thank Tim Ridley and Nick Goodall for their excellent studio photography and inspirational company.

To the following I extend my thanks for assistance throughout the project: Louise Greenwood, Ali Edney, and Tracey Turner of Liberty; Martin Ephson of Farrow & Ball; Richard Foxell and Martin James of Foxell & James; Alex Portelli of World's End Tiles; Karen Buswell of Mulberry at Home; Stephen Bunce of London Lighting; Annabel Lewis of V. V. Rouleaux; Martin Long at The Carpet Library; Beattie and Trish at Rossiters; Dave Marsh; Lyn Sherwood and Ian Mankin of Ian Mankin Ltd.; Caroline Brandenberger; Liz Crouch; Harrington Evans; Diana Ekins; and The Stencil Library.

When in London I was made welcome by the generous hospitality of James and Jennie Merrell, Mike and Carol Wilson, and Andrew and Margot Hawkins.

The following have kindly supplied props for photography:

Patrizia Antonicelli, P & A Collection rugs 247; **Gloria Birkett** tapestry cushion cover 121; **Carpet Library, London** natural floor coverings 245; **Crossleys, Somerset** soft furnishings and carpet samples 245; **Designers Guild** 51, edging 70, check fabric 73 and 74–75, patterned wallpaper 212–218; **Diana Lampshades, Hampshire** supplies and advice 162–171; **Christopher Farr, London** rugs 247; **Farrow & Ball, Dorset** all latex, gloss, and eggshell paint; **Foxell & James, London** specialist decorating tools and materials; **Frome Feather Company, Somerset** filled cushions; **Habitat UK** chair 124–125 and 126–127, chair 128–129, round and rectangular tables 148–155; **Christopher Legge, Oxford** rugs 247; **Liberty, London** all patterned fabric 40–41, 43, 44–45, patterned fabric 46–47, 48, 51, all patterned fabric 52–53, 55, 56–57, patterned fabric 58–59, 60–61, 97, 113, 117, floral fabric 156, wallpaper border 217; **Litvinoff & Fawcett, London** bed and mattress; **Lumiance UK** and **London Lighting** light fixtures 266–267; 268–269; **Dave Marsh Hardware, Somerset** tools and decorating materials; **Malmic, Nottingham** lace edging on curtain 42 and pillow 86; **Mr. Light, London** light fixtures 266–267; **Mulberry at Home** patterned fabric 18–19, 62–63, patterned fabric 73, fabric 76–77, 98, 150, 154–155, printed voile 157, 164–165, 166–167; **Papyrus, Bath & London** 168–169; **Rossiters, Bath** brass fixtures 36; **V. V. Rouleaux, London** all ribbons and edging; **Rufflete** heading tapes; **Shaker Shop, London** candles and candle fixtures 268; **Sussex House, London** stool frames 142–143; **Swish** curtain hooks, hanging and track systems 35; **Alice Taylor, R.T. Herbs, Somerset** culinary herbs 275; **Tile and Flooring Centre, Bath** wood and cork floor samples; **Wagner Spraytech (UK) Ltd.** power paint roller, paintbrush, and sprayer; **Westbury Wallpapers, Wiltshire** wallpapers; **World's End Tiles, London** majority of wall tiles 224–225, all tiles 226–235, and all floor tiles 239.

Publisher's Acknowledgments

Editorial assistance:
Mark Ronan, Candida Ross-MacDonald, and Sharon Lucas

Design assistance:
Tim Scott and Colette Ho

Picture research:
Emily Hedges

Page make-up and computer assistance:
Noel Barnes and Doug Miller

Index:
Pat Coward

Modeling:
Tracey Strudwick-Williams (134-135)

Artwork:
Andrew Macdonald

Set builders:
Simon Moore, Ben Pulsford, and Charlie Cork

PHOTOGRAPHIC CREDITS
key: t top, c center, b bottom, l left, r right

All photography by Tim Ridley, Steve Gorton, Andy Crawford, and Nick Goodall except:

Arcaid: Richard Bryant/Gwathmey Siegel Architects 82b; Jeremy Cockayne/Rusland Hall Hotel 200; Ken Kirkwood 32tl, 160t, 161tr; Ken Kirkwood/John Wright 262tr; Lucinda Lambton/Abbey Hotel, Penzance 178b; Lucinda Lambton/Mrs. Henry Keswick 82tl; Sally-Ann Norman 222; Justin Paul/Thorp and May 105b; Julie Phipps 263cl

Simon Brown: 161bl, 203b

Camera Press: 240b; Bo Appeltofft 147t, 160 br; Brigitte 253c; Simon Brown/SHE 104tl, 252; IMS 146t; James Merrell/SHE 64, 66tr, 83t, 130, 146b, 253tr; Rej/Schoner Wohnen 262b; C. Simon-Sykes 102; Stradtmann/Schoner Wohnen 80

Habitat UK: 161br

Robert Harding Picture Library: 133cl; Bo Appeltofft 133b; Brock 132t, 160bl; Peo Eriksson 179tl; Brian Harrison 82r, 263tr; Mike Newton 238tr

Robert Harding Syndication/IPC Magazines Ltd.: 244cr; Jan Baldwin 133cr, 179b, 240tl; Tim Beddow 202, 244b; Henry Bourne 133tl, 244tr; Simon Brown 203cl; Christopher Drake 67tr, 83cl, 161tl, 223bl, 272b; Michael Dunne 178t; James Merrell 158, 161c, 176, 203cr, 250, 253b; Trevor Richards 66b, 144; Pia Tryde 273b

Houses and Interiors: Jon Bouchier 33tr; Simon Butcher 223tl; David Markson 203tr

Paul Ryan: International Interiors 83cr, 223tr & br; JB Visual Press 67tl & cl, 246b, 253tl

Thames and Hudson: James Merrell 2, 30, 32tr & b, 66tl, 83b, 104b, 147b, 238b, 246tl, tr & cr, 263tl, 273tl

Elizabeth Whiting & Associates: 105cl, 244tl, 273tr; Tommy Candler 104tr; Nick Carter 133tr; David Cripps 240cr; Michael Dunne 105cr, 223c, 260, 262tl, 272tl & tr; Andreas V. Einsiedel 105t, 242; Rodney Hyett 263b; Tom Leighton 179tr; Di Lewis 33b, 236, 270; Neil Lorimer 67b, 238tl; Spike Powell 132b; Dennis Stone 33tl, 203tl; Peter Woloszynski 147cr, 220, 240tr